Global Fashion Brands

Global Fashion Brands
Style, Luxury & History

Edited by

Joseph H. Hancock, II   Gjoko Muratovski
Veronica Manlow   Anne Peirson-Smith

intellect Bristol, UK / Chicago, USA

First published in the UK in 2014 by
Intellect, The Mill, Parnall Road, Fishponds, Bristol, BS16 3JG, UK

First published in the USA in 2014 by
Intellect, The University of Chicago Press, 1427 E. 60th Street,
Chicago, IL 60637, USA

A catalogue record for this book is available from the
British Library.

Copy-editing: MPS Technologies
Cover design: Stephanie Sarlos
Production manager: Bethan Ball
Typesetting: Contentra Technologies

ISBN: 978-1-78320-357-4

Printed and bound by Hobbs, UK

To our family, friends and colleagues ... we appreciate your love and support.

And to the memory of Masoud Yazdani, who believed in us as editors of fashion, style and popular culture. We will never forget you welcoming us into the Intellect family.

Contents

FOREWORD

ALLEN SABINSON
Dean, Antoinette Westphal College of Media Arts & Design
Drexel University

When I began my career in the film and television industry in 1973, branding was something you did to cattle. In the parlance of the times, the professions were known as: publicity, advertising and public relations. By the mid-1980s, the media were beginning to transform, and marketing became the word du jour encompassing all three disciplines. But *branding* and *brand identity* are something altogether different. Whether it's a fashion design label like Burberry or Chanel, a performer like Beyoncé or Lady Gaga, a media giant like Disney, or sports teams like Manchester United or the New York Yankees, a truly global brand resonates on a far deeper level. You only need to hear the name Chanel to know that it represents the highest level of design, unique in its vision and produced to the highest standards of quality. In the minds of consumers – successful brands like Chanel exist as shorthand – transmitting a whole array of brand attributes that cast a favourable glow over entire product lines as with Chanel and their perfume, cosmetics, haute couture and ready-to-wear lines. In sports the world over, Manchester United is known as an international powerhouse, the best of the best, year-in year-out, regardless of which star is in this year's lineup or even whether they've won the most important tournaments. Branding is the story and identity that comes to exist in people's minds, and successful companies are beyond vigilant in their efforts to build stories that reinforce brand identities.

Those who are most successful in branding understand that every aspect of their operations – their products and packaging, their stores, their e-commerce and social media efforts, their advertising and associations with celebrities – all must be consistent with the brand image. In successful branding, the whole is greater than the sum of its parts, but there are downsides too. When a company's actions appear to be departures from accepted core values, whether through products that depart too radically from expectations or are of lesser quality, or are superseded by new technologies, they run the risk of alienating consumers from every aspect of their business. Consider the rapid rise and

ix

precipitous fall of mobile phone makers Nokia and Blackberry's Research in Motion, the decline of Dell as smart phones and tablets decimated the demand for personal computers, or how Gap has struggled to regain market share in the face of new competition and poorly received product lines. Then there's the impact of scandal, be they the inappropriate public statements of a CEO, a credit card breach, or an association with third world manufacturers with little regard for their workers' safety and well-being. Any misstep can cause a brand to suffer and in today's globalized, connected worlds, brands must be continually focused on protecting their brand identity while being mindful of consumers quest for the next big thing, which can easily turn today's hot brand into yesterday's news.

Drexel University's Westphal College of Media Arts & Design is very proud of Dr. Joseph H. Hancock II, whose research addresses branding, national and international trends, and cultural influences. In the classroom and through his publications, he is a major contributor to our nationally ranked Department of Fashion Design/Design & Merchandising and Product Design. I would also like to thank and acknowledge his highly esteemed colleagues Gjoko Muratovski, Auckland University of Techonology, Veronica Manlow, Brooklyn College, and Dr. Anne Peirson-Smith from the City University of Hong Kong, all of whom are known for their global reputations in the areas of fashion, design and branding scholarship, as well as consulting. Without them this book, with its diverse array of topics addressing style, luxury and history, would not have been possible.

Global Fashion Brands: Style, Luxury & History

© 2014 Intellect Ltd Introduction. English language. doi: 10.1386/GFB.1.xi_7

INTRODUCTION

JOSEPH H. HANCOCK, II
Drexel University

GJOKO MURATOVSKI
Auckland University of Technology

VERONICA MANLOW
Brooklyn College

ANNE PEIRSON-SMITH
City University of Hong Kong

Global fashion brands: Style, luxury and history

Fashion, style, dress and appearance in the broadest sense are universal, and as such have transcended time and space. The German sociologist Georg Simmel (1954) defined fashion as a form of both segregation and social equalization that is in constant flux. He argued, fashion was a product of social demand and acting as a reflection of a class-driven society where needs for differentiation and imitation are high. In his seminal work, 'Fashion', he suggests the well-to-do initiate fashion in order to define themselves as the upper social class and to segregate themselves from others. While the mass populace may try to imitate them to reduce the distinctions between the classes, as soon as it becomes apparent that styles of the wealthy are becoming common, those with financial means abandon current fashion styles and replace them with newer ones. Thus, the elites are able to keep up their appearances of class distinction somewhat out of reach from the masses.

But fashion has evolved since the early twentieth century and is constantly changing amongst all consumer groups. It is a driving force that utilizes the latest technologies and encompasses ever more sectors of society. It is at once material culture and transitory, inhabiting the realm of concepts and images and linked to production and industry. The socio-economic shifts that occurred were exemplified post-World War II through the marketing efforts behind rapidly mass-produced, mass-communicated fashion garments that allowed for a shift in financially urban working class and style-driven youth from the 1960s, to become the fashion leaders of global trends (Peirson-Smith and Hancock 2013: 166).

From haute couture across ready-to-wear global fashion production, commodities required a uniqueness to gain the almighty consumer dollar and success in the apparel industry. Fashion branding is the process that brought all this together. As Joseph Hancock states, 'Fashion branding is the process by whereby designers, manufacturers, merchandisers, buyers, strategists, creative directors, retailers and those responsible for selling fashion create campaigns and give fashion garments a unique identity' (2009: 6). It involves the cast of cultural intermediaries across the spectrum of fashion practices whose work transcends the product and communicates a consistent brand story in the interests of 'creating a clear vision and strategy for a company' (Hancock 2009: 7). Having a specific target market in mind, while exhibiting variations in clothing collections, the power of mass fashion brands provides continuity by popular appeal, and through branding sometimes even creates a perceived national identity of a country. For example, globally recognized fashion brands such as Ralph Lauren, Tommy Hilfiger, American Apparel are a reflection of American life both real and imagined, and have been a persuasive force in shaping the international perceptions of the American lifestyle (Manlow 2011).

Yet even today, fashion branding is still often misrepresented as being only about the logo, the brand name, and the tangible design aspects of the brand created and communicated in a linear way as often the 'message-weary, sophisticated consumer tunes out all of these superficial aspects of the brand architecture' (Devereux and Peirson-Smith 2009: 66). The intangible aspects and the emotional attachments of the consumer to the brand in terms of its recognizable identity or personality is the most compelling in developing the all-powerful 'mindshare' (Devereux and Person-Smith 2009: 66). The chapters presented in the four sections of this work capture fashion brands as they exist today, underscoring their most important dimensions and indeed their power as a means to move fashion and continue its evolutionary processes.

I. FROM THE EDITORS: MASS FASHION BRANDS

The first section of the book concentrates on mass market brands and the adoption and implementation of various branding strategies to assure their survival in competitive and often saturated markets. In 'Rebranding American men's heritage fashion through the use of visual merchandising, symbolic props and masculine iconic memes historically found in popular culture', Kevin Matthews, Joseph H. Hancock, II and Zhaohui Gu employ a critical interpretation of how culturally influenced thematic props and icons from the rebel to the jock, historically reflective of American culture, are used to promote and sell men's mass fashion brands. As a consequence, they observe that this popular culture inspired merchandising as a successful and iconic fashion branding practice has had a significant impact on street style and everyday menswear.

Next, D. J. Huppatz and Veronica Manlow turn their attention to North American mass market brands such as Ralph Lauren, Gap and American Apparel in 'Producing and consuming American mythologies: Branding in mass market fashion firms', which actively create hyper-real representations

Joseph H. Hancock, II   *Gjoko Muratovski*   *Veronica Manlow*   *Anne Peirson-Smith*

of a mythic American nation and lifestyle that global consumers aspire to be part of. The chapter examines the emergence, development and the inherent differences in brand strategies amongst the companies residing in this middle market segment across four decades.

Taking a different angle in Chapter 3, 'Co-branding strategies for luxury fashion brands: Missoni for Target', Edwina Luck, Gjoko Muratovski and Lauren Hedley use a case study approach to assess the collaborative relationship between Italian luxury knitwear company Missoni and North American retail company, Target. This is a co-branding story with mixed benefits for the partners involved following the frenetic pre-launch media hype and overwhelming consumer response. Whilst the collection was a huge commercial success, significantly raising consumer awareness of, and demand for, Missoni, the risks of an uncontrolled or confused brand image for both parties provides a cautionary tale for luxury brands involved in this marketing strategy.

On a related theme, Anne Peirson-Smith analyses H&M's well established co-branding partnerships with a range of luxury brands in 'Comme on down and Choos your shoes: A study of consumer responses to the use of guest fashion designers by H&M as a co-branded fashion marketing strategy'. The chapter analyses the sustained validity of these symbiotic 'massclusive' relationships that borrow interest from each other as high-end and high-street brands cohabit in the interests of establishing brand visibility and credibility amongst aspirational global consumers turning them from customers into 'lustomers'. Using ethnographic evidence from in-depth consumer interviews, the chapter questions whether in view of changing economic conditions and evolving consumer needs there is evidence of increasing consumer agency, cynicism and saturation with regard to this co-branding strategy despite the media hype and apparent commercial success.

II. BRANDS, STYLE AND INNOVATION

In section two the spotlight is placed on emerging and innovative trends in fashion branding from social media engagement, 'trashion' and cultural re-appropriation. Kendra Lapolla's chapter, 'ModCloth: A case study in co-creative branding strategies' uses observational research methods to analyse the co-branding strategies of North American vintage retailer,

ModCloth, to encourage consumer involvement. The trend from product to customer centred engagement with the brand is examined across the company's e-commerce website and interaction with its online customer community highlighting the importance of transactional dialogue when co-creating and sustaining a brand.

Following on from this in Chapter 6, 'Juicy (contradiction) couture: The Starburst Prom Gown and female teens' appropriation and emotional branding of a candy label', Tara Chittenden tracks the fascinating 'trashion' DIY phenomenon of the prom gown made from Starburst candy wrappers. This often involves hundreds of hours of folding and weaving by the teen wearer's family and friends. The Starburst gown is analysed as a cultural text shedding light on female teen identity and its interface with and affective expression through crossover branding practices.

The beleaguered, mid-range American department store J. C. Penney is the subject of Chapter 7 'It's all inside: J. C. Penney and 'cut 'n' paste' as branding practice' for author Myles Ethan Lascity. The chapter details the 2012 rebranding strategy for the store under its former CEO applying the cut 'n' paste concept to the store-within-a-store approach that can be identified either as an innovative branding departure or as a weak market position. The author concludes that the resulting brand identity for the store resulted from a combination of these two interpretations in the public domain.

Next, the online followers of multi-channel lifestyle brand Anthropologie are under the spotlight in 'Effortless consumption: The "Anthropologie" of a brand-focused online shopping community', by Lauren Downing Peters, and Anya Kurennaya. Taking a close investigation of the online posts made by the Effortless Anthropologie blogging community, the chapter contends that this is a coherent, like-minded community bonded by trust and loyalty that retailers and marketers ignore at their peril.

Concluding this section, Christina Lindholm details how the *abaya* – the all-covering black outer robe typically worn by observant Muslim women in the Arabian Gulf – is being adapted into a more fashion conscious garment in 'Visible status: Couture and designer *abayas*'. This trend, adopted by Muslims and non-Muslims alike, is being reworked by couturiers and designers into garments with an aesthetic appeal that still remains within the boundaries of cultural acceptability.

III. BRANDS IN THE LUXURY MARKET

The subject of this section is the evolving role of luxury brands across time, space and place and the importance of heritage and authenticity in these brand narratives. In this regard, Tasha Lewis and Brittany Haas in their chapter 'Managing an iconic old luxury brand in a new luxury economy: Hermès handbags in the US market', examine the operations of the French family-owned heritage brand Hermès founded in 1837. World renowned for its quality leather luxury goods, and in particular the covetable Birkin 'it' bag, the chapter highlights how Hermès faces the challenges of maintaining control over, and ensuring the quality of its distribution practices across the United States market, in addition to jockeying for position across the luxury brand market with its competitors.

Following on from this focus on luxury branding, the influence of the appearance of a designer's home, flagship store and fashion collection on consumer perceptions towards a designer's brand is the focus of Osmud

Rahman and Lauren Petroff's chapter on 'Communicating brand image through fashion designers' homes, flagship stores and ready-to-wear collections'. Using in-depth ethnographic interviews, the findings from this exploratory investigation highlight the importance of the designer's home to their overall persona and design aesthetic representing a new factor influencing the fashion brand that has only recently begun to reach the attention of the broader public. This unique study tested the degree to which the consumer perception of a brand concept is influenced by the way in which the designer's collection and their personal domestic interiors are used as a communication strategy to engage with consumers in order to promote and reinforce the brand image.

In their chapter, 'Leveraging designer creativity for impact in luxury brand management: An in-depth case study of designers in the LVMH brand portfolio', RayeCarol Cavender and Doris H. Kincade offer a business/producer case study focus on luxury goods company LVMH's competitive brand management strategies in an increasingly saturated luxury goods market. The winning formula for a premier luxury brand such as LVMH involves the coming together of an innovative creative director with farsighted management who value creativity at the core of the brand ethos. This strategic pairing of designer creativity and directive brand management, the chapter suggests, is a benchmark for sustained success to withstand the rigours of a highly competitive marketplace.

Bringing this section to a close, in the chapter entitled, 'Narratives of Italian craftsmanship and the luxury fashion industry: Representations of Italianicity in discourses of production', Alice Dallabona addresses how luxury Italian fashion labels embody Barthian representations of national identity or 'Italaianicity' as a way of adding value and cultural capital to their garments. Using a series of case studies, the chapter examines the discourses of Italian fashion production centred on authenticity and craftsmanship that are also often appropriated by non-Italian brands to enhance the status of an international brand by association. The chapter argues that this hybridization of the 'made in Italy' narrative from any source has a positive effect on the Italian fashion system and its resulting brands.

IV. BRANDS IN THEIR HISTORICAL CONTEXTS

The next section looks at the evolution of fashion branding though a historical lens. Given that many of the luxury brands predominating in the market today originated in the seventeenth and eighteenth centuries, Shaun Borstrock in 'Do contemporary luxury brands adhere to historical paradigms of luxury?' addresses the origins of the concept of luxury brand heritage and its unique contribution to current luxury brands. Stripping away contemporary brand and marketing practices that tend to rely on the rhetoric of heritage and exclusivity to engage with the consumer, the chapter highlights the authentic historic roots of luxury brands. The chapter explains how this originated in skilful craftsmanship forming an indelible part of the brand story for many contemporary luxury brands.

Going further back in time, the quest for an appropriate brand persona (BP) for contemporary fashion brands is located in mythical Sumerian goddess Inanna in Linda Matheson's chapter, 'The "age of enchantment", the "age of anxiety": Fashion symbols and brand persona'. Using social theory as a framework for analysis, Matheson proposes that in the current age of uncertainty modern brand icons and their impossibly glamorous associations, often heightening personal concerns and widespread anxiety, may not be as effective in tapping into the consumer psyche. Alternative narratives and symbolic associations with more postmodern attributes represented by Inanna such as unpredictability, fragmentation and heterogeneity may offer more relatable realities for the globalized fashion consumer.

Finally, the evolution of modern branding and visual merchandising to determine the unique qualities of goods is traced back to the seventeenth-century reign of Louis XIV, King of France, by Ellen Anders. In 'Louis XIV: Le marketing, c'est moi' the focus is on a highly productive reign of a king who created a brand for his royal house comparable to contemporary marketing practices across the fashion industry. Within the context of an 'Age of Discovery' the king expanded this approach as a way of systematizing the import and export trade and the methods of production and consumption across a range of industries, including textiles. The echoes with present day commercial activities are carefully drawn revealing striking similarities in mercantile and fashion branding practices both old and new.

REFERENCES

Devereux, Mary and Peirson-Smith, Anne (2009), *Public Relations in Asia-Pacific: Communicating Effectively Across Cultures*, London and Singapore: John Wiley & Sons.

Hancock, Joseph (2009), *Brand/Story: Ralph, Vera, Johnny, Billy and Other Adventures in Fashion Branding*, New York: Fairchild Books.

Manlow, Veronica (2011), 'Creating an American mythology: A comparison of branding strategies in three fashion firms', *Fashion Practice*, 3: 1, pp. 85–110.

Peirson-Smith, Anne and Hancock II, Joseph H. (2013), 'Editorial', *Fashion Practice*, 5: 3, pp. 165–70.

Simmel, Georg (1954), 'Fashion', *The American Journal of Sociology*, 62: 6, pp. 541–58.

PART I

From the Editors

Global Fashion Brands: Style, Luxury & History
© 2014 Intellect Ltd Chapter. English language. doi: 10.1386/GFB.1.3_1

KEVIN MATTHEWS
Drexel University

JOSEPH H. HANCOCK, II
Drexel University

ZHAOHUI GU
Xi'an Polytechnic University

*Re*branding American men's heritage fashions through the use of visual merchandising, symbolic props and masculine iconic memes historically found in popular culture

ABSTRACT

This article takes a critical examination of how merchandising inspired by popular culture communicates various notions of history, and in this case, to display and sell heritage fashion lines. In specific retail locations popular and historically

KEYWORDS

men's fashion
American culture
masculinity

fashion branding
visual display
memes

cultural-influenced visual displays and aesthetic merchandising strategies are stud-ied to ascertain and interpret the importance of visual display as one vehicle of fashion branding. A careful interpretive analysis, determines that retailers associ-ate cultural-influenced thematic props and icons reflective of America culture to sell men's mass-fashion garments and give them an aura of authenticity and American heritage. These displays and the branding stories convey conceptual (pop) cultural masculine icons or noted historical memes *of US historical masculine imagery that include such male icons as the rebel, the cowboy, the Ivy Leaguer, jocks and blue-collar workers, revealing how these worn styles have infused into American culture and men's mass fashion as contemporary street style.*

INTRODUCTION

Men's fashion styles are influenced by, and have inspired, American culture. Throughout history, men's clothing has teetered between ostentatious as well as conservative styles (López-Gydosh and Hancock 2009). During the early twenty-first century, men's mass-fashion sportswear has been stylized by social constructions of work- and sports-influenced principles in order for contemporary men to appear culturally accepted as masculine (Edwards 2006: 99–115). Retailers selling these garments have realized men are important consumers to pursue; and, by doing so, successful retailers gain dollars and market share (Pellegrin 2009: xv–xxii).

As competition among men's mass-fashion retailers grows, brand-ing becomes an essential component in the retailing strategy (Hameide 2011: 178). One method of a branding strategy utilized to enhance mass fash-ion in the retailing context is visual merchandising and display. One goal of visual display is to convey a cohesive story-like theme to the consumer in order to gain his attention. Through the use of various types of props, found objects, furniture, and other such items, a visual merchandiser can create a selling context for mass-fashion garments giving them a centralized meaning (Diamond and Litt 2009: 361–64). A brand-like storytelling context and association to pop-cultural meanings often overshadows the actual product consumers are purchasing (Hancock 2009a: 28–31).

Because the men's mass-fashion retail industry provides similar prod-ucts such as T-shirts, jeans, khaki pants, woven shirts, sweaters, shorts, etc. to consumers, a branding technique such as visual display becomes the primary means used to sell these products to the consumer (Hancock 2009a). With differences in the logo, style, price or colour as negotiable to some consumers, a men's 100% cotton piqué polo shirt may look quite similar at Rugby, Club Monaco, Abercrombie & Fitch, American Eagle, Polo Ralph Lauren, or even Tommy Hilfiger. Devoid of retailing or visual-selling context, a product as ostensibly basic as a cotton piqué polo shirt does not convey the brand message or meaning (Barthes 1967: 3–18). Yet the brand insignia or label may conjure images of fashion hierarchy or associations in a consumer's mind; thus influencing his purchase decision (Hancock 2009a). The process of contextual display, such as visual merchandising, allows for mass-fashion garments to establish, change and reorganize their position in relation to other clothing items.

By discerning the various intended visual themes created through artistic display, story-like brand narratives often reflect contemporary cultural mark-ers of what appears to be acceptable masculine dress (Pellegrin 2009: 38–56).

Figure 1: Ralph Lauren Double RL store in New York City's Nolita Area. Note the various icons associated with Western wear and the blatant use of the cowboy as a marker for acceptable men's fashion. Photo courtesy of Kevin Matthews and Joseph Hancock, 2012, All Rights Reserved.

In recent years, greater numbers of men's fashion focused clothiers have been opening across the nation. For example, in 2009, J.Crew opened one of its newest concept stores for men in a former liquor store at 235 Broadway in New York City. This store represents a packaging of J.Crew's somewhat insignificant mass-fashion garments in an homage to mid-century nostalgia and style giving them a new selling context and style (www.jcrew.com). Other such stores include nationwide retailers Ralph Lauren's Double RL Stores (Figure 1), Penguin, and the Brooklyn Circus, in addition to regional shops such as Isle of Man in Chicago, IL and Cable Car Clothiers in San Francisco, CA.

With the rise of these stores, a return to what has been referred to as vintage; clothes associated with 'Made in the USA' authentic, legendary and retro-American fashion have risen among male shoppers. The metrosexual has vanished and a new image of a more hunky masculine man has taken his place in such magazines as *Fantastic Man*, *V-Man* and *Hercules*. In his *New York Times* article, 'From Boys to Men', author Guy Trebay (2010) states:

> On catwalks and in advertising campaigns the prevalent male image has long been that of skinny-rat, a juvenile with pipe-cleaner proportions [...] Suddenly evidence of a new phase in the cycle of evolving masculinity imagery was all over the catwalks in the runway season [...] where the boys of recent memory have been transformed overnight into men.

Jim Nelson, the editor of *GQ* Magazine, was noted as suggesting that the twink movement is over and men do not enjoy looking at boys who appear to be 16. The fashion industry is moving towards a male model with heft on him and a few years marking his face.

Mid-range to high-end menswear has shown an increasing trend in American heritage styling. With historical references to pioneering images, blue-collar workwear, and idealized notions of a rugged masculinity, branding has taken on the arduous task of maintaining the market value of these garments, their production and distribution. For some consumers, these historical references are sufficient to provide a feeling of Americanism through authenticity to a particular legendary brand and the product. The more discerning consumer, as men are increasingly engaging in fashion consumerism, will probe deeper, searching for the particular trait on which their purchase hinges to understand why the brand is so important (Wu and Ardley 2007: 302–03). The recent revival of Carter's men's jeans for J. Crew is an example of this. Since 1865, Carter's of Wisconsin, normally associated with children's clothing, has decided to revitalize their historical line of men's jeans through the J. Crew company, charging consumers US$199 to US$225 for their 'Made in the USA' products. This return to a truly Americana brand allows consumers to recognize a time when the United States was a strong producer of fashion products.

In the height of a recession and in a current labour market where most work is digital, a return to an era when labour actually produced goods and services is becoming desirable and men want to be reminded of what labour used to be like through images and icons of popular culture. In Trebay's article Jim Nelson, editor of *GQ* Magazine, states, 'that we as men do work, we do labour, we do still make things' (2010). Designers have been inspired by these ideas of retro-branding 'heritage' labels and workwear where the models for these garments are manly men, with hairy bodies, hunky builds and mature looks – men who do not appear to have been waxed and manicured (Trebay 2010). It is a rugged, masculine return to a work and labour era gone by that is influencing fashion, when men went hunting, joined a bowling league, and learned to play the guitar under the night sky.

PURPOSE OF THIS STUDY

This article takes a critical examination of how merchandising inspired by popular culture communicates various notions of history, and in this case, to display and sell heritage fashion lines. In specific retail locations popular and historically cultural-influenced visual display and aesthetic merchandising strategies are studied to ascertain and interpret the importance of visual display as one vehicle of *fashion branding*. A careful interpretive analysis determines that retailers associate cultural-influenced thematic props and icons reflective of America culture to sell men's mass-fashion garments and give them an aura of authenticity and American heritage. These displays and the branding stories convey conceptual (pop) cultural masculine icons or noted historical *memes* of US historical masculine imagery that include such male icons as the rebel, the cowboy, the Ivy Leaguer, jocks and blue-collar workers, revealing how these worn styles have infused into American culture and men's mass fashion as contemporary street style.

FASHION BRANDING

Culturally branded scenarios in the fashion industry, and those companies with the ability to communicate appealing narratives seem to be the most successful (Hancock 2009a; Manlow 2011). Interpretive branding through the concepts of visual storytelling allows the consumer to feel that the brand is concerned specifically with them and their needs as an individual (Vincent 2002: 15). Fashion companies aim at producing images that reflect people, narratives or myths in popular culture (Hancock 2009b). Branding allows the company to create an image that is based upon functional and hedonic characteristics that identify a product to a specific market (Brannon 2005: 405). At times this is achieved through business strategies, such as creating thematic fashion marketing, which reflect the image of the company (Schultz and Hatch 2006: 15–33).

Douglas Holt defines cultural branding as a method and a strategy utilized by businesses to sell products and services to consumers (2004: 218–19). Cultural branding is about reflecting the cultural context or the *zeitgeist*. Holt believes cultural activists and individuals who understand popular culture develop successful brands. He posits that the problem with many brands is ignorance with regard to art, history, popular culture and trends. He calls for a new focus on consumer research that examines individuals instead of target markets. Rather than worry about traditional consumer research, brand leaders should assemble cultural knowledge (Holt 2004: 219).

As the branding relationship develops, the successful cultural-branding agent will listen to and understand the consumer, producing the goods a consumer desires. A successful brander will understand the historic equities of products and position them according to a strategic marketing rank toward the most advantageous customers. Brands that become iconic brands develop a reputation for revealing an appropriate narrative (Holt 2004: 219). Holt states that new brands earn higher profits when they are woven into social institutions and political awareness (Holt 2006b: 300). For example, the men's fashion industry's re-releasing of what are known as American 'heritage brands' through mass retail-outlet collaborations. Chippewa Boots, an established brand and noted for its roots in workwear and blue-collar labour, has recently done a collaboration with J.Crew. Chippewa, with their 'Made in the USA' line of boots for men, allows J.Crew to be associated with their notions of quality and authentic American craftsmanship. J.Crew's new upscale line of 'Made in the USA' boots from Chippewa are accepted into social life because it provides customers with what Holt has called 'real informational, interactional, and symbolic benefits' (Holt 2006b: 300). In this case, the customer purchasing the boots may feel attachments to American heritage and thus feelings of quality. Additionally, J.Crew becomes associated with a 'heritage brand' allowing the company to be perceived as better than just another mass-fashion producer.

In *Legendary Brands: Unleashing the Power of Storytelling to Create a Winning Marketing Strategy*, Laurence Vincent demonstrates how each company creates a brand culture through myths and brand narratives that give their products a consumer perception that their brand is the best (2002: 25). Also, each brand situates itself within popular culture in the hopes of becoming part of the social order and cultural context. Vincent's research reveals that brand narratives must have four parts: aesthetics, plot, character and theme. Aesthetics includes any part of the brand that stimulates one of the five senses. Vincent suggests that spectacle (what you see), song (what you hear musically) and diction (how words are constructed to convey meaning) are important elements for visual and performing arts. Brands can also stimulate taste and touch, and these are powerful narrative devices (Vincent 2002: 19). Making a connection to the consumer through brand narrative is key to success. The narrative must relate to the consumer both culturally and personally and the consumer must develop a personal attachment to the brand's narrative (Vincent 2002: 127). The brand narrative attracts customers when the audience follows the characters used in the brand advertising and marketing.

Consumer brand knowledge relates to cognitive representation of the brand. Interpretations of fashion-branding strategies are necessary to understand a company's advertisements and their relationships to consumers (Heding, Knudtzen and Bjerre 2009: 205). The cultural approach to branding relies on interpreting how brand meaning impacts consumers and how, in turn, consumers influence future meaning and branding techniques (Heding, Knudtzen and Bjerre 2009: 215). Increasingly competitive marketplaces demand that companies associate their brands with other people, places, things or brands as a means of building or leveraging knowledge that might otherwise be difficult to achieve through product marketing programs (Keller 2003: 597). Linking the brand to another person, place, thing or cultural movement affects how consumers view the brand or 'primary brand knowledge'. A deeper understanding of how knowledge of a brand and other linked entities interact is of paramount importance. The linkages to the originating or primary brand become 'secondary' brand associations such as other brands, people, events, places, social causes and/or other companies. To provide comparable insight and guidance, a conceptually visual model demonstrates this leveraging process (Figure 2).

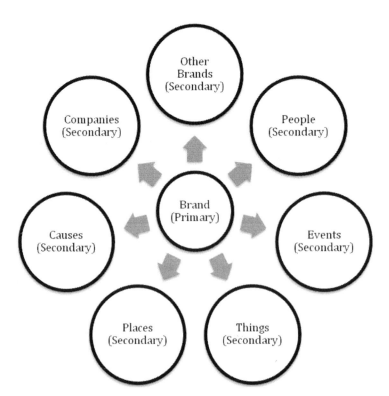

Figure 2: Examples of Brand Linkages to Popular Culture. Modified from Keller (2003: 598).

Linking the brand (primary source) to various parts of culture (secondary source) creates new primary brand knowledge (Keller 2003: 598). The linking of brand-A to other aspects of popular culture creates recognition and association with other causes and meanings thereby creating new narratives (primary brand + secondary brand = new meanings). While a consumer may know nothing about the retailer where they are shopping, they may be aware of secondary branding sources associated with the retailer, such as props and display design, and this could entice them to become more knowledgeable about the store and what they are about to purchase.

Jeff B. Murray and Julie L. Ozanne argue in 'Rethinking the Critical Imagination' (2006: 46) that interpretative methods of consumer research are acceptable methods for understanding how a company is creating meaning and understandings of culture for consumers. They call for researchers to examine brands from a critical perspective. This is accomplished through analysing the branding process where layers of multiple meanings and negotiations are created with the customer. Elements such as advertising are used to create such meaning (Moor 2007: 5–7). The researcher's eyes and experiences become a voice in what is possible. The researcher may examine the branding based upon life experiences that may not have been experienced by other consumers; therefore, interpretation and meaning will be different depending on the perspective. In other words, the precise meaning of the branding strategy is not so important. More crucial are the stories and narratives generated in the mind of the viewer, rather than that of the advertiser (Murray and Ozanne 2006: 51).

In order to understand and interpret the visual meanings and associations of new iconic forms, an individual must investigate the appearance of the icon, history of the icon, evolutionary changes of the icon, iconic groups associated with that icon and exploitation of that particular icon. By understanding contemporary popular culture and the general history of an icon the viewer can begin to interpret meanings and how new visual messages are generated (Nachbar and Lause 1992: 178–79). Through fashion, 'B' becomes a new context for the exploitation of historical and popular-culture icons generating a new brand story (Hancock 2009a) that is seen in men's fashion narrating to them an understandable message that allows them to make connections.

VISUAL RETAIL SPACES AND MEMES

Visual merchandising can be defined as the features and characteristics of a retail space that create an inviting and exciting environment for the consumer (Diamond and Litt 2009: 213–14). Elements of store design and display such as colour, furnishings, props, artwork, signage, and more all contribute to visual merchandising. Stores may have an in-house design team, corporate visual-merchandising branch, or can employ freelance merchandisers to positively impact sales. Balance is of utmost importance in all aspects of visual merchandising, as the proper message and story must be conveyed at all levels of brand communication. Without visual merchandising, stores might look unappealing or find it difficult to compete with other retailers carrying similar products (Diamond and Litt 2009: 214).

Establishing a retail store using visual display is imperative to discuss the system for understanding how consumers create associations for brand meaning (Hancock 2009b). Utilizing certain props in a store is shown to be effective to explain the phenomenon of how a brand can become associated with notions of authenticity or masculinity. For example, a trade-magazine article exploring the use of props in retail stores found that bikes and motorcycles were a common theme in several successful fashion retail brands in London (Anon. 2012), directly linking the display of a non-fashion object to successful visual merchandising.

Another example illustrates how, the icon and display of the American Flag was common in many of these stores. Whether it was tattered or brand new, retailers used this icon to associate garments with preconceived notions of Americana. Presented with iconic sportswear, it is unquestionable that the American flag displays notions of patriotism and national identity. The American flag creates a visual display that could be deceiving to most consumers who might perceive that they are supporting American workers by purchasing garments 'Made in the USA' because the garments are featured in front of the flag. This aura of Americana is supported with the various uses of denim blue jeans, khaki pants, or even traditional patterns and cargo pants such as camouflage displayed next to or with the flag (Figure 3). Additionally, these iconic mass-fashion garments are transnational and associated with notions of what attire men wear, reinforcing ideas of what could be perceived as socially acceptable and masculine no matter when they are utilized or how they are contextualized.

Figure 3: A visual display from the retailer Brooklyn Circus in Brooklyn, New York. The reader will note the use of the flag behind such iconic garments as camouflage cargo pants, khakis and denim blue jeans. Photo courtesy of Kevin Matthews and Joseph Hancock, 2012, All Rights Reserved.

USING MEMES IN RETAIL BRANDING SCHEMES

The importance of creating an inviting and appropriate retail space is not a novel concept. Utilizing meme theory, however, affords the opportunity to evaluate the methods by which brand identity and meaning can be created through visual merchandising. A team of researchers in the United Kingdom developed an approach to retail brand creation through visual merchandising by conducting interviews (Kerfoot, Davies and Ward 2003: 143–52). They found that by focusing on consumer answers to merchandising strategies, several brand associations were discovered to have common visual identities and characteristics. Entailing several components, the importance of visual merchandising is recognized immediately as it creates and sustains consumer interest in the location where retail sales are made. While an overview of visual merchandising will note such important features as lighting, displays, mannequins, window designs and themes, it is important and relevant to note that these areas can have different emphases for different retail brands. In stores like the Ralph Lauren Double RL in New York and Isle of Man in Chicago, mannequins were rarely a point of focus in their merchandising arrangement. Instead, props and themes created and conveyed brand narratives at the retail level.

One theory in marketing research is *memetics*, or the study of memes. In business and marketing application, meme theory has been used to explain the success of certain management strategies, advertising campaigns and brand identities (Pech 2003; Marsden 2002; Williams 2000; Wu and Ardley 2007). Russell Williams, in his exploration of memes involved in each of these categories, inadvertently integrates the concept of brand icons and the proliferation of a meme by referencing the 'Marlboro Man' (2000: 276). The Marlboro Man was created in the 1950s to advertise filtered cigarettes and give them a masculine identity by using a cowboy. The iconic image resonates with Americans in a far different, but no less pleasing, way than it does with West Africans. However, though the cultural digestion of this meme is associated with different notions, the brand is successful in both markets. This is a positive example of an accidental brand evolution: much like genes, memes can mutate through their dissemination.

Brand meme creation and mutation can occur from the actions of the producer or the consumer. Yufan Wu and Barry Ardley discuss the difficulty and importance of recognizing the power of the meme, noting that its memetic transmission must be carefully followed if the brand is to maintain an appropriate identity (2007: 307). In this case, it is important to note that the vehicles for meme transmission can be auditory, visual and linguistic (Pech 2003: 173–74). In the context of the retail store, all three sensory types are engaged. Thus, brand meme creation, mutation and even confusion can occur at a much higher rate through a customer's interaction in a store.

Joseph Hancock's study of Abercrombie & Fitch (2009b) highlights this concept. His exploration of the flagship store on 5th Avenue in New York City describes the dance music and erotic imagery set amongst rugged preppy clothing and other signs of the great outdoors (2009b: 79–80). Because the Abercrombie brand focuses on notions of masculinity and sex, these seemingly conflicting memes serve to bombard the customer with enticing brand messages.

Another crucial element of Hancock's study was the comparison of gay clone culture to the *hypermasculine* imagery of the Abercrombie store (2009b: 76–83). In Martin Levine's landmark study on gay clone culture in

Butch image	Sign vehicles
Western	Cowboy hat, denim jacket, cowboy shirt, Western belt, leather chaps, Frye or cowboy boots, farmer bandanas, rawhide thongs
Leather	Black leather motorcycle cap, jacket, pants and boots. Black or white T-shirts, studded black leather belt and wrist band, chains, tattoos
Military	Green army cap, flight jacket, red belt and fatigues. Brown leather bomber jacket, khaki army shirt, combat boots
Labourer	Hardhat, denim jacket, plaid flannel shirt, painter's pants, construction boots, keys
Athlete	Team jacket, sweatshirt, Lacoste shirt, tank top, sweatpants, gym shorts, jock straps, white crew socks and running shoes

Figure 4: Butch Sign Vehicles in Clone Fashion. Taken from Martin Levine (1998: 60).

the 1970s, several archetypes of masculinity are identified with accompanying clothing styles (1998: 60; see Figure 4). Levine notes that gay men in clone culture overemphasize masculine images to create sexual appeal, and refers to this concept as hypermasculinity (1998: 56–60). These cultural markers of masculinity, or memes of masculinity, are not new; many are historical references to various aspects of American history. Another book, *Jocks and Nerds*, by Richard Martin and Harold Koda, also details these masculine style tropes (1989: 7–9). Using the work of Martin and Koda alongside Levine proves the cultural importance and longevity of these memes. Levine's study, conducted in the 1970s, and Martin and Koda's work, published in 1989, provide a continuity in the study of cultural masculinity as it relates to fashion and the use of repetitive archetypes.

Of the twelve style icons in *Jocks and Nerds*, five are consistent with Levine's study and the various memes referenced by the visual merchandising of the menswear stores that were surveyed for this study. Levine uses the terms *Western, Leather, Military, Labourer* and *Athlete*. The roughly corresponding chapters in *Jocks and Nerds* are 'The Cowboy', 'The Rebel', 'The Military Man', 'The Worker' and 'Joe College'. Each meme has associated signposts that serve to conjure notions of masculinity, authenticity and heritage. Though multiple memes can be referenced while creating a visual-merchandising strategy, these five have a storied cultural history that is associated with American heritage and masculinity.

MEME ONE: THE REBEL

'The adult who purchases a Harley-Davidson may be fulfilling a different kind of dream – the dream of freedom perhaps not yet achieved for the baby boomer who has become a stalwart member of society' (DeLong and Park 2008: 177). This quote, from an article on the black leather jacket, paints a clear picture of the rebel that could never be found.

Two iconic symbols are discussed in this article, both separately and in tandem: the motorcycle and the black leather jacket. Though focusing primarily on the garment, Marilyn DeLong and Juyeon Park discuss the notions that these symbols create for both the wearer and the viewer. Interestingly, many of the stores that featured motorcycles as prominent points of visual display also featured or sold leather jackets. One store in particular, The Isle of Man in Chicago, was almost solely designed and merchandised around this concept. Ostensibly inspired by the treacherous annual motorcycle race on the namesake British island, this boutique sold a mix of vintage and new leather jackets, motorcycle gear and various accessories, shoes and cosmetics for men. As if the rampant display of motorcycle symbols was not enough, two large posters of Steve McQueen hung in the store, an actor noted for creating an impenetrable 'bad boy' image.

Another actor noted for perfectly stylizing the rebel look was Marlon Brando in the film, *The Wild One* (Benedek 1953). Not only was his leather jacket and motorcycle look complete with a plain white T-shirt and cuffed jeans, but his character also was part of a youth gang (DeLong and Park 2008: 174). Beyond style, his cool and detached attitude fully formed the icon of the rebel, an icon that continues to be revived in modern culture. Mike Salisbury describes the experience of LA-area bikers congregating regularly outside the city to enjoy a ride in, much like a gang of cool rebels (2004: 93).

The iconic appearance of the rebel, though inextricably linked, in some cultural references, to the motorcycle, can also stand alone as fashion inspiration for an entire subculture. The coiffed hair, leather jacket, plain white T-shirt, cuffed jeans and black boots ensemble has clothed bikers, punks, skinheads and even Fonzie on ABC's television show *Happy Days* (Garry Marshall, 1974–84). Because each of these groups has adopted and altered this basic palette, it is important to reference the icon of the rebel more generally. Even when using a motorcycle to evoke the entire look and feel of the rebel, a merchandiser must be conscious not to place a heavily embellished leather jacket nearby that could suggest the uniform of a Hell's Angels member. The rebel, being far less distinct in apparel choices than the cowboy, has significant symbols in his own right; however, image management and discretion can provide the best allure for consumers.

By committing strongly to the iconic image of the leather-clad motorcycle rider, the Isle of Man (Figure 5) evokes notions of masculinity and authenticity from both the jacket and the motorcycle that a male customer might be seeking. Especially considering the price point of the store, the quote above might accurately represent its clientele. In this case, these men who have worked diligently to create comfortable lives for themselves can purchase the identity of the rebel through the items at the store. In doing so, they are solidifying the process that began when the first motorcycle picture was hung on the store's wall: these men are validating the notions of freedom that are assigned from the visual display and store signage onto the goods.

As an icon, the rebel stands inherently opposed to the consumerism that drives the world of fashion. However, by referencing symbols such as the motorcycle and the leather jacket, retailers can retro-brand a store's visual display to highlight distinctly masculine attributes. By showcasing a worn biker jacket haphazardly strewn on a vintage motorcycle, the message is not a disdain for the world. Rather, this image would underscore the rugged outsider aspect of the rebel, encapsulating it in the essence of cool. The themes of ruggedness and the appeal of the outsider are also consistent in other iconographic memes of masculinity, such as the cowboy.

Figure 5: Isle of Man, a boutique in Chicago, features a motorcycle prominently in the store, creating notions of masculinity and authenticity linked with the icon of the rebel. Photo courtesy of Kevin Matthews and Joseph Hancock, 2012, All Rights Reserved.

MEME TWO: THE COWBOY

Ever present in American culture since the first few rode out in the late nineteenth century, the cowboy has become an iconic image that is easy to reference in visual display (Martin and Koda 1989: 77). A simple touch of a red paisley-print cotton bandana can evoke images from pop culture of the brave pioneers who travelled out to conquer the West. Though photographic accounts throughout the cowboy's history have shown considerable changes in dress, there are some garment styles and details that will always be attributed to Western wear: snap-front shirts, fringe jackets, ten-gallon hats and leather chaps. No matter which cultural groups have adopted these into their uniform, they still ring true to the nostalgic image of the cowboy. Just as the Marlboro Man was a successful branding tool to make cigarettes appear masculine, other brands can also use aspects of the cowboy to create notions of masculinity and authenticity.

In her article titled 'The Evolution of Western Style in Menswear', Laurel Wilson uncovers important aspects of the history of the cowboy that firmly solidify its presence as uniquely American (2009: 465–79). First, the discrepancies in depictions of what cowboys wore can be attributed to several key factors: cowboys operated in different areas of the United States with very different climates; cowboys adopted dress from Spain, Mexico and the Native American tribes; cowboy style was appropriated by performers and dude ranchers while working cowboys were still on the plains. In this brief historical account, it becomes clear as to why Western-inspired dress was synonymous with ostentatious decoration and flamboyance. Meanwhile, the outfits that working cowboys wore included aspects borrowed from several cultures that all spawned from function. Even the slight changes in garment details, like fabric choice and belt-loop size, were of utmost importance to the working cowboy.

Recent references to the cowboy in popular film have had a significant impact on the revival of the cowboy as a fashion icon. Films like *3:10 to Yuma* (Mangold 2007) and *Brokeback Mountain* (Lee 2005) have received critical acclaim, and present an authentic cowboy image in the costume choices. Notable items in the apparel of the cowboy include the cowboy hat, otherwise known as a ten-gallon hat or Stetson; bandana or cotton scarf, usually in a paisley print; Western-style plaid button-up shirt with defined yoke and snap buttons; denim; leather chaps; and cowboy boots with spats (Martin and Koda 1989: 77–80). Saddlebags and patterned blankets, inspired by Native American tribes, complete the look and provide clear symbols that can be used to evoke the iconic cowboy image. Though the characters and the action in the two films above are vastly different from each other, they provide two important qualities for the viewer. First, differences in cowboy apparel relate to the functionality of each garment; the gunslingers in *3:10 to Yuma* need a holster for their pistols, while the two main characters in *Brokeback Mountain* frequently wear large field jackets to protect themselves from the cold nights in the mountains of Wyoming. Second, despite the differences, each portrayal of the cowboy presents a grittiness and authenticity that is difficult to rival. Also, because both films are set in the past, this may suggest that the true cowboy is no longer present in the American landscape.

As suggested by the visual display of several key men's fashion retailers, however, the *image* of cowboy is far from obsolete. In the conclusion of her article, Wilson notes that the cowboy style tends to have resurgences when Americans need a solemn, nostalgic, heroic figure (2009: 476). Because the profession of a working cowboy is no longer part of our cultural landscape, the image of the cowboy is the perfect locus for retro-branding a retail experience. Men who purchase Western wear in New York City at Ralph Lauren's Double RL store are not going to herd cattle in Wyoming (Figure 1); therefore there is safety in this fantasy and illusion. Figure 6, showcasing hunting gear and aspects of the pioneering is an example of how the icon of the cowboy is conjured by visual merchandising.

Much of the definitive aspects of cowboy dress are rooted in function – namely protection. The cowboy is, of course, a lone ranger. In a retail marketplace saturated with identical styles from different makers, utilizing Western themes in visual display creates the perfect attraction for the consumer that he feels he needs to stand out. In doing so, he is also protecting his masculinity by adopting that of a cowboy.

MEME THREE: JOE COLLEGE

When describing the origin of the term 'Joe College', Martin and Koda refrain from precise historical placement (1989: 137). Instead, they focus on the defining cultural characteristics of collegiate men's style and the iconic symbols they produced. While fashion dictates change in acceptable dress, collegiate style has focused on, and created, classic styles that speak to the irreverence of youth. Even styles that transcend generations, such as the button-down shirt, are worn and styled in a way to defy conventional modes of dress. Thus, Joe College has been symbolized through several college symbols, including sports, books and typewriters.

Figure 6: Welcome Stranger, menswear boutique in San Francisco, CA, uses props to create notions of masculinity and authenticity related to the cowboy. Photo courtesy of Kevin Matthews and Joseph Hancock, 2012, All Rights Reserved.

Unlike other men's fashion icons, which begin from functional garments and become associated with the masculine traits of their usage, Joe College represents a lifestyle that is seeped in tradition, elitism and knowledge. As lifestyle branding has taken off in the fashion world in recent years, preppy has gone from a singular garment, such as a sweater vest, to an entire brand, such as a menswear store designed like a lavish study. Wall shelves that display shoes can be filled with encyclopedic books, such as in the Brooklyn Circus flagship store in New York City. Directly opposite the shelves is an antique leather couch. This playful interior juxtaposition can easily allude to the Ivy League frat house, or perhaps a campus library. In the college context, this creates a notion of authenticity very different from the cowboy or military man.

The notion of authenticity ascribed by college symbols is of class rather than gender. In the case of the cowboy, class has been dissolved in historical references in favour of the strong masculine attributes that every man can strive to achieve. In the case of gender, symbols that allude to Joe College also speak to a gentleman in the making. Perhaps this freshness of masculinity, even potential masculinity, is what draws today's consumer to the lifestyle.

The Brooklyn Circus store in San Francisco, CA, creates a perfect image of the symbols associated with Joe College. Importantly, the brand specializes in producing varsity jackets, a staple garment of the Joe College wardrobe.

Figure 7: The Brooklyn Circus boutique in San Francisco uses a typewriter and antique desk to convey the image of Joe College. Photo courtesy of Kevin Matthews and Joseph Hancock, 2012, All Rights Reserved.

In Figure 7, this garment is juxtaposed with a typewriter, desk and American flag, drawing on notions of school spirit. By situating a garment with masculine qualities above an object that reflects intellect and achievement, the Brooklyn Circus uses a meme of masculinity that is distinct from other icons, and distinguished. Rather than ruggedness, this brand is historical, reflective and educated. This can entice a consumer by presenting a hyperreality that they never experienced, or a nostalgic moment that they can engage in.

MEME FIVE: BLUE-COLLAR WORKER

When Martin Levine was conducting fieldwork for his landmark study on gay clone culture in the United States, he explored the danger and sex appeal of rough-trade gender presentation among gay males (1998: 77–99). Many of the gay clones in Levine's book are middle class; yet gay clone culture dictated the fashion choices of these cities (namely New York and San Francisco) to be distinctly blue-collar, rugged and hypermasculine. Shaun Cole explores clone fashion as well as other trends in recent history to describe the cycle of gay men adopting working-class dress (2000: 93–106, 169–81). With regards to masculinity, and concurrently sexuality, there is certainly a virility that is ascribed to working-class symbols, from the hardhat of a construction worker to the faded blue jeans of a trucker. With regards to American heritage, however, these symbols take on different meanings. In the context of men's fashion retail stores, the blue-collar symbols used in visual display were often celebrated as antiquated symbols of America's past as opposed to sexualized definitions of masculinity.

One of the strongest symbols of blue-collar dress is a pair of jeans. Though now available at every tier of fashion, this garment has a long history that is inextricably linked to America's working class (Sauro 2005). Pioneered by Levi Strauss in 1873 for use in mining and other labour-intensive industries, denim jeans have evolved into a ubiquitous garment throughout most of the world. Styles used in blue-collar industries are still produced and worn today; alongside the various denim boutiques showcasing different levels of distressing in denim, however, the mark of an authentic pair of jeans may vary completely depending on the viewer.

Another symbolic garment of blue-collar labour is the apron (Gau n.d.). Used in a variety of labour-intensive jobs, the apron has several important similarities to jeans: both garments are generally constructed of a thick-weight fabric, such as canvas or twill; both are of utmost importance in function and protection; both will show signs of wear due to regular use. Unlike fine suiting that white-collar labour calls for, aprons and jeans are not meant to stay pressed or clean. Though the apron is less likely to make a strong revival as a fashion item, its use as a tool for branding and retro-branding is eminent. As men's fashion retail branding begins to adopt these and other staples of workwear, it is important to evaluate the shift in American culture that occurs alongside these trends.

With most revivals in American heritage style, there is a strong social nostalgia present (Wilson 2008: 476; Cole 2000: 171). The prevalence of men's fashion retailers celebrating the working class seems to coincide with a rapidly

Figure 8: By placing this loom in a museum-like way in its headquarters, Levi's strengthens its brand notions of historical authenticity and associations to manly industrial labour. Photo courtesy of Kevin Matthews and Joseph Hancock, 2012, All Rights Reserved.

shrinking manufacturing sector and an increasingly virtual globalized economy. By presenting objects from labour-intensive industries as antiques, and by using them as part of a retro-branding motif, it seems as if men's fashion retailers believe the remaining textile and apparel manufacturers to be novel. Instead of truly celebrating the working class of America, men's fashion retailers are idolizing the 'blue-collar heroes' of times past. The Levi's Headquarters in San Francisco features a loom on which original denim fabric was woven (Figure 8). The disconnect between nostalgia and present reality will likely create the same cyclical confusion that both Cole and Levine explore with sexual identity and gender performance.

CONCLUSION

The concepts and fieldwork conducted in this study conclude that strong visual merchandising can aid men's fashion retailers in creating a solid brand identity by conjuring cultural memes. These iconic memes convey notions of authenticity and masculinity for the retail brands in which they are presented. If referenced properly by way of visual display, a men's fashion brand can build a strong identity and create multiple meanings and associations for the consumer. In a competitive marketplace, this type of branding will help to set a retailer apart from its peers. As men continue to engage in fashion consumption, narrative branding will not only ensure higher profits, but also reflect and inspire cultural standards of masculinity and authenticity.

By evaluating brands through the visual display of retail stores, scholars can continue to unpack the cultural signifiers of brand narratives. Though much scholarship in the area of branding, including fashion branding, is focused on advertisements, it is important to continually evaluate the retail store. As the location of commodity and cultural exchange, retail stores provide a tangible, defined boundary in which men can exercise not only performances of gender, but also reveal their understanding of brand identities and meanings.

As research continues in the field of fashion retail, it may also become necessary to explore brand meme discrepancies and inappropriate associations. Considering the plethora of props used in certain locations during this study, one might contemplate the line between retail branding and clutter. Though many male consumers are now delighting at the retail shopping experience, it is imperative, both culturally and financially, not to burden the consumer with an array of mismatched objects, leading to conflicting memes and muddled brand associations. It is also important to explore the notion of brand loyalty as it relates to retail branding, especially considering the recent abundance of men's fashion-only retail stores. The fashion industry is constantly adapting to protect the profits of its businesses – so too must fashion scholarship continue to examine these changes.

ACKNOWLEDGEMENTS

The authors would like to thank the following individuals who have made this article possible. They include, the Drexel University's Steinbright Coop Center who funded this project; Drexel University's Honors College; Dean David Jones; Custom Design Major Program Coordinator Kevin Egan; the Antoinette Westphal College of Media Arts and Design; Dean Allen Sabinson; Program Director Anne Cecil; and the Design and Merchandising programme. A special thanks goes to the Drexel University Office of International Programs for allowing Zhaohui Gu, Xi'an Polytechnic University in China, to be the first visiting scholar in the Design and Merchandising programme. The authors would also like to recognize their families, for all their support.

REFERENCES

Anon (2012), 'What are 2012's visual merchandising trends?', *Retail Week*, http://www.retail-week.com/stores/what-are-2012s-visual-merchandising-trends/5033405.article. Accessed 9 August 2013.

Barthes, Roland (1967), *The Fashion System*, New York: Columbia University Press.

Benedek, Laslo (1953), *The Wild One*, USA: Stanley Kramer Productions.

Brannon, Evelyn, L. (2005), *Fashion Forecasting: Research, Analysis and Presentation*, New York: Fairchild Publications.

Cole, Shaun (2000), *'Don We Now Our Gay Apparel': Gay Men's Dress in the Twentieth Century*, Oxford: Berg.

DeLong, Marilyn and Park, Juyeon (2008), 'From Cool to Hot to Cool: The Case for the Black Leather Jacket', in Andrew Reilly and Sarah Cosbey (eds), *The Men's Fashion Reader*, New York: Fairchild, pp. 166–79.

Diamond, Jay and Litt, Sheri (2009), *Retailing in the Twenty-First Century*, New York: Fairchild.

Edwards, Tim (2006), *Cultures of Masculinity*, Routledge: London.

Gau, Colleen (n.d.), 'Conventional Work Dress and Casual Work Dress', *Berg Encyclopedia of World Dress and Fashion: Volume 3 – The United States and Canada*, http://www.bergfashionlibrary.com/view/bewdf/BEWDF-v3/EDch3042.xml, Accessed 18 November 2012.

Gelb, Betsy D. (1997), 'Creating "Memes" While Creating Advertising', *Journal of Advertising Research*, 37 (6), pp. 57–59.

Hameide, M. Kaled (2011), *Fashion Branding Unraveled*, New York: Fairchild.

Hancock, Joseph H, (2009a), *Brand/Story: Ralph, Vera, Johnny, Billy, and Other Adventures in Fashion Branding*, New York: Fairchild.

Hancock, Joseph H. (2009b), 'Chelsea on 5th Avenue: Hypermasculinity and Gay Clone Culture in the Retail Branding Practices of Abercrombie & Fitch', *Fashion Practice*, 1: 1, pp. 63–86.

Heding, Tilde, Knudtzen, Charolette F. and Bjerre, Mogens (2009), *Brand Management: Research, Theory and Practice*, London: Routledge.

Holt, Douglas B. (2002), 'Why Do Brands Cause Trouble? A Dialectical Theory of Consumer Culture and Branding', *Journal of Consumer Research*, 29: 1, pp. 70–90.

Holt, Douglas B. (2004), *How Brands Become Icons*, Boston: Harvard Business School Press.

Holt, Douglas B. (2006a), 'Jack Daniel's America: Iconic Brands as Ideological Parasites and Proselytizers', *Journal of Consumer Culture*, 6: 3, pp. 355–77.

Holt, Douglas B. (2006b), 'Toward a Sociology of Branding', *Journal of Consumer Culture*, 6: 3, pp. 299–302.

Keller, Kevin L. (2003), 'Brand Synthesis: The Multidimensionality of Brand Knowledge', *Journal of Consumer Research*, 29: 4, pp. 595–600.

Kerfoot, Shona, Davies, Barry and Ward, Philippa (2003), 'Visual Merchandising and the Creation of Discernible Retail Brands', *International Journal of Retail & Distribution Management*, 31: 3, pp. 143–52.

Lee, Ang (2005), *Brokeback Mountain*, USA: Universal Studios.

Levine, Martin P. (1998), *Gay Macho: The Life and Death of the Homosexual Clone*, New York: NYUP.

López-Gydosh, Dilia and Hancock, Joseph (2009), '*American Men and Identity: Contemporary African American and Latino Style*', 32: 1, pp. 16–28.

Mangold, James (2007), *3:10 to Yuma*, USA: Lionsgate.

Manlow, Veronica (2011), 'Creating an American Mythology: A Comparison of Branding Strategies in Three Fashion Firms', *Fashion Practice*, 3: 1, pp. 85–110.

Marsden, Paul (2002), 'Brand positioning: Meme's the word', *Marketing Intelligence & Planning*, 20: 5, pp. 307–12.

Martin, Richard and Koda, Harold (1989), *Jocks and Nerds: Men's Style in the Twentieth Century*, New York: Rizzoli.

Moor, Elizabeth (2003), 'Branded Spaces: The Scope of New Marketing', *Journal of Consumer Culture*, 3: 1, pp. 39–60.

Moor, Elizabeth (2007), *The Rise of Brands*, Oxford: Berg.

Murray, Jeff B. and Ozanne, Julie L. (2006), 'Rethinking the Critical Imagination', in Russell W. Belk (ed.), *Handbook of Qualitative Research Methods in Marketing*, Cheltenham: Edward Elgar Publishing.

Nachbar, Jack and Lause, Kevin (1992), *Popular Culture: An Introductory Text*, Bowling Green: Bowling Green State University Popular Press.

Pech, Richard J. (2003), 'Memes and Cognitive Hardwiring: Why are Some Memes More Successful Than Others?', *European Journal of Innovation Management*, 6: 3, pp. 173–81.

Pellegrin, Bertrand (2009), *Branding the Man*, New York: Allworth Press.

Salisbury, Mike (2004), 'Hey Johnny, What Are You Rebelling Against?', *Forbes FYI, FYI*, 092–97, http://search.proquest.com/docview/200845645?accounti d=10559. Accessed 18 November 2012.

Sauro, Clare (2005), 'Jeans', A–Z of Fashion', *Berg Fashion Library*, http://www. bergfashionlibrary.com/view/bazf/bazf00329.xml. Accesssed 18 November 2012.

Schultz, Majken and Hatch, Mary Jo (2006), 'A Cultural Perspective on Corporate Branding: The Case of Lego Group', in Jonathon E. Schroeder and Miriam Salzer-Mörling (eds), *Brand Culture*, London: Routledge.

Trebay, Guy (2010), 'From Boys to Men', *New York Times*, 15 October, http:// www.nytimes.com/2010/10/17/fashion/17MANLY.html?pagewanted=all &_r=0. Accessed 4 August 2013.

Vincent, Laurence (2002), *Legendary Brands: Unleashing the Power of Storytelling to Create a Winning Market Strategy*, Chicago: Dearborn Trade Publishing.

Williams, Russell (2000), 'The Business of Memes: Memetic Possibilities for Marketing and Management', *Management Decision*, 38: 4, pp. 272–79.

Wilson, Laurel E. (2009), 'The Evolution of Western Style in Menswear', in Andrew Reilly and Sarah Cosbey (eds), *The Men's Fashion Reader*, New York: Fairchild, pp. 465–79.

Wu, Yufan and Ardley, Barry (2007), 'Brand Strategy and Brand Evolution: Welcome to the World of the Meme', *The Marketing Review*, 7: 3, pp. 301–10.

CONTRIBUTOR DETAILS

Kevin Matthews is the second student in the history of Drexel University to complete the Custom Design Major programme in Global Fashion Industry. As a recent graduate he is already working full-time at the home office of Urban Outfitters in buying. He craves an educational track that allows him to look at fashion on a more theoretical basis. Matthews has been working in industry for over seven years and wished to have his education complement his work experience, and also allow him to indulge in the process of research and academic investigation. The custom-designed major allowed Matthews to evaluate the fashion industry using multiple outside lenses to figure out such phenomena as how fashion occurs and why it changes. In March 2013, Matthews presented this paper at the annual Popular Culture Association/ American Culture Association (PCA/ACA) conference in Washington DC.

Contact: Drexel University, 3141 Chestnut Street, Urbn Center #110G, Philadelphia, PA. 19104, USA.
E-mail: kevinpmatthews@gmail.com

Joseph H. Hancock, II, Ph.D., teaches, publishes and conducts scholarly activities at Drexel University in the Department of Fashion, Product Design and Merchandising. He has a twenty-year retailing background having worked for the Gap Corporation, the Limited Inc. and the Target Corporation and continues to do publishing and merchandising consulting work on an international level. He has published numerous articles in such journals as the *Journal of Popular Culture*, *Journal of American Culture*, *Fashion Practice* and the *Australasian Journal of Popular Culture*. He is the author of the book *Brand/ Story: Ralph, Vera, Johnny, Billy and Other Adventures in Fashion Branding* (Fairchild/Bloomsbury, 2009). His most recent edited book *Fashion in Popular Culture* (Intellect, 2013) was the inspiration for his new journal *Fashion, Style and Popular Culture* (Intellect, 2013).

Contact: 64 Stuart Drive, Norristown, PA 19401, USA.
E-mail: joseph.hancockii@gmail.com

Zhaohui Gu is a visiting scholar at Drexel University in the Antoinette Westphal College of Media Arts and Design. He is the first visiting scholar in the Design and Merchandising Program. Gu teaches and conducts scholarly research at Xi'an Polytechnic University in Xi'an, China. His courses are related to merchandising and branding. He will be a visiting scholar at Drexel University until March 2014, when he will return to his home country. Gu is the author of various publications in China and this article represents his first publication with Intellect. Both Hancock and Matthews wish to thank Zhaohui Gu for his insightful ideas on how to make this manuscript a more well-researched publication.

Contact: 4203 Chester Ave, APT 2D Philadelphia, PA 19104, USA.
E-mail: lightgu2012@gmail.com

Global Fashion Brands: Style, Luxury & History
© 2014 Intellect Ltd Chapter. English language. doi: 10.1386/GFB.1.23_1

D. J. HUPPATZ
Swinburne University of Technology

VERONICA MANLOW
Brooklyn College

Producing and consuming American mythologies: Branding in mass market fashion firms

ABSTRACT

The majority of contemporary fashion encompasses a vast middle ground comprised of popular and influential brands whose designs are neither haute couture nor trendy. These mass-market brands rely on intensive marketing and advertising to evoke ideals of an American national identity and lifestyle. In this article, we employ a holistic analysis of Ralph Lauren and Tommy Hilfiger's lifestyle branding strategies aimed at creating coherent American mythologies, Gap, J. Crew, Abercrombie & Fitch and Hollister's less coherent approach and American Apparel's new 'authenticity' in its portrayal of American ideals. In their respective branding strategies, each of the brands constructs a hyperreal American world based on appearances and associations, in which contradictory ideologies are conflated and consumed by global audiences. The companies produce coherent systems of signification through advertising and promotional strategies in which consumers are invited to become a part of their mythological constructs. Through the kaleidoscopic lens of the production-branding-consumption cycle, an examination of several mass-market brands exposes

KEYWORDS

branding
American fashion
mythologies
national identity
massmarketing
lifestyle

variations on American national identity and differing responses to broader cultural and political changes over the last four decades.

INTRODUCTION

Ready-to-wear mass fashion, produced in large quantities by a variety of manufacturers and designers, represents the bulk of industry sales. While couture level clothing is expensive, made to measure, and employs craftspeople with high technical skills such as cutters, seamstresses, or embroiderers, the mass produced clothing of Ralph Lauren, Tommy Hilfiger, Abercrombie & Fitch, Hollister, J. Crew, Gap, and American Apparel is not, for the most part, exclusive in design, reliant on craft skills or material innovation but instead is characterized by its accessibility, affordability and above all, lifestyle branding. In constructing lifestyles over the past 40 years, these mass fashion labels have contributed to the generation of both individual and collective identities, but their common thread is a particular emphasis on the creation and dissemination of a mythological America.

PRODUCING LIFESTYLES

Although the concept of lifestyle is often understood in individual terms, the assemblage of goods, practices and experiences that are stitched together to comprise a modern lifestyle express collective as well as individual identities. How can we take account of the role fashion companies and consumers play in producing and consuming both products and discourses around lifestyle brands? Yuniya Kawamura (2005) proposes a sociological study she calls 'fashion-ology' that separates fashion from the material product of clothing and the act of production. Fashion and the merchandising and promotional processes that work towards its diffusion in society are part of a conceptual system. Design is part of the tangible world of production but when conceived of as fashion is made to appear mystical. In a survey of the economic and social science literature on consumption within modern capitalism, Ben Fine and Ellen Leopold (1993) argue that most scholars fail to consider consumption in relation to production, and to cultural and historical contexts. For Joanne Entwistle (2000) lived experience intersects with political, technological, economic and cultural spheres. In her most recent work Entwistle (2009) proposes actor network theory (ANT) as a method to study networks linking such systems as aesthetics and the marketplace. Fields of knowledge are tacit and often based on intangible practices.

How does this connect to questions of identity and to the overall experience people have with fashion? Ana Marta González (2010: 81) quotes Laura Bovone (2007), who argues that 'most of us have relatively little to do with fashion designers' suggestions, high fashion images, or prêt-à-porter purchases, but for all of us clothing is a duty, for some of us a pleasure, and for many of us a problem' but González highlights another key factor: the construction of identity vis-à-vis fashion. While it may seem free from certain long-standing social constraints, modern self-conceptualized identity is constructed with 'the materials offered by the consumer society' (González 2010: 80) in relation to social considerations. While it is difficult to grasp the complex interrelations between production, consumption and identity, at the same time, it seems impossible to separate them entirely, and we believe that by analysing branding in popular fashion brands in a holistic manner, we can begin to understand them.

Fashion scholars have long noted that modern fashion communicates 'nonverbal cultural and social ascriptions such as class, gender, education, lifestyle affinities, and political affiliations' (Niederer and Winter 2008: 689). Susan B. Kaiser et al. (1991) contend that fashion change is driven by fashion's ambivalence – even confusion and chaos – in defining a self and creating cultural codes satisfactory to the agent. Perhaps more than most fashion, mass-market fashion embodies an exaggerated version of a fundamental modern conundrum – the paradoxical desire to be at once an independent individual and part of a social collective (Simmel 1904). Gregory P. Stone (1962) cites a long intellectual tradition, including William James, George Herbert Mead, Charles Horton Cooley and Harry Stack Sullivan who all argue the central role of clothing in defining a modern sense of self. Fred Davis (1991), following Herbert Blumer, situates fashion in a new logic of modernity characterized by social change where individual expression asserts itself though the symbolism of clothing rather than as a functionalist mechanism of class differentiation. However, in a post- or hypermodern context, a new question arises when considering the average consumer: how does one construct an identity using mass-marketed brands that offer ideals fabricated in boardrooms?

Ruth P. Rubinstein (1995) analyses how clothing expresses signs and subtle symbols which signal social membership and personal preferences in American culture. Clothing and fashion, argues Malcolm Barnard (2002: 39), 'as communication, are cultural phenomena in that culture may itself be understood as a signifying system, as the ways in which a society's beliefs, values, ideas and experiences are communicated through practices, artefacts and institutions'. Barnard states that fashion does not simply reproduce an existing social order, but is actively 'constitutive of … social groups, and of the identities of individuals within those groups, rather than merely reflective of them'. Diana Crane (2000) characterizes fashion as part of a cultural and global industrial system; once a precise marker of social position, it is no longer limited solely by class hierarchies but has become rather a statement of personal identity. Jean Baudrillard (1993), and later Gilles Lipovetsky (2002), envision fashion itself as an active and originating force in forming identity, liberated from societal constraints.

NATIONAL IDENTITY

National identity, though complex and multifaceted, is defined by Anthony D. Smith as 'bonds of solidarity among members of communities united by shared memories, myths and traditions that may or may not find expression in states of their own but are entirely different from the purely legal and bureaucratic ties of the state' (1991: 15). While shifting and elusive in character, politically, writes Smith, the 'appeal to national identity has become the main legitimation for social order and solidarity today' (1991: 16). As a fundamental form of collective identity, national identity also functions in the socialization of individuals – through, for example, the public school system or national media – and this collective bond is expressed via repertoires of shared values, symbols and traditions. As a continual reminder of a sense of belonging, visible symbols of national identity such as flags, anthems, uniforms, monuments and ceremonies, function to reinforce a shared history and cultural identity.

Importantly, national identity, as an outward expression of nationalism, is commonly understood as something natural and self-evident rather than consciously (or unconsciously) constructed. However, sociologists and historians alike confirm nationalism as an invented doctrine – thus Elie Kedourie's classic opening line, 'Nationalism is a doctrine invented in Europe at the beginning of the nineteenth century' – and national identity as equally constructed (1960: 1, see also Gellner 1964, 1997; Anderson 1991). Eric Hobsbawm and Terence Ranger (1983: 12) argue that what passes for timeless, continuous tradition is frequently invented and mostly relatively recently. While he contends that all cultures are in a state of change and development, Homi K. Bhabha (1990: 208) describes a norm by which the dominant culture locates others within their 'grid'. For Bhabha ([1994] 2005: 247) other cultures are defined with respect to the dominant logic within a 'unifying discourse of 'nation', 'peoples', or authentic 'folk' tradition…' in 'embedded myths'.

In a more recent American context, Betty Jean Craige has analysed the tension between national identity and globalization in the 1980s and early 1990s – a period characterized by the 'intensification of nationalist patriotism' in the United States (1996: 49). Threats to national cultural hegemony, she argues, were due to demographic changes, particularly increased immigration from Latin America and Asia, the threat of multiculturalism (Craige 1996: 61–64), globalization (Craige 1996: 64–66) and military campaigns–to which we could add increasingly globalized trade, loss of manufacturing industries overseas, and significant technological changes in everyday life. In such a climate of profound social and cultural change, the nation itself emerged as a potent source of stability, and visible patriotic symbols and myths help reinforce collective identity. Within an increasingly postmodern culture, characterized by homogeneity in certain sectors (Rutherford 1990), symbolic investment in a stable and coherent nation with timeless values and traditions is both appealing and readily accessible. Iconic American brands such as Coca Cola, Disney, Marlboro, McDonalds, Ford and Apple came to function as seemingly stable vehicles to transmit ideas and ideals both within America and globally functioned as visible symbols of 'Americanization'. In a contemporary consumer society, such brands have a profound influence on the social representations that become rooted in consciousness.

NATIONAL IDENTITY AND FASHION

While scholars are in general agreement that modern fashion continues to function in some sense as an expression of collective identity, there is relatively little scholarship on the important and pervasive issue of fashion's interrelationship between national identity, individual identities and global brands. Wendy Parkins' anthology (2002), *Fashioning the Body Politic: Dress, Gender, Citizenship* comprises a series of historical studies on this issue, but offers little insight into contemporary identity. Valerie Steele and John S. Major (1999) explore the history of Chinese design and the impact it has had on designers outside China, while other scholars such as Steele (2003), Eugenia Paulicelli (2004) and Nicola White (2000) have considered national identity and its role in Italian fashion. Alice Goodrum's (2005) *The National Fabric: Fashion, Britishness, Globalization* reveals the importance that cultural nuances and ambiguities play in defining a British look. Paulicelli and Hazel Clark (2009) explore the links between body, self and the economic and cultural facets of society in the context of national and global identity with a series of contributions which address fashion's role in establishing local style and national narratives, and the role of aesthetic imagination in incorporating a multiplicity of signifiers. Karen Tranberg Hansen (2009) has written extensively about the secondhand clothing market in Zambia. She contends that young people, while desiring the most up to date fashions, do not simply accept and emulate western norms but rather make choices that reflect their own cultural context, such as adapting clothing to fit norms of modesty and respectability. In *Fashions: Exploring Fashion Through Culture* (Feitsma 2012) we see how national identity is upheld historically and in a contemporary context in a variety of nations but most often by those more concerned with fashion design or with fashion subcultures (Carriger, for example, explores the 'Japanese Lolita' and McFarlane fashion in Jamaican reggae dancehalls). Maaike Feitsma (2012) in providing the reader with a historical analysis of Dutch values and attitudes towards self presentation in clothing shows through fashion editorials how French fashions were adapted to Dutch sensibilities. Valéria Brandini (2009) too discusses how elements of Brazilian style in the 1990s become part of the global fashion narrative by following the 'fundamental rules' of European fashion. What we seem to see is a widespread global acceptance of western norms with a variety of local adaptations.

In a variety of blogs young American people exchange information on what their international counterparts are wearing. In a blogpost about fashion and self presentation in Brazil for example, an American is told not to worry, Brazilians buy the same brands though there are some subtle differences in terms of what is worn and when. Men wear soccer shirts and women would not wear sneakers and sweats unless they are exercising. Another blogger writes 'Brazil is not as exotic as Americans believe it to be' (Yahoo Answers 2012). An American is assured by an Italian that they dress like people everywhere else but with 'more class' and 'more fashionable'. One can wear jeans and a t-shirt but with nice shoes, a bag, and makeup, the blogger is advised (Yahoo Answers 2007).

Another area little explored is the means by which companies create a branded identity by drawing on and marketing elements of national identity such as heritage, tradition and attitudes. Not only does fashion shape identity, animate interaction and link the individual to collective life, but firms that produce fashion create both signs of distinction that reproduce and reconstruct hierarchies, as well as mythologies and products that define national and global identities. Davis (1991) calls attention to the fashion's role as a 'social world' containing many 'overlapping' and 'interpenetrating' sectors: manufacturers, merchandisers, designers, models, customers who themselves connect to other social worlds and subworlds. It is within fashion's social world where visual/symbolic and material/productive realities meet. Joseph Henry Hancock II (2009), in discussing advertisers' goals which revolve around creating scenarios and meanings, cites Jean Hamilton's (1997) assertion of the lack of research on how 'macro' forces influence consumer purchase decisions. She argues that this is accomplished through 'selling stories'.

AMERICAN FASHION AND NATIONAL IDENTITY

In the United States, fashion's link to industry has historically yielded simpler clothes for a more active, independent lifestyle. Caroline Rennolds Milbank (1989) describes how a practical American style emerged in the 1940s with designers such as Claire McCardell and Bonnie Cashin. A consumer economy in which mass produced clothing was perfected and later expertly promoted paved the way for a casual sportswear industry which would sweep across the world allowing jeans and t-shirts to carry a popular and seductive ideology founded on a notion of freedom severed from local traditions. David A. Hounshell (1984) contrasts European craftsmanship with the interchangeability of American mass produced clothing and the possibility for continuous innovation and improvement available to a mass market that became synonymous with America. Fashion, and other cultural products embody ideals of democracy, freedom and pragmatism, though they may be combined with a number of other elements as we will see when we consider American fashion brands. Lane Crothers (2010) has analysed the appeal that American popular culture has across class, cultural and ethnic/national boundaries, through music and films that were simple to understand and infused with sex, violence and consumerist content.

Despite changing appearances in garments, the ideological tradition of appealing to American national identity remains. Through fashion, for example, first lady Michelle Obama can be said to have traded a revolutionary and countercultural identity for that of a fashionable woman who embodies traditional American values (Braithwaithe 2012). And this is not an entirely new phenomenon. George Washington, at the first Presidential inauguration of the new nation in 1789, for example, consciously chose to wear home-spun clothing made in America's first wool factory (Bachelor 2010). For Thorstein Veblen ([1899] 1973) and other nineteenth century writers on American fashion, the leisure classes were the key drivers in fashion as they needed to differentiate themselves from the lower classes and thus continually reinforce their difference. In the late twentieth century, however, fashion became less class-based and more about broader conformity to collective identities (Barnard 2002: 131).

In an American context the 1980s and 1990s saw a 'revolution in consumerism' (Smith 2008: 764) as changes in global capitalism saw production shift offshore and consumption intensify in wealthy nations. For fashion, the response involved, 'developing mass designer fashion, extending and expanding the role of mass-produced clothing, affecting all kinds of cultural arenas and encouraging the construction of cultural identities by way of apparel choices' (Smith 2008: 765). While exhibiting variations in clothing collections, mass fashion brands provide continuity by popular appeal to national identity. American fashion brands are both a reflection of American life – real and imagined – for Americans, and an influential force in shaping global culture. For Manlow, 'American fashion projects an American identity that can be readily identified through a variety of elements' (2009: 261).

Just as Roland Barthes ([1957] 1972) holds that myths acquire their meaning through culture, Jean Noël Kapferer (1992) refers to brands as 'meaningless' apart from the cultural content they inhabit. It is through communication, originating in companies and extending to consumers that brands are 'authored'. The brand culture is a discourse comprised of stories, images and associations (Holt 2001). Brands must be positioned correctly vis-à-vis carefully constructed identities so that there will be coherence between products, the spaces they inhabit, and the experiences and narratives they generate. In a world where meanings are often ambiguous, brand mythologies order reality, providing a way to frame the brand's products. This happens at every level in the fashion industry. As Hancock (2009) explains, branding is inextricably linked to mass-produced fashion.

Borrowing from Bhabha's ([1994] 2005: 247) concept of the grid in which a 'natural(ized), unifying discourse of "nation"', can be found, one can argue that the following brands operate as dominant cultures, claiming America as their own and 'othering' outsiders. However, unlike colonizers intent on exercising hegemony and weeding out any subversive responses, fashion brands are a lot less powerful and more flexible in their ideologies, employing an element of frivolity and fantasy, as the following analysis reveals.

RALPH LAUREN AND TOMMY HILFIGER

The first two brands to self-consciously promote an American identity and achieve global success were Ralph Lauren and Tommy Hilfiger. Both brands create a social order, a basis for solidarity on which bonds can be formed. They provide 'technologies' to animate one's self concept and being. Hilfiger reappropriates some of the icons and ideologies of American culture that Lauren so skilfully extracted and reconfigured: the individual freedom and democracy the New World offered, embodied in the West and the Protestant ethic, truncated and commercialized. Success once reliant on hard work, or inherited wealth, is made aspirational and immediately accessible, the old markers of elite heritage severed from a closed system and worn on one's sleeve. The Ivy League, the polo club or beach house are encapsulated in props in flagships stores and in visual images that 'stage' identity (Huppatz 2010: 553). Representations of a once private life are circulated widely through digital media.

Ralph Lauren markets this lifestyle to status-conscious consumers desirous of being affiliated with notions of tradition, good taste and success.

Figures 1 and 2: Ralph Lauren store window in New York City. Photo courtesy of John Ricasoli, 2013. All Rights Reserved.

Lauren's American master narrative of wealth, privilege and freedom draws on elements of traditional and conservative realms of American culture to create an all encompassing mythology, open to people everywhere, of any age, who see value in this nostalgic yet timeless America. Embodied in a vast range of products a lifestyle of privilege can be worn or painted on one's living room wall.

In contrast, Tommy Hilfiger's brand draws upon the world of popular culture to create a more multicultural and inclusive American experience. While Lauren shows deference to elite heritage by way of an appreciation for the leisurely life of the New England Protestant and the aesthetic of the Ivy League university, Hilfiger's mythology incorporates popular sports, film, television and music into the brand. Within these constructed paradigm, Ralph Lauren can be seen as a precursor to Tommy Hilfiger, a lighter, diluted and more inclusive version of the elite, Ivy League preppy universe created by Ralph Lauren. For those who take this world to be real the Hilfiger universe appears to be a third order signifier.

The leaders behind these two brands share a middle class family background in which neither man attained a college diploma, let alone a privileged Ivy League experience. Yet, rather than rebelling against a system that largely shut them out they achieved success through a belief in the American dream; a dream that was later reinvented for others through branding. At the

Figure 3: Tommy Hilfiger store window in New York City. Photo courtesy of John Ricasoli, 2013. All Rights Reserved.

intersection of fashion, branding and advertising strategies, both Ralph Lauren and Tommy Hilfiger emerged in the 1980s and 1990s as successful companies built on particular versions of a mythological America.

GAP AND J. CREW

Running parallel with Lauren's rise to national and then global success, Gap has also built a brand on characteristically American ideals without the 'designer fashion' designation. Founded in San Francisco, California in 1969 by the Fishers, a married couple, Gap Inc. comprises several brands including Gap (with Baby Gap and Gap Kids), Banana Republic, and Old Navy. On its website Gap Inc. describes its 'inventive American style' as: 'Clean, classic clothing and accessories help customers express their individual sense of style'. Gap Inc. prides itself as a brand not reliant on mythology. In some ways one might describe it as a 'generic' brand. Its simple, casual American style is presented as allowing the wearer's individual identity to shine through. However, in the last months of 2011 in particular the brand's success was questioned, with store closures in the US efforts increasingly focused overseas (Duxbury 2011).

The Gap initially sold one item of clothing: Levis jeans. Levis' democratic heritage and association with workers made them appealing to young people eager to demonstrate an 'antipathy to corporate America' (Funding Universe). Ironically, due to the Gap's mainstream success, the company went public in 1976, expanding its range to include basic sportswear, and the small company grew into global brand that marketed a distinctive American sportswear look. However, by the early 2000s, negative publicity over sweatshop conditions and child labour threatened to tarnish the brand (Klein 2000). While it may have lost its countercultural edge, going full circle from anti-corporate to what Teri Agins (1999) refers to as the end point in fashion when a firm goes public and produces commodity merchandise, Gap kept its associations with the countercultural movements of the late 1960s, and added to its identity an American-style success story vis-à-vis the ingenuity of its founders who built a successful empire. The Gap Inc. become a global youth brand and indeed had a profound influence on fashion in promoting comfortable, functional casual American sportswear, the antithesis of 'high' fashion.

Comparing Gap, Inc. to Disney and Coca Cola, Nina Munk (1998) credits former Gap, Inc. CEO Mickey Drexler (like Lauren, a child of Jewish parents who grew up in the Bronx) with having more influence on American style than anyone else. Meryl Gordon (2005) argues that he changed the way the world dressed with the invention of 'casual chic'. Munk (1998) considers that while 'Most clothing companies want their products to be a sign of something else – money, power, class, virility, sex, privilege, access ... Drexler knows instinctively that Americans aren't all that comfortable with class. ... Gap is democratic and familiar. Ordinary, unpretentious, understated, almost lowbrow'. Drexler reads the *New York Post* and does not know the name of the photographer whose work decorates his office walls. He believes that wearing and buying clothing should not be complicated and believed that 'Gap was about wardrobing America'. He took the CEO position in 1983 (Groth and Aquino 2011). In 1996 he recounts his shock at seeing an ad campaign, featuring a young blond androgynous male with a piercing that did not reflect the values of the Gap. The ad director soon left, as did some of her staff. Drexler began purging the brand; he went through each piece of clothing, removing everything that was not 'pure Gap' (Munk 1998). In search of authenticity and an unmarketed look he recruited marketing and advertising executives, and designers he believed would better represent the brand (Groth and Aquino 2011). By 2002, Drexler had to deal with intensifying competition from 'imitators' such as Abercrombie and Fitch and decided to move Gap away from basics into more 'trendy looks', cropped tees and low-rider pants described as 'Britney-esque'. He moved Gap into the domain of more stylish yet still affordable clothing. Gap seemed lost, and indeed it had expanded too quickly. Drexler was abruptly fired and soon after was hired by J. Crew (Gordon 2005; Gaudoin 2010).

Brendan Sauray studied Gap for his semester-long project in a fashion marketing course at Brooklyn College. Analysing advertising, the clothing itself, and the brand's communications in stores and on various social media platforms, Sauray concluded that Gap 'embodies wholesome family values'. Messages are always simple: 'Keep it Simple', or 'Let's Gap Together', for example. He describes the branding message as 'conservatism, freedom, fun, non-political and never sexual'. When men and women are depicted together the mood is 'playful and innocent'. Stores and the website embody the brand's stance that clothing should be simple in design, wellorganized and colour coordinated. Stores feature white, brown and beige decor, in simple surroundings. Websites have easy to read text and neatly organized tabs. Customer service online and in-stores is efficient and pleasant. Summing up The Gap Inc.'s brand identity Sauray concludes that it is 'Everyday casual. Bland and basic'.

In November 2010, The Gap Inc. began its launch in China. Photographer Annie Liebovitz, who had previously worked for the brand, was hired to create the Chinese 'Let's Gap Together' campaign. The marketing director in China states that the brand has always been a supporter of self-expression and embracing one's own individual style. The campaign, says Young & Rubicon China's chief creative officer, is about 'breaking boundaries' between Chinese and US approaches to freedom. In this way, we see a vague American notion of freedom, and its appeal to young Chinese. This young generation, argues Nils Andersson, equates freedom with consumer choices: 'In contrast to previous generations, today's "Golden Generation" is more free to choose what they wear, which is a fundamental expression of new found freedoms'. Y&R China's campaign for Gap won the Brand of the Year Award from the Campaign Asia-Pacific Agency of the Year Awards with black and white images ranging from choreographer and dancer Twyla Tharp, actress Lucy Liu, and comedian Sarah Silverman modelling Gap's Fall line of clothing (Yr. com 2011). In a journey from an authentic experience provided in its single San Francisco store that had a connection to history, ideals and place, the Gap has become flexible in its significations, identity and values.

Mickey Drexler picked up where he left off at Gap. Applying his logic of allowing the masses to look good without going broke, he took the same basics, khakis and tee-shirts to J. Crew, but increased the quality quotient. He describes his vision for J. Crew as 'a better fashion image than the Gap'. His aim is to make the brand more upscale and appeal to a customer who 'graduated from the Gap' in search of something better, more stylish and worth the extra money. He tells Tina Guadoin (2010) that he liked the J. Crew 'preppy vibe' – the broken-in chino pant – that was not so different from the Gap. He believes there are two types of fashion firms 'price-players' or 'quality-players'. 'The only way to go with J.Crew was quality'. He decided to create more 'up-market' pieces: Italian cashmere for the cardigans, and leather from the same Italian firm that supplied Prada (Groth and Aquino 2011). Gaudoin explains Drexler's vision as simple and not unlike his original vision for Gap: quality basics, the perfect T, the perfect pair of khakis, the perfect sweater – but he took it further by increasing the quality to create more upmarket pieces. … His theory being: Customers will pay more for well-made clothing.

(2010)

As a specifically American brand, J. Crew occupies a place paved by Ralph Lauren and Tommy Hilfiger. Continuing the success of American sports and casual wear, J. Crew grew during the 1980s and 1990s to become a major label. Like Lauren, there was a strong emphasis on brand image and identity rather than the distinction of the clothing. Matthew DeBord argued that J. Crew's mail order catalogue was integral to establishing an identity, 'a brand of New York/ Los Angeles casual cool' (1997: 265). He notes the influence of Lauren's Ivy League look and early catalogues influenced by the Bruce Weber-style of expansive images comprising the tableaux of natural looking models with minimal text (DeBord 1997: 269), combined with the convenience of mail order. What DeBord termed the 'visual rhetoric of ease' produced in the catalogue appeals to an American anxiety of having to shift from professional to casual wardrobes (1997: 266–67). In this way, J. Crew anticipates a significant shift in working patterns with little distinction between work and leisure spaces or work time and leisure time, a shift intensified by the rise of personal mobile technologies. The absence of a designer further simplifies the brand, establishing it as a look or lifestyle given an identity through the wearer and not vis-à-vis, an identification with a designer whose presence figures in the brand in a prominent manner.

While not specifically nationalist in the overt manner of Tommy Hilfiger or Ralph Lauren, J. Crew's imagery is specifically American. For DeBord:

For most, American style is linked with freedom, and the J. Crew catalog – without resorting to the usual Laurenisms or Hilfigerisms of plastering the Stars and Stripes on everything in sight or of bedecking everyone in red, white, and blue – sustains the idea of freedom, in the weave of its catalog aesthetic, at such a lovely, low hum that the political aspect of its message becomes like oxygen, indispensible.

(1997: 275)

Attributed to the threat of foreign styles (DeBord 1997: 274) as well as an affirmation of American values – the ease of a casual, seemingly timeless lifestyle indifferent to elitist haute couture or lowbrow street fashion, J. Crew is emblematic of the Protestant work ethic made manifest in complete control yet ease that suggests no effort – 'It is then classically American of this transcendence that J. Crew, in its vision of style and merchandizing, is innovative, self-made, and (on the dark flipside) perhaps more than a little scary, as all unified messianic visions must be' (DeBord 1997: 276). Both Gap and J. Crew's contemporary casual tableaux are unified design visions derived from earlier mass brands such as Lauren and Hilfiger whereby the branding creates a total, desirable lifestyle supposedly attainable by purchasing clothes.

ABERCROMBIE AND FITCH AND HOLLISTER

Shifting its sights from the rugged outdoors customer to the youth market, Abercrombie and Fitch redesigned garments and rebranded itself, selecting Bruce Weber to photograph its cargo pants and tee-shirts for its catalogues

Figure 4: Abercrombie and Fitch sales associates. Photo courtesy of Joseph Hancock, 2009. All Rights Reserved.

(Hancock II 2009). Abercrombie and Fitch attempts to create a clear, simple idea, built symbolically around, and supported by, visual and textual structures: objects, images, texts, events. Advertisement, stores and products, for example, carry ideals and evoke the youthful America of the Ivy League, prep school or fraternity/sorority life. These associations evoke emotions and trigger behaviour, taking Abercrombie and Fitch from its origins as an outdoor sporting goods company to a powerful global lifestyle brand. Abercrombie uses sexualized salespeople to make its statement. In a reversal of the typical female sexual object, half-dressed males parade around. Sales people can be found dancing as if in a nightclub; posing suggestively for photos with shoppers. Indeed with boarded up shutters replacing shop windows the brand relies on sales people and visual display in the store for entertainment.

The Hollister brand was created in Ohio in 2000, a sister brand of Abercrombie and Fitch. The brand posts nothing about its history on its website. It describes itself as 'So Cal Prep'. 'Crisp. Classic Style.Undeniably Preppy and Elite'. In several articles on the topic of its fabricated history one learns that John M. Hollister did not exist but was created to provide a more 'authentic' experience to customers. Hollister was born into a 'high class' lifestyle in Manhattan, and graduated from Yale, but decided to become an adventurer, eventually buying a rubber plantation before settling in California where he founded the brand in 1922. When the BBC contacted the brand for comment they were told: 'Due to our policies regarding press, we choose not to provide any comment on your questions' (BBCnews.com 2009). Lower priced than Abercrombie, Hollister is aimed at the High School aged market. Rather than to appeal to those who engage in the sport of surfing, Hollister appeals to the aspirational consumer with its huge screens displaying the Huntington Beach surf scene, loud music, lounge areas with palm trees and a beach club environment. The rise of Abercrombie and Fitch and Hollister in

the last decade reflects the continuation of a strategy based on national identity and particularly American mythologies.

AMERICAN APPAREL

Recently, a shift in public consciousness away from overt branding has seen
the American Apparel brand highlight global production processes that have
been systematically obscured by earlier labels such as Ralph Lauren and
Tommy Hilfiger, a trajectory that we associate with the emergence of a new
discourse of authenticity. American Apparel aggressively rejects the norms of
proper comportment in a wholesome American world upheld by the above-
mentioned brands. Freedom of expression, individuality and democracy are
embraced by all three brands but they take on a confrontational rather than
conformist tone for American Apparel. Indeed the company directly addresses
labour issues: fair wages, working conditions and immigrant rights, in an
industry where this discourse has been largely ignored and repressed, save for
a brand having no choice but to confront allegations.

Through its highly visible leader Dov Charney who unlike Lauren and
Hilfiger does not evoke the mystique associated with the fashion designer,
American Apparel positions itself as both left leaning and libertarian, a cham-
pion of free expression, the free market, hedonistic sexuality, fair wages, an
end to oppression and discrimination, particularly for immigrants, both legal
and illegal. However, its 'selective engagement with 'ethical concerns' create
a 'carefully constructed brand identity, which is thematically organized around
the notion of 'transparency' (Moor and Littler 2008: 703–04). Its vertically integrated production differentiates the company from the others we have analysed
above and, along with the name of the brand, helps reinforce an identity that
ties it to production. The brand highlights the underside of American culture,
ignored or polished up and sentimentalized by Tommy Hilfiger, Ralph Lauren,
the Gap and J. Crew. In some ways it shares with the Gap a basic, even working
class aesthetic but for American Apparel it becomes gritty, no longer dressed in

Figure 5: Ralph Lauren menswear displayed in store window in New York City.
Photo courtesy of John Ricasoli, 2013. All Rights Reserved.

a neat 'super service' jumpsuit. The nascent defiant attitude that disappeared in Gap with celebrity models and art photographers is let loose by American Apparel. 'Real girls' with flaws and deliberately downgraded photographic images reinforce a sexual appeal that rejects conventional, highly scripted notions of prettiness we see in the Guess pin up or the well-sculpted collegiate Abercrombie male whose sexually is always under control. While some US customers may identify with the persona that American Apparel cultivates through its marketing, others may focus on the brand's simple t-shirts and casual wear and the fact that these products are made in America may allay ethical anxieties. Abroad the brand is more likely to be seen as directly marketing itself in connection to an American national identity.

CONCLUSION

Globalization creates shared practices brought about in large measure by a common material and virtual culture: the Internet, technology, music, film, novels and fashion create new values, boundaries and distinctions that are not as sharply defined by national identity. All brands investigated in this article provide clothing that contributes to homogenize differences through reinforcing mythical American ideals as the norm against which all others are measured. Branding within these firms is a process through which mass-produced clothing meets what Agins (2009) has called 'lifestyle merchandising'. As McCracken (2005) has also described, this invigorates a fashion system which turns out a lot of ordinary merchandise. Categories such as gender, status and occupation contribute to the script in which brands are linked to cultural and mythological ideals.

Semiotic constructs emerge around symbols specific to a particular nation vis-à-vis brands acting as sign vehicles and referring to objects that resonate with people, creating something that is easily interpreted and understood. In a process of myth-making, brands act as vectors, infused with cultural meaning from places, practices and attitudes. Prevailing notions of national identity, particularly American identity, are thus embodied in the mass fashion and branding strategies of these firms, creating aspirations for idealized lives. Debord (1997) asserts that consumers long for placed identities and placeless times, a powerful emotional desire that may lead to an acceptance of these fictions as real, or at least to an emotional identification leading to purchases. However, it is important to note that mythologies created by the brands analysed above are never completely accepted, but may be renegotiated or even rejected by consumers. This is an important issue worth exploring in further research.

REFERENCES

Agency of the Year Awards, 'Editorial Awards: Brand of the Year. Gap China', http://www.aoyawards.com/winners/2011/219. Accessed 1 June 2012.

Agins, Teri (2009), *The End of Fashion. How Marketing Changed the Clothing Business Forever*, Collingdale, PA: Diane Publishing Company.

Anderson, Benedict (1991), *Imagined Communities: Reflections on the Origin and Spread of Nationalism*, London: Verso.

Bachelor, Rosemary E. (2010), 'Washington's American made inaugural clothes', 16 March, http://rosemary-e-bachelor.suite101.com/washingtons-american-made-inaugural-clothes-a213962. Quoted 6 May 1789 in John Fenno's *Gazette of the United States*. Accessed 15 November 2012.

Barnard, Malcolm (2002), *Fashion as Communication*, 2nd ed., London and New York: Routledge.

Barthes, Roland ([1957] 1972), *Mythologies*, New York: Hill and Wang.

Baudrillard, Jean (1993), *Symbolic Exchange and Death*, London: Sage.

BBCNews.com (2009), 'Hollister Branding "Fictitious"', 10 November, http://news.bbc.co.uk/2/hi/business/8340453.stm. Accessed 12 December 2012.

Beaudoin, Pierre, Moore, Mary Ann and Goldsmith, Ronald E. (1998), 'Young fashion leaders' and followers' attitudes toward American and imported apparel', *Journal of Product and Brand Management*, 7: 3, pp. 193–207.

Bhabha, Homi K. (1990), 'The third space: Interview with Homi Bhabha', in J. Rutherford (ed.), *Identity: Community, Culture, Difference*, London: Lawrence and Wishart, pp. 207–21.

—— ([1994] 2005), *The Location of Culture*, Oxford and New York: Routledge.

Braithwaithe, Alisa K. (2012), 'First lady fashion: How the U.S. has embraced Michelle Obama', in Jacque Lynn Foltyn (ed.), *Fashions: Exploring Fashion Through Culture*, Oxford: Inter-Disciplinary Press, pp. 3–22.

Brandini, Valéria (2009), 'Fashion Brazil: South American style, culture, and industry', in E. Paulicell and H. Clark (eds), *The Fabric of Cultures: Fashion, Identity, and Globalization*, London and New York: Routledge, pp. 16–76.

Craige, Betty Jean (1996), *American Patriotism in a Global Society*, Albany: State University of New York Press.

Craik, Jennifer (1993), *The Face of Fashion: Cultural Studies in Fashion*, London: Routledge.

Crane, Diana (2000), *Fashion and its Social Agendas: Class, Gender, and Identity in Clothing*, Chicago and London: University of Chicago Press.

Crewe, Louise and Goodrum, Alison (eds) (2008), *Fashion Cultures: Theories, Explorations, and Analysis*, London: Routledge.

Crothers, Lane (2010), *Globalization and American Popular Culture*, Plymouth, UK: Rowman and Littlefield.

Davis, Fred (1991), 'Herbert Blumer and the study of fashion: A reminiscence and a critique', *Symbolic Interaction*, 14: 1, pp. 1–21.

—— (1992), *Fashion, Culture, and Identity*, London and Chicago: University of Chicago Press.

DeBord, Matthew (1997), 'Texture and taboo: The tyranny of texture and ease in the J. Crew catalog', *Fashion Theory*, 1: 3, pp. 261–78.

Duxbury, Sarah (2011), 'Gap brand closing 34% of U.S. stores; Piperlimetest store coming', *San Francisco Business Times*, 13 October, http://www.bizjournals.com/sanfrancisco/blog/2011/10/gap-brand-closing-34-of-us-stores.html. Accessed 13 June 2012.

Entwistle, Joanne (2000), *The Fashioned Body: Fashion, Dress, and Modern Social Theory*, Cambridge: Wiley-Blackwell.

—— (2009), *The Aesthetic Economy of Fashion: Markets and Values in Clothing and Modelling*, London: Berg.

Feitsma, Maaike (2012), 'Don't dress to impress', in Jacque Lynn Foltyn (ed.), *Fashions: Exploring Fashion Through Culture*, Oxford: Inter-Disciplinary Press, pp. 35–58.

Fine, Ben and Leopold, Ellen (1993), *The World of Consumption*, New York: Routledge.

Funding Universe, 'Company histories and profiles. Gap Inc', http://www.fundinguniverse.com/company-histories/The-Gap-Inc-company-History.html. Source: *International Directory of Company Histories*, Vol. 55, St. James Press, 2003. Accessed 11 June 2012.

Garingalao, Nicole (2006), 'Branding the national interest, December 15', symposium paper *The International Symposium*, Institute for Cultural Diplomacy, May 2011, http://www.culturaldiplomacy.org/culturaldiploma-cynews/content/articles/participantpapers/2011-symposiumusa/Branding-the-National-Interest--Nicole-Garingalao.pdf.

Gaudoin, Tina (2010), 'The Big Interview. Mickey Drexler: Retail Therapist', *WSJ Magazine*, 10 June, http://magazine.wsj.com/features/the-big-interview/retail-therapist/. Accessed 2 January 2012.

Gellner, Ernest (1964), *Thought and Change*, London: Weidenfeld & Nicholson.

—— (1997), *Nationalism*, London: Weidenfeld & Nicolson.

Goodrum, Alice (2005), *The National Fabric: Fashion, Britishness, Globalization*, Oxford and New York: Berg.

Gordon, Meryl (2005), 'Mickey Drexler's redemption', *New York Magazine*, 21 May, http://nymag.com/nymetro/news/bizfinance/biz/features/10489/index1.html. Accessed 12 August 2012.

Groth, Aimee and Aquino, Judith (2011), 'Meet the guy who saved Ann Taylor, made Gap Cool and Put J. Crew in the White House', *Business Insider*, 9 June, http://www.businessinsider.com/mickey-drexler-turnaround-2011-6?op=1. Accessed 1 January 2012.

González, Ana Marta (2010), 'On fashion and fashion discourses', *Critical Studies in Fashion and Beauty*, 1: 1, pp. 65–86.

Hall, Ann C. and Bishop, Mardia J. (eds) (2007), *Pop-Porn: Pornography in American Culture*, Westport, CT and London: Praeger.

Hancock II, Joseph Henry (1997), 'Brand storytelling: Context and meaning for cargo pants', in Peter McNeil, Vicki Karaminas and Cathy Cole (eds), *Fashion in Fiction: Text and Clothing in Literature, Film, and Television*, Oxford and New York: Berg, pp. 95–104.

—— (2009), *Brand/story: Ralph, Vera, Johnny, Bill, and Other Adventures in Fashion Branding*, New York: Fairchild Books.

Hansen, Karen Tranberg (2009), 'Youth, gender, and secondhand clothing in Lusaka, Zambia: Local and global styles', in E. Paulicelli and H. Clark (eds), *The Fabric of Cultures: Fashion, Identity, and Globalization*, London and New York: Routledge, pp. 112–27.

Hobsbawm, Eric and Ranger, Terence (1983), *The Invention of Tradition*, Cambridge and New York: Cambridge University Press.

Holt, Douglas B. (2001), 'Brands and branding', Harvard Business School, Teaching Note No. 9-503-045, http://douglasholt.org/?page_id=243. Accessed 6 January 2012.

Hounshell, David A. (1984), *From the American System to Mass Production: 1800–1932*, Baltimore: John Hopkins University Press.

Huppatz, D. J. (2010), 'Fashion branding: Ralph Lauren's stage', in Giorgio Riello and Peter McNeil (eds), *The Fashion History Reader: Global Perspectives*, London and New York: Routledge, pp. 553–555.

Joseph, May (1999), *Nomadic Identities: The Performance of Citizenship*, Minneapolis: University of Minnesota Press.

Kaiser, Susan B., Nagasawa, Richard H. and Hutton, Sandra S. (1991), 'Fashion, postmodernity and personal appearance: A symbolic interactionist formulation', *Symbolic Interaction*, 14: 2, pp. 165–85.

Kapferer, Jean-Noël (1992), *Strategic Brand Management: New Approaches to Creating and Evaluating Brand Equity*, London and Paris: Kogan Page.

Kawamura, Yuniya (2005), *Fashion-ology An Introduction to Fashion Studies*, 5th ed., New York: Berg.

Kedourie, Elie (1960), *Nationalism*, London: Hutchinson.

Klein, Naomi (2000), *No Logo, No Space, No Choice, No Jobs: Taking Aim at the Brand Bullies*, London: Flamingo.

Lipovetsky, Gilles (2002), *The Empire of Fashion: Dressing Modern Democracy* (trans. Catherine Porter), Princeton, NJ: Princeton University Press.

Lopez, Carmen and Ying Fan (2009), 'Internationalization of the Spanish fashion brand Zara', *Journal of Fashion Marketing and Management*, 13: 2, pp. 279–96.

Manlow, Veronica (2009), *Designing Clothes: Culture and Organization of the Fashion Industry*, New Brunswick, NJ: Transaction Publishers.

McCraken, Grant (2005), *Culture and Consumption II: Markets, Meaning and Brand Management*, Bloomington, IN: Indiana University Press.

McDowell, Colin (2000), *Fashion Today*, London: Phaidon Press.

Milbank, Caroline Rennolds (1989), *New York Fashion: The Evolution of American Style*, New York: Harry N. Abrams.

Moor, Liz and Littler, Jo (2008), 'Fourth worlds and neo-fordism: American apparel and the cultural economy of consumer anxiety', *Cultural Studies*, 22: 5, pp. 700–23.

Munk, Nina (1998), 'Gap gets it. Mickey Drexler is turning his apparel chain into a global brand', *Fortune*, 3 August, http://money.cnn.com/magazines/fortune/fortune_archive/1998/08/03/246286/index.htm. Accessed 6 January 2012.

Newman, Andrew J. and Patel, Darshika (2004), 'The marketing directions of two fashion retailers', *European Journal of Marketing*, 38: 7, pp. 770–89.

Niederer, Elizabeth and Winter, Rainer (2008), 'Fashion, culture, and the construction of identity', in Michael Ryan (ed.), *Cultural Studies: An Anthology*, Malden, MA and Oxford: Blackwell Publishing, pp. 687–697.

Parkins, Wendy (2002), *Fashioning the Body Politic: Dress, Gender, Citizenship*, Oxford and New York: Berg.

Paulicelli, Eugenia (2004), *Fashion Under Fascism: Beyond the Black Shirt*, Oxford and New York: Berg.

Paulicelli, Eugenia and Clark, Hazel (eds) (2009), *The Fabric of Cultures: Fashion, Identity, and Globalization*, London and New York: Routledge.

Rubinstein, Ruth P. (1995), *Dress Codes: Meaning and Messages in American Culture*, Boulder, CO: Westview Press.

Rutherford, Jonathan (ed.) (1990), *Identity: Community, Culture, Difference*, London: Lawrence and Wishart.

Sarracino, Carmine and Scott, Kevin M. (2008), *The Porning of America: The Rise of Porn Culture, What it Means, and Where we Go from Here*, Boston: Beacon Press.

Simmel, Georg ([1904] 1957), 'Fashion', *American Journal of Sociology*, 62: May. Rpt in *International Quarterly*, 10: October, pp. 130–55.

Smith, Anthony D. (1991), *National Identity*, London and New York: Penguin Books.

Smith, Paul (2008), 'Tommy Hilfiger in the age of mass customization', in Michael Ryan (ed.), *Cultural Studies: An Anthology*, Malden, MA and Oxford: Blackwell Publishing, pp. 764–72.

Steele, Valerie (2003), *Fashion, Italian Style*, New Haven and London: Yale University Press.

Steele, Valerie and Major, John S. (eds) (1999), *China Chic: East Meets West*, New Haven and London: Yale University Press.

Stone, Gregory P. (1962), 'Appearance and the self', in Arnold M. Rose (ed.), *Human. Behavior and Social Proceuer*, Boston: Houghton Mifflin, pp. 86–118.

Veblen, Thorstein ([1899] 1973), *The Theory of the Leisure Class*, Boston: Houghton Mifflin.

White, Nicola (2000), *Reconstructing Italian fashion: America and the Development of the Italian Fashion Industry*, London and New York: Berg.

Yahoo Answers (2007), 'How do people dress in Italy, and other questions', http://answers.yahoo.com/question/index?qid=20070529203012AAKxBRo. Accessed 5 May 2012.

—— (2011), 'What kinds of clothes do Brazilians wear?', http://answers.yahoo.com/question/index?qid=20110912160918AAYTkFs. Accessed 3 April 2012.

Yr.com (2011), 'Y&R's Shanghai's "Let's Gap Together" Nets GAP China Brand of the Year', http://www.yr.com/content/yr-shanghais-lets-gap-together-nets-gap-china-brand-year.html. Accessed 1 March 2012.

CONTRIBUTOR DETAILS

D.J. Huppatz is a Senior Lecturer within the Faculty of Design, Swinburne University of Technology, Melbourne, Australia. His recent publications have focused on American designer Russel Wright's design project Manitoga, contemporary design and design history. He is a founding member of the Design History Australia Research Network (DHARN) and a contributing editor of the DHARN website. Since returning from New York in 2007, he has maintained a strong interest in American design, architecture and fashion.

Contact: Faculty of Design, Swinburne University of Technology, 144 High Street, Prahran, Victoria 3181 Australia.
E-mail: dhuppatz@swin.edu.au

Veronica Manlow is an Assistant Professor of Business in the Finance and Business Management Department of the School of Business at Brooklyn College. She is a sociologist and is interested in the fashion industry from an organizational standpoint as well as considering its role as a social, cultural and interpersonal force. Recent work on branding focuses on luxury and mass produced fashion, and on the important changes brought about by digital and social media.

Contact: Brooklyn College, School of Business, Department of Finance and Business Management, 2900 Bedford Avenue, Brooklyn, NY 11210, USA.
E-mail: veronica.manlow@gmail.com

Global Fashion Brands: Style, Luxury & History

© 2014 Intellect Ltd Chapter. English language. doi: 10.1386/GFB.1.41_1

EDWINA LUCK
Queensland University of Technology

GJOKO MURATOVSKI
Auckland University of Technology

LAUREN HEDLEY
Carolina Herrera

Co-branding strategies for luxury fashion brands: Missoni for Target

ABSTRACT

Missoni is a luxury Italian knitwear brand that partnered with Target in September 2011 releasing a large, one off, mass-market collection that ranged from apparel to home wares. The collaboration received extensive media coverage and was consequently extremely sought after. The online sales site crashed within hours of opening while shelves were cleared in stores minutes after trading began. Within hours more than 40,000 items from the collection were posted for sale online at greatly inflated prices. Evaluation of the case study revealed that sales of the Missoni collection increased following the collaboration and the value of the publicity generated at estimated US$100 million. The lack of available stock, despite the enormous hype created, reinforced Missoni's luxury image. Missoni was able to gain massive awareness of the brand despite not employing any of its own communication channels in the promotion of the collaboration. However the co-branded collaboration was distinctively Missoni, potentially inciting comparison and confusion with the signature line. Nevertheless, this study shows that co-branding strategies can offer

KEYWORDS

luxury
fashion
branding
co-branding
Missoni
target

a viable opportunity for luxury brands to increase their market share, while they maintain their market position.

INTRODUCTION

Marketers have long held onto the illusion that wealthy customers are immune to the ebb and flow of economic uncertainty and, thus, luxury is a recession-proof game (Atsmon et al. 2010). However, this was nothing but a myth as the 2008 financial crisis hit and the *Luxury Consumption Index* fell to its lowest levels since records began (Danziger 2008). The industry experienced an 8 per cent decline in demand to result in 2009 revenues of US$200 billion, in line with 1995 levels (KPMG International 2011). While the international luxury market continues to grow, it is becoming harder for luxury brands to market themselves on status alone. As it will be argued here, a well-established brand name is no longer enough to sustain sales, and strategic developments such as co-branding alliances are options for future success.

For many luxury fashion brands, forming co-branding alliances with high street retailers has emerged as a popular additional revenue stream (Hosea 2008; Ahn et al. 2010). For example, the multinational retail chain Debenhams can be credited with pioneering the trend in 1993 when renowned milliner Philip Treacy collaborated with the British high street chain to release a small collection of hats. This was followed by the first major fashion collection by Jasper Conran in 1996 (Mower 2011). The last decade has seen the trend accelerate rapidly involving some of the fashion industry's most eminent designer houses – including Karl Lagerfeld, Stella McCartney, Jimmy Choo, Lanvin, Versace and Missoni. This global trend has also taken a hold in some smaller markets, such as Australia, where selected Australian designers – including the global luxury brand Collette Dinnigan – have also taken part in similar local collaborations (Lee 2011). However, it has to be noted that this kind of strategy can put the brand's luxury position in jeopardy if not executed correctly; therefore it should be conducted rarely and it cannot be universally applied by all luxury brands. As it will be discussed further, co-branding in a luxury fashion context should only be considered as a momentary opportunity to gain significant awareness and build the brand's reputation beyond its core market.

When designers work in collaboration with retailers to produce a line that offers the style and design creditability expected of a luxury label at a high street price point, the designers' luxury appeal could be consequently compromised. However, such partnership often allows designers to experiment with previously unexplored brand extensions in a low risk environment. For example, in collaboration with H&M, Jimmy Choo was able to extend beyond their core accessories product line to women's clothing, while Matthew Williamson used the same opportunity to venture into menswear (Marketing Week 2011).

In their examination of the practice, S. Ahn et al. (2010) discerned that such co-branding strategies 'leverage entire fashion business concepts that transform their branding strategy into not only "sleeping with enemies", but also to "talking to strangers"' (2010: 6). Therein lies the appeal for luxury fashion brands: in addition to the extraordinary publicity and brand awareness gained from the strategy, this exposes them to an entirely new and untapped market to exploit revenue from (Marketing Week 2011). Generally these collaborations produce a single collection before the high street retailer moves onto a new designer (Benigson 2010). However, the long-term implications for luxury fashion brands engaging in such co-branding strategies remain largely unassessed.

With this in mind, we have to ask what is the impact for the luxury brand in the long term. Such low-end co-branding strategies veer dramatically away from the brand's core luxury positioning in terms of price, quality, distribution and ultimately exclusivity (Bold 2002). Thus, it is imperative that luxury brands recognize and establish the true implications for such a strategy. Particularly as a new customer base is exposed to the brand, luxury fashion brands must understand the impact on overall brand perception (Liu and Choi 2009). Hence, this case study seeks to gain insights to resolve the following managerial problem: To what extent the customer's perception of a luxury fashion brand is impacted by the implementation of a co-branding strategy with a high street retailer?

The main object of this study is the co-branding alliance between Missoni and Target in 2011. As a means of rationalizing the results of this retrospective analysis, we have reviewed he luxury fashion branding literature in relation to marketing and brand management theory. In the process, we have focused on four aspects: (1) the implications of customer perception of co-branding collaborations between luxury fashion brands and high street retailers, (2) luxury fashion branding, (3) co-branding strategies and (4) the market implications of such strategies. In this study we have highlighted some of the key factors that determine the implications for customer perception of luxury fashion co-branding strategies and we have presented a list of recommendations for planning such strategies.

THE ETHOS OF LUXURY FASHION BRANDING

By reviewing the literature on luxury, it can be concluded that there is a difficulty in defining the concept of luxury. For some authors, the idea of luxury sits in a social context (Nueno and Quelch 1998); for others, luxury can be seen as a form of cultural evolution (Amatulli and Guido 2009) that is changeable and subjective (Phau and Prendergast 2000), and it is one that often lacks clarity (Miller and Mills 2012). In a fashion context, luxury has also described as a type of 'uniqueness' (Surchi 2011).

Recent research into luxury fashion branding has attempted to identify specific elements that in combination have been the foundation for success for the market's leading brands with regard to perceptions of leading brands and equity (Zhan and He 2012), teen attitudes (DeAraujo Gil et al. 2012), and value perceptions (Shukla and Purani 2012). While researchers appear to agree on certain individual factors such as distribution exclusivity and targeted communication strategies, other elements such as appropriate price and brand positioning strategies appear to be in contention. Moreover, disagreement emerges over the level of importance placed on individual elements in comparison to the cohesive collaboration of all contributing factors.

The literature clearly identifies the necessity for a strong focus on developing a clear and distinct brand identity focusing and agreeing on intangibility brand elements such as history, culture, spirit, corporate identification and reputation of a brand (Atwal and Williams 2009; Beverland 2004; Dubois and Paternault 1995; Fionda and Moore 2009; Kapferer and Bastien 2009; Keller 2009; Nueno and Quelch 1998; Wetlaufer 2004). Along these lines, A. M. Fionda and C. M. Moore (2009) argue that brand identity is reflective of brand values such as 'fashionability' and heritage, which then determine a brand's unique approach to distribution, awareness and positioning. This is consistent with the factors identified by Okowono (2007) that work to develop both functional and emotional appeal for consumers through heritage of craftsmanship and a global reputation.

The importance of developing a unique and compelling brand image is championed by J.-V. Kapferer and Bastien (2009). They argue that traditional approaches to positioning, in which brands develop a unique selling proposition relative to other competitors in the market, goes against what is at the heart of luxury. Rather than carving out a niche based on a recognized business opportunity, a brand's image must be 'born of itself' and founded on its individual creative eccentricities (2009: 316). This, however, is in direct contrast to the observations of C. M. Moore and G. Birtwistle (2004), suggesting that luxury fashion brands must compete with rivals particularly by developing a high fashion collection necessary to facilitate editorial content. Furthermore, they also recognized the importance of a flagship store located amongst other luxury fashion brands and participation in major fashion shows hosted in New York, Milan, London or Paris as both present crucial opportunities for the brand to interact with the media and a perception that is a reflection of perceptions that holds strong consumer associations of uniqueness (Keller 1993).

While the brand identity forms the brand's existence (Louis and Lombart 2010), creating a personality for a brand allows for meaning to be encompassed (Kapferer and Bastien 2009. This allows for other emotive elements such as loyalty (Southgate 1994), trust and relationships to be established. On the basis of this, it can be argued that successful luxury fashion branding likely lies somewhere in between branding elements and personality aspects. However, the boundaries of high-end fashion and luxury are being blurred as brands are extending their exclusivity by creating limited edition collections. This allows short-term value-conscious customers access to a high-end brand. In comparison, the studies that we have outlined in Table 1 are based on theoretical models that are seen as critical to a luxury brand's success factor.

In order for luxury brands to maintain their status, they must ensure that they are offering outstanding products at a premium price, alongside

Fionda and Moore (2009)	Kapferer and Bastien (2009)	Moore and Birtwistle (2004)	Okonkwo (2007)
• Clear brand identity • Luxury communications strategy • Brand signature • Prestige price • Exclusivity • Luxury heritage • Environment and consumption experience • Luxury culture	• Brand identity over positioning • Be superlative, never comparative • No flaws, no charm • Resist client demands • No equality with clients • Make it difficult for clients to buy • Role of advertising not to sell • Advertise to those not targeted • Raise prices continuously to increase demand	• Clearly defined brand positioning • Coordinated distribution ensuring maximum market coverage • Brand extension facilitated by strong brand identity • Flexible management to allow foreign market opportunities • Media relations management to build and maintain brand reputation	• A distinct brand identity • Innovative, creative, unique and appealing products • Consistent delivery of premium quality • Exclusivity in goods production • Tightly controlled distribution • A heritage of craftsmanship • A global reputation • Emotional appeal • Premium pricing • High visibility

Table 1: Success factors of luxury fashion brands.

targeted marketing communications (Fionda and Moore 2009; Okonkwo 2007). Furthermore, studies show that luxury fashion consumers seek unique and exceptional products that are reflective of the brand's individual aesthetic and heritage (Dion and Arnould 2011). In addition to this, Fionda and Moore (2009) have identified product quality, craftsmanship and attention to details as key features that, alongside innvoation and creativity, reflect the status of a luxury fashion brand and differentiate it from less prestigious counterparts.

Nevertheless, the thirst for luxury is built on the desire for exclusivity with a luxury fashion brand's communications strategy integral in creating and maintaining this desire beyond the target market. This strategy aims to engage consumers who do have the means to seek out the brand above all others (Kapferer and Bastien 2009). However, I. Phau and G. Prendergast (2000) argue that exclusivity must be maintained, through both premium pricing strategies and limited distribution, so as to prevent erosion of the brand's prestigious identity. In addition to this, M. Chevalier and G. Mazzalovo add that a luxury brand is founded from the process of maintaining 'well-controlled scarcity' while the brand itself remains highly desirable and recognisable (2008: 14).

According to K. L. Keller (2009), abiding by such a model can limit a luxury fashion brand's growth potential, particularly in the trade-off between exclusivity and accessibility in an effort to maximize market coverage. Furthermore, Keller (2009) asserts that it is necessary to differentiate across market segments and price points in order to achieve growth in sales and brand equity. In essence, this entails following the branding guidelines presented by the studies discussed above in that each sub-brand develops a unique brand identity and strategy. In addition to this, Y. Truong et al. (2009) argue that luxury status must be maintained relative to each market so that consumers at every level perceive the brand as aspirational because it remains somewhat inaccessible. However, a successful 'massitge' strategy of this kind could prevent brand dilution if middle-class consumers are only allowed to access the brand infrequently (Truong et al. 2009).

CO-BRANDING STRATEGIES

Co-branding is a strategy in which two existing brands are paired together to create a single product offering. S. J. Dickinson and T. Heath (2008) qualified that co-branding can apply to the cooperation of two brands extending to advertising, product distribution or product development activities. Researchers in the field generally agree that the recent increase in popularity of co-branding strategies is founded on the notion that leveraging an existing brand to achieve growth is more efficient that creating a new brand (Dickinson and Heath 2008; Chang 2008). Spefically, J. H. Washburn et al. (2000) highlighted co-branding strategies as a means of gaining additional market exposure, sharing costs with a partner, and defending against competitors. Moreover, each brand engaging in a co-branding strategy seeks to capitalize on its partner's reputation and core competencies in order to create a competitive advantage (Dickinson and Heath 2008; Chang 2008, 2010).

In Table 2 we can see a more comprehensive set of objectives for brands engaging in this strategy. This includes organizational objectives of gaining financial and operational benefits, expansion of the brand's customer base, and strengthening of the brand's competitive position (Chang 2008; Dickinson and Heath 2008).

Chang (2008)	Dickinson and Heath (2008)
• Expand customer base • Achieve financial benefits • Respond to expressed and latent needs of customers • Strengthen competitive position • Introduce new products with a strong image • Create new customer perceived value • Gain operational benefits	• Achieve market place exposure • Share expenses • Gain access to new markets • Enhance reputation

Table 2: Identified aims of co-branding strategies.

Studies into co-branding have largely focused on the success factors for brands engaging in this strategy, with partner selection and suitability widely identified as critical in ensuring successful branding alliances. For example, research conducted by Ahn et al. (2010) investigated the dimensions that determine the suitability of brand pairings, identifying the importance of complementarity, substituability and transferability of brands engaging in the alliance. The study emphasized the importance of partnering with a brand that maintains the same usage situation, user identity and perceived brand equity. W.-L. Chang (2010) additionally highlighted the importance of evaluating and selecting partners based on business criteria such as financial and operational feasibility considerations and complementary business cultures. Furthermore, L. Leuthresser et al. (2003) asserted that successful co-branding alliances are based on the idea that both brands contribute value by pairing their potentail customer bases with the new product. In line with this, their study championed the importance of clearly defining the co-brand's customer base, comprehensive evaluation of the benefits to the customer, and clear division of responsibilities for deliviering these benefits to the end customer.

Leuthresser et al. (2003) identified achieving market response, in terms of sales profits and market reach, as potential advantages of this strategy. However, the study also argued that potential disadvantages include giving a competitive advantage to the alliance partner, creating potential competition, trusting the alliance partner with important product characteristics, and limiting potential market reach in comparison to a line or brand extension strategy. On another note, in their study on the issue, A. d'Astous et al. (2007) highlighted the benefits of sharing costs associated with launching the co-branded product. For example, the new product has the advantage of being offered to existing customers of both partner brands and can further benefit from the increased brand recognizability over other products. Nevertheless, this study also identifies the risk of potential customer confusion between the individual partner brands, affecting the partner brand image in the long term. The implications for customer perception of this strategy in conjunction with luxury fashion branding is evaluated in the following section.

IMPLICATIONS FOR CUSTOMER PERCEPTION

Co-branding strategies tend to strongly affect customer perceptions. Ahn et al. (2010) argue that partnering with a strong brand with high brand equity is vital in creating a positive evaluation of the co-branding alliance. The nature of such partnership can be crucial to the success of the luxury brands that engage in this strategy, or can lead to their detriment. However, researchers have different views around what the exact nature of this partnership should look like. Dickinson and Heath implore that 'partners require positive parent brand attitudes as a precondition' for positive evaluation of the co-branded offering (2008: 22). This comes in agreement to an earlier study by Washburn et al. (2000) who also argue that consumer perception of partner brands prior to the alliance signficantly affects attitudes towards the co-branded offering. If both partners already have positive customers perceptions, than they will both experience an increase in brand equity. However, what has also been noted in their study is that combinations of two high equity brands, or one high and one low equity brand, are perceived more positively than the combination of two low equity brands.

Conversley, Leuthresser et al. (2003) presented less definitive findings about the positive impact of co-branding on partner brand equity. The study asserts that consumer attitudes towards co-branded offering are determined by averaging attitudes towards the respective parent brands. Similarly, the findings are less optimistic about the positive affect for existing strong brands, suggesting such brands are less likely to be positively impacted. However, the study does agree that the combination of a high equity brand with a low equity brand does not nessecarily denigrate the high status brand.

Along these lines, T. Geylani et al. (2008) assert that the greater the distance between the status of partner brands the greater the uncertainty for consumers in evaluating the co-branded offering. Hence, the study maintains that it may not be in a brand's best interest to partner with a brand with far greater brand equity. Finally, in contradiction with all other literature reviewed, Geylani et al. (2008) found that consumer uncertainty increases for strong brands who choose to follow a co-branding alliances. This conclusion was made due to the transferance of uncertainty from the less reliable brand and the perceived inconsistency of co-branded product with the original brand. This comes to a direct contrast of the findings outlined by the other researchers, such as those outlined above.

In addition to this, there are several other things that need to be factored in when planning co-branding strategies. Research into perceptual theory surrounding luxury brands has highlighted distribution as a primary factor in determining positive customer perception of luxury. S. Kemp (2008) found that consumers expect the distribution of luxury goods to be left to the forces of the market despite its scarcity, highlighting the difference in perception of luxury versus necessity. This comes in line with C. Wu and S.-S. Hsing (2006) who advocated engineered scarcity as a viable luxury brand strategy, exercised through premium pricing with emphasis placed on product quality, as a way of achieving improved customer perception of value. Also, in terms of product offerings, J. Berger et al. (2007) found that brands with greater product line variety were perceived by customers to be of higher quality, and in return, this has lead to increased likelihood of purchase. This decision was made on presumed category expertise. In terms of pricing, on the other hand, K. Rajagopal (2008) found that while a price reduction strategy may result in immediate increase of sales, it may eventually lead to erosion of customer perception and reduced long-term profitability for the luxury brand. Therefore, it can be argued that by venturing in a temporary co-branding alliance with a high street retailer, luxury brands could increase their sales without causing a significant risk to their status.

CASE STUDY: MISSONI FOR TARGET

The following section addresses the 'Missoni for Target' co-branding example. This is a prominent example of a co-branding collaboration between a luxury fashion brand and high street retailer. Here we will examine the Missoni brand prior to the co-branding partnership with Target; the collaboration experience; and the outcomes from this partnership for Missoni.

Brief history of the brand

Missoni is an Italian brand, established in 1953 by husband and wife Ottavio and Rosita Missoni. In 1947, Ottavio Missoni established a knitwear venture that focused on sports apparel, with Rosita joining in 1949 to take on creative duties. By 1953, the Missoni fashion brand was established and the label continued to grow over the following decades. With time, Missoni demonstrated an ongoing specific focus on machine technology used to improve the quality of the label's knits (Missoni 2012). By the 1960s, Missoni began to attract the interest of the fashion media. This was aided by the label's first presentation to the press in Milan in 1966. In 1969 Missoni successfully entered the lucrative US market gaining important stocklists and editorial coverage (Martin 2012). The brand's rapid international growth continued as flagship stores were established across the globe, with production remaining in Italy. The Missoni signature knitwear remained highly recognizable by the vivid colours and zigzag pattern. The brand expanded its range with perfumes, footwear, home, and a diffusion line – M Missoni. The expansion has been widely attributed to daughter Angela Missoni, who took over creative control in 1997 (LxKnitwear 2012). Missoni revenue estimates for 2010 vary from US$42 million to US$74 million (Moore 2011), which is relatively small in comparison to the market leaders in luxury fashion.

The Missoni brand maintained its reputation as a strong family owned and operated fashion label with continued focus on innovative yet distinctive knitwear. This aesthetic has since been translated to Hotel Missoni, established on the back of the success of Missoni Home, which is still creatively controlled by Rosita Missoni. Hotel Missoni has been launched in Edinburgh and Kuwait, in 2009 and 2011 respectively, with up to 30 more locations planned (Swerdloff 2011). Missoni's co-branding with Target is a part of this brand extension strategy.

Collaboration with Target

The collaboration between Missoni and Target was announced on the 21st of July 2011 via an otherwise non-descript fashion blog titled All the way up here. The blog was authored by a blogger named Marina' with posts dating back to early April 2011. The blog went on to exclusively release the date when the collaboration was to hit stores and included a preview of the collection. The blog became a platform for promotion of the collaboration leading up to, and immediately following its release date. Eventually, the brand ambassador

'Marina' was introduced to the public as a seven-metre tall doll dressed in Missoni clothing (Hutzler 2011).

This seemingly anonymous blog allowed for the utilization of the re-blog function of Tumblr blogging and the real-time nature of Twitter to generate enormous buzz around the collaboration amongst the fashion media and the new customers (Connor 2011). Such was the hype created, that long queues of customers were formed outside Target stores prior to their opening on the day of the launch – 13 September 2011. The collection was released online two hours prior to in store but the website subsequently crashed due to the overwhelming demand before stores had even opened. The scene was similar in store with shelves cleared within twenty minutes of opening in some locations (Bickers 2011).

The collection included 400 distinctively Missoni pieces. This was the largest of Target's co-branding collaborations, encompassing men's, women's and children's apparel, home items luggage, and even bicycles. Prices ranged from US$2.99 to US$599.99 for a patio set. Apparel pieces averaged under US$40, significantly less than the Missoni signature collection with most pieces retailing for in excess of US$1000 (Abraham 2011).

The unanticipated demand for the collection meant that the promotion lasted for days rather than for more than a month as was originally intended, despite additional stock made available in some stores (Stych 2011). This gross underestimation was despite exceptionally high demand already experienced in the pop-up store established in New York one week prior to the collection's national release. The temporary store, also 'Marina's' location, was expected to remain open for three days but instead sold out of stock after six hours and was forced to close (D'innocenzio 2011).

Ongoing implications of the co-branding strategy: The backlash

Angela Missoni identified building awareness as a key objective of the co-branding collaboration, which appears to be achieved with estimates that the strategy generated publicity to the value of AU$100 million. That strategy also appears to have succeeded in the immediate term with sales for following collection of the Missoni signature line increasing by 10 per cent on the previous season (Moore 2011).

However, many customers of the co-branded collection were left disgruntled by the overall consumer experience, generating significant backlash on social media channels (Brooks 2011). Many online customers had their orders cancelled by Target due to unavailability of stock despite already being charged for the items. Adding to customer frustration, within hours of selling out, Missoni for Target pieces began to be posted for resale online. By the 15th of September up to 44,000 items were listed as for sale on eBay, with many sellers demanding extraordinarily inflated prices. Bicycles that retailed for US$399.99 were sold within days for US$2500, a more than 600 per cent mark up, and remain available on the site for up to US$1000 (Bickers 2011).

The implications of this backlash were immediately debated and while some theorized that Missoni loyalists may now reject the brand as it is now in reach of a mass audience with concern that their original signature pieces may be confused with the co-branded collaboration (Bickers 2011). Conversely, others insist that the relative inaccessibility achieved a 'digital velvet rope' effect that was able to preserve the Missoni exclusivity, even at the mass market level (Dishman 2011).

EVALUATION AND ANALYSIS

This co-branding strategy afforded Missoni to expand its customer base into new markets with significant financial gains, in line with generic objectives of co-branding strategies (Chang 2008; Dickinson and Heath 2008). The venture, however, did not respond to the needs of the brand's existing customers. Missoni did not deliver a unique product to this new market with an individually strong brand image; instead it offered a mass market adaptation of its existing product line.

Missoni's signature line is perhaps one of the most recognizable labels within the luxury fashion industry. Hence, for any co-branded collaboration to be identified as Missoni it was imperative that the offering remain faithful to the uniquely vibrant zigzag knitwear pattern synonymous with the Missoni aesthetic. This therefore complicates the creation of differentiation and separation between the signature and co-branded offerings necessary to ensure that inexpensive co-branded pieces are not perceived as equal alternative to the luxury priced signature line (d'Astous et al. 2007).

The luxury fashion branding literature clearly identifies the importance of developing and maintaining a distinct brand identity (Fionda and Moore 2009; Okonkwo 2007). The positioning of the Missoni for Target collection was in stark contrast with the luxury position traditional to the Missoni brand. The collaboration maintained the brand aesthetic of the Missoni main line, though the quality was undoubtedly compromised. Similarly, the pricing strategy of the co-branded collaboration did not align with its standard prestige strategy and distribution to the mass market contradicted the main line's exclusive distribution.

However, the execution of the strategy brings into question potential disparity between the superficial positioning of the co-branded collaboration and the intended perception outcome. In reality, the Missoni for Target collection was exclusive relative the proportion of customers aspiring to buy (Keller 2009). The promotion of the collaboration was extremely successful in gaining mass awareness despite the limited merchandise available. In this sense, Missoni for Target adopted a luxury communications strategy by appealing to customers that were outside of the target market. Moreover, the exorbitant prices demanded for pieces of the collection that were later posted online further served to position the offering as out of reach for many customers (Kapferer and Bastien 2009). By creating massive hype prior to the collections release, Missoni for Target ensured that offering was inaccessible in a similar manner to standard luxury fashion brands (Wu and Hsing 2006); this in return created the emotional allure, which is usually reserved for its signature line. The mass communications strategies to ensure extensive brand awareness was further aided by the enormous media coverage following the collections dramatic sell out.

Perhaps most ingeniously, Missoni did not use any of its own communication channels to gain awareness for the collaboration. Instead information was disseminated through the *All the way up here* blog and Twitter feed in combination with high profile events held to generate further publicity. The media coverage of this collaboration was unprecedented and likely meant that the total publicity achieved through the venture was an enormous return on investment. For Missoni this also meant that distance was maintained between the high street collaboration and its signature line communications.

The immediate repercussions for customer perception appear to be positive, as demonstrated by increased sales in for Missoni's signature line. The

Missoni for Target collaboration was, in reality, all about Missoni, with Target acting as a trusted distribution channel for the collection. While the line was priced at a Target level, all of the merchandise and communications spoke of Missoni. Hence, Target's reputation as a reliable high street retailer brought credibility to the collaboration, with the Missoni parent brand remaining unaffected by its lower budget image (Washburn et al. 2000). The consequential backlash regarding the online sales bungle and lack of merchandise was ultimately aimed primarily at Target as it was recognized as responsible for this aspect of the collaboration, further shielding Missoni from any negativity.

For existing Missoni customers this collaboration served to reinforce the brand's desirability, while for new customers who are now aware of the brand, it continues to remains out of reach. The potential concern for existing customers may be that their signature Missoni pieces may now be compared or confused with the low priced co-branded collection (d'Astous et al. 2007). This is the pitfall of co-branding. While the co-branded offering must be truly reflective of the signature brand, association that is too close may offend existing customers who bought the signature collection on the basis of its prestigious reputation, and much higher price.

Perceptual theory gives reason to the extreme success in achieving sales of the co-branded collaboration. As observed by Berger et al. (2007), likelihood of purchase of a new product variety is expressly linked to perceived category expertise. Missoni has demonstrated its proficiency in luxury fashion over its lifetime, and hence consumers perceive that its co-branded lower-end offering can be trusted to also be of high quality.

It is imperative that such co-branding ventures be implemented by luxury fashion brands on an extremely rare basis. If entering the mass market is seen as a long term, ongoing opportunity, the brand puts its luxury position in significant jeopardy. Co-branding in a luxury fashion context must be considered only as a momentary opportunity to gain significant awareness and build the brand's reputation.

RECOMMENDATIONS AND CONCLUSIONS

This study examined the consumer experience as a valuable tool for evaluating co-branding strategies, while raising questions about the implications related to brand credibility. Based on the preceding evaluation of the Missoni for Target collaboration, several recommendations have been developed for luxury fashion brands seeking to implement a successful co-branding venture in the future:

Co-branding strategy is a single opportunity

Maintaining a luxury fashion brand's prestige positioning is determined by a cohesive brand image. Venturing into the mass market too frequently, or as an ongoing brand extension has the potential to erode a brand's luxury status and alienate its primary target market (Truong et al. 2009; Rajagopal 2008).

Communicate beyond target market

The primary objective of implementing a co-branding strategy must be to gain mass market awareness of the luxury fashion brand (Dickinson and Heath 2008). As such, it is necessary for communications to reach beyond the co-branded collaboration's target market in order to gain maximum ongoing awareness of the signature line and consequently increase its desirability (Kapferer and Bastien 2009).

Maintain inaccessibility

A co-branded collaboration must be positioned as a prestige brand relative to the mass market (Keller 2009). Luxury positioning is founded on creating desire among those who are not able to obtain the brand (Chevalier and Mazzalovo 2008). Rationing of the co-branded collection not only increases desire for the collaboration but also the signature collection as its inaccessibility is further highlighted.

Differentiate from signature line

It is imperative that luxury fashion brands create separation between their signature and co-branded collections to minimize confusion between the two and demonstrate value to existing customers (d'Astous et al. 2007). Nevertheless, the co-branded collection must be recognized that it comes from a luxury fashion brand, but it should not replace the luxury line (Dion and Arnould 2011).

Choose the right partner

Luxury fashion brands should seek to align with a high street retailer that is experienced in delivering similar co-branding collaborations and trusted by the new target market. Ensuring credibility with a high street partner is significant, though luxury fashion brands must maintain prominence in the collaboration with the high street retailer acting as a trusted distribution channel (Ahn et al. 2010).

This case investigation found that engaging in a co-branding strategy could positively impact customer perception of a luxury fashion brand. Missoni's success is contingent on the brand adhering to the recommendations presented, which articulates to creating exclusivity despite trading in the mass market. Therefore this strategy has been found to be viable for luxury fashion brands for the future, based on the condition that it is only implemented fleetingly. For the fashion industry, this strategy presents as feasible in creating mass awareness while maintain luxury positioning: something that has not been examined in great detail in this fierce industry.

REFERENCES

Abraham, Tamara (2011), 'Sneak preview of Missoni's designer style at Target prices (so will you be bagging the babygro or the bicycle?)', *Daily Mail*, 11 August, http://www.dailymail.co.uk/femail/article-2024687/Sneak-preview-Missonis-designer-style-Target-prices-bagging-babygro-bicycle.html. Accessed 8 December 2013.

Ahn, SooKyung, Kim, Huenjung, and Forney, Judith (2010), 'Fashion collaboration or collision? Examining the match-up effect in co-marketing alliances', *Journal of Fashion Marketing and Management*, 14: 1, pp. 6–20.

Amatulli, Cesare and Guido, Gianluigi (2009), 'Determinants of purchasing intention for fashion luxury goods in the Italian market: A laddering approach', *Journal of Fashion Marketing and Management*, 15: 1, pp. 123–136.

Atsmon, Yuval, Pinsent, Demetra, and Sun, Lisa (2010), *Five trends that will shape the global luxury market*, McKinsey & Company, http://csi.mckinsey.com/Knowledge_by_topic/Consumer_and_shopper_insights/globalluxury.aspx. Accessed 7 December 2011.

Atwal, Satnam and Williams, Alistair (2009), 'Luxury brand marketing – the experience is everything!', *Journal of Brand Management,* 16: 1, pp. 338–46.

Benigson, Moira. (2010), 'The key to successful collaboration', *Retail Week*, 17 September, http://www.retail-week.com/comment/the-key-to-successful-collaboration/5017134.article. Accessed 12 December 2013.

Berger, Jonah, Draganska, Michaela, and Simonson, Itamar (2007), 'The Influence of Product Variety on Brand Perception and Choice', *Journal of Marketing Science,* 26: 4, pp. 460–472.

Beverland, Michael B. (2004), 'Uncovering "Theories-in-use": the case of luxury wines', *Journal of Management Studies,* 42: 5, pp. 1003–29.

Bickers, James, (2011), 'Missoni for Target line sells out, raises questions', *Retail Customer Experience*, 15 September, http://www.retailcustomerexperience.com/article/184615/Missoni-for-Target-line-sells-out-raises-questions. Accessed 12 December 2013.

Bold, Ben (2002), 'Is Gucci for the masses damaging the brand?', *Marketing Magazine*, 10 October, p. 15.

Brooks, Tory (2011), 'Missoni for Target – Challenges of Online Retailing', *The Online Economy*, 4 November, http://www.onlineeconomy.org/missoni-for-target-challenges-of-online-retailing. Accessed 12 December 2013.

Chang, Wei-Lun (2008), 'A Typology of Co-branding Strategy: Position and Classification', *Journal of American Academy of Business,* 12: 2, pp. 220–226.

—— (2010), 'A Taxonomy Model for a Strategic Co-Branding Position', *The Journal of American Academy of Business,* 16: 1, pp. 165–170.

Chevalier, Michel, and Mazzalovo, Gerald (2008), *Luxury Brand Management,* Singapore: John Wiley & Sons.

Connor, Emily (2011), 'Marina – Doll, Blogger, Celebrity – Target's Unique Approach to Missoni Fashion Line Launch', *Business2Community,* 14 September, http://www.business2community.com/trends-news/marina---doll-blogger-celebrity---target's-unique-approach-to-missoni-fashion-line-launch-058944. Accessed 12 December 2013.

Danziger, Pam (2008), 'Luxury Consumption Index (LCI) in Free Fall', *Marketwire*, 31 October, http://www.marketwire.com/press-release/luxury-consumption-index-lci-in-free-fall-915650.htm. Accessed 7 December 2011.

d'Astous, Alain, Colbert, François & Fournier, Marilyne (2007), 'An experimental investigation of the use of brand extension and co-branding strategies in the arts', *Journal of Services Marketing,* 21: 4, pp. 231–240.

Dickinson, Sonja and Heath, Tara (2008), 'Cooperative Brand Alliances: How to Generate Positive Evaluations', *Australasian Marketing Journal,* 16: 2, pp. 22–38.

D'innocenzio, Anne (2011), 'Shoppers furious as Target's Missoni problems continue', *Today (Style)*, 22 September, http://www.today.com/id/44624643/. Accessed 12 December 2013.

Dion, Delphine and Arnould, Eric (2011), 'Retail Luxury Strategy: Assembling Charisma through Art and Magic', *Journal of Retailing,* 87: 4, pp. 502–520.

Dishman, Lydia (2011), 'The Genius of Target's Missoni Madness', *Forbes,* 14 September, http://www.forbes.com/fdc/welcome_mjx.shtml. Accessed 12 December 2013.

Dubois, Bernard and Paternault, Claire (1995), 'Understanding the world of international luxury brands: the dream formula', *Journal of Advertising Research*, 35: 4, pp. 69–77.

Dwyer, Michael (2011), 'Anti-crisis in the bling economy', *The Australian Financial Review*, 15 November, p. 61.

Fionda, Antoinette. M. and Moore, Christopher. M. (2009), 'The anatomy of the luxury fashion brand', *Journal of Brand Management*, 16: 5, pp. 347–363.

Geylani, Tansev, Inman, J. Jeffrey and Ter Hofstede, Frankel (2008), 'Image Reinforcement or Impairment: The Effects of Co-Branding on Attribute Uncertainty', *Journal of Marketing Science*, 27: 4, pp. 730–744.

Hosea, Maeve (2008), 'Couture collaborations: Hitting the street', *Brand Strategy*, 8 April , pp. 50–51.

Hutzler, Kayla (2011), 'Missoni avoids brand dilution with secret Target partnership', *Luxury Daily*, 19 August, http://www.luxurydaily.com/missoni-maintains-luxury-status-by-keeping-quiet-about-target-line/. Accessed 12 December 2013.

Kapferer, Jean-Noel and Bastien, Vincent (2009), 'The specificity of luxury management: Turning marketing upside down', *Journal of Brand Management*, 16: 5, pp. 311–322.

Keller, Keith L. (1993), 'Conceptualizing, measuring, and managing customer-based brand equity', *Journal of Marketing*, 57: 1, pp. 1–22.

—— (2009), 'Managing the growth tradeoff: Challenges and opportunities in luxury branding', *Journal of Brand Management*, 16: 3, pp. 290–301.

Kemp, Simon (2008), 'Perceiving luxury and necessity', *Journal of Economic Psychology*, 19: 5, pp. 591–606.

KPMG International (2011), 'Resurgence in demand for luxury goods', *Issues Monitor*, 9: 1, pp. 9–16.

Lee, H. (2011), 'Designer's rack up their high street credentials', *Sassybella*, http://www.sassybella.com/designers-rack-high-street-credentials/. Accessed 7 December 2011.

Leuthresser, Lance, Kohli, Chiranjeev and Suri, Rajneesh (2003), '2 + 2 = 5? A framework for using co-branding to leverage a brand', *Journal of Brand Management*, 11: 1, pp. 35–47.

Liu, Shuk-ching and Choi, Tsan-ming (2009), 'Consumer attitudes towards brand extensions of designer-labels and mass-market labels in Hong Kong', *Journal of Fashion Marketing and Management*, 13: 4, pp. 527–540.

LxKnitwear (2012), 'Missoni History', *Lx Knitwear*, 14 February, http://www.lxknitwear.com/articles/44-article/66-missoni-history.html. Accessed 8 December 2013.

Marketing Week (2011), 'Fashion designers reaching out to the high street cultivating new consumers or losing their edge?', *Marketing Week*, http://www.marketingweek.co.uk/sectors/retail/fashion-designers-reaching-out-to-the-high-street-cultivating-new-consumers-or-losing-their-edge?/3024742.article. Accessed 12 December 2013.

Martin, Richard (2012), 'Missoni', *Fashion Encyclopedia*, 14 February, http://www.fashionencyclopedia.com/Ma-Mu/Missoni.html. Accessed 12 December 2013.

Miller, Karen W. and Mills, Michael K. (2012), 'Fashion Marketing and Consumption of Luxury Brands', *Journal of Business Research*, 65: 10, pp. 1471–1479.

Missoni (2012), 'History', *Missoni*, http://missoni.com/ing.html. Accessed 2 February 2012.

Moore, Booth (2011), 'Sitting down with three generations of Missoni', *Los Angeles Times*, 30 October, http://articles.latimes.com/2011/oct/30/image/la-ig-missoni-20111030. Accessed 12 December 2013.

Moore, Christopher M. and Birtwistle, Grete (2004), 'The Burberry business model: Creating an international fashion luxury brand', *International Journal of Retail & Distribution Management*, 32: 8, pp. 412–422.

Mower, Sarah (2011), 'Preen reigns supreme at Debenhams', *The Telegraph*, 13 April, http://fashion.telegraph.co.uk/news-features/TMG8446339/Preen-reigns-supreme-at-Debenhams.html. Accessed 12 December 2013.

Nueno, Jose, L. and Quelch, John, A. (1998), 'The mass marketing of luxury', *Business Horizons*, 41: 6, pp. 61–68.

Okonkwo, Uche (2007), *Luxury Fashion Branding: Trends, Tactics, Techniques*, Hampshire: Palgrave Macmillian.

Phau, Ian and Prendergast, Gerard (2000), 'Consuming luxury brands: The relevance of the "Rarity Principle"', *Journal of Brand Management*, 8: 2, pp. 122–138.

Rajagopal (2008), 'Measuring brand performance through metrics application', *Measuring Business Excellence*, 12: 1, pp. 29–38.

Schiffman, Leon, Bednall, David, O'Cass, Aaron, Paladino, Aangela and Kanuk, Leslie (2005), *Consumer Behaviour*, Frenchs Forest: Pearson Education Australia.

Shukla, Paurav. and Purani, Keyoor (2012), 'Comparing the importance of luxury value perceptions in cross-national contexts', *Journal of Business Research*, 65: 10, pp. 1417–1424.

Stych, Ed (2011), 'Target says some stores will restock Missoni collection', *Business Journal*, 14 September, http://www.bizjournals.com/twincities/news/2011/09/14/missoni-target-more-stock-coming.html. Accessed 12 December 2013.

Surchi, Micaela (2011), 'The temporary store: a new marketing tool for fashion brands', *Journal of Fashion Marketing and Management*, 15: 2, pp. 257–270.

Swerdloff, Alexis (2011), '60 Seconds With: Rosita Missoni', *The Wall Street Journal*, 12 February, http://online.wsj.com/news/articles/SB1000142405274870442220457613031398837862. Accessed 12 December 2013.

Truong, Yann, McColl, Rod and Kitchen, Phillip J. (2009), 'New luxury brand positioning and the emergence of Masstige brands', *Journal of Brand Management*, 16: 5, pp. 375–382.

Van Praet, Nicholas (2011), 'Luxury brands start feeling the pinch', *Financial Post*, 29 November, http://business.financialpost.com/2011/11/29/luxury-brands-start-feeling-the-pinch/. Accessed 12 December 2013.

Washburn, Judith H., Till, Brian D. and Priluck, Randi (2000), 'Co-branding: Brand equity and trial effects', *Journal of Consumer Marketing*, 17: 7, pp. 591–604.

Wetlaufer, Suzy (2004), 'The perfect paradox of star brands: an interview with Bernard Arnault of LVMH', *Harvard Business Review*, October, pp. 79–117.

Wu, Couchen and Hsing, San-san (2006), 'Less is More: How Scarcity Influences Consumers' Value Perceptions and Purchase Intents through Mediating Variables', *Journal of American Academy of Business*, 9: 2, pp. 125–132.

Wu, Shwu-Ing and Lo, Chen-Lien (2009), 'The influence of core-brand attitude and consumer perception on purchase intention towards extended product', *Asia Pacific Journal of Marketing and Logistics*, 21: 1, pp. 174–194.

Zhan, Lingjing. and He, Yanqun (2012), 'Understanding luxury consumption in China: Consumer perceptions of best-known brands', *Journal of Business Research*, 65: 10, pp. 1452–1460.

CONTRIBUTOR DETAILS

Dr Edwina Luck has been with Queensland University of Technology (QUT) Business School within The School of Advertising, Marketing and Public Relations since 2002. Her research specialist areas include Consumer Behaviour, IMC, Marketing Education, Virtual Social Networks, Not for Profit, Generation Y and is published in these areas. She has attended many international conferences, been interviewed in local and State media and her opinion is sought after in aspects of social media. She has participated in expert panels regarding social media. She has won two QUT's Vice Chancellor's Awards for Excellence in Teaching and Innovation.

Contact: Queensland University of Technology Business School, School of Advertising, Marketing and Public Relations, Brisbane, 4001, Australia.
E-mail: e.luck@qut.edu.au

Dr Gjoko Muratovski holds a Ph.D. in Design Research and Corporate Communication Strategies, with specialization in Branding and Public Opinion Management. He has over twenty years of international experience spanning from Europe and Asia, to the USA and Australia working with a broad range of businesses and organizations. Dr Muratovski is currently the Head the Communication Design Department at the Auckland University of Technology (New Zealand) and a Chairman at the agIdeas International Design Week (Australia). Dr Muratovski has been an Advisor on Brand Development Strategies for the European-based agency IDEA Plus Communications whose clients include brands such as Porsche, Audi, Volkswagen, McDonald's and the Heineken Group.

Contact: Auckland University of Technology, School of Art and Design, WE521 / 27 St Paul Street, Auckland, 1010, New Zealand.
E-mail: gjoko.muratovski@aut.ac.nz

Lauren Hedley is working with Carolina Herrera in Marketing and Communications in New York. She has graduated with a Double Degree in Marketing and International Business from QUT. Hedley was a Dean's Honours student and has a keen interest in the fashion industry.

Contact: 64 W 70th St Apt 4A, New York, NY, 10023, USA.
E-mail: lfhedley@gmail.com

Global Fashion Brands: Style, Luxury & History

© 2014 Intellect Ltd Chapter. English language. doi: 10.1386/GFB.1.57_1

ANNE PEIRSON-SMITH
City University of Hong Kong

Comme on down and Choos your shoes: A study of consumer responses to the use of guest fashion designers by H&M as a co-branded fashion marketing strategy

ABSTRACT

This chapter focuses on the current fashion retail trend to use guest celebrity fashion designers by high street fashion brand H&M from 2004 onwards as a commercial promotional strategy resulting in global urban scenes of customers queuing for hours in all weather conditions pre-opening, followed by locust-like scenes of frenzied shoppers emptying racks and shelves of designer branded items in seconds with resulting media buzz. This form of social construction is intended to concretize the abstract symbolic nature of fashion in the global marketplace. As the fashion system is increasingly image driven, designers are personified, individualized

KEYWORDS

fashion co-branding
Hennes and Mauritz
  (H&M)
celebrity designers
fashion consumers
massclusivity
fashion branding

and aestheticized, whilst also branded and co-branded by the cultural intermediaries whose job it is to align and position them within a consumer niche of shared values and lifestyles. These symbiotic relationships borrow interest from each other as trickle-down and bottom-up brands cohabit in the interests of establishing brand visibility and credibility amongst aspirational consumers. A qualitative study of H&M consumers using focus groups and interviews will suggest that whilst the intentions of co-branding strategies to motivate consumers to trade upwards by implementing celebrity designer crossover collections has been largely successful in engaging fashion brand fans, there is evidence of increasing consumer agency, cynicism and saturation with regard to this strategy in view of changing economic conditions and evolving consumer needs.

INTRODUCTION: H&M STREETSCENE

Picture the scene – actually it is not too difficult and does not take too much imaginative effort – as it has rapidly become a regular media story – much editorialized and photographed, blogged and tweeted about and now an established

Figure 1: H&M window display showing designer collaboration with Marni, March 2012. Photograph by author.

part of the fashion consumer Zeitgeist. It is Saturday in a major global city – take your pick – New York, London, Paris, Shanghai, Seoul, Hong Kong. Imagine – there you in are in your city of choice and you're walking down the street at 7:30 a.m. Here you see a long queue of shoppers snaking round the block of a mall at street level in the central shopping area. Curious as to what's behind this collective show of dedication to some strange cause – and ever the street anthropologist (or is it frustrated investigative journalist?) – you make your way to the front of the queue – to the source of this magnetic draw. After passing a long line of a hundred or more anticipatory females of varying demographic profiles, you find yourself at the gleaming plate glass, red and white plastic portals of that current temple of high street consumerism – H&M. Most of the worshippers appear good humoured despite the cool, overcast morning with a hint of rain in the air, and you can feel the sense of anticipation in the air like that of children eagerly awaiting the arrival of Santa Claus or the Easter Bunny. Reaching the front of the queue, but not joining it, you ask one of the pole-positioned twenty-something girls in skinny jeans, Hello Kitty t-shirt, BAPE customized denim jacket and Ugg boots (and wait – is that a sleeping bag that you can see peeping out from her Coach leather backpack) how long has she been waiting to get to the front of the queue? 'Oh I've been here all night', she smiles casually pushing her Ray-Ban aviators back up onto her well-groomed hair. 'It's so worth it you know, because I'm about to purchase my big dream fashion item – a pair of Jimmy Choos!' Her voice rises to a state of frenetic, breathy ecstasy as she adds, 'Look there they are in the window!' You crane your neck to see above the heads of the couple of girls immediately behind her who scowl at you grimly as if you are attempting to pull off some kind of subtle queue-jumping stunt. You gasp and raise your eyebrows in response to what you can see. There in the window is a sight to make even the most hard-bitten urban Cinderella's heart melt. Before you is a high pyramid of purple Jimmy Choo monikered shoe boxes displaying five styles of shoe (two stiletto-style sandals, two stiletto high boots and a low kitten heeled shoe) surrounded by sleek mannequins intently pawing each others' shoes, whilst also adorned with the said objects of desire. 'Which ones will you buy then?' you ask. 'Oh those leopard skin and black patent super high stilettos – they'll be mine – and my friends will be so like, "Wah! You look amazing" when I wear them out tonight'! She responds with an almost religious fervour and reverence for the object of her desire, mixed with more than a hint of lustful glee.

As you walk away from the worshipful mob, the uniformed guards remove the metal barriers protecting the double doors of the storefront and we leave our informant as she is carried into the store on a tidal wave of frenzied and aggressive shoppers, disappearing into the temple of current consumer heaven to satisfy her heartfelt desire and shoe fetish.

The contemporary retail trend to use guest celebrity fashion designers notably by high street fashion brands as a central promotional marketing strategy is the focus of this article. Specifically, this article examines the efficacy of the current fashion retail trend to use guest celebrity fashion designers by high street fashion brand, mass market retailer, Hennes & Mauritz (H&M) from 2004 onwards as a co-branding promotional strategy resulting in global urban scenes of customers queuing for hours in all weather conditions pre-opening, followed by locust-like scenes of frenzied shoppers emptying racks and shelves of designer branded items in seconds with resulting media buzz. The analysis will be based on a qualitative, ethnographic investigation into

Figure 2: Customers queue up and sleep outside H&M store in Hong Kong for the H&MxMMM designer collection, November 2012. Photograph by author.

H&M's designer crossover collections launched in its major global flagship stores such as Hong Kong based on feedback from a series of focus groups and on the spot interviews at the launch of selected H&M co-branded designer collections.

Co-branding fashion collections

Co-branding refers to the practice of pairing the brand names of two or more different companies with

> potential economic and commercial rewards for participating parties …
> showcasing and communicating the brand in collaboration with another
> different company … regarded as both a communication and growth
> strategy. It opens new venues to showcase the brand, and it also creates
> opportunities to extend and expand the brand through these collabora-
> tions.
>
> (Hameide 2011: 85)

The benefits of this close design collaboration relationship appear to facilitate a win-win commercial outcome promising benefits for both parties in terms of heightened brand visibility and increased sales (Chang 2009). Conversely, there are risks in these commercial liaisons including the inability to control the consumer response to the relationship and, as H&M have found, not all co-branding relationships are equally successful.

This branding collaboration is not a brand new approach to fashion brand-ing dating back to Pierre Cardin's presentation of his prêt a porter collection in French supermarket Printemps in 1959 to the consternation of the fashion world of the day who viewed this as a debasement of his core brand ethos followed by his extensive licensing agreements resulting in his expulsion from the governing body of French fashion La Chambre Syndicale (Coleridge 1989). The emergence and acceptance by the industry of what became known as the commercialization of exclusive fashion, had to wait until 1973 with the crossover relationship between sportswear brand adidas and Japanese luxury designer Yoji Yamamoto, for whom the latter designed the long-running Y3 sportswear collection.

This was a practice previously avoided by luxury brands fearing that their prestigious reputation would be downgraded by this base association with mass fashion. Credited with championing designer collaborations as a successful branding strategy, H&M has racked up the partnerships as an annual event with top designers such as Stella McCartney, Roberto Cavalli, Matthew Williamson, Jimmy Choo, Viktor & Rolf, Comme des Garçons, Lanvin, Versace, Sonia Rykiel, Marni and Maison Martin Margiela (MMM) and Isabel Marant, in addition to celebrity collections with Madonna, Kylie Minogue, Anna dello Russo and Beyonce. These symbiotic relationships borrow interest from each other as trickle-down and bottom-up brands cohabit in the interests of establishing brand visibility and credibility amongst aspirational consumers. As Tungate observes

> few ordinary folk could afford a Prada suit or a Dior dress even if they could stretch to a handbag or a pair of sunglasses, where do they get clothes to match? Enter Zara, H&M, Top Shop – high street brands.
>
> (Tungate 2006: 22)

This form of social construction by the brand producer is intended to concretize the abstract symbolic nature of fashion in the global marketplace. As the fashion system is increasingly image driven, designers are personified,

Figure 3: Queues form overnight in Hong Kong for the launch of the H&M Versace collection.

individualized and aestheticized, whilst also branded and co-branded by the cultural intermediaries (Negus 2002) whose job it is to align and position them within a consumer niche of shared values and lifestyles as a way of enhancing the brand identity.

To this end, the ratification of designer genius and their alignment with strategic fashion brand partnerships is visibly played out in globalized urban spaces and places and in the less rarefied arena of the high street fashion store with the emergence of this phenomenon of 'masstige' and 'massclusivity' (Hogue 2005). In a broader frame, this legitimating process, although seemingly critical to the survival and success of the fashion brand and individual designer in the global cultural marketplace, underlines the latent contradictions of the fashion system whereby the cult of personality and celebrity designer label deliberately obscure the significant collaborative efforts underpinning the cultural production and promotion of branded garments (Peirson-Smith 2013). The fashion system has critically and historically relied from the end of the nineteenth century across Worth, Poiret, Dior, Chanel and YSL on the push of marketing strategies and mediated visual representations by fashion brands to locate, nurture and direct consumers to engage and enter into a lifelong relationship with the brand in the interests of increasing sales. In turn, the engaged fashion consumer fuels the fashion marketing machine in their search for individual identity formation and change, and in the process of fulfilling their collective dreams and aspirations through the dominant symbolic markers of identity and belonging (Craik 2009) found in the welcoming arms of global fashion brands and the nurturing spaces and places of shopping malls and retail zones in which they are located from advertising campaigns to point of sale.

Whilst the push of marketing and fashion branding has become increasingly competitive over the past decade, then so has the pull of consumer demand and response in the form of protracted queuing and doing in-store

Figure 4: Daytime queues outside H&M for launch of Versace H&M collection, Hong Kong. November 2011. Photograph by author.

battle for special offers from designer collections to the traditional January and Black Friday sales (Simpson et al. 2011). This reaches its apogee in the case of H&M's guest fashion designer co-branding strategy where we see customers transubstantiating into 'lustomers' (Brown 2007), 'who drool over the latest H&M designer launch, engage in ferocious fistfights between fashionistas in H&M, all testament to the intensity of the acquisitive impulse and the associated loss of emotional equipoise, we witness consumers driven wild by insatiable marketer induced desire' (Brown 2007: 150).

Yet, these hyper-enthusiastic fashion fans that every fashion marketer dreams of are actually the marketing and branding exception, rather than the rule. Given the highly competitive nature of the fashion universe, high street fashion shoppers in general across global urban fashion centres such as London, New York and Hong Kong are more sophisticated consumers, well informed about their fashion brand options and very demanding of quality and value for money when they do decide to enter into a purchase agreement. These consumer sophisticates are not to be underestimated. They are like endangered species – highly difficult to locate and ensnare. By the same logic, 'lustomers' for most fashion brands are almost mythical creatures who are seemingly downright impossible to locate and make real. As a measure of this, the fashion universe is filled with the corpses of fashion brands that failed to maintain their customer base, let alone attract and connect with the elusive fashion brand fan.

Yet, the fashion brand fanatic appears connected emotionally to the brand of their choice given their dedication that manifests itself in their willingness to queue up overnight whatever the weather outside the H&M stores pre-launch of the cross over collections and once inside to exhibit passionate behavioural displays often resulting in fighting and injuries (Kirova and Winter 2013). In response to this, H&M more recently have implemented a strict crowd control system, not only by employing

Figure 5: Customers gain access to the H&M store for guest designer collections in carefully controlled, timed sessions. Photograph by author.

security guards and erecting barriers outside the stores sectioning customers off from passers-by, but also by organizing a carefully policed, militaristically staged store entry system on the day of each of the collection's launch, which normally starts at 8 a.m. This is executed by issuing colour-coded wrist bands to each queuing customer and a fifteen-minute purchasing time restriction limiting each consumer to only purchase one item in each category of the collection. Whilst appearing as a system of consumer control, this also can be seen as adding to the 'special' symbolic nature of the latest limited designer collection where visible queues signify demand and generate collective desire. In addition, to heighten this exclusive experience in a tangible way, H&M have specially designed carrier bags for each collection such as the Versace launch or hangers for the Marni and the MMM collection, for example, complete with brand logo, which also serves as street-level advertising for the launch as they exit the store with significant numbers of carrier bags that serve to promote the launch and generate further desire amongst potential shoppers who might visually encounter this consumption spectacle and be persuaded to investigate this scenario for themselves. Further, this consumption fest also becomes a media spectacle as news and broadcast journalists and bloggers also wait outside the store to photograph and interview the first wave of customers weighed down with their purchases. More recently, H&M have also launched these new collections online resulting in a parallel universe of virtual queues, a website crash and frustrated online shoppers (Sidell 2013).

This leads us then to probe H&M's success in pushing the cognitive and emotional buttons of its customers by transforming them into fashion brand fans as reflected in its ability to consistently rank in the past few years as the top performing European retail brand.

H&M history

Swedish-based, family-owned Hennes & Mauritz (H&M) one of the world's largest fast fashion empires has 75,000 employees and approximately 2000 stores in over 40 countries worldwide including China, Japan, Russia and Korea. Its successful operations to date are reflected in its market capital of $586 billion and annual sales of $21 billion (Milne 2013) on the back of selling over 600 million items per year. Since being founded in 1947, H&M's corporate vision is 'to offer fashion and quality at the best price' (H&M Annual Report 2008: 13). This sentiment aligns with original founder Erling Persson's notion of building a retail chain with 'fashion at prices that will suit everyone' (Giertz-Martenson 2012: 110). Across corporate literature and CEO media interviews, the company claims to have democratized fashion given that 'H&M's business concept is to offer fashion and quality at the best price. H&M should always have the best customer offering in each and every market ... With a strong offering that appeals to customers around the world, H&M is able to grow successfully in all its existing markets as well as in new ones, with growth among all its brands and through new concepts' (H&M Annual Report 2012: 7). H&M's fast fashion philosophy, whereby the store is run like a fashion supermarket with a high turnover of stock to ensure its freshness and professed customer focus, is reworked in the designer collaboration in the interests of the market as current CEO Karl-Johan Persson, claims of H&M's democratizing fashion mantra: 'The main focus is on the customer – just to make sure they get a better offer all the time' (White 2011).

CREATIVE BRANDING STRATEGIES

Whilst some critics may suggest that this marketplace success is down to chaos theory (Lewin 2001) chance, good fortune (Roberts 1989) or evidence of cultish, unfathomable fads of collective display whose day will soon pass, the argument presented here suggests that strategic creative branding at the heart of the brand's ethos lies at the heart of the successful fashion brand. In addition, significant creative branding strategies, such as the incorporation of guest fashion designers, appear to be a winning lustomer driver. It is suggested that this results in positioning the fashion brand in a unique and impactful way, thereby activating the consumer–brand relationship and elevating it to another, hyper-level of engagement. Yet, this depends on the careful management of this type of branding strategy to ensure quality garment control and alignment with consumer need.

Name culture

As in the evolution of many of the creative industries – the fashion world has been built on the backs of designer names and the history of fashion in the past 150 years is personified through famous individuals – fashion stars – who are lauded as the benchmark or exemplars of creative fashion genius in terms of their ability to create and style a signature garment or collection. In this regard, the fashion world parallels that of the art world, architecture and design and the wider sphere of entertainment and media where star systems are central to their operations (Peirson-Smith 2013).

Figure 6: Gold dress in the H&M Versace collection, November 2011. Photograph by author.

The celebrity – commodity nexus is a modern phenomenon showing no let up in the twenty-first century as there is an ongoing cycle of famous people being attached to new goods and services or in case of fashion designers producing these goods. As Rojek notes, 'market organization is actually founded on the perpetual replenishment and development of desire through commodity and brand innovation' (2001: 187). Thus, the contemporary creative industries from which fashion emerges are largely subject to the workings of an influential publicity-driven system, which trades on the discourse of novelty as evidenced in the constantly revolving fashion production and consumption cycle (Nystrom 1928).

DEMOCRATIZATION OF FASHION – WHERE HAUTE COUTURE AND HIGH STREET COLLIDE

Yet, a number of factors emerging across the past decade have attempted to democratize the fashion system as fashion designers such as Jacobs, Ford and Galliano reinvented and reworked old fashion brands into luxury brands in the full glare of a media machine, centred on generating coverage around the cult of celebrity in the name economy (Moeran 2003). In this name game, celebrities also willingly act as clothes horses or walking advertisements for luxury fashion brands, visually representing them across acres of global magazine pages and newspaper columns, thereby fuelling the desire of hordes of wannabe young women and men to emulate them in the never-ending quest for celebritydom (Church Gibson 2012). In addition, celebrities become fashion designers and launch their own branded lines or become the face of fashion retail outlets.

If the hierarchically ordered fashion system had already been changing shape over the past 50 years with youth and street styles exerting a bubble-up influence on the Veblenesque top-down flow of style trends, it now resembles Table Top mountain rather than Mount Olympus. So, the fashion gods fell or came down to earth, or in most cases descended from the mountain to play with the mortals as luxury fashion brands such as Gucci under Ford's direction, established massluxe, massclusivity or masstige diffusion lines carrying near affordable accessories and designer fragrances to cater for the desires of the brand conscious, style-savvy, fashion-aware masses. As if by magic the fairy godmothers H&M, Zara, Topshop and Target appeared laden with armfuls of trendy, catwalk-inspired outfits and now everyone is invited to the ball. Equally, consumer tastes in developed urban fashion centres changed across the past decade with a more postmodern, mix-and-match approach to compiling outfits, mixing H&M jackets with Hermès scarves, partly due to an economic downturn resulting in a more cash-strapped consumer and partly because the fashion consumer is more informed by an unending flow of fashion coverage and advice via traditional, digital and social media channels.

Retailers such as H&M have seemingly stood out from the crowd and survived the test of time for over 50 years in a highly competitive sector because they have been adaptive and also adhered to branding's golden rules becoming active customer owners by positioning the brand, closely managing the brand image and identity and aligning it with new market needs amongst young fashion leaders for fast fashion based on opportunity-pulled responses across weeks rather than months. The brand identity – the core ethos or essence of the brand that the company wants to convey and its resulting brand image – the perceptions of the brand in the mind of the consumer are candidly defined by H&M's Chief Marketing manager Jorgen Andersson as 'fashionable, exciting and accessible' (Tungate 2006: 39). Here design principle and quality fashion through efficient distribution at the best possible price are coherently encapsulated in H&M's communications efforts. This is based on high-profile, multimodal promotional campaigns and strategic public relations management generating significant global media coverage in the industry and business press whilst operating customer-focused web loyalty programmes, producing its own free customer magalog and ensuring that the store experience is bright and cheerful.

Differentiation and being distinctive in the marketplace for design, quality and cost and aligning this with on-trend customer aspirations for fast-paced, glamorous lifestyles is a large part of this brand-winning formula as encapsulated in the recent guest designer relationships that it has courted, which are founded on a symbiotic relationship as trickle-up and bottom-down influences cohabit, albeit fleetingly, in the interests of establishing brand visibility for both couture and high street brands to satisfy the seemingly insatiable demand for new looks and imagined lives.

The fashion celebrity designer appears to reside between the push of the cultural intermediaries and the pull of the consumer in the market for their products in both their social and socio-economic roles. Contradictions emerge and significant tensions exist between the fashion designers' desire for authenticity and the socio-economic demands of their commodity status. Yet the guest designers clearly enter willingly into the relationship – albeit after significant negotiation – seemingly happy to present their manufactured

Figure 7: Successful customers are interviewed by the media on exit from the H&M Versace collection, Hong Kong, November 2011. Photograph by author.

identity in another frame. In this sense, they are packaged and positioned by and across a range of media that the consumer audience identifies with and desires to be part of. So, the question is why does this celebrity fashion designer crossover work so well by seemingly turning customers into avid brand fans and what motivates them to think, feel and behave in this way? It appears that all players involved – customer, fast fashion retailer and couture designer or celebrity are responsible for collectively constructing this phenomenon where the push responds to the pull in the business of selling dreams of owning luxury goods to those who have an insatiable desire for them.

FASHION BRANDING

A brand is based on the association that people make with a company in addition to its tangible material aspects so that it exists in the minds and hearts of the consumer (Olins 2000; Ind 2001). The rationale of branding 'is to establish a differentiated identity for the line of clothing being marketed in a highly competitive, crowded marketplace niche so that Zara's knitwear, for example, sets itself apart from H&M's or Mango's version' (Peirson-Smith 2013: 180). Brand management focuses on brand identity (logo, name) created by the designer encapsulating the brand mission or rationale and the brand image – the resulting perception in the mind of the consumer. Hence, brand managers aim to establish a relationship with consumers and control their perception of the brand identity through multi-modal communicative forms and channels from print to social media. This brand identity is managed in three ways: through the brand's ethos or what it represents at its core, the values that it ascribes to and the brand personality 'that enable the brand to be instantly recognisable and much desired' (Devereux and Peirson-Smith 2009: 66). Brand managers attempt to control the overall character of the brand, making it unique from others, bringing it alive, giving it a raison d'etre with a consistently identifiable look and feel (Peirson-Smith and Hancock 2013).

In response to this brand product positioning, the brand image is the overall consumer perception of the brand (ethos, values and personality) driven by the brand personality and its relative positioning in the market (Aaker 1997). Branding is the result of interplay between these different elements in the push from the producer and the pull of the consumer affecting the values and symbolic meanings attached to the brand and its acceptance or rejection by the consumer as active agent (Arvidsson 2005). Effectively, branding 'takes a lifeless garment and transforms it into something with a desirable and irresistible power to persuade the customer to acquire it' (Peirson-Smith 2013: 181).

So, brand managers create a universe in which to situate the brand, project its identity intertextually and invite the consumer to exercise creative agency by engaging within the co-creation of meaning for the brand (Bridson and Evans 2004; Lury 1999). In the specific case of fashion branding, the designer's creative output and the strategy of using a 'celebrity' designer crossover will set in motion the material and intangible 'platforms for action that enable the production of particular immaterial use-values: an experience, a shared emotion, a sense of community' (Arvidsson 2005: 248). Arguably, the brand in itself is not important. Rather, it is what it can do for the consumer, or more precisely it is what the consumer does with it that is important.

Frame and narrative theory

Frame theory is also useful here in attempting to understand the production process and consumption response that underlies this celebrity guest designer strategy adopted by H&M. Frames are the fundamental cognitive structures signposting the representations of reality, which Goffman saw as a basis for understanding how we 'locate, perceive, identify and label a seemingly infinite number of concrete occurrences defined in its terms' (Goffman 1974: 21) in the process of making sense of the vast array of mediated information processed on a daily basis. Goffman considered that frames are unconsciously assimilated into communication exchange as he saw framing as an innate social and communicative process. Yet, this only accords with one part of the picture – and places emphasis on the creator of the discourse and the sender of the message. These are the cultural mediators – actively and professionally responsible for selecting and positioning the visual and verbal message. As Gitlin notes, 'frames are principles of selection, emphasis and presentation composed of little tacit theories about what exists, what happens, what matters' (1980: 6). The emphasis on the selection of frames by the promotional intermediaries accords with their professional brief as Entman observes,

> To frame is to select some aspects of perceived reality and make them more salient in communicating text, in such a way as to promote a particular problem, definition, causal interpretation, moral evaluation and/or treatment recommendation.
>
> (1993: 54)

In this way, the promotional intermediaries responsible for the marketing campaigns and how it is communicated to the consumer and consciously communicate using frames or schemata to reflect their position (and convey their belief system) using cognitive devices such as keywords, issues, stereotyped images, which thematically reinforce their position in competing stakeholder markets.

Clearly, the views articulated through the framing of designers will on the one hand represent the world-view of those representing the case, and also the choice of frame is based on professional considerations of what will capture media attention and connect cognitively and affectively with consumers – especially pushing their emotional buttons and linking them to the brand more closely.

For the H&M co-branding campaigns, we can identify some common frames that have assisted in effecting meaning behind this persuasive retailing endeavour in the process of signalling their difference from the high street competition – both the brands being promoted and the consumer once they have bought into this cultural system emotionally and functionally.

Framing the celebrity brand narrative

Storytelling as a sense-making device (Weick 1995) is a human trait and a communicative tool that is used rhetorically to persuade others and to influence events (Fisher 1984) premised on audience identification and involvement. Hence, stories are often used to make sense of organizational life and to communicate that sensibility created through a range of communication channels and modes. In many ways, brand identity building is all about storytelling (Hancock 2009). In an age of celebrity culture (Marshall 1997), consumers aspire towards and buy into celebrity brands to be part of their dream story or to make that story part of their own lives as they want to cast themselves in leading roles or live like they imagine their favourite celebrities do.

RESEARCH METHODOLOGY

As an active agent the consumer will interpret the brand's signifiers or image in their own way. In anticipation of this, brand managers ensure that all brand communication and messages are consistent and coherent. Hence, as Fisher (1987) suggested, all narratives form the basis of our sense-making and fail or succeed on the basis of their ability to be internally structurally consistent and credible for their audience. This suggests that the crossover designer brand relationships with H&M must attain some sort of credibility and credence with the consumer in order to make sense and to align with the brand's identity and impact on the brand's image all based on consumer perceptions as 'the effects of co-branding on the consumer should be paramount in decisions concerning this strategy' (Okonkwo 2007: 171).

The next section will test this notion out by presenting qualitative research findings from the consumer's perspective by matching up eight promotional frames or narratives identified as being embedded in the H&M crossover campaigns 2004–2012 with the consumer response elicited in the focus groups (Morgan 1988, Kawamura 2011). The intention was to determine the prospects' responses to the H&M designer collaborations, and to identify the range of motivations underpinning the consumer's cognitive, affective and behavioural engagement. To elicit this data, twenty student respondents (5 males and 15 females) across five focus groups representing an age range from 18–23 and featuring a range of representative ethnicities (from Hong Kong, Mainland China, the Philippines, India, Sweden, Poland, United Kingdom, North America, Australia, Canada, France, Germany and New Zealand) were interviewed. In addition, on the spot open-ended interviews with customers (Weiss 1984) were conducted both outside and inside H&M stores during the M for Madonna, H&M loves Kylie (July 2007), Comme des Garçons (November 2008), Jimmy Choo (November 2009), Versace (November 2010), Matthew Williamson (S/S 2008), David Beckham (2012), Sonia Rykiel (December 2008), Marni (November 2011), and H&MxMMM (November 2012) collection launches in Hong Kong. Responses were coded and analysed according to the themes covered below (Harding 2010). These include: limited edition; affordable luxury; glamour; quality, uniqueness, fashion heritage, design principle and reciprocity.

1. Limited edition

H&M's foray into guest-designed lines from Lagerfeld's A/W 2004 to Maison Martin Margiela (MMM) A/W 2012 collection have not only been limited in stock numbers as 'one-off' phenomena and also only released in selected global stores. This constructed scarcity principle articulated through the frame of 'get it now whilst stocks still last' – a frame originally borrowed from low price point retailing – appears to add to the special value of the branded items on offer arousing the intensity of the desire to purchase (Cialdini 2001). It intends to add excitement to the purchasing experience at point of sale, with most of the H&M guest designer lines being emptied from racks and shelves within a few hours and usually resold on eBay within the day.

The interviewees did generally concur that the idea that the items from each collection would be highly desirable, certainly adding to H&M's brand cachet and to their desirability as one of the focus group respondents observed:

> People always like limited editions because they are unique, and if you get that, it means that … for example if there are 10 items, and you get one of them, then it means that just 9 of the others can have that, and you will feel like you are so privileged and I can tell you that makes me feel really good and superior to everyone else.
>
> (Janice, Hong Kong, student, 20)

Another respondent also supported this idea regarding the worth of the superior affect afforded by accessing and purchasing the celebrity crossover item and speculated that this motivated H&M customers to withstand the rigours of standing in line for hours on end outside of the H&M store:

> I think that people are prepared to sacrifice their time and comfort to queue overnight and sleep outside in the street to get a chance to buy the H&M Versace jeans or the H&M Matthew Williamson suit and tie because it really matters to them to be seen as unique and special and to stand out from the crowd because they have been able to get something that no-one else has. Exclusivity really works and matters in this place.
>
> (James, Hong Kong, student, 21)

Outside the store for the Versace-H&M launch, one respondent said, 'In this life when everything is the same it's great to be able to find something different and exclusive. I'm planning to buy the big Versace cushions as they will dress up my home in a unique way' (Eunice, Thailand, 20).

The exclusive nature of the designer collections also yields a significant exchange value beyond the symbolic value. As a measure of this, another respondent queuing for the Comme des Garçons collection explained that this collection had real commercial value in the marketplace,

> Quite a few people will buy as many outfits as they can from this collection as it's a famous Japanese designer and Hong Kong people admire Japanese designers. So, many of us will put these items straight onto the internet for sale as it's the start of the day and I will most likely make a profit today … maybe three times the price that I will pay and that will be a good money.
>
> (Den, Hong Kong, 22)

Another respondent from the Philippines explained as she emerged from the store with ten large white bags with items worth over HK$5000 that she had travelled specially to Hong Kong to select pieces from the Marni collection for her customers of her boutique in Manila as 'their desire for these items is so high and they are more than willing to pay the price which covers the cost of my travel expenses too. They will be so happy'.

2. Affordable luxury

The notion of affordable luxury and fantasy is encapsulated in the framing of most of the H&M crossover collections including the Roberto Cavalli guest designer relationship in 2007, for example, who promised as the first invited Italian designer to 'add a dash of festivity and dreams' to H&M customers' life.

The focus group respondents largely believed this to be a major driver in the success of the celebrity collections, as noted by Stephen (Australia, 19):

> Yes the pricing really works, especially when H&M cross-over with famous brands like Comme des Garçons because people usually have to spend like thousands on items for Comme des Garçons, so now they only need to spend HK$200–300, so they will think they will have to have this because it is a rare opportunity to get a high luxury fashion item.

This sentiment was mirrored by the interviewees lining up for many of the collections as Dot (Hong Kong, 26) said 'We would never be able to afford the real thing in the Versace shop so we can have a luxury outfit at non-luxury prices'. Equally, as Candice (Singapore, 24) noted:

> In our age group (i.e. 20s to 30s), we normally cannot afford high-end fashion brands such as Roberto Cavalli, Jimmy Choo, or Sonia Rykiel. Therefore, we may not take the initiative to search for the information about these brands. However, when they have crossover fashion lines with H&M, the price of the products become affordable for us, so the distant between the brands and us has shortened.

There also appeared to be an expectation that the exchange value of the designer goods would not exceed a certain threshold and should be good value as if the H&M brand principle was also a critical part of the commercial exchange relationship:

> I noticed that people still tend to buy the designer clothes at a cheaper price, even in the cross-overs with the famous brands because I saw the $2000 Comme des Garçons cross-over with the H&M trench coat, and no one bought it, because it was slightly more expensive because the customers have the perception of, although you are Comme des Garçons but with H&M, but H&M doesn't deserve this amount of money.
>
> (Win, China, 23)

3. Glamour and lifestyle aspirations

> 'Celebrity culture, the art, movie and music world … As a designer you must have your eyes, ears, everything open'.
>
> (Margareta van den Bosch in Fisher 2009)

Glamour was feted as the hallmark of both the Versace and Jimmy Choo inaugural shoe and accessory range offering consumers the borrowed interest and brand identity associations from A-List designers.

In a similar manner, Madonna's womenswear (S/S 2006) and Kylie's beachwear (Summer 2007) invested their respective pop celebrity crossover collections with a rock chick and pop princess quality that adds other cultural systems – the music and pop culture industry – to this aspirational frame.

Queuing overnight for the Versace collection, Dina from India explained that she had a long list of items from friends and family that she was intending to buy for them in time for the Christmas season as 'some of the pieces are so sexy and so Versace and we love that'.

4. Quality lines

One of the core brand values of quality that H&M places great emphasis on in all of their external communications and promotional collaterals is a key promotional frame encapsulated in the guest designer relationships with Stella McCartney and Matthew Williamson, for example. McCartney's aesthetic of cool, feminine, wearable designs most typically aligns with the target H&M customer who are also offered sharp tailoring in the process for A/W 2005 – from the frame of her own signature line or her former Chloé wardrobe. Similarly, Matthew Williamson's men's and womenswear line offered in all featured stores for two seasons in 2009 was framed as an opportunity for the designer to benefit from H&M's penchant for matching quality and crafts-manship in the signature line to educate the consumer about fashion and style (Dehn 2012). Yet, many are keen to note, including Lagerfeld and Jimmy Choo themselves, that this was a specially invited line with a different finish, and was not a diffusion line for their brand whose signature shoes are made in Italy.

The focus group respondents questioned the quality of the fabric and production of the garments and one shared a disappointing experience when the hem of a Marni skirt came unravelled after one wear whilst another said that the buttons on the Matthew Williamson jacket had fallen off after a few weeks. As Janice (Canada, 20) observed:

> In fact, like last time I went to H&M for that Sonia Rykiel collection, I don't know why, but the bangles are not well produced – such cheap plastic and disappointing as it looked like they came from a cheap market stall.

There was a sense with the interviewees at the store that they had convinced themselves of the superior quality of the goods that they were lusting after and buying into. 'Look at that bag' Tammy (from Beijing, China) noted point-ing at the black Versace tote, 'It's such good leather – you could not get any better in the actual shop'.

5. Uniqueness

A more esoteric and conceptual frame was crafted for the Comme des Garçons winter 2009 avant garde and intellectual collaboration, 'founded on artis-tic inspiration and her philosophy of pursuing the ultimate form of creation based on a sense that H&M is surprising and educating consumers – even taking them outside of their comfort frame and broadening its target base', which was also the case with the 2012 MMM collection.

In the same vein, the Viktor & Rolf 2006 collection was aimed at a more discerning fashion crowd or at brining a new one up to speed, as Tim Blanks at Style.com noted,

> Viktor and Rolf suggest a number of opportunities for customers as well as designers at H&M. This is a clever collaboration. The challenge: V&R are cherished within the international fashion crowd but still a bit

unknown outside it. This will put an end to that. Whilst V&R, whose roots are based in couture, but love to play with opposites, embraced the opportunity to 'communicate our vision to such a large audience of H&M devotees'.

(Blanks 2006)

The unique liaison between high street and haute couture was seen by many respondents as an interest generator and one that creates significant desire. Yet, other respondents in the focus group viewed it as a cynical marketing ploy that duped the consumer into thinking that they had acquired the real designer item. 'The consumers are fooled into thinking that the designer and atelier have had a big input into the collection but in reality it's not true and it's like buying fake goods really' (Jac, France, 20).

On a pragmatic note, some of the focus group respondents were also keen to point out that whilst the MMM collection was interesting, it was essentially unwearable for most young people given the sizing as Matt (Hong Kong, 21) noted:

I really admire Maison Margiela and its really fascinating to see a reworking of the collection across the decades like a museum but I tried the men's coats and jackets on and I looked like a crazy person or a clown as even the XS size drowned me.

Significantly, much of this collection including the iconic duvet coat remained on the racks to become remainders or were relocated back to other global stores.

6. Fashion heritage

In a sense, the entire guest designer relationship is premised on the notion of providing customers with a rare gift or opportunity to buy into the story of the couture fashion brand of the moment as was the case with the recent Spring 2010 collection with Sonia Rykiel knits that evoked the 1960s modernist Parisian left bank look and origins of her original boutique. Equally, the most recent A/W 2012 MMM collection featuring replicated selected pieces such as the sock jumper from 1998 and other past collections from the 1980s onwards offered the chance to acquire a piece of fashion history.

There was a sense amongst the focus group respondents that the range of crossover collections representing a variety of styles and taste determined their level of cultural capital amongst the consumers who had to be in the know about many of the less well-known designers such as Sonia Rykiel or MMM. 'I think why it works is because the customers show their knowledge of fashion. You must be in the know about style, and knowing that you're in the know so you're part of a club'. The idea of a fashion club was also highlighted by the responses from the on-site interviews and observations as quite a number of customers from a range of countries across the collections said that they had checked on the H&M app, website and also with local fashion blogs to determine the content and to plan their personal or commercial purchases beforehand.

7. Design principle

H&M's CEO is on record as saying that H&M is committed to good design: garment design was allegedly one of the reasons that Lagerfeld entered into the strategic crossover alliance (Tungate 2006).

Figure 8: Customers with their Versace H&M purchases, November 2011. Photograph by author.

Whilst most respondents and interviewees admitted that the design of the products would not be the same as the actual designer brand, they all believed that the collections represented good design and felt and looked well designed.

However, the focus group respondents were more cynical and savvy about the design process: 'H&M shoppers just don't know that perhaps things they get in H&M with those famous designers, they just don't know that maybe these collections are not designed by that designer but it's designed by their team or associate' (Karly, Hong Kong, 21).

8. Reciprocity – gift giving

Some focus group respondents noted that H&M's celebrity collections could be interpreted as a gift for their customers, given that they were the first high street brand to launch and continue this strategy. As such, there seemed to be a recognition that this impacted on the brand image in a favourable way.

As one respondent noted, 'Now that I think of it – Zara don't do it, Mango don't, Cotton On and Forever 21 so they are giving their consumers something special I guess' (Carmen, China, 20).

DISCUSSION

Throughout all of these promotional frames or brand stories runs the notion that H&M attempts to position itself as the key fashion driver with its finger on the pulse of style and fashion trends of the now as it is in control of the selection and invitation process for each of the guest designers who to a person gush gratefully in the news releases and media interviews arranged around the launch of their one-off collections as to how enthusiastic and grateful they are to be occasioned this creative opportunity and chance to widen their market as the ultimate credibility booster.

Significantly, some designers such as Vivienne Westwood have gone on record stating that she would never be seen dead on the H&M rails. Yet, the fact that this is a regular question asked of couturiers often in media interviews demonstrates the impact that H&M have on the collective consumer consciousness. In turn, H&M frame this strategy as the ultimate and unique gift to its consumers – an act designed to stimulate brand loyalty.

In response from the consumer perspective, it would appear that these eight frames and brand narratives are largely recognized and bought into both symbolically and tangibly by H&M consumers. In addition, they go a significant way to explaining the cognitive, affective and behavioural responses that do appear to turn regular consumers of H&M merchandise into avid fans of the designer crossover collections. They appear to be successful in aligning with the aspirations of the consumer in terms of providing access to limited-edition, well-designed, affordable luxury items that appear to make sense of their lives given the current prevalence of celebrity culture. Beyond that, these collections also appear to increase H&M's brand equity on the back of the existing high-end designers' credibility, thereby strengthening H&M's brand equity and loyalty. Respondents appeared to associate value for money and good design with the H&M brand, which is also aligned with H&M's mission as a consequence of the content of both the designer and the regular collections, suggesting that the former transfers associational or symbolic value to the latter enhancing brand loyalty in the process.

Many of the focus group consumers and customers at the site of the designer collections appeared to be affectively connected to the celebrity designer crossover collections in terms of how it made them feel more positive about themselves with regard to others. In many ways, being able to purchase from the designer collections empowered them and made them feel more 'superior' and 'in the know about fashion unlike people who just throw on clothes' (Ang, Philippines, female shopper, 36). Yet, there was no evidence that H&M's regular customers would become the designer's customers other than in an aspirational way, although one shopper did say that having 'bagged my Versace gold party dress I'm now off to cosmetics store, Sasa, to buy my Versace perfume to complete the outfit' (Tara, United Kingdom, 38), suggesting that the designer buying relationship could be extended to related affordable designer diffusion lines. On the other hand, it was interesting to encounter consumers wearing designer outfits or bags who were in line to supplement their authentic designer wardrobes with the crossover items as one well-informed respondent in the store explained,

I'm here to buy a few Marni H&M items and I love the look of the pea coat and the graphic fabric of the skirts as they add an interesting twist to the collection and it was worth the wait in line to get my hands on these items. I think that we've all got over the head to toe designer look that was so prevalent here in the 1980s and 1990s. Actually, that looks so over the top and dated now and it was all so insecure. But you do see it in some Asian cities still and in Mainland Chinese first and second tier cities but their time will come too and that look will evolve as mine has.

(Cath, Canada, 33)

However, the 'lustomers' also appear to have their own frames or agendas when participating in the performance of queueing and frenzied shopping at the crossover launches. As we have seen, some of the participants' motivations in this spectacle are more cognitively and less affectively oriented, purely purchasing their quota of designer goods in each size to either sell in their own local or regional boutiques, sell on eBay or the Internet and to take them home as gifts in a variety of geographic and cultural locations. In this way, the designer collections fully represent the global commodification of fashion items with a high exchange value.

CELEBRITY CROSSOVER SATURATION

The question remains as to whether the 'lustomer' syndrome is sustainable or a passing fashion fad? In addition, are customers likely to get bored with the celebrity circus or just come to expect it so that the marketing buzz will fail to activate the manic desire for affordable and fleeting luxury that we have seen with previous collections?

Despite doubling income from 1998 to 2003, the recent economic downturn suggests that H&M returns over the past financial year have not been as robust as Wood (2012) observes:

H&M may need bouncers to control the crowds when it launches its high street collections by famous designers such as Karl Lagerfeld and Donatella Versace, but analysts warned on Thursday that Swedish fashion chain was losing its lustre after it reported a surprise fall in quarterly profits.

Furthermore, from personal observations the lengths of the queues from 2007 to 2012 with each collection appeared to get smaller. In addition, some of the focus group respondents as a younger demographic appeared to be more cynical and critical of these collaborative efforts.

Does this crossover promotional activity run the risk of actually tarnishing and debasing the luxury brand that becomes street smart, as some suggested with Viktor & Rolf and others? Or might it even signify a desperate act both of fading brands and celebrities to gain visibility. In fact, some blogs suggested that Madonna was past her prime, which generated unintended meanings and consumer responses to the Madonna H&M crossover collection. The focus group respondents also seemed to be more bemused by the recent H&MxMMM liaison, with few admitting to actually purchasing anything from that collection or being aware of anyone who had been a customer.

Finally, there is a sense that the designer collections have been successful thus far for H&M because of the affordance of cultural capital, where customers as part of a fashion club with an appreciation for, and understanding of, the brand backstory can indulge their desire for and their knowledge of the elite brands for their own personal consumption or as gifts for others. On another level, economic capital is also a stake here, turning some consumers into active economic agents who are using the collections to source garments, and style clients for a profit in retail outlets

Figure 9: Multiple purchases by customers from the H&M Versace collection November 2011. Photograph by author.

or by generating sales on eBay. On the surface, it all appears to be a win-win relationship, with the co-producers and consumers getting what they want out of the frenzied performance of consumption. Yet, at the end of the day, H&M is all about fast assembly line produced fashion. So, the process of turning rags into designer gowns is a collusion between the professional guardians of brand identity and consumers as fashion brand fans who are exercising various forms of agency and affect under the illusion of democratized fashion.

BACK AT STREET LEVEL

So, it is a Saturday afternoon in late November 2009 and I am entering the HK flagship H&M store on Queens Road Central with my 12-year-old daughter to spend her birthday vouchers in her notion of the coolest place on earth, and on entry we see a rugby scrum of fashion-frenzied people in front of us. People are pushing, pulling, arms flailing, cameras flashing. Every now and again a person will emerge from the shopping scrum with a pile of purple shoe boxes looking ruffled but ecstatic and head for the cash register. One man is carrying a six-box tower of silver and gold Jimmy Choos in every size from 35 to 40. 'These are gifts for all my sisters back in Delhi' he tells me with a triumphant smile. 'Come on then – let's take a closer look!' I instruct my hapless daughter as I realize it is the actual Jimmy Choo-H&M launch. We make it to the front line of boxes – and I scan them closely in between grasping hands and falling boxes as shoes are deftly fitted to foot and whisked away – this is fast fashion like no other. And I spot mine – size 40, leopard skin stiletto with patent trim – before I know it I've tried them on, secured the box and run for the till pulse racing, handing over US$130 (HK$1000) to seal the deal. 'Mummy, you'll never wear them,' my daughter yells above the noise of the shopping skirmish. 'Darling – I'll never wear them out' I retort, 'but at last I have my own pair of Jimmy Choos – and all in the name of research of course!'

REFERENCES

Aaker, David A. (1991), *Managing Brand Equity*, New York: The Free Press.

Aaker, Jennifer (1997), 'Dimensions of brand personality', *Journal of Marketing Research*, 34: August, pp. 347–56.

Arvidsson, Adam (2005), 'Brands: A Critical Perspective', *Journal of Consumer Culture*, 5: 2, pp. 235–57.

Blanks, Tim (2006), 'Viktor and Rolf for H&M', *The Fashion Spot.com*. http://forums.thefashionspot.com/f60/viktor-rolf-h-m-44141-16.html. Accessed 3 March 2011.

Bourdieu, Pierre (1993), *The Field of Cultural Production*, Cambridge: Polity Press.

—— (1984), *Distinction: A Social Critique of the Judgment of Taste*, Cambridge, MA: Harvard University Press.

Bridson, Kerrie, and Evans, Jody (2004), 'The secret to a fashion advantage is brand orientation', *International Journal of Retail and Distribution Management*, 32: 8, pp. 403–11.

Brown, Stephen (2007), 'Turning customers into lustomers: The Duveen proposition', *Journal of Consumer Behaviour*, 6: 2, July, pp. 143–53.

Chang, Wei-Lun (2009), 'Roadmap of co-branding positions and strategies', *Journal of American Academy of Business, Cambridge*, 15: 1, September, pp. 77–84.

Church Gibson, Pamela (2012), *Fashion and Celebrity Culture*, London: Bloomsbury.

Ciadini, Robert B. (2001), *Influence: Science and Practice*, 4th ed., Boston: Allyn & Bacon.

Craik, Jennifer (2009), *Fashion: Key Issues*, Oxford: Berg.

Coleridge, Nicholas (1989), *The Fashion Conspiracy: A Remote Journey Through the Empires of Fashion*, London: Mandarin Press.

Dehn, Georgia (2012), 'Margarita van den Bosch on the Marni for H&M range', 18 February, *The Telegraph.co.uk*, http://fashion.telegraph.co.uk/news-features/TMG9088781/Margareta-van-den-Bosch-on-the-Marni-for-HandM-range.html. Accessed 20 March 2012.

Devereux, Mary and Peirson-Smith, Anne (2009), *Public Relations in Asia Pacific: Communicating Effectively Across Cultures*, London and Singapore: John Wiley & Sons Ltd.

Entman, Robert M. (1993), 'Framing: Towards a Clarification of a Fractured Paradigm' *Journal of Communication*. 43(4), pp. 51–58.

Fisher, Alice (2009), 'Woman who gave us the A-List look', *The Guardian*. Sunday 22 March, http://www.theguardian.com/lifeandstyle/2009/mar/22/margareta-van-den-bosch. Accessed 3 March 2011.

Fisher, Walter R. (1984), Narration as Human Communication Paradigm: The Case of Public Moral Argument, *Communication Monographs*, 51, pp. 1–22.

—— (1987), *Human Communication as Narration: Toward a Philosophy of Reason, Value, and Action*, Columbia: University of South Carolina Press.

Giertz-Martenson, Ingrid (2012), 'H&M – documenting the story of one of the world's largest fashion retailers', *Business History*, 54: 1, pp. 108–15.

Gitlin, Todd (1980), *The Whole World Is Watching: Mass Media in the Making and Unmaking of the New Left*, Berkeley, CA: University of California Press.

Goffman, Erving (1974), *Frame Analysis: An Essay on the Organization of Experience*, London: Harper and Row.

Hameide, Kaled K. (2011), *Fashion Branding Unraveled*, New York: Fairchild.

Hancock, Joseph (2009), *Brand Story*, New York: Fairchild Books.

H&M (2008), *Annual Report Part 1: H&M in Words and Pictures*, Stockholm: H&M.

H&M (2012), *Annual Report*, Stockholm: H&M.

Harding, Jamie (2010), *Qualitative Data Analysis from Start to Finish*, London: Sage.

Hogue, Stuart (2005), 'Making designs dissonant', *Design Management Review*, 16: 4, pp. 34–38.

Ind, Nicolas (2001), *Living the Brand*, London: Kogan Page.

Kawamura, Yuniya (2011), *Doing Research in Fashion and Dress: An Introduction to Qualitative Research*, London: Bloomsbury.

Kirova, Deni and Winter, Katy (2013), 'Hysteria at H&M as shoppers queue from 4am for Isabel Marant collection and STILL miss out (then have to snap it up at THREE times the price on eBay)', *Mail Online*, http://www.dailymail.co.uk/femail/article-2507088/Hysteria-H-M-shoppers-queue-4am-STILL-miss-Isabel-Marant--eBay-already.html. Accessed 30 November 2013.

Lewin, Roger (2001), *Complexity: Life at the Edge of Chaos*, Chicago: University of Chicago Press.

Lury, Celia (2004), *Brands: the logos of a global economy*, New York: Routledge.

Marshall, P. David (1997), *Celebrity and Power*, Minneapolis: University of Minnesota Press.

Milne, Richard (2013), 'Karl-Johan Persson, chief executive, Hennes & Mauritz' *FT.com/management. The Monday Interview*, May 19, http://www.ft.com/intl/cms/s/0/d0c93d1a-be6b-11e2-bb35-00144feab7de.html#axzz2n4yQDcN9. Accessed 2 October 2013.

Moeran, Brian (2003), 'Celebrities and the name economy', *Research in Economic Anthropology*, Volume 22, pp. 299–321.

Morgan, David L. (1988), *Focus Groups as Qualitative Research Methods*, Volume 16, Thousand Oaks, CA: Sage Publications.

Negus, Keith (2002), 'The work of cultural intermediaries and the enduring distance between production and consumption', *Cultural Studies*, 16: 4, pp. 501–15.

Nystrom, Paul Henry (1928), *Economics of Fashion*, New York: Ronald Press Company.

Okonkwo, Uche (2007), *Luxury Fashion Branding: Trends, Tactics and Techniques*, London: Palgrave Macmillan.

Olins, Wally (2003), *On Brand*, London: Thames & Hudson.

Peirson-Smith, Anne (2013), 'Wishing on a star – promoting and personifying designer collections and fashion brands', *Journal of Fashion Practice: The Journal of Design, Creative Process and the Fashion Industry. Special Issue: Fashion Branding*, 5: 2, November, pp. 171–202.

Peirson-Smith, Anne and Hancock II, Joseph H. (2013), 'Editorial', *Journal of Fashion Practice: The Journal of Design, Creative Process and the Fashion Industry. Special Issue: Fashion Branding*, 5: 2, November, pp. 165–170.

Roberts, Royston M. (1989), *Serendipity: Accidental Discoveries in Science*, New York: John Wiley & Sons, Inc.

Rojek, Chris (2001), *Celebrity*, London: Reaktion Books.

Sidell, Misty White (2013), 'Isabel Marant collection overwhelms H&M U.S. website leaving thousands of shoppers disappointed by 'virtual queue'. Mail Online, 14 November. http://www.dailymail.co.uk/femail/article-2507403/Isabel-Marant-collection-overwhelms-H-M-U-S-website-leaving-thousands-shoppers-disappointed-virtual-queue.html. Accessed 1 December 2013.

Simpson, Linda, Taylor, Lisa, O'Rourke, Kathleeen and Shaw, Katherine (2011), 'An analysis of consumer behavior on Black Friday', *The American Journal of Consumer Behaviour*, 1: 1, July, pp. 1–5.

Tungate, Mark (2006), *Fashion Brands: Branding Style from Armani to Zara*, London: Kogan Page.

Weick, Karl (1995), *Sensemaking in Organizations*, Thousand Oaks, CA: Sage.

Weiss, Robert (1984), *Learning from Strangers: The Art and Method of Qualitative Interview Studies*, New York: The Free Press.

White, Belinda (2011), 'Versace to design a range for H&M', *The Telegraph*, 21 June. http://fashion.telegraph.co.uk/article/TMG8588618/Versace-to-design-a-range-for-HandM.html. Accessed 12 March 2012.

Wood, Zoe (2012), 'H&M surprise fall in profits', *The Guardian*, 26 January, http://www.theguardian.com/business/2012/jan/26/h-and-m-profits-fall. Accessed 10 October 2013.

CONTRIBUTOR DETAILS

Anne Peirson-Smith, Ph.D., is an assistant professor in the Department of English, City University of Hong Kong. She teaches and researches fashion culture and communication, popular culture, public relations, advertising and branding. She has also published articles in *Fashion Theory: The Journal of Dress, Body and Culture, Fashion Practice: The Journal of Design, Creative Process and the Fashion Industry* and *World Englishes* and contributed various book chapters on fashion and style. She has also recently co-authored a book, *Public Relations in Asia Pacific: Communicating Beyond Cultures* (Singapore, New York: Wiley, 2009). In addition, she is an associate editor of the new peer-reviewed journal *Fashion, Style & Popular Culture* (Intellect) and is also on the advisory board of the *East Asian Journal of Popular Culture* (Intellect).

Contact: City University of Hong Kong, 83 Tat Chee Avenue, Kowloon Tong, Hong Kong.
E-mail: enanneps@cityu.edu.hk

PART II

Brands, Style and Mass Market

Global Fashion Brands: Style, Luxury & History

© 2014 Intellect Ltd Chapter. English language. doi: 10.1386/GFB.1.85_1

KENDRA LAPOLLA
Kent State University

ModCloth: A case study in co-creative branding strategies

ABSTRACT

This article examines how to integrate co-creation into the foundation of a brand for female millennials by using ModCloth as an innovative example. ModCloth is an American online clothing retailer that specializes in vintage, vintage-inspired and indie designer apparel. The observational research uses the building blocks of co-creation (dialogue, access, risk assessment and transparency) defined by C. K. Prahalad and V. Ramaswamy as an initial framework for understanding approaches that invite and encourage customer participation in a brand. According to Prahalad and Ramaswamy, value creation is shifting from product-centric to personalized consumer experiences based on interactions between consumers, consumer communities and companies. An analysis of ModCloth's company, e-commerce website and online community provides insights for opportunities to enhance company/customer interaction. This analysis extends the building blocks of Prahalad and Ramaswamy and is simplified into a new framework that places dialogue at the centre of a co-creative branding strategy. As a result of this research, the framework serves to illustrate dialogue as an entry point to access, risk assessment and transparency.

KEYWORDS

co-creation
branding
dialogue
brand communities
e-commerce
user innovation

INTRODUCTION

Consumers want to interact through dialogue with brands and become active members of the brand community. These people are no longer satisfied with just being 'consumers' and are looking for deeper user engagements to fulfil a demand for more creative ways of living (Sanders 2006). Company-customer interaction must now provide more than 'small incremental choices in product or service customization' (Prahalad and Ramaswamy 2004:16). This increase in co-creative communication is gaining attention beyond product innovation and starting to spread into branding (Hatch and Schultz 2010).

Successful co-creative experiences in product innovation have encouraged active dialogue in branding. Past research shows consumers involved in interactive creation are providing value for companies (Fueller and von Hippel 2008; von Hippel 2005). Initially customers participated in product innovation by gaining control of customized choices in colour, fit, and style. This can be seen in a rise of mass customization retailers like NikeID, Shoes of Prey, Blank Label and Laudi Vidni. NikeID was a pioneer in this movement for athletic shoes, but since Shoes of Prey has launched the first customizable women's shoe brand. Shoes of Prey allows consumers to customize heel height, style, leather, fabrics, stitching and decorations. Mass customization has also moved into the men's apparel market on the e-commerce website Blank Label where consumers can design a dress shirt by selecting fabric, collar, cuff, plackets, pockets and tailored sizing. Laudi Vidni has brought mass customization to the accessories market by allowing consumers to select fabric, hardware, shape and overall design of a personalized bag. The success of these mass customized experiences has opened the door for further co-creation through use of social media. Online communities have given way to collaborative product design creation on websites like Threadless and Designbyhumans. Both of these T-shirt retailers allow consumers to submit designs and vote for their favourites on a crowdsourcing platform. Threadless and Designbyhumans both have forums where designs can be critiqued and users can ask for advice from the online community to make the designs better. These collective experiences go beyond minimal mass customization and engage a wider community in the design process. Co-creative product innovation experiences are now triggering a shift in brand research to focus on active customer participation. This article begins with establishing support for a new brand paradigm and provides understanding of co-creation. Additional information about the new creative customer illustrates a need for consumer participation in branding. Further, the co-creation building blocks (dialogue, access, transparency and risk assessment) by C. K. Prahalad and V. Ramaswamy (2004) are explained and used in a case study of the ModCloth brand to illustrate a need for dialogue as the foundation in co-creative branding strategies. An investigation of the ModCloth brand shows dialogue as the gateway to access, risk assessment and transparency.

From an observational approach, this research examines co-creative branding opportunities within a female millennial online community using the website, ModCloth. In this way, co-creative ideas are extended into branding by using the co-creation building blocks defined by Prahalad and Ramaswamy (2004). These building blocks (dialogue, access, risk assessment and transparency) serve as a preliminary framework to understand co-creative branding strategies. A. F. Payne et al. (2008) cite Prahalad and Ramaswamy's building blocks as a rare/singular existing framework useful for helping to manage the co-creation process. Thus, this article attempts to build additional research using the co-creation building blocks by Prahalad and Ramaswamy (2004) for brand co-creation. This article addresses research questions, such as, how do consumers actively participate in co-creative branding? What are potential access points for encouraging brands to become more co-creative?

CO-CREATION AND BRANDING

Researchers acknowledge a demand for new information regarding co-creation and branding. Specifically, brand researchers recognize social, inclusive and interactive qualities of co-creation as a new paradigm for branding (Hatch and Schultz 2009; Lusch and Vargo 2006; Payne et al. 2009). For example, R. F. Lusch and V. L. Vargo (2006) express a need for shifting to a Service-Dominant logic based on the value of active relationships built in co-creation. Prahalad and Ramaswamy (2004: 2) also reinforce the need for a shift from the 'traditional system of company-centric value creation' used in the past 100 years to a 'premise centered on co-creation of value'. Attempts should be made to push thinking 'away from the traditional consumer-brand dyad to the consumer-brand-consumer triad' (Muniz and O'Guinn 2001). The concept of 'enterprise branding' proposed by M. Hatch and M. Schultz (2009) explains this new brand paradigm as co-creation between all stakeholders 'engaged by its purpose and in its activity'.

Co-creation employs engaged participation and communication skills between brand and consumer. S. Abbott (2007) explains co-creation as a way to bring 'consumers into a closer relationship with the brand by inviting them to take part in the creative process'. I. Nam et al. (2008) agree that a co-creative experience includes an active consumer who is able to contribute to the 'design, delivery, and creation of the customer experience'. This is also supported by E. B.-N. Sanders and C. T. William (2001) that state participation in the 'fuzzy front-end of the development process' is necessary for human-centred co-creation. While the literature contains varying degrees of co-creation, the common thread is that co-creation requires active participation and interaction from all members involved. Hatch and Schultz (2010) recognize this as a full stakeholder approach that ensures all members have responsibility for the co-creation. In a co-creative experience, the roles between a company and consumer merge into an 'experience of one' (Prahalad and Ramaswamy 2004: 16).

Communities provide an opportunity for members to actively participate in co-creation through a series of collaborative conversations. Past brand community studies focus on the interaction and dialogue of all members involved in the community (Hatch and Schultz 2010; Muniz and O'Guinn 2001). Specifically in some branding studies, the term co-creation is used to describe 'customer-supplier dialogue and interaction' (Payne et al. 2009: 381). The co-creation of value framework created by Payne et al. (2008) stresses the need for these encounters between customer and supplier that will contribute to a 'long-term view of customer relationships' through individualized communication. A. M. Muniz and T. O'Guinn (2001) further support this by explaining brands are socially constructed through actively involved consumers. This literature stresses that co-creation is built through a series of connected dialogues.

THE CREATIVE CUSTOMER

A change in the mindset of customers is causing online retailers to be more creative and collaborative in the communication of the brand. The shifting position of these new customers is 'from isolated to connected, unaware to informed, from passive to active' (Prahalad and Ramaswamy 2004: 2). This transition is generating customers that are more knowledgeable and resourceful than those compared to in the past (Bhalla 2010). These new consumers want to be more involved and assertive with their purchasing power (Quillin and Peck 2012). Through years of generative research, Sanders (2006) has found a deeper user engagement may come from the idea that everyday people don't want to be just 'consumers'. What they really desire, is to become 'creators'.

The desire to be a more creative consumer manifests itself in a demand for a variety of new fashion online retail experiences. These new retail experiences give consumers an active voice in the brand and provide a social platform to interact. J. Wu (2010) identified Zazzle and Threadless as specific examples that support consumer co-creation through the interactive features used by their online communities. Design contests also promote dialogue within the online community. In a study of online design competitions, J. Füller et al. (2011) examined a jewelry competition titled 'Swarovski Enlightened™' and found that co-creation experiences can positively impact quality and quantity of design submissions, as well as the likelihood of participating in a future co-creative competition. J. Quillin and K. Peck (2012) support this by saying, 'Information-hungry customers want to feel like they are a part of a brand's intimate circle and want to take part in how a brand takes shape and the products it markets'.

Online retailers are using new interactive spaces to communicate with consumers in hopes of strengthening relationships through co-creation. Specifically marketers in e-commerce are using co-creative experiences to engage in discussions with consumers to build trust. Nam et al. (2008) empirically tested customer satisfaction of co-creative marketing approaches and found both satisfaction and trust can be achieved from co-creation and as a result relationship strength and loyalty would be affected positively. Giving consumers the ability to create individual designs and vote on favourite ideas is a way to support brand co-creation. J. Lee et al. (2012) found online apparel stores offering mass customization can enhance relationships with consumers by supporting participation in design, production and delivery. In these studies, co-creation experiences provided an open dialogue to build relationships between brand and consumer.

CO-CREATION BUILDING BLOCKS

According to Prahalad and Ramaswamy (2004), there are four main building blocks for value creation in a co-creation process. These four building blocks are Dialogue, Access, Risk Assessment and Transparency. In this framework, the building blocks provide new 'points of interaction between the consumer and the company – where the co-creation experience occurs, where individuals exercise choice, and where value is co-created' (Prahalad and Ramaswamy 2004: 33). The co-creation building blocks were also used by Hatch and Schultz (2010) to generate a new framework for company/stakeholder engagement in brand co-creation.

DIALOGUE

Prahalad and Ramaswamy (2004: 23) identify dialogue as 'interactivity, deep engagement, and a propensity to act-on both sides'. It requires more than just listening to a customer. Dialogue requires a conversation between both the customer and the company. It should focus on common interests and issues. This in turn builds a loyal community that is maintained by additional dialogue and conversation. Prahalad and Ramaswamy (2004: 23) further describe dialogue by saying, 'It entails empathic understanding built around experiencing what consumers experience, and recognizing the emotional, social, and cultural context of experiences. It implies shared learning and communication between two equal problem solvers'. For a strong dialogue, both the customer and company should be equally heard.

Online retailers initiate dialogue with their customers through social media, blogs and online customer service options. Free People has a Free People Me Style Gallery which allows an online community to submit photos of themselves wearing Free People stylized outfits. Not only does this initiate communication between the brand and customers, it creates conversation between the online community members to share ideas, comment, and like others' outfits. Free People's BLDG 25 blog is another way the brand creates a dialogue with its customers by encouraging customers to comment and discuss posted articles. Another example, Zappos is an online retailer with a successful online customer service feature that uses customer initiated dialogue. The live help feature allows customers to ask questions or give comments about products.

ACCESS

Access is the second building block of co-creation. Access in this case refers extensively to the access customers have for involvement with the brand. In a traditional value chain, a company would focus on creating a product the customer could own through a purchasing process. This was the main access for gaining ownership with the brand and products. Prahalad and Ramaswamy (2004: 25) say, 'Increasingly, the goal of consumers is access to desirable experiences-not necessarily ownership of the product. One need not own something to access an experience. We must uncouple the notion of access from ownership'. For successful co-creation, companies should understand that customers want more than access to ownership. They want access to experiences with the company as well. In this way, access should be understood from a broader perspective.

Mass customization is a form of access that online retailers are providing to consumers. Letting consumers select from different options to customize a product is an inviting experience for consumers to interact with the brand. NikeID is a recognized example of successful co-creative interaction that uses mass customization. With NikeID consumers are able to select the desired colour, material and width of shoe. Another example, Laudi Vidni, is an online retailer that allows consumers to create custom leather handbags by selecting shape, leather and details. Laudi Vidni, which is 'individual' spelled backwards, focuses on the consumer's personal wants. These made-to-order bags are hand-crafted in Chicago, Illinois by skilled crafts-people and individually customized by the consumer. The opportunity to co-create through a variety of selections gives consumers access to interact with a brand in a new experience.

RISK ASSESSMENT

Prahalad and Ramaswamy (2004) identify Risk Assessment as the third building block for value co-creation. Risk refers to how it could harm the customer or company. Traditionally, internal managers were thought to better handle a company's risk more than its customer. This is why marketers often focus on only communicating the benefits to customers. It is thought, if customers are active co-creators they may assume more responsibility for risk and subsequently, demand more information about the products and services offered (Prahalad and Ramaswamy 2004: 27). Customers as active co-creators may assume more responsibility for the success of the company. In turn, strategies that seem risky may have less perceived risk if the customers are closely involved in a co-creation process.

Crowd-sourcing is an example of how online retailers are using consumer input to lessen the risk of offering new products. Threadless is one of the earliest examples of crowdsourcing fashion merchandise online. Here, members of the online community can submit graphic designs ideas for apparel and other members of the online community can vote on their favourites. The design with the most votes gets produced. A similar website, CutOnYourBias.com, engages consumers in a virtual collaboration with select fashion designers. Consumers create designs from set selections of fabric and styles on a crowdsourced social commerce platform. The winning designs are then manufactured in an upcoming collection.

TRANSPARENCY

The last building block of co-creation according to Prahalad and Ramaswamy (2004) is Transparency. Information about all aspects of the company must be transparent to the customers. Prahalad and Ramaswamy (2004: 30) further state, 'Firms can no longer assume opaqueness of prices, costs, and profit margins. And as information about products, technologies, and business systems becomes more accessible, creating new levels of transparency becomes increasingly desirable'. Companies used to benefit from 'information asymmetry between the consumer and firm', but that mentality is quickly disappearing (Prahalad and Ramaswamy 2004: 30). A new sense of transparency helps to encourage co-creation and build trust between the customer and company. Transparency also creates a comfortable, open environment for the customers to co-create with the company.

Online retailers create transparency of the brand through unbiased online product reviews. Product reviews often allow customers to comment on the fit, price and even quality of the garment. Other customers can use the reviews as a way to evaluate purchasing decisions. American Apparel offers this option to their customers through the online store giving them the ability to discuss fit, give height and weight, recommend to a friend and let others reply to the review. Other online retailers like Zappos and Amazon also feature product reviews to illustrate transparency about the details of the product.

MODCLOTH CASE STUDY: COMPANY PROFILE

In the short history of ModCloth, the company has quickly grown with a consistent co-creative focus. ModCloth is an online retailer equipped with a trendy, user-centred website that sells hip clothing to millennial women (Hesseldahl et al. 2010). In 2006, Susan and Eric Koger started ModCloth to manage Susan's vintage clothing collection (Barnard et al. 2012). They worked from a family member's living room selling clothing online and using a cell phone number for customer service (Hesseldahl et al. 2010). J. Barnard et al. (2012) say, 'The site blossomed naturally to include both independent and major designers, and is flourishing in sales and in social spaces'. ModCloth now has three offices in Pittsburgh, San Francisco and Los Angeles with 350 full-time employees (Gannes 2012). Inc. Magazine identified ModCloth as 'America's Fastest-Growing Retailer' for 2010, and founders Susan and Eric were named in 'Forbes 30 under 30' list (Brennan 2012).

Barnard et al. (2012) say, 'Armed with a staff of young, hip, Millennials, Modcloth has been at the forefront of the social shopping wave, naturally thinking ahead of their competitors'. ModCloth's success was reported in over ten different stories in November 2012 on various blogs ranging from business to design. A. Plichta says,

> It is building a platform that empowers its global community to directly collaborate on the production of unique and inspiring merchandise, with the mission to change the way fashion is discovered, developed, and delivered around the world. ModCloth has gained media attention for cultivating one of the most active communities in fashion through groundbreaking engagement strategies that extend from its site to social networks like Facebook, Pinterest, and Twitter (2012).

There is a strong online social presence with over 692,000 Facebook fans, 97,000 Twitter followers, and over 1,300,000 Pinterest followers (Barnard et al. 2012). Currently, ModCloth has nearly two million visitors to their website each month (Hesseldahl et al. 2010). ModCloth is on the forefront of digital shopping by focusing on opportunities for consumers to shop on their smartphones. They are able to deliver convenience, choice and value for money in a quick click, faster than mortar franchises like Gap and Limited Brands (Barnard et al. 2012). Beyond shopping, this growing access to the Internet has provided ModCloth with the ability to develop new platforms for co-creation activities with its customers.

ModCloth's co-creative platform is different from some other online retailers who are targeting young, millennial women because the brand is rooted in consistent dialogue and social engagement between the consumers and company. For example, online retailers like Gilt, ideeli and Blue Fly provide flash sales and discounts on designer merchandise. This is a trickle down approach to telling the consumer what they want to buy with giving them little input to effect product innovation or advertising. In the case of ModCloth, the consumers are able to initiate design inspiration for new products, marketing, social media and more. These social experiences work especially well with these young, millennial women because they prefer collective and communal shopping experiences (Dias 2003; Dennis et al. 2010).

MODCLOTH CASE STUDY: A NEW CO-CREATIVE FRAMEWORK FOR BRANDING

For this research, a case study was created by using observational research of ModCloth. The main objective of the data generation was to show examples that illustrate how consumers participate in co-creation and to look for accessible opportunities to enter into co-creation. Data was collected from the company website, online community comments, and additional secondary sources. Analysis of the data supported a new co-creative framework that emphasizes dialogue as the foundation of co-creative branding strategies. Examples from ModCloth show dialogue is the connection to access, risk assessment and transparency.

DIALOGUE: A FUNDAMENTAL ENTRY POINT

Dialogue is the initial gateway to becoming more co-creative as a brand. As a model example, ModCloth illustrates the importance of dialogue in the new co-creative branding framework. ModCloth encourages open dialogue with their customers through contests. The 'Name It & Win It' Contest engages customers in naming the styles of garments soon to be for sale online (Figure 1). The winner of the best name for the garment receives that garment in their size (ModCloth 2012b). In December 2012 when the winners were released, members of the online community responded with enthusiasm. Even those who didn't win were in support of the contest and felt their contributions added to the co-creative dialogue. In the comment section of the blog, one member says to the winner, 'ooh! I was going for the day 5 dress but congrats :) do you know the next time one of these will be happening? I love ModCloth so much :)' (ModCloth 2012b).

Figure 1: Screenshot of ModCloth's Name It & Win It Contest featured on the ModCloth Blog, 7 December 2012. © ModCloth, All Rights Reserved.

ModCloth also initiates open dialogue with customers through social media and an online style gallery. With ModCloth's new style gallery, customers are able to communicate new outfit ideas by posting styled outfits on the website. This online style gallery combines user content, commerce and community in one place (Gannes 2012). Other customers can view the outfit ideas and be directly linked to the garment item and price if they would like to purchase it (ModCloth 2012a). L. Gannes (2012) says, 'The "Style Gallery" ties into ModCloth's efforts to make customers feel the site is their online home'. This gives the customer responsibility for visual merchandising and demonstrates their strong voice within the company dialogue. Some visitors access the page more than ten times a day (Gannes 2012). ModCloth is also using social media websites, like Pinterest, to further create a dialogue. C. Horton (2012) says, 'ModCloth joined Pinterest in the fall of 2011, but it's already one of ModCloth's top unpaid referral sites in terms of traffic and revenue'. There are approximately 7000 pins that have been tagged on Pinterest, and '99 per cent of them are from advocates of the ModCloth brand' (Horton 2012). This ability to communicate ModCloth product has become a shared responsibility between the company and customer which keeps an open conversation going within the brand.

DIALOGUE + ACCESS

Access to the brand is created from a preliminary dialogue between the brand and consumers. ModCloth offers access to their brand by inviting the customers into the creative process with their 'Make the Cut' Contest (Figure 2). This private label collection is a collaboration between the company and the customers, offering access to a new design experience. The brand initiated communication by inviting aspiring designers to submit their sketches and ideas for garments. Co-founder, Susan Koger, then selected 25 finalists from the 1900 submissions and continued the dialogue by asking customers to vote for their favourites on the ModCloth Facebook page (Joyner 2012). The 25 finalists were narrowed down to seven designs based on more than 10,000 votes, 1000 comments, and two of the founder's favourites (Joyner 2012). These seven designs went through 'extensive development, from selecting fabrics to construction samples and creating dress patterns' (Paranjpe 2012).

This proved to be a successful opportunity for customers to have access to a creative experience and maintain influential communication with the brand. Selection of the final designs came from a connected dialogue between the brand and customers. There were initially 200 garments produced of each of the seven designs by a third-party manufacturer in California (Joyner 2012). About 40 per cent of the available inventory was sold on the first day (Plichta 2012). The garments were available for purchase on the ModCloth website each with a custom 'Make the Cut' tag that included the designers name (Paranjpe 2012).

ModCloth has continued the 'Make the Cut' Contest as a beneficial opportunity for access in co-creation. The second 'Make the Cut' Contest, titled 'Retro Honor Roll', was inspired by 1960s back-to-school styles and resulted in five fan-chosen designs (Vretos 2012). For the third instalment of the contest, ModCloth has partnered with Teen Vogue for a Winter Garden Gala collection (Vretos 2012). A. Joyner (2012) says, 'ModCloth has long sought new ways to engage customers and better cater to their tastes'. ModCloth's 'Make the Cut' Contests are an essential element to the company's mission 'to empower its

Figure 2: Screenshot of ModCloth's 'Make the Cut' Contest that encourages customers to submit illustrated designs to be voted for future production. © ModCloth, All Rights Reserved.

community to directly impact apparel production and democratize fashion' (Vretos 2012). In an interview with Joyner, co-founder Eric Koger says,

> The way most of the industry works is, they produce a design on a large scale, then they send it out to stores and hope customers buy it. Ours is a more lean and agile approach. We involve the customer and get feedback earlier in the process (2012).

Allowing customers to participate and give feedback early on in the process provides additional access to the company through diverse experiences. This encourages customers to become more invested in the brand, both emotionally and financially.

DIALOGUE + RISK ASSESSMENT

ModCloth uses dialogue to evaluate the risks of new products and ideas for the brand. There is an inherent risk in predicting what to buy for future seasons as the fashion industry is in a constant state of fluctuation. Further, for those in the retail business it can be difficult because of 'minimum purchase requirements, travel limitations, and sometimes buying stock based on technical sketches, it's difficult to determine what, how many, which color to buy six months in advance of the season' (Barnard et al. 2012). In 2010, ModCloth launched 'Be the Buyer' to collect customer interest and feedback on potential styles before placing an order as a way to lessen the risk (Barnard et al. 2012).

ModCloth's 'Be the Buyer' programme can better predict the potential best sellers by inviting the customers to give feedback and help assess the risk of each style (Figure 3). Through this programme, customers are given

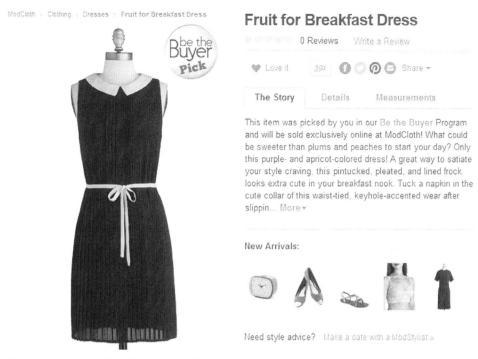

fourteen days to vote on potential designs that ModCloth might consider selling (Bennett 2012). By using a 'Pick It' button customers can vote for the designs they like, and those with the highest amount of votes are produced and sold (Bennett 2012). ModCloth produces in smaller quantities that creates less waste because only the most popular styles are produced in limited, predetermined quantities (Barnard et al. 2012). One month after the launch of the 'Be the Buyer' programme, there was a 25 per cent increase in traffic to the ModCloth website (Bennett 2012). Barnard et al. (2012) suggest, 'Customers are more apt to purchase something they provided input for, and ModCloth makes the extra effort to alert them if an item they voted for has gone into production'. This further illustrates how dialogue can decrease the risk of buying if customers are more invested in the process. These customers will also tend to share their favourite styles on Facebook, personal blogs and Twitter to further promote their involvement with the company (Bennett 2012).

DIALOGUE + TRANSPARENCY

Transparency becomes visible through dialogue between the brand and consumers. ModCloth illustrates transparency within their company through the online reviews of their products. Customer reviews and the option to upload photos have been a part of e-commerce for awhile, but ModCloth takes this further (Barnard et al. 2012). ModCloth has an interactive review space that upholds transparency about the company and its products (Figure 4).

Barnard et al. say, 'Reviews are not only uncensored, both glowing positive reviews and scathing poor reviews are often met with responses from staffers, indicating to buyers that their input is taken into consideration' (2012). For example, a customer, wrote 'I bought this shirt and fell in LOVE! I'm a 36DD so I bought a large and the fit was pretty good, but I wore it once and it tore on the seam on my forearm :(I'd like to return it but threw the box away)'. In response the ModCommunity replied,

> Hi there! I am so very sorry that this shirt hasn't held up as expected. :(I do see that you've already received additional assistance from our 24/7 Customer Advocates though, and am glad that we were able to offer a super speedy solution.
>
> (ModCloth 2012a)

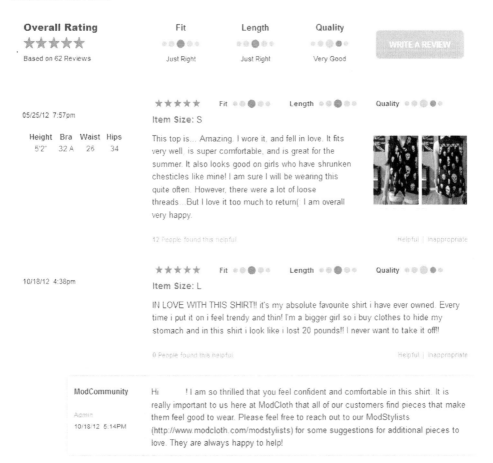

Figure 4: Examples of Customer Reviews for ModCloth's products include a social aspect that encourages customer to help provide information about their purchase to other customers. © ModCloth, All Rights Reserved.

ModCloth customers converse in online reviews and become active members of the online community. Because ModCloth has encouraged participation with their brand, they along with their customers have built an online environment that is supportive and non-judgmental (Brennan 2012). These ModCloth reviewers 'even share pictures of themselves in the actual clothing, enabling potential buyers to see how the clothes might actually look on them' instead of a thin model (Bennett 2012). There is such a strong sense of support with this online community that over two-thirds of the customers will include their body measurements in their product reviews (Brennan 2012). Customers want to help other customers make good choices and feel a sense of trust within the online community. B. Brennan (2012) says, 'Enabling customers to give and receive advice from their peers has a strong draw for millennials, who actively seek input from their peer group, both pre- and post-purchase'. ModCloth also has a team of 'Social Butterflies' that respond to positive and negative reviews posted on their Twitter account (Bennett 2012). The openness with ModCloth's product reviews builds a sense of trust and transparency about products customers may potentially purchase.

A FRAMEWORK TO ENTER IN CO-CREATION BRANDING

As shown in observation of ModCloth, dialogue should be the core of a co-creative brand. This new co-creative branding framework emphasizes dialogue as a connection to access, risk assessment and transparency. Figure 5 illustrates the new proposed framework by rearranging the building blocks. Placing dialogue at the foundation of the framework provides focus for introduction into brand co-creation. Literature supports the significance of dialogue in brand co-creation. Abbott (2007) defines co-creation as an open dialogue that gives consumers more influence over the direction of the brand. This is further supported by Rajah et al. who describe co-created value as 'a sum of the derivation of the dialogue, interactions, personalized treatment, and level of customization co-created in the experience network' (2008). Payne et al. (2008: 84) highlight dialogue as an important interaction between supplier and customer in 'each stage of product

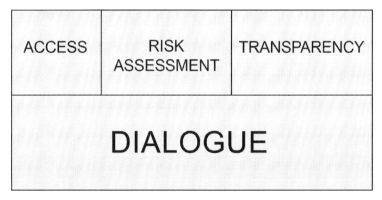

Figure 5: Extension of Prahalad's and Ramaswamy's (2004) co-creation building blocks into a new framework for brand co-creation that places dialogue at the foundation.

design and product delivery'. In this way, the proposed co-creative branding framework organizes the building blocks in a supportive way to the brand literature and observations of co-creative branding opportunities in the ModCloth case.

Any entry point into co-creative brand experiences should use dialogue as the gateway. For example, brands wanting to venture into assessing risk through crowdsourcing should first start with smaller contests to test consumer response, build trust and further initiate a dialogue with the online community. P. Aggarwal (2004) says, 'consumer interactions with brands can be characterized as relational'. The start to building these relationships is by encouraging an open dialogue between members of the online community. In another example, brands could strengthen the relationship by following up in additional conversations with online product reviews. This way the dialogue continues and others are encouraged to join the conversation. The need for dialogue is further supported by J. Winsor (2010: 19) who says consumers, 'have too little time to research everything they buy and are less willing to purchase from companies that are not prepared to engage them in a dialogue'.

CONCLUSION

The shift to consumer experience branding with a creative customer are causing researchers to consider co-creation as an important focus in branding (Hatch and Schultz 2009; Lusch and Vargo 2006; Payne et al. 2009). This differs from other traditional branding strategies that focus on company-centric approaches. Increasing amounts of research are now engaging the customer perspective instead (Payne et al. 2009). Thus, this article adds to the research that references co-creation as being influential in a new brand paradigm.

The co-creation building blocks (dialogue, access, transparency and risk assessment) by Prahalad and Ramaswamy (2004) provide a background to study co-creation in branding. As a result, a new co-creative branding framework is created from supporting literature and an observational case study of ModCloth. The case study of ModCloth illustrates examples of consumers actively participating in co-creation and suggests that dialogue provides an entry to co-creative experiences. Exposure to access, risk assessment and transparency are initiated using dialogue as a bridge. ModCloth is unique in this way because all co-creation starts with a dialogue between every stakeholder involved. In some experiences the communication is company initiated, but in others it may be completely customer driven. ModCloth does not preplan or control the conversation in this way. It remains an open discussion for collaboration, which guides the co-creation experience. In each case, the dialogue opens co-creative opportunities for access, risk assessment and transparency.

This case study of ModCloth serves as an example of co-creative implementation in branding and additionally supports the modified co-creation building blocks originally introduced by Prahalad and Ramaswamy (2004). Other brands may pull from this example or generate new co-creative experiences. Sanders (2006) says, 'These new design spaces will be living, thriving, diverse, and probably somewhat messy. And that is ok'. Further research may question quality of dialogue or frequency of dialogue in co-creation experiences.

REFERENCES

Abbott, Susan (2007), 'Customer experience crossroads: Co-creation and fashion brands', 5 April, http://www.customercrossroads.com/customercrossroads/2007/04/cocreation_and_.html. Accessed 20 March 2010.

Aggarwal, Pankaj (2004), 'The effects of brand relationship norms on consumer attitudes and behavior', *Journal of Consumer Research*, 31: 1, pp. 87–101.

Barnard, Jonathan, Ladds, Jennifer and Kim, Jinah (2012), 'How to do social shopping right: A case study – moxie pulse', 9 November, http://www.zenithoptimedia.com/zenith/how-to-do-social-shopping-right-a-case-study-moxie-pulse/. Accessed 3 December 2012.

Bennett, Hubert (2012), 'Social commerce case study: ModCloth', 7 November, http://insparq.com/social-commerce-case-study-modcloth-2/. Accessed 4 December 2012.

Bhalla, Gaurav (2010), *Collaboration and Co-creation: New Platforms for Marketing and Innovation*, New York, New York: Springer.

Brennan, Bridget (2012), 'The retailer winning the battle for millennial women', 16 November, http://www.forbes.com/sites/bridgetbrennan/2012/11/16/the-retailer-winning-the-battle-for-millennial-women/. Accessed 4 December 2012.

Dennis, Charles, Morgan, Alesia, Wright, Len Tiu and Jayawardhena, Chanaka (2010), 'The influences of social e-shopping in enhancing young women's online shopping behaviour', *Journal of Customer Behaviour*, 9: 2, pp. 151–74.

Dias, Laura Portolese (2003), 'Generational buying motivations for fashion', *Journal of Fashion Marketing and Management*, 7: 1, pp. 78–86.

Füller, Johann and von Hippel, Eric (2008), 'Costless creation of strong brands by user communities: Implications for producer-owned brands', MIT Sloan School of Management Working Paper 4718–08.

Füller, Johann, Hutter, Katja and Faullant, Rita (2011), 'Why co-creation experience matters? Creative experience and its impact on the quantity and quality of creative contributions', *R&D Management*, 41: 3, pp. 259–73.

Gannes, Liz (2012), 'ModCloth Launches an In-House Pinterest', 19 November, http://allthingsd.com/20121119/modcloth-launches-an-in-house-pinterest/. Accessed 4 December 2012.

Hatch, Mary Jo and Schultz, Majken (2009), 'Of bricks and brands. From corporate to enterprise branding', *Organization Dynamics*, 38: 2, pp. 117–30.

—— (2010), 'Toward a theory of brand co-creation with implications for brand governance', *Journal of Brand Management*, 17: 8, pp. 590–604.

Hesseldahl, Arik, Kharif, Olga, MacMillan, Douglas and King, Rachael (2010), 'Best Young Tech Entrepreneurs 2010', 4 April, businessweek.com/ss/10/04/0419_best_young_tech_entrepreneurs/index.htm. Accessed 3 December 2012.

Horton, Chris (2012), 'Case Study: 4 Brands that Use Pinterest the Right Way', 25 April, marketing-technology-for-growth/bid/136311/Case-Study-4-Brands-that-Use-Pinterest-the-Right-Way. Accessed 30 November 2012.

Joyner, April (2012), 'ModCloth: Getting customers to design their own clothes', 3 May, http://www.inc.com/magazine/201205/modcloth-democratizing-fashion-company-watch.html. Accessed 30 November 2012.

Lee, Jihyun, Lee, Yuri and Lee, Yoon-Jung (2012), 'Do customization programs of e-commerce companies lead to better relationship with consumers?', *Electronic Commerce Research and Applications*, 11: 3, pp. 262–74.

Lusch, Robert F., and Vargo, Stephen L. (2006), 'Service-dominant logic: Reactions, reflections and refinements', *Marketing Theory*, 6: 3, pp. 281–88.

ModCloth (2012a), 'Just the Fox, Ma'am Sweater', www.modcloth.com/shop/pullovers-sweaters/just-the-fox-ma-am-sweater. Accessed 18 December 2012.

—— (2012b), 'The winners of name it & win it: Good tidings & titles', http://blog.modcloth.com/2012/12/07/the-winners-of-name-it-win-it-good-tidings-titles/. Accessed 15 December 2012.

Muniz Jr., Albert M. and O'Guinn, Thomas C. (2001), 'Brand community', *Journal of Consumer Research*, 27: 4, pp. 412–32.

Paranjpe, Anjelika (2012), 'Be the Designer: ModCloth's Brand New User-Generated Clothing Collection', 29 May, Brit.co www.brit.co/be-the-designer-modcloth-s-brand-new-user-generated-clothing-collection/. Accessed 3 December 2012.

Payne, Adrian F., Storbacka, Kaj and Frow, Pennie (2008), 'Managing the co-creation of value', *Journal of the Academy of Marketing Science*, 36: 1, pp. 83–96.

Payne, Adrian, Storbacka, Kaj, Frow, Pennie and Knox, Simon (2009), 'Co-creating brands: Diagnosing and designing the relationship experience', *Journal of Business Research*, Advances in Brand Management, 62: 3, pp. 379–89.

Plichta, Aire. (2012), 'Modcloth continues mission to democratize fashion; launches second crowdsourced clothing collection', 20 August, http://www.prweb.com/releases/2012/8/prweb9812715.htm.

Prahalad, C. K. and Ramaswamy, Venkat (2004), *The Future of Competition: Co-creating Unique Value with Customers*. Boston, MA: Harvard Business School Publishing.

Quillin, Jessica and Peck, Krista (2012), 'Digital emotiveness: The new key to participatory marketing', 4 April, http://fashionscollective.com/FashionAndLuxury/04/digital-emotiveness-the-new-key-to-participatory-marketing/. Accessed 9 December 2012.

Rajah, Edwin, Marshall, Roger and Nam, Inwoo (2008), 'Relationship glue: customers and marketers co-creating a purchase experience', *Advances in Consumer Research*, 35, pp. 367–373.

Sanders, Elizabeth B.-N. (2006), 'Scaffolds for building everyday creativity', in Frascara, Jorge (ed.), *Design for Effective Communications: Creating Contexts for Clarity and Meaning*, New York, NY: Allworth Press, pp. 65–77 .

Sanders, Elizabeth B.-N. and William, Colin T. (2001), 'Harnessing people's creativity: Ideation and expression through visual communication', in J. Langford and D. McDonagh-Philp (eds), *Focus Groups: Supporting Effective Product Development*, New York, New York: Taylor and Francis, pp. 137–148.

Von Hippel, Eric (2005), *Democratizing Innovation*, Cambridge, MA: MIT Press.

Vretos, Pamela (2012), 'ModCloth launches second crowdsourced clothing collection', 20 August, http://www.fashionotes.com/content/ 2012/08/

modcloth-launches-second-crowdsourced-clothing-collection/. Accessed 30 November 2012.

Winsor, John (2010), *Flipped: How Bottom-Up Co-Creation is Replacing Top-Down Innovation*, Chicago, Illinois: Agate B2.

Wu, Juanjuan (2010), 'Co-design communities online: Turning public creativity into wearable and sellable fashions', *Fashion Practice*, 2: 1, pp. 85–104.

CONTRIBUTOR DETAILS

Kendra Lapolla is an Assistant Professor at Kent State University in the Fashion Department and has past industry experience in technical design at Express and Victoria's Secret. She has also taught design coursework at Albright College, Ohio State University and co-taught Continuing Education courses at Columbus College of Art and Design. Her research interests include co-creation, participatory design, branding and emotional design. She is a member of the International Textiles Apparel Association (ITAA) where she has presented. Kendra also has presented at several conferences including the Wardrobe Ethnographies Conference sponsored by The Wardrobe Network and the Copenhagen Business School, the Design & Emotion Conference sponsored by the Design & Emotion Society, and the Fashion & Health Symposium sponsored by the University of Minnesota.

E-mail: klapolla@kent.edu

Global Fashion Brands: Style, Luxury & History
© 2014 Intellect Ltd Chapter. English language. doi: 10.1386/GFB.1.103_1

TARA CHITTENDEN
The Law Society

Juicy (contradiction) couture: The Starburst Prom Gown and female teens' appropriation and emotional branding of a candy label

ABSTRACT

A growing trend for 'Trashion' means that branded labels from a variety of products and packaging are finding their way into fashion design, where the visuality of colours, fonts and textures make labels an attractive 'fabric' for fashion creation. The Starburst Prom Gown is a prime example of branded candy wrapper as fashion resource, as female teens take the brand out of the marketing context and into the 'fashion show' that is prom night. The prom is an important milestone in the lives of American teens and how female teens brand themselves for this night can tell much about the relationship between branding and teen identity formation in contemporary popular culture. As such, the Starburst gown offers a prime opportunity to study and begin to understand cultural forces in teen brand utilization and the ways in which a mix of fashion/non-fashion brands becomes imbued with emotional significance during these years.

KEYWORDS

prom
teen
candy wrappers
Starburst
Trashion
emotional branding

1. John Palfrey and Urs
Glasser (2008) use the
term 'Digital natives'
to describe people
born after 1980, when
social interaction
technologies, such as
Usenet and bulletin
board systems, came
online. For digital
natives, 'major
aspects of their lives –
social interactions,
friendships, civic
activities – are
mediated by digital
technologies. And
they've never known
any other way of life'
(Palfrey and Glasser
2008: 3).

2. Companies such as The
Ecoist (www.ecoist.
com) and Terracycle
(www.terracycle.
com) aim to eliminate
waste through
creative solutions
to items normally
sent to landfill. The
Ecoist makes bags
from recycled candy
wrappers and Coca-
Cola cans – a lot of
the wrappers are
hand folded and sewn
in Peru and Mexico.
Terracyle's display
pieces include a dress
commissioned from
Chicago couture
designer Christina
Liedtke; it took over
100 hours to cut and
sew more than 1800
flower shapes from 600
peanut M&M wrappers
(http://www.ecouterre.
com/gown-made-from-
recycled-mm-wrappers-
fronts-terracycle-pop-
up-shop/).

INTRODUCTION

The impact of American popular culture on teens, fashion and visual identity is considerable and in the last decade American teenagers have had
one of the greatest disposable incomes of teenagers in history to spend on
'branding' themselves (Reid 2012). 'Brand image' is central to the formation
of personal and social identity in popular culture, and especially so during
the teen years (Bhattacharya et al. 2012; Hollenbeck and Kaikati 2012). The
body serves as a critical site of identity performance and having access to
designer clothing affords some teen girls a 'popularity', which gives them
social power and leverage over others in their school or neighbourhood.
According to Kit Yarrow, today 'the bar is higher for what it takes to get attention, and therefore, (teens) really need to have something exclusive, original,
unique to them in order to get attention from other people' (in Malcolm
2012). Teen girls' sources of style and fashion inspiration have evolved with
greater access to information through fashion blogs (Chittenden 2010; Gilles
and Nairn 2011; Rocamora 2011) and other websites that put an emphasis
on individuality.

The 'mash-up' of cultural industries prevalent amongst teen digital natives[1]
denaturalizes the modes of differentiation that have been institutionalized in
the fashion (and other) industries as 'brand'. A growing trend for 'Trashion' –
fashion designs made from packaging and other discarded items, supported
by a 'green fashion' movement towards upcycling landfill items – means that
branded labels from a variety of products are finding their way onto and into
outfits and accessories (Simon 2009).[2] Brands are inherently visual; logos,
packaging and advertising all draw upon visual statements to create a distinctive identity, and it is this visuality of colours, fonts and texture that is part
of what make brands an attractive 'fabric' for fashion creation. Jessica Bugg
(2009) examines how fashion is understood within interdisciplinary contexts
and where its boundaries lay in relation to other disciplines; I argue for the
value in asking the same question in relation to fashion's intersection with
non-fashion brand labels, as literally woven together by female teens.

In the following pages, I focus on the branded candy wrapper as material fashion resource, looking in detail at the Starburst Prom Gown – a dress
crafted from Starburst candy wrappers. Teen girls view prom as their 'red-
carpet moment' and, for Yarrow and Jayne O'Donnell (2009), prom has
replaced weddings, debutante balls and coming-out parties as the formal occasion of a young adult's life. Sandra Weber and Claudia A. Mitchell suggest that
'because it is so highly ritualized, the prom experience is replete with symbols
that provide a shorthand for interpreting and reflecting on the cultural forces
and psychological processes that constitute who we become' (2000: 248); arguably, brands, and fashion labels in particular, are an important part of these
'cultural forces and psychological processes' for teen girls. So the idea that a
girl would turn up to this pivotal night dressed in candy wrappers does not fail
to raise a few eyebrows, and yet there have been at least eight Starburst prom
gowns in different parts of the United States since 2010, each favouring a
different design and combination of folding, weaving and layering techniques;
and these are only the gowns known about, which received coverage in local
press and on the web. Discussion in this article is based on a content analysis of all found web and media reports around these eight dresses, further
informed by e-mail exchanges with two of the dress makers; my thinking was
yet further honed by informal e-mail 'interviews' with female teen fashion

bloggers[3] around prom age (in the six months prior to/post prom night) to understand more about prom fashion choices and perceptions.

In considering the Starburst Gown as a teen fashion creation, I discuss what happens to brand associations when translated from one space or material to another. The terms of commodity exchange from the realm of confection to the realm of fashion engage teens in the active production and exchange of meanings, and in particular I look at the emotional connections and potential for nostalgia, which arises by associating this candy brand with prom night. Through analysis of the Starburst Prom Gown, I argue for a more nuanced way of reflecting on the ways in which the relationship between branding and teen identity formation is manifest – here in the lived experience of the prom.

Following a brief introduction to the context of prom night in popular culture, I focus on examples of the Starburst Prom Gown as worn by five teens in 2010–2012, proceeding to examine the emotional branding of the wrappers used in this way. I argue that the ways in which female teens utilize a mix of fashion/non-fashion brands in their self-styling is critical to understanding how teens imbue these resource brands with personal and emotional significance, and in ways that strengthen their concept of self.

3. Some of these contacts came via previous research with the teen fashion blogging community (Chittenden 2010); others were located via discussion thread posts and links on sites such as Facebook, http://blog.missesdressy.com, http://www.teenspot.com/boards/showthread.php?313917-Rate-my-prom-dress-please!! and http://blog.promgirl.net.

PROM NIGHT

In the United States, the prom is a formal dance or gathering of high school students, typically held near the end of the senior year. Boys usually dress in black or white formal wear, paired with brightly coloured ties and vests or cummerbunds. Girls wear traditional dresses or gowns and a corsage, given to them by their dates. The prom is an iconic, integral part of the high school experience and features prominently in popular culture, becoming more common in the United Kingdom and Canada due to the influence of American TV shows and movies (Best 2000). Popular movies such as *Prom* (Nussbaum, 2011); *Pretty in Pink* (Deutch, 1986); and *10 Things I Hate About You* (Junger, 1999) attest to the importance of prom themes, dates and, above all for teen girls, dresses.

The prom is an important milestone in the lives of American teens; Weber and Mitchell describe 'an over-hyped but significant rite of passage that few high school students or teachers can successfully ignore. Certain stock images, myths and ideologies of prom dresses and prom night permeate' (2000: 248). Teen magazines provide 'expert advice on how to pick the perfect outfit' for the prom (Seventeen Prom 2004: 124); for Natalie Zlatunich (2009: 357); these magazines 'define the prom as an event that requires girls to invest time and money in order to achieve success'. Girls are 'very aware of the cultural and social expectations placed upon them by the larger culture and by the prom, more specifically' (Zlatunich 2009: 370), and for Weber and Mitchell (2000: 249) the prom dress functions 'as an example of how women dress their bodies to express both personal and social aspects of their identity'. As Levy describes:

there's a general sense of people wanting to be differentiated. Going to a national chain and getting the same dress that 18 other girls have is not a chance for me to differentiate myself or express my individuality, which is such an important part of my social experience today.

(in Malcolm 2012)

According to Kathryn Lively (2011), the overall top prom fashion brands for 2011 included: Mori Lee, Jovani Designs, BG Haute, Sherri Hill and La Femme. However, in certain pockets, competition between teen girls is couture driven; one teen explained:

> when I realized there was a Facebook group for prom dresses that was up, I posted a picture of an Alexander McQueen dress as a joke. A few days later, girls were coming up to me in the hallway actually looking a bit worried, and kept asking me if I was really wearing the dress.
>
> (Cills in Meltzer 2011)

Issues around prom fashion seemed to intensify and hold greater significance for girls than for their male dates, suggesting in many instances that fashion branding on this night could be a gender or generational issue more than a 'teen' one. The *New York Times* reported that whilst boys remained oblivious to the designer brand trend, renting tuxedos from local shops, girls' tastes were escalating to brands such as Galliano, Yves Saint Laurent, Roland Mouret and Herve Leger (Meltzer 2011), fuelled by popular culture and by prom issues of *Seventeen* and *Teen Vogue* showcasing prom dresses by high-end couture designers, although it by no means follows that the Starburst gown (as an expression of individuality) would be considered only by those girls who could not afford couture labels.

For many teens, worrying over what to wear to the prom starts months or even years before the actual night. Growing up in a society where a presence on the web via Facebook and other social media platforms is an almost mandatory part of socialization, teens are concerned with the impression they communicate (Yarrow and O'Donnell 2009) and will go to great lengths to create their 'perfect wow moment' on prom night. As the amount of money spent on this night steadily grows (in the United States to an average of $1078 per family in 2012; Malcolm 2012), teens recognize that making their own dresses cannot only earn them the admiration of peers, but can save money as well, although this approach is not taken lightly: 'appearance is everything, and for prom, appearance really matters … It's like your Cinderella night, so you pull out all the stops' (Levy in Malcolm 2012).

THE STARBURST PROM GOWN

Starburst is the brand name of a fruit-flavoured soft taffy candy manufactured by The Wrigley Company, a subsidiary of Mars. The brand began as 'Opal Fruits' in the United Kingdom, in 1959, when the four original flavours were strawberry, lemon, orange and lime (the latter subsequently replaced by cherry). In 1967, the candy was introduced to the US market as 'Starburst' and in 1998 Mars phased out the brand name 'Opal Fruits' to standardize the product as 'Starburst' in a globalized marketplace. Today, Starburst comes in several assortments, including 'Retro Fruits', 'Tropical' and 'Strawberry Mix'. Each candy comes wrapped in a brightly coloured wax paper wrapper, bearing the word 'Starburst', and a large 'S' inside a teardrop shape to convey its juiciness. In the United States, the current brand slogan for Starburst is 'It's A Juicy Contradiction' or 'It's A Pack of Contradictions' to highlight the experience of eating the candy – solid, yet also juicy like a liquid.

Douglas Holt (2002: 87) suggests that 'consumers will look for brands to contribute directly to their identity projects by providing original and relevant cultural materials with which to work'. The postmodern branding paradigm 'is premised upon the idea that brands will be more valuable if they are offered not as cultural blueprints but as cultural resources, as useful ingredients to produce the self as one chooses' (Holt 2002: 83); the Starburst Prom Gown is a prime example of candy wrapper as a fashion resource, as these teens take the brand out of the marketing context and into the 'fashion show' that is prom night.

Kelly Henriksen made her prom dress from 'duct tape, masking tape and about 450 individual wrappers and 20 packages of Starburst candy' (Jones 2010). She had already used the wrappers to create an ipod case and was inspired to translate the technique after seeing a dress made out of newspaper. She explained her choice of candy, 'I picked Starburst because the wrappers are made of wax-covered paper, it's more sturdy, and the candy doesn't stick as much' (in Jones 2010). On one level, consumer choice is critical to understanding why certain brands become more successful than others. Teens favour Starburst for the colours and waxed paper, which makes the wrapper cleaner and more durable than other wrappers. These teens do not appear to have chosen Starburst specifically – they could have used any candy with a similar wrapper – so this journey does not begin with the significance of Starburst as a candy brand, and yet what these teens do with the wrapper transfers meaning and associations to the candy brand by connecting it with emotionally charged prom night and by 'selling' the idea, and in association selling the candy, to other teens inspired to make their own wrapper dress or accessories.

On completion of her dress, Henriksen made her date's bow tie out of Starburst candy wrappers, and he continued the brand association by spelling out her invitation to the prom in the actual candies (Jones 2010). Collecting the wrappers, as for all of the teen Starburst gown makers, became a communal effort; for Henriksen, her mother purchased economy-size bags and friends helped to eat the candy. It took three days for Henriksen and her friends to provide more than 1000 of the pink, red, yellow and orange wrappers (Jones 2010).

Tara Frey's prom dress and matching accessories (Figure 1) took six years[4] from initial idea to completion. The outfit was made by her mother, who conceived the idea whilst watching her friend fold wrappers together during a hockey game. Frey's mother contacted the brand to ask whether she could buy the wrappers directly, but was told 'no', so she began to buy twenty bags of starburst at a time and called on the neighbourhood to help eat them: 'The whole community gave us wrappers … My mom would hand [Starburst] out to people and ask for the wrappers back, and don't rip them!' (Tara Frey in Murray 2011). Each wrapper was folded eight times and pressed with tweezers for a tight weave, then the wrappers were braided together, joined with hot glue and sewn onto fabric.

Diane McNease had the idea for her Starburst gown when she saw a friend folding Starburst wrappers into bracelets. She claims to have already been collecting wrappers for her design when pictures of Frey came out in the news. It took McNease a year and a half to collect the 18,000 wrappers needed, and five months to create the bodice of her gown; this period of nearly two years, following on from Frey's six years, challenges notions of teens as an 'instant gratification generation' with a shallow or flickering attention span (Weiss 2012). For the first month, McNease ate all the candy herself, but then she 'got sick of it' and enlisted friends at school to help (Weir 2012), and her

4. And this in itself is bizarre – when teens are often depicted as fickle or at the mercy of fashion trends it seems strange to think of a teen committed to a particular style/approach for six years.

5. http://www.dailymail.
co.uk/femail/
article-2141433/
Eat-heart-Missoni-
Teenagers-prom-gown-
Starburst-wrappers-
dead-ringer-designer-
style.html.

6. See image at: http://
www.eacourier.com/
news/local-youths-
create-fashion-
phenomenon-prom-
with-a-side-of/
article_0181c05a-
9c92-11e1-92ca-
0019bb2963f4.html.

Figure 1: Tara Frey prom dress and accessories (2011). Photo Courtesy of Ripley Entertainment Inc.

father helped to sew the strips of folded wrappers together. For Kristie Lau (2012), the resulting weave design, made into a bodice, headband and purse, 'resembles a brightly-coloured Missoni print'.[5]

Hannah Stiles-Culver spent nearly a year collecting wrappers for her gown, calling on her college-age sister to help supply wrappers: '[my sister] and her roommates would send me packages full of Starburst wrappers' (Robinson 2012). She used 800 wrappers for her dress, and additional wrappers to decorate a parasol and shoes.[6] This teen used her prom dress as a part of a programme at her church, which 'encourages young women to set and accomplish goals in several areas'; her mother described: 'I saw Hannah grasping onto something that was so expressive of who she is. That dress

Figure 2: Starburst bracelets. Photo courtesy of justByou. (http://www.flickr.com/photos/justbyou/5986468512/).

became a voice and outlet for Hannah' (Robinson 2012). Hannah's date was inspired by her creativity and she taught him various folding and sticking techniques; he said: 'I told her I was going to make a vest to go with her dress and then we could go to prom together' (Robinson 2012) – he also made her a wrist corsage out of the wrappers and she made him a Starburst boutonniere.

The dress in Figure 3 took Annie-Marie three months to make: 'I used probably umm close to 50ish bags idk, and the whole thing is glued to a dress that i sewed the whole thing' (http://anniemarie88.deviantart.com/#/d4aj2j9). This is her second consecutive year making a dress from Starburst wrappers, but the first worn to the prom; she also made a matching tie for her date.

The making of these dresses engages teens and their immediate social circles in ways (both qualitative and quantitative) that extend far beyond the idea of saving money or trying to find a unique dress for the prom: quantitatively, in the money spent on candies, in the time put into calculating and collecting the needed number of wrappers and in making the dress; qualitatively, through communicative interaction engaging friends to help eat the candy and collect wrappers; and in efforts spent folding, stitching and sticking the various parts of the dress in collaboration with friends and family. Whilst prom-dress-making may seem a more female-oriented activity, in at least two

7. http://www.
candywarehouse.
com/candy-type/
bulk-wrapped-candy/
products/starburst-
fruit-chews-candy-3lb-
bag/. Price at time of
writing in October 2012.

Figure 3: Annie-Marie dress. Photo by Annie-Marie. (http://anniemarie88.
deviantart.com/#/d4aj2j9).

examples the date became involved in making Starburst accessories, and one
teen's father also helped to work the wrappers.

The actual monetary cost of making such a dress is negligible next to the
social and emotional value of using the brand in this way; yet when considering escalating costs of prom night for American families, it is possible to
give some indication of what these wrapper dresses might have cost. Candy
Warehouse sells 3lb bags containing 300 pieces of Starburst candy for $12.90.[7]
This is one of the cheaper retail prices, but means that for an 800 wrapper
dress Stiles-Culver spent at least $34.40; 450 wrappers for Henriksen would
come in at $19.35; and $774.00 to purchase the 18,000 wrappers needed by
McNease. And these estimates do not even account for spare wrappers or for
the amount of time and effort taken to fold wrappers or the emotional significance woven into the whole process.

THE EMOTIONAL BRANDING OF THE STARBURST PROM GOWN

Teens construct and perform identities, creating their self-image within, and in collaboration with, brand culture (Holt 2002; Wikstrom 1996). Previous studies acknowledge brands' representational and rhetorical power both as valuable cultural artefacts and bearers of meaning that reflect cultural and ideological codes (Askegaard 2006; Cayla and Eckhardt 2008; Roberts 2011). Brands are not only mediators of cultural meaning, but for Jonathan Schroeder (2009: 124) 'brands themselves have become ideological referents that shape cultural rituals, economic activities, and social norms'. School, nights out and events such as the prom are all situations where girls can show their skills to create a look in accordance with what is expected of the occasion. The Starburst gown offers a prime opportunity to study and begin to understand cultural forces in teen brand utilization. For John Storey, 'the symbolic value of objects in the information system is not inherent in the objects themselves ... To understand the value of one object, it is necessary to locate it in the information system as a whole' (1999: 43). Thus, to 'understand' a brand or branded item is to understand how it is located, used and tailored in society. Here teens are upcycling the value of the wrapper from potential litter to one-off bespoke creation; in so doing, they are not just patching the brand logo onto an existing garment, but weaving it through the gown to its very core.

C. K. Prahalad and V. Ramaswamy (2004: 5) identify the locus of brand value creation in the interaction between the producer and consumer, or, as Holt (2010: 2) describes, 'as they interact with the product, customers create consumption stories involving the product, which they often share with friends'. A brand represents a mark of ownership and a means of product differentiation. When a brand generates a strong bonding experience, it is 'an emotional point that transcends the product' (Webber 1997: 100). According to Holt:

> customers get three types of symbolic value from brands: they viscerally experience desired values and identities when they consume the brand; they use the brand symbol to create social distinction, to make status claims; and they use the brand symbol to forge solidarity and identification with others.
>
> (2010: 6)

Applied to the example of the Starburst gown, teens: literally consume the candy; plan their dress as a social distinction amidst their peers; and forge solidarity with close friends/family through the collecting/making, and with other teens through media representations. According to Elizabeth Wissinger (2009: 248), 'brands work as platforms for action that enable the production of particular immaterial use-values: an experience, a shared emotion, a sense of community'. Consequently, narratives evolve out of teen experiences with brands, as these brands enter into social rituals such as the prom. Adam Arvidsson (2005: 237) suggests that consumers, active and creative, produce 'a social relation, a shared meaning, an emotional involvement that was not there before' in their use of branded goods, producing a communicative context within which brands can acquire multiple use-values. The emphasis on brand 'experiences', and how brands are used beyond the intention of the producer, reflects the idea of an 'experience economy' (Pine and Gilmore 1999), in which companies build brand image and forge 'an emotional and memorable connection with consumers' (Schmitt 1999: 85).

8. The connection between candy and fashion industries offers numerous avenues for further exploration, although all beyond the scope of the immediate article; for example: the branding, marketing and packaging of fashion products, as well as debates around young teen models, the age-appropriateness of designs aimed at young teens/children and the trend for 'Lolita fashion' in some magazine shoots, and in the Japanese market in particular (see, e.g.: blinded for reviewA; Merskin 2004; http://www.teenvogue.com/beauty/2012-11/sweet-beauty-products).

By using these Starburst wrappers to create fashion items, and the prom dress in particular, teens embed potential for nostalgia in the brand – they form an emotional bond associated with planning, collecting and making their prom dress, which links with the candy and lodges a memorable experience. For Marc Gobe (2001: xxvi), 'the emotional connector is what differentiates one brand from another' and Holt advises that brands should 'always connect with the consumer on an intimate level' (2010: 21). For these teens, looking back on their prom or encountering these candies in the future will bring a mix of nostalgia for their rite of passage and for the effort and processes involved in collecting and shaping the wrappers. Candy wrappers are a big part of popular culture; candy is one of the first brands and visual identities (colours, logos, tastes) that become familiar (and desired) from early age. This connection breeds a nostalgia, as seen in adults who have fond memories of the revived 'olde candy shoppe' and the reappearance of discontinued candies.

In my example, the candy wrapper becomes a transitional object in Donald Winnicott's (1971) sense, as these young adults use the shell of childhood tastes to display their emerging adult taste at this rite of passage. Significance might also be drawn from the choice of candy wrappers. Candy is a product that potentially fattens (changes the shape of) the body – something in stark contrast to the idealized 'size zero' model body, but perhaps more closely allied to the growing curves of the changing teen female body. There is a hint towards other changing tastes as the wrapper dress presents a fetish display of selves wrapped enticingly as candy for their date. The boundaries between candy and fashion industries are already blurred. Teen magazines feature make-up as sweets – brightly coloured cosmetic products that look juicy and chewy (Quart 2003) – packaged/named to imply candy; for example, Too Faced's set of eye-shadows with names like 'Gum Drop', 'Marshmallow' and 'Malted Milk Ball', presented in a bon-bon tin (Marcus 2012).[8]

Starburst becomes a brand name that links different artefacts – candy, dresses and fashion accessories. For C. Lury (2006: 95), 'increasingly the brand name is not the mark of an originary relationship between producer and products, but is rather the mark of the organization of a set of relations between products in time' – how consumers evolve the product to make other statements and meet other needs. The candy wrapper implies a dynamic 'economy of qualities', an economy in which the wrapper is defined by the characteristics attributed to it in successive qualifications and re-qualifications, including those enacted by consumers – for these teens, relationships with the brand have evolved from something they eat to something they wear, from a product purchased for its candy to one bought for the wrapping.

CONCLUSION

The Starburst Prom Gown showcases a conceptual and experimental use of candy wrappers as fashion, exposing an interdisciplinary branding at the edges of the bespoke fashion creation. So, how does this work? If a teen made their own prom dress, using fabric and a pattern from a store, they may be ridiculed for not having the latest labels/brands, or wearing 'homemade'; yet because the creation is made from candy wrappers, it speaks to new trends, exciting and different ways of self-branding. Equally, if Starburst produced their wrapper material via the roll, to be bought and used as fabric, again it would not have the same status or reaction. There is something key here in collecting the wrappers, in the collaborative work to assemble the dress and in putting wrappers to unpredicted use.[9] The Starburst gown not only demonstrates how teens are (literally) consuming (for) fashion in new ways, but also questions the extent to which contemporary manifestations of candy wrapper dresses within popular culture,[10] and especially this gown, function to refashion/rebrand perceptions of the candy and of personal identities. Such questioning provokes a reconsideration of branding processes and shifts attention from brand producers towards consumer response in order to understand how branding inspires fashionable meanings (e.g. Aaker 1997; Fournier 1998; Holt 2010). The appearance of such prom dresses, presented to mass culture through the media and web, arguably place 'Trashion' in a highly popular context, beyond the runway or shop [or school art project]: 'presentation provides fashion with a platform, like a work of art … the clothes themselves are less important than the environment created using fashion' (2000: 53). And yet, whilst my inclination was to view these wrappers as 'trash', a reviewer raised an important point that for these girls the wrappers never actually reach trash status and, furthermore, the link to sustainability and 'green fashion' (as in my example of The Ecoist and Terracycle; endnote 2) is never an overtly articulated concern for teens in the making of the Starburst dresses. In all of my teen examples, Mars still benefit from product sales. For those who buy thousands of packages to complete their dresses and end up giving away the candy, this indicates a change in value, whereby they are buying the brand for the packaging, not the product.

For Michael Serazio, hybridization, recycling and irony are 'the holy trinity of pop culture today' (2008: 79). It is within this cultural milieu that the candy wrapper dress emerges as creative fashion invention and nod to precedents such as American Pop Art of the 1960s. Andy Warhol's soup can series (1962) questioned the boundaries between brand culture and high culture, celebrating the aesthetics of brand design, packaging and mass production. Warhol isolates the Campbell brand image, reducing it to the familiar white and red label, in the same way these teens reduce Starburst to the small brightly coloured wrapper. In both instances, the taste of the food product is sublimated to the taste of fashion/style.

Germano Celant (1998: 18) advises fashion to 'maintain a relationship with the extra-disciplinary, it must be open to every sort of innovation and unexpected development'. Teens are seeking out (social/media) spaces in which they can produce their own cultural statements; these spaces 'allow people to continually rework their identities rather than let the market dictate identities for them' (Holt 2002: 72). Individuals can now order personalized candy wrappers (e.g. for weddings/birthdays), raising the possibility that these personalized wrappers could be used to further raise the bar on the candy wrapper dress.

The overriding theme in the stories of these Starburst dresses is that the ease of making (and disseminating via the web) opens up cultural expression to those excluded from the competition of 'who's wearing which high-end designer' that dominates some school cliques. Fashion itself is now involved in a creative world in which designers are no longer confined to a brand hierarchy, but work across the disciplines of creativity (e.g. Karl Lagerfeld, Versace and Viktor & Rolf designing lines for H&M). Arguably, this signifies a blurring of the divisions between high and popular brand culture, where couture fashion has become associated with high street brands and with adopting and changing the associations of those brands. This removal of boundaries

9. Although as awareness of these gowns grows and more teens engage in their own wrapper creations, the singular uniqueness of this gown wanes – perhaps prompting teens to search for other unusual fabrics.

10. It is beyond the scope of this article to examine such dresses, beyond pointers to, for example, the Terracycle dress (see endnote 2), also to: Project Runway, which featured two challenges for contestants to make dresses from candy/ wrappers from the Hershey Store (2008) and from Dylan's Candy Bar Store (2012); Katy Perry's California Dreams tour costumes (www.katyperry.com); and Michelle Rosen and David Zornitsky's wedding at Dylan's Candy Bar store in New York (2009), the bride wearing a dress made out of Hershey wrappers: http://www.nytimes. com/2009/04/26/ fashion/ weddings/26VOWS. html?_r=0.

between different forms of culture and brand sectors encourages a rethinking of the ways in which brands carry meaning and, in particular, to the social practices by which individuals transform products into artefacts 'invested with particular inseparable connotations' (Miller 1987: 190). The mash-up of established brands, via the upcycling process and/or teen creators offers potential for future research to explore how brand use/meaning shifts across different sectors/industries and in ways meaningful to twenty-first-century teens.

REFERENCES

Aaker, Jennifer L. (1997), 'Dimensions of brand personality', *Journal of Marketing Research*, 34: 3, pp. 347–57.

Arvidsson, Adam (2005), 'Brands: A critical perspective', *Journal of Consumer Culture*, 5: 2, pp. 235–58.

Askegaard, Søren (2006), 'Brands as a global ideoscape', in J. E. Schroeder and M. Salzer-Mörling (eds), *Brand Culture*, London: Routledge, pp. 91–102.

Best, Amy (2000), *Prom Night: Youth, Schools, and Popular Culture*, New York: Routledge.

Bhattacharya, Debasis, Saha, Dipak and Dey, Shuvendu (2012), 'Predicting brand loyalty and product involvement behaviour of Indian teenagers incorporating the moderating effect of brand influence score', *World Journal of Social Sciences*, 2: 1, pp. 54–73.

Bugg, Jessica (2009), 'Fashion at the interface: Designer-wearer-viewer', *Fashion Practice*, 1: 1, pp. 9–32.

Cayla, Julien and Eckhardt, Giana (2008), 'Asian brands and the shaping of a transnational imagined community', *Journal of Consumer Research*, 35: 2, pp. 216–30.

Celant, Germano (1998), *Biennale di Firenze/Florence Biennale*, 1st ed., Milan: Skira Editore, pp. 18–387.

Chittenden, Tara (2010), 'Digital dressing up: Modelling female teen identity in the discursive spaces of the fashion blogosphere', *Journal of Youth Studies*, 13: 4, pp. 505–520.

Deutch, Howard (1986), *Pretty in Pink*, Los Angeles, CA: Paramount Pictures.

Fournier, Susan (1998), 'Consumers and their brands: Developing relationship theory in consumer research', *Journal of Consumer Research*, 24: 4, pp. 343–73.

Gilles, Marion and Nairn, Agnes (2011), '"We make the shoes, you make the story" Teenage girls' experiences of fashion: Bricolage, tactics and narrative identity', *Consumption Markets & Culture*, 14: 1, pp. 29–56.

Gobe, Marc (2001), *Emotional Branding: The New Paradigm for Connecting Brands*, New York: Allworth Press.

Hollenbeck, Candice and Kaikati, Andrew (2012), 'Consumers' use of brands to reflect their actual and ideal selves on Facebook', *International Journal of Research in Marketing*, 29: 1, pp. 395–405.

Holt, Douglas (2002), 'Why do brands cause trouble? A dialectical theory of consumer culture and branding', *Journal of Consumer Research*, 29: 1, pp. 70–90.

—— (2010), 'Brands and branding: Teaching note', Cultural Strategy Group, Harvard Business School, http://culturalstrategygroup.com/wp-content/uploads/2010/10/brands-and-branding-csg.pdf. Accessed 14 November 2012.

Juicy (contradiction) couture

Jones, Tiffany (2010), 'Starburst not just sweet anymore; it's stylish too', 15 May, http://www.news-record.com/content/2010/05/14/article/starburst_not_just_sweet_anymore_it_s_stylish_too. Accessed 12 September 2012.
Junger, Gil (1999), 10 Things I Hate About You, Burbank, CA: Touchstone Pictures, Mad Chance and Jaret Entertainment.
Lau, Kristie (2012), 'Eat your heart out Missoni! Teenager's prom gown made from Starburst wrappers is dead ringer for designer style', Daily Mail, 8 May, http://www.dailymail.co.uk/femail/article-2141433/Eat-heart-Missoni-Teenagers-prom-gown-Starburst-wrappers-dead-ringer-designer-style.html. Accessed 8 October 2012.
Lively, Kathryn (2011), 'Top prom dress designers for 2011', http://ezinearticles.com/?Top-Prom-Dress-Designers-for-2011&id=5862330. Accessed 12 October 2012.
Lury, Celia (2006), '"Contemplating a self-portrait as a pharmacist": A trade mark style of doing art and science', in C. Lury and S. Kember (eds), Inventive Life: Approaches to the New Vitalism, London: Sage, pp. 93–110.
Magdanz, Fee (2000), 'The new language of fashion', Form, 172: 2, pp. 51–53.
Malcolm, Hadley (2012), 'Prom spending rises to average $1,078 this year, survey says', http://usatoday30.usatoday.com/money/industries/retail/story/2012-04-12/high-school-prom-spending/54224068/1. Accessed 9 October 2012.
Marcus, Lilit (2012), 'Holiday beauty trend report: Why does all this makeup look like candy?', Racked, 5 November, http://racked.com/archives/2012/11/05/holiday-beauty-trend-report-why-does-all-this-makeup-look-like-candy.php. Accessed 12 November 2012.
Meltzer, Marisa (2011), 'The prom dress moves into the designer leagues', The New York Times, 1 June, p. E5.
Merskin, Debra (2004), 'Reviving Lolita?: A media literacy examination of sexual portrayals of girls in fashion advertising', American Behavioural Scientist, 48: 1, pp. 119–29.
Miller, Daniel (1987), Material Culture and Mass Consumption, New York: Basil Blackwell.
Murray, Michael (2011), 'Wisconsin teen wearing prom dress made from Starburst wrappers', 22 April, http://abcnews.go.com/WN/prom-dress-made-starburst-river-falls-wisconsin/story?id=13437383. Accessed 8 October 2012.
Nussbaum, Joe (2011), Prom, Burbank, CA: Walt Disney Pictures and Rickshaw Productions.
Palfrey, John and Glasser, Urs (2008), Born Digital: Understanding the First Generation of Digital Natives, New York: Basic Books.
Pine, Joseph and Gilmore, James (1999), The Experience Economy, Boston: Harvard Business School Press.
Prahalad, Coimbatore K. and Ramaswamy, Venkat (2004), 'Co-creation experiences: The next practice in value creation', Journal of Interactive Marketing, 18: 3, pp. 5–14.
Quart, Alissa (2003), Branded: The Buying and Selling of Teenagers, London: Random House.
Reid, Jason (2012), '"My Room! Private! Keep Out! This Means You!": A brief overview of the emergence of the autonomous teen bedroom in Post–World War II America', The Journal of the History of Childhood and Youth, 5: 3, pp. 419–43.

115

Roberts, Kathleen Glenister (2011), '"Brand America": Media and the framing of "Cosmopolitan" identities', *Critical Studies in Media Communication*, 28: 1, pp. 68–84.

Robinson, Stephanie Mae (2012), 'Candy wrapper prom', Eastern Arizona Courier, 13 May, http://www.eacourier.com/news/local-youths-create-fashion-phenomenon-prom-with-a-side-of/article_0181c05a-9c92-11e1-92ca-0019bb2963f4.html. Accessed 9 October 2012.

Rocamora, Agnès (2011), 'Personal fashion blogs: Screens and mirrors in digital self-portraits', *Fashion Theory*, 15: 4, pp. 407–24.

Russell, Rachel and Tyler, Melissa (2005), 'Branding and bricolage – gender, consumption and transition', *Childhood*, 12: 2, pp. 221–37.

Schmitt, Bernd H. (1999), *Experiential Marketing: How to Get Customers to Sense, Feel, Think, Act and Relate to Your Company and Brands*, New York: The Free Press.

Schroeder, Jonathan (2009), 'The cultural codes of branding', *Marketing Theory*, 9: 1, pp. 123–26.

Serazio, Michael (2008), 'The apolitical irony of generation mash-up: A cultural case study in popular music', *Popular Music and Society*, 31: 1, pp. 79–94.

Seventeen Prom (2004), New York: Hearst Magazines.

Simon, Stephanie (2009), 'Trashion trend: Dumpster couture gets a boost at Green Inaugural Ball', *Wall Street Journal*, 13 January, http://online.wsj.com/article/SB123180107217975103.html. Accessed 11 October 2012.

Storey, John (1999), *Cultural Consumption and Everyday Life*, 1st ed., London: Arnold.

Webber, Alan (1997), 'What great brands do', *Fast Company*, August/September, http://www.fastcompany.com/29056/what-great-brands-do. Accessed 18 October 2012.

Weber, Sandra J. and Mitchell, Claudia A. (2000), 'Prom dresses are us? Excerpts from collective memory work', in J. Loughran and T. Russell (eds), *Exploring Myths and Legends of Teacher Education, Proceedings of the Third International Conference on Self-Study of Teacher Education Practices*, Kingston, ON: Queen's University, pp. 248–51.

Weir, Sarah (2012), 'Michigan teen makes prom dress out of Starburst wrappers', 9 May, http://shine.yahoo.com/summer-kick-off/michigan-teen-makes-prom-dress-starburst-wrappers-162500376.html. Accessed 9 October 2012.

Weiss, Laura B. (2012), 'Study predicts always-on generation will excel at multitasking; lag in patience and focus', The Digital Shift, 29 February, http://www.thedigitalshift.com/2012/02/research/study-predicts-always-on-generation-will-excel-at-multitasking-lag-in-patience-and-focus/. Accessed 24 January 2013.

Wikstrom, Solveig (1996), 'The customer as co-producer', *European Journal of Marketing*, 30: 4, pp. 6–19.

Winnicott, Donald (1971), *Playing and Reality*, London: Routledge.

Wissinger, Elizabeth (2009), 'Modelling consumption: Fashion modelling work in contemporary society', *Journal of Consumer Culture*, 9: 3, pp. 273–96.

Yarrow, Kit and O'Donnell, Jayne (2009), *Gen Buy: How Tweens, Teens and Twenty-Somethings Are Revolutionizing Retail*, London: John Wiley & Sons.

Zlatunich, Natalie (2009), 'Prom dreams and prom reality: Girls negotiating "Perfection" at the high school prom', *Sociological Inquiry*, 79: 3, pp. 351–75.

CONTRIBUTOR DETAILS

Tara Chittenden is a qualitative researcher in the Research Unit of The Law Society in London. Her Ph.D. examined strategies used to interpret the body of a virtual reality mummy displayed at the British Museum. Prior to her current employment, she worked at the British Museum. Her research interests include practices of interpretation, semiotics, teen identity formation, spatial narratives and technological interventions at museums and heritage sites. Recent publications have discussed teen identity formation in the discursive spaces of the fashion blogosphere and the use of projected images in the interpretation of La Venaria Reale in Italy.

Contact: Research Unit - Room 201, 113 Chancery Lane, London WC2A 1PL, UK.
Tel: 44 207 320 9552
E-mail: tara.chittenden@lawsociety.org.uk

Global Fashion Brands: Style, Luxury & History
© 2014 Intellect Ltd Chapter. English language. doi: 10.1386/GFB.1.119_1

MYLES ETHAN LASCITY
Drexel University

It's all inside: J.C. Penney and 'cut 'n' paste' as branding practice

ABSTRACT

Struggling mid-range department store, J.C. Penney embarked on an ambitious rebranding plan in 2012 with the help of its (now former) CEO Ron Johnson. Following successes in turning Target's big box stores into a more 'hip' destination and giving rise to Apple's tech-heavy 'Genius Bars', Johnson was drafted to turn around the ageing chain. During Johnson's reign, the company instituted a series of changes, including a plan to break down many of the chain's store into a series of branded shops. This article seeks to understand J.C. Penney's turn in retailing and branding practice and argue that the company utilized a new aesthetic for its branding efforts. By applying the concept of cut 'n' paste to the store-within-a-store concept, it may be argued that companies are deploying a traditionally resistive aesthetic. Further, the practice may signal a weakness in the market position of the adoptee and creates an intertwined dialogue between brand images.

KEYWORDS

brands
branding practice
brand image
cut 'n' paste
department store
J.C. Penney
rebranding
store branding
store image

INTRODUCTION

Struggling mid-range department store, J.C. Penney embarked on an ambitious rebranding plan in 2012 with the help of its (now former) CEO Ron Johnson. Following successes in turning Target's big box stores into a more 'hip' destination and giving rise to Apple's tech-heavy 'Genius Bars', Johnson was drafted to turn around the aging chain. During Johnson's reign, the company instituted a series of changes that included phasing out sale prices, stylizing the name into 'jcpenney', revamping the logo and featuring comedian and talk show host Ellen DeGeneres as a company spokeswoman. The hallmark of the turnaround plans included redesigning nearly two-thirds of the company's stores to include a 'Main Street' and 80 to 100 branded shops (J.C. Penney 2012b, 2012c).

The 'Shops', as the company called them (J.C. Penney 2012c), started in 2006 with an alliance between Sephora and J.C. Penney (Associated Press 2006). This branding strategy was amped up with Johnson's addition to the company and during the second half of 2012, J.C. Penney unveiled shops from Levi's, Liz Clairborne, Buffalo and Izod (J.C. Penney 2012a, 2012c). The redesign would also include shops for home goods, wider aisles, activities for children and food and drink options (Thompson 2012).

Some analysts had questioned Johnson's changes initially (Surowiecki 2013) and following Johnson's departure after seventeen months and millions in losses (J.C. Penney 2013), more journalists piled onto the criticism (Buffett 2013; Denning 2013; Herbold 2013; Tuttle 2013b). However, the Shops strategy pushed by Johnson garnered some praise early on (Thau 2012) and appears to be a retail trendsetter with Best Buy and Target also debuting shops (Tuttle 2013a). Results for such experiments seem mixed: J.C. Penney's shops have been outselling the rest of the store (D'Innocenzio 2013; Tuttle 2012) even though same-store sales have faltered (Boesler 2013). Meanwhile, Target discontinued their smaller-scale, yet similar efforts (Lee 2013).

It is probably still early to tell whether these practices will help the department store concept. However, using J.C. Penney as a lens, it is possible to assess whether this is a turn in the development of the department store or whether this is business as usual. If J.C. Penney was, in fact, embarking on a new path for department stores, it leads to significant branding questions. What does turning over significant amounts of floor space do to a brand identity? Is J.C. Penney still a cohesive brand, or does the process fracture the brand imagery, reducing the brand to little more than a sum of its parts?

This article seeks to understand this J.C. Penney's turn in retailing and branding practice and argue that the company is utilizing a new aesthetic for its branding efforts. By applying the concept of cut 'n' paste to the store-within-a-store concept, it may be argued that companies are deploying an aesthetic that has traditionally been used as a resistance to cultural dominance (Luvaas 2010: 2–5). The practice may signal a weakness in the market position of the adoptee and creates an intertwined dialogue between brand images.

DEPARTMENT STORES: THEN AND NOW

Historians often highlight the 1852 opening of Le Bon Marché in Paris as the birth of the modern department store (Pasdermadjian 1954: 3). Le Bon Marché's founder, Aristide Boucicaut, developed several tenets of modern-day department stores. Boucicaut aimed to lower markups on items in order to sell more merchandise; offer fixed prices instead of bartering; permit shoppers and window shopping for those who may not purchase goods; and offer returns on goods. The success of these tenets allowed Bourcicaut to grow Le Bon Marché quickly and within eight years Le Bon Marché could be considered a 'real department store' by today's standards. From 1860 to 1870, Le Bon Marché expanded its annual sales fourfold, from five million francs to twenty million francs (Pasdermadjian 1954: 4).

The success of Le Bon Marché inspired imitators in Paris and abroad – especially within the US retail market. US retailers followed Le Bon Marché's mold as A.T. Stewart opened in New York City, and John Wanamaker and Marshall Field followed suit in Philadelphia and Chicago respectively (Pasdermadjian 1954: 6). These urban department stores moved into the US suburbs following World War II. Some, such as Macy's and Marshall Field's developed into full-fledged chains, and were greeted by less affluent, department store chains. Chains such as Sears, Montgomery Ward and J.C. Penney expanded their offerings to compete with department stores (Pasdermadjian 1954: 66). The J.C. Penney chain had been created by pulling innovations from department stores, variety stores and mail-order business (Whitten and Whitten 2006: 48–49).

The rise of the department store has been linked into several different historical developments including both advertising and merchandising techniques (Chaney 1983: 24–25; Longstreth 2010: 41–49; Pasdermadjian1954: 32), labour development and female empowerment (Benson 1986: 200–16; Chaney 1983: 24) and overall a sense of modernization (Chaney 1983: 26; Longstreth 2010: 37). David Chaney argues that the department store inspired a significant development towards modern day consumer culture by forming a more egalitarian system of purchasing (1983: 27).

As department stores grew larger and expanded to more locations, they also began to reinvent their spaces. Stores originally relied on windows for natural lighting and climate control, however, the development of air conditioning made windows unnecessary. Retailers began to turn customers inward, keeping windows for outside appearance, but often using the perimeter space for storage and other non-selling activities (Longstreth 2010: 47).

Inside, retailers began to section off the sales floor into numerous departments or shops. In 1938, retail designer Raymond Loewy said:

> The up-to-date department store is actually a series of specialty or internal shops. When one enters a modern department store, one is no longer confronted with a vast seething sea of merchandise. Departments have become intimate, dramatic, individual and personalized.
>
> (quoted in Longstreth 2010: 45)

Loewy's strategy was soon adopted nationwide (Longstreth 2010: 45). To varying degrees, this strategy is still common in department stores today. While big box stores such as Walmart and Target have more of a unified theme across the store, department stores such as Macy's differentiate product spaces areas by age, gender and product type.

Today, there are few department stores in the vein of giants of the nineteenth and twentieth centuries. While there are certainly large department stores – such as Macy's, Saks and Bergdorf Goodman in New York – the majority of department stores are located within shopping centres. Macy's maintains several notable downtown locations, including the former Marshall Field's store in Chicago and the former Wanamaker store in Philadelphia. However, the stores are now held together in a more unified system with the major urban locations acting as 'flagship stores' for the rest of the chain.

THE STORE AS A BRAND

The branding of stores and retail spaces has been the topic of academic interest for decades. Jay D. Lindquist outlined nine distinct characteristics that helped to create the 'store image' (1974: 31). According to Lindquist, attributes such as convenience and post-transaction satisfaction played a part in building a store image alongside more commonly assumed attributes such as physical facilities and merchandise (1974: 32).

A second line of research regarding consumers understanding of a store was developed as 'atmospherics' (Kotler 1973: 52). Phillip Kotler built the concept of atmospherics off of a concept of a sensory atmosphere, including not only visual stimuli, but also aural, olfactory and tactile dimensions. Later applications of atmospherics can be seen in Mary Jo Bitner's concept of 'servicescapes' (1992: 58–59), John Sherry's 'brandscapes' (1998: 109–47) and various experiments on consumer behaviour (Turley and Milliman 2000: 193–95).

Ko Floor has presented a more recent discussion on store branding (2006). Taking a wide approach, Floor discusses different store types such as grocery stores, specialty retailers and – most relevant for the discussion at hand – department stores. Floor points out that consumers 'are no longer only looking for a certain product, but also looking for a store experience' (2006: 13). Other writers have noted the importance of experience within the retail environment (Kim et al. 2007: 3; Hamiede 2011: 270), especially in regard to singularly branded stores (Borghini et al. 2009: 365–66; Kozinets et al. 2002: 20–24).

Moreover, stores selling products of different manufacturers are seeing a shift in power from manufacturers to retails, according to Floor, forcing stores to create their own brand identities instead on simply relaying on their products. Floor recognizes that manufacturers and retailers are co-dependent with their branding efforts, despite a tension between the two. Issues of price, exclusiveness and product placement are some sticking points between the manufacturers and retailers (Floor 2006: 36–39). Moreover, Floor points out that when a 'shop-in-a-shop' is built, 'retailers are searching for the right balance between manufacturer brands and their own retail brand' (2006: 59).

J.C. Penney's Shops strategy plays with the dialogue between product brand and store brand. The strategy promotes the brand identity of the store's merchandise. By doing so, J.C. Penney is playing with the dialogue between its own brand identity and the brands it sells. The high-profile fight between J.C. Penney and rival Macy's over Martha Stewart branded products (Clifford 2013b; Tuttle 2013c) shows how this dialogue is important to all department stores, even if other stores are not as overt in the brand interplay as J.C. Penney.

BRANDING, SPACE AND J.C. PENNEY

Floor suggests that the in-store experience is the most important medium to communication brand identity (2006: 266–72). Physically, store design and visual merchandising converge with merchandise and service to create the in-store experience (Kim et al. 2007: 336–43). In some ways, J.C. Penney is returning to an older way of retailing by moving from a sea various merchandise into more heavily constructed space (Longstreth 2010: 41–49). In J.C. Penney, each branded space has a unique identity that relates to the merchandise in question and embellishes the product's brand image.

Competitors continue to section their stores into different departments allowing for vastly different atmospheres when shopping for men's clothing, women's clothing, jewellery and home goods. However, they still sell athletic wear brands such as Nike and The North Face next to each other. At times, there may be a change in display signage – as is often the case with Ralph Lauren merchandise – but the surrounding environment remains the same.

This is vastly different from J.C. Penney's new strategy. In the young men's department, J.C. Penney's Levi's Denim Bar (Figure 1) comes not only

Figure 1: J.C. Penney offers a different look and special services in the Levi's Denim Bar. Image courtesy of J.C. Penney Corporation Inc., 2013.

with a change in signage, but with a change in flooring, display and even service as employees who work at the denim bar are 'specially-trained Levi's Fit Specialists', according to the company (J.C. Penney 2012c). The rustic, Americana feel of the Levi's area is a stark comparison to the IZOD area (Figure 2), which includes white flooring and displays, bright lighting and meticulously pressed shirts. Each of these amplifies the unique brand identity sold within J.C. Penney.

Figure 2: IZOD shops have a clean look at feel inside J.C. Penney stores that contrasts with other areas of the store. Image courtesy of J.C. Penney Corporation Inc., 2013.

Celia Lury refers to the disparate parts that come together to form a brand as the 'interface of the brand' (2004: 49). The interface works as a communicative medium between producers and consumers and, as such, brands need to be understood as an object at work. Lury suggests brands can be built 'inside out' or 'outside in' (2004: 53). Both these of processes, Lury points out, should not be equated to real consumers and real producers but are a means of understanding the brand as a media artefact.

The process of 'outside in' is built upon the idea that a brand can be understood with little input from an organization. The brands are linked to some outside identity – like, Swatch with Switzerland and Nike with sports – that helps to frame the brand through outside associations. A further example can be made in the fashion industry where lines such as Calvin Kline and CK One target different market segments, but keep their original ties to the famed designer (Lury 2004: 61). Lury's 'inside out' method suggests that brands are developed through the process of managing the aspects of the brand that cannot be dictated solely through price. While these actions change over time, they also alter the temporality of a brand, allowing it to develop in different times and in a non-liner fashion (2004: 69).

If we apply the ideas of 'outside in' and 'inside out' to the J.C. Penney brand, it is possible to see a change in the way the company constructed the brand. From its inception until its 2012 rebranding, J.C. Penney did not rely on an outside association to gain its identity. The brand was constructed through Lury's 'inside out' fashion, where the brand took on different associations over its history.

The Shops strategy shows that J.C. Penney aims to build its brand on the backs of other brands. As discussed previously, the company is making a significant investment in each brand it decides to bring into its fold through a shop. By devoting a significant portion of floor space to other brands, J.C. Penney is becoming an 'outside in' brand that works to tie the store's brand to its merchandise brands.

Two of J.C. Penney's earliest shops illustrate this point. Sephora and J.C. Penney originally agreed upon opening branded Sephora spaces in 2006 and Levi's stores started opening in late 2012. However, both of these brands have a complex brand identity of their own that gets brought into the J.C. Penney's image through the branded shops.

Sephora is already known as an upscale cosmetics destination. The company is owned by LVMH and operates more than 1,750 stores in 30 countries around the world. Sephora's logo, along with the familiar white and black décor helps keep the upscale feel to the brand (see Figure 3). The Sephora stores inside J.C. Penney keep the same look and feel as the company's stand-alone stores (see Figure 4). By replicating the brand's identity with the confines of its stores, J.C. Penney is able to draw upon the high-end associations of Sephora in a way to burnish its own brand.

Likewise, J.C. Penney's association with Levi's comes with a set of associations. Levi Strauss & Co. has a storied history and deep associations with the American West and cowboy culture. While Levi's was an integral part of the counterculture throughout the second half of the twentieth century, the brand has had notable issues becoming a go-to brand for younger consumers (Elliot 2009). Still the air of Levi's provides a rugged association to the J.C. Penney brand, which can be useful in J.C. Penney's quest for a younger customer. This ruggedness can be seen in Levi's own stores (see Figure 5) and is clearly mimicked in the J.C. Penney denim bar.

Figure 3: Sephora shops within J.C. Penney replicate the cosmetic chain's distinctive appearance. Image courtesy of J.C. Penney Corporation Inc., 2013.

Figure 4: The clean, white-and-black décor is noticeable at this Sephora location at the King of Prussia Mall, King of Prussia, Pa. Image Courtesy of Myles Ethan Lascity, All Rights Reserved 2013.

Figure 5: The rugged, American-feel can be seen in the Levi's storefront at the King of Prussia Mall, King of Prussia, Pa. Image Courtesy of Myles Ethan Lascity, All Rights Reserved 2013.

THE CULTURAL PRACTICE OF CUT 'N' PASTE

The process of copying and reassembling disparate parts has its roots in other cultural processes. Studying the Indonesian indie scene in 2006 and 2007, Brent Luvaas noticed fashion designers would co-opt the look of international corporations. However, often these appropriations often included a manipulation of the logo and/or imagery. Luvaas saw this process as a '[…] repudiation of the classic Western notion of individual authorship and, a defiant assertion of the sociality of production […]' (Luvaas 2010: 2). This aesthetic, Luvaas shows, works to visually manipulate existing images and messages to create something new and unique.

Luvaas positions the practice of cut 'n' paste' along a continuum of bricolage practices he traces back to Claude Levi-Strauss (1966). Presenting a dichotomy between Dick Hebdige's use of bricolage (1979) and Fredric Jameson's version of pastiche (1991), Luvaas suggests both manage to over-reach (2010: 5–6). Luvaas sees bricolage as having the *potential* for reworking dominant cultural meanings, however, he notes that it also offers 'complex positionalities' for 'the ambivalence and "inbetweenness" of contemporary consuming subjects' (2010: 6).

Those in the Indonesian indie scene apply this logic to the cultural products they produce. Luvaas sees this both as a denial of authorship (2010: 11) to the original producers and a form of resistance that gives Indonesian youth a means to exert cultural agency (2010: 12–13). Luvaas sums up the practice, explaining:

> These designers are not trying to throw off the conceptual shackles of cultural imperialism; they are trying to assert some degree of direct control over the new commercial world they live in. Designers … are less concerned with subverting international commercial culture than working with in, or perhaps more accurately, inserting themselves into it.
>
> (2010: 13)

There are three important points to note of Luvaas' discussion of cut 'n' paste for the discussion at hand. First, practice of cut 'n' paste, as Luvaas notes, allows for a resistance but does not require overt resistance to employ the practice (Luvaas 2010: 12–13). Therefore, it may be argued that those who practice cut 'n' paste are not required to follow the practice in a malicious manner. Those who engage in cut 'n' paste *may* seek to subvert the dominant meanings, but may also simply be reproducing in a form of imitation or flattery.

The second issue to note is that once cut 'n' paste – or any form of bricolage – is undertaken, there is an intertextual linking of meaning between the original and the bricolage creation. Luvaas ties this interexuality to that of Bakhtin (Luvaas 2010: 12), but an equally apt linkage could be made to Barthesian myths. For Roland Barthes (1972), a myth is created through a chain of signification. The original meaning of the sign is dropped and the sign is given additional meaning within the new system. Cut 'n' paste appears to work much the same way: the original meanings are still present, but a second layer of signification adds meaning beyond the original message.

Finally, the third point to note of Luvaas' discussion of cut 'n' paste is the idea of a power inequality between the two parties (Luvaas 2010: 13; 2012: 122–23). Indonesian designers build from the production of Western corporations. As Luvaas points out, the Indonesian designers are already being inundated with the messages of western companies (2010: 7). Indonesian public spaces are overrun with messages from powerful multinational companies forcing Indonesian designers to resort to bricolage as a way of presenting their own voices and self-interests.

J.C. PENNEY: A CUT 'N' PASTE BRAND

J.C. Penney's branding effort aligns well with Luvaas' discussion of the practice of cut 'n' paste. As has already been discussed, J.C. Penney has moved from an inside-out brand to an outside-in brand as the brand is drawing its current identity in relation to not only its own history but also from the brands on its sales floor. However, examining the brand through the lens cut 'n' paste illustrates how a brand can utilize this practice.

First, cut 'n' paste does not need to be utilized as a resistive act (Luvaas 2010: 12–13). While cut 'n' paste – like other forms of bricolage – has resistive capacities, resistance does not need to be a goal of the aesthetic. If, as Luvaas asserts, bricolage happens on a spectrum from simple reproduction to malicious subversion, the can be assumed that cut 'n' paste also falls within such a spectrum. In the case of J.C. Penney, the practice of cut 'n' paste is much closer to – if not complete – reproduction, as opposed to subversion.

J.C. Penney is building branded spaces within their sales floor, but they are doing so with the consent of the brands being used. This helps to replicate the brand identity of the merchandise, but also tie the J.C. Penney brand to the associations of the merchandise brands.

A simple comparison of the Levi's Denim Bar within J.C. Penney to a Levi's branded store shows that the aesthetic is similar. Both are aiming for a American West aesthetic, full of rugged masculinity. The wood and metal replicate this both from the branded store and within J.C. Penney. Similarly, the same can be seen for Sephora. J.C. Penney shops have produced the well-known black and white strips and the clean, femininity of Sephora's company stores.

This intertwining of brand identities creates a dialogue between the J.C. Penney brand and the brands built into the store. While J.C. Penney is drawing off of the other brands for their identity, this interplay alters both J.C. Penney's image and the brands in use. Levi's lends J.C. Penney youth and ruggedness and Sephora lends higher-class femininity. Likewise – and perhaps in a less faltering way – both Levi's and Sephora are being tied to the low-middle-class, suburban imagery that previously made up J.C. Penney's traditional consumer (Parekh and Zmuda 2011; Thompson 2013).

This happens through the cut 'n' paste process, which, as mentioned above, has some similarities to the Barthesian myth. Though J.C. Penney is using similar imagery to reproduce the messaging of brands like Levi's and Sephora, it cannot fully reproduce the message. Levi's Denim Bar will always be the Levi's section of J.C. Penney, while the Levi's branded store will remain a Levi's branded store; the imagery cannot fully make the brand.

However, as the original meaning is dropped from the first-level signification, the form remains and the myth takes on an altered meaning. Luvaas linked the altering of corporate logos by Indonesian designers to intertextuality between the original logo and the altered product. Likewise, in that process the original imagery remained – even if altered – while a new meaning was added to it. In the case of Levi's and Sephora, the brands keep some of their original connotations, while also picking up additional meaning through being so closely associated with J.C. Penney. The imagery is there, but the chain of signification allows for a new level of meaning.

This leads to the power dynamic as Luvaas pointed out with regard to Indonesian designers. These designers, Luvaas argues, are at a disadvantage when attempting to compete with the much more powerful multinational corporations. Instead of attempting to fight against the system, these designers simply carve out their own niches through the process of cut 'n' paste.

The power dynamic is slightly different, but still at work in J.C. Penney's use of other brand imagery. While some journalists have questioned the viability of department stores (Norris and Barbaro 2007; Wieffering 2011), J.C. Penney has been seen to be in an especially tenuous position seeing a significant drop in sales from 2006 to 2010 (Clifford and Helft 2011; Holmes and Lublin 2011). Even ignoring the statistics since brand value is difficult to quantity (Lury and Moor 2010), Luvaas' discussion can be used as a lens to see J.C. Penney's brand difficulties.

Instead of attempting to build a brand identity that might compete with the likes of Levi's and Sephora, J.C. Penney sought to bring these well-known brands under the same tent. Just as the Indonesian designers decided to carve their own voice from the discourse of multinationals, J.C. Penney is using the brand identity of others in an attempt to strengthen their own brand. This tactic implies J.C. Penney's weak brand position in comparison to more fashionable brands. The question remains, however, of whether creating a brand of brands strengthens or weakens a brand identity.

CUT 'N' PASTE AS HIP CONSUMERISM

Stepping back from the intricacies of J.C. Penney's branding process, it is also possible to see some wider implications of this branding practice. Some brands work as a cultural product that can work to resolve cultural contradictions, and compete with other cultural products such as films, music and books (Holt 2004: 39). Often through intertextuality – as Luvaas noted – brands can be tied back to cultural production at large.

Constantine V. Nakassis explored the role of brands in the context of India and was especially interested in the 'counterfeit' or 'surfeit' culture of branding (Nakassis 2012: 706–10, 2013: 111–13). Nakssis sees a tension between 'authentic' and 'counterfeit' and argues that such tensions helps to provide brands with meaning (2013: 112). The tensions are made possible by the immateriality or destabilization of the brand and allow more actors to influence the brand meanings.

Turning Nakassis' argument back to J.C. Penney allows for a different dynamic to be understood. Accepting the notion that brand meaning comes from the incredibly blurred line of what is 'authentic', it may be argued that brands in the J.C. Penney context are surfeits giving the brands outside of the department store more credibility. One is left to wonder whether merchandise from a Levi's branded store is seen as more desirable than Levi's branded merchandise from J.C. Penney? Such a process would occur on a continuum with Levi's branded merchandise being sold in a big-box setting – i.e. Walmart – likely to be understood very differently than in a highly branded environment. J.C. Penney's retailing practices could be assumed to be moving from less branded to more branded spaces, and thus, from less 'authentic' to more 'authentic'.

Douglas B. Holt has argued that the key to iconic branding is to position a brand as a cultural product – a myth that consumers can relate to and incorporate into their daily lives. For Holt, the many well-known brands – such as Budweiser, Mountain Dew and Harley-Davidson – become a cultural product through their branding efforts. Often, these cultural strategies aim to bridge a gap between a rebellious or otherwise alienated group and the dominant culture. Mountain Dew appealed to the 'hillbilly' and later 'slacker' myths (Holt 2004: 40–56); Budweiser aimed for working-class men (Holt 2004: 96–100); and, Harley-Davidson worked with the outlaw culture (Holt 2004: 177–83).

There is a link between appealing to subcultural groups and 'hip consumerism' as outlined by Thomas Frank. Frank (1997) traced marketing and branding back to the cultural revolution of the 1960s. In an attempt to stay a step ahead of the cultural movement, companies began to adopt the same ethos that the counterculture was espousing. In doing so, companies were able to bring 'cool' into the marketing mix.

Following Frank and Holt, it is possible to envision the J.C. Penney's cut 'n' paste as an attempt at hip consumerism. Luvaas points out the practice of cut 'n' paste is tools to manipulate culture and could provide a means of resistance to the dominant cultural forms (2010: 10–12). This process aligns closely with Frank's conquest of cool (Luvaas 2012: 156), as brands use the tools of counter cultural or subcultural groups in an attempt to be 'hip' and relevant (Frank 1997: 217–23).

In this case, J.C. Penney tried to grow its credibility through countercultural means. The adoption of cut 'n' paste was aimed to appeal to an edgier or trendy demographic – perhaps the US equivalent to Indonesian indie designers. The change in target demographic – from 'moms' to younger, wealthier consumers – was well documented by retail journalists (Thompson 2012; Tuttle 2013b; Wahba and Gupta 2011). Using a cut 'n' paste aesthetic was an attempt to achieve this goal.

CODA

The Shops strategy at J.C. Penney seems to have been pushed to the backburner after the company experienced heavy losses during Ron Johnson's seventeen-month tenure that led to his ouster in early 2013 (Clifford 2013a; D'Innocenzio 2013). While this appears like a damning indication of a shops-within-a-store strategy, it should be noted that it was just one of several rebranding strategies Johnson undertook at the same time (J.C. Penney 2012b). Further, many of these strategies were implemented with little to no customer feedback (Tuttle 2013b), opening the door to wide speculation on what went wrong (Buffett 2013; Hsu and Hamilton 2013; Lahart 2013; Moin and Clark 2013; Tuttle 2013b).

However, even if the shops-in-a-store strategy was not successful in this instance, the tenants of such practices outlined still hold true. By following the practice of cut 'n' paste, brands become intertwined with the stronger brand – usually the 'shop' in the store – lending some credibility to the weaker brand – usually the store housing the shop. This relationship *may* be beneficial for both brands.

In the case of J.C. Penney, the department store chain has been a destination for middle-class and Middle American consumers for a century. By tying the J.C. Penney brand image to younger, trendier brands – and doing so in quick pace – the store alienated a majority of its customer base (Mattioli 2013). The moral of the story may be that if cut 'n' paste is utilized, it should be done carefully and with the current customer in mind.

REFERENCES

Associated Press (2006), 'Sephora to open in J.C. Penney Stores', *Los Angeles Times*, 12 April, http://articles.latimes.com/ 2006/apr/12/business/fi-briefs 12.3. Accessed 11 November 2013.

Barthes, Roland (1972), *Mythologies*, New York: Hill and Wang.

Benson, Susan Porter (1986), *Counter Cultures: Saleswomen, Managers, and Customers in American Department Stores, 1890–1940*, Chicago: University of Illinois Press.

Bitner, Mary Jo (1992), 'Servicescapes: The impact of physical surroundings on customers and employees', *Journal of Marketing*, 56: 3, pp. 57–71.

Boesler, Matthew (2013), 'JCPenney earnings disaster – same-store sales tank 32%', http://www.businessinsider.com/jc-penney-q4-2012-earnings-2013-2. Accessed 29 November 2013.

Borghini, Stefania, Diamond, Nina, Kozinets, Robert V., McGrath, Mary Ann, Muñiz Jr., Albert M. and Sherry Jr., John F. (2009), 'Why are themed brandstores so powerful? Retail brand ideology at *American Girl Place*', *Journal of Retailing*, 85: 3, pp. 363–75.

Buffett, Mary (2013), 'Why did JC Penney stumble so badly under Ron Johnson? It's culture, stupid', http://www.huffingtonpost.com/mary-buffett/why-did-jc-penney-stumble_b_3103698.html. Accessed 29 November 2013.

Chaney, David (1983), 'The department store as cultural form', *Theory, Culture & Society*, 1: 1, pp. 22–31.

Clifford, Stephanie (2013a), 'J.C. Penney ousts chief of 17 months', http://www.nytimes.com/2013/04/09/business/ron-johnson-out-as-jc-penney-chief.html. Accessed 29 November 2013.

—— (2013b), 'J.C. Penney wins ruling in dispute with Macy's', http://www.nytimes.com/2013/04/13/business/interim-martha-stewart-ruling-favors-jc-penney.html. Accessed 29 November 2013.

Clifford, Stephanie and Helft, Miguel (2011), 'Apple stores chief to take the helm at J.C. Penney', http://www.nytimes.com/2011/06/15/business/economy/15shop.html. Accessed 29 November 2013.

D'Innocenzio, Anne (2013), 'JC Penney looks to old CEO to secure its future', http://bigstory.ap.org/article/jc-penney-shares-jump-report-ceo-out. Accessed 29 November 2013.

Denning, Steve (2013), 'J.C.Penney: Was Ron Johnson's strategy wrong?', http://www.forbes.com/sites/stevedenning/2013/04/09/j-c-penney-was-ron-johnsons-strategy-wrong. Accessed 29 November 2013.

Elliot, Stuart (2009), 'Levi's courts the young with a hopeful call', http://www.nytimes.com/2009/06/30/business/media/30adco.html. Accessed 29 November 2013.

Floor, Ko (2006), *Branding a Store: How to Build Successful Retail Brands in a Changing Marketplace*, Philadelphia: Kogan Page.

Frank, Thomas (1997), *The Conquest of Cool: Business Culture, Counterculture, and the Rise of Hip Consumerism*, Chicago: University of Chicago Press.

Hamiede, Kaled K. (2011), *Fashion Branding Unraveled*, New York: Fairchild Books.

Hebdige, Dick (1979), *Subculture: The Meaning of Style*, New York: Routledge.

Herbold, Bob (2013), 'Why trying to apple-fy your brand won't work', http://www.fastcompany.com/3007448/why-trying-apple-fy-your-brand-wont-work. Accessed 29 November 2013.

Holmes, Elizabeth and Lublin, Joann S. (2011), 'Penney picks boss from apple', http://online.wsj.com/news/articles/SB10001424052702303848104576385510781132614. Accessed 29 November 2013.

Holt, Douglas B. (2004), *How Brands Become Icons: The Principles of Cultural Branding*, Boston: Harvard Business School Press.

Hsu, Tiffany and Hamilton, Walter (2013), 'J.C. Penney ousts CEO Johnson, brings back his predecessor', http://articles.latimes.com/2013/apr/09/business/la-fi-0409-penney-ceo-20130409. Accessed 29 November 2013.

Jameson, Fredric (1991), *Postmodernism or The Cultural Logic of Late Capitalism*, Durham, NC: Duke University Press.

J.C. Penney (2012a), 'JC Penney CEO reveals newest installment of shops for Liz Clairborne, Izod and jcp', http://www.jcpmediaroom.com/media/1258/JCPENNEY-CEO-REVEALS-NEWEST-INSTALLMENT-OF-SHOPS-FOR-LIZ-CLAIBORNE,-IZOD-AND-JCP. Accessed 29 November 2013.

—— (2012b), 'jcpenney's transformation plans revealed at launch event in New York City', http://www.jcpmediaroom.com/posts/18/JCPENNEY%27S-TRANSFORMATION-PLANS-REVEALED-AT-LAUNCH-EVENT-IN-NEW-YORK-CITY. Accessed 29 November 2013.

—— (2012c), 'jcpenney unveils first shops just in time for back to school', http://www.jcpmediaroom.com/posts/101/JCPENNEY-UNVEILS-FIRST-SHOPS-JUST-IN-TIME-FOR-BACK-TO-SCHOOL. Accessed 29 November 2013.

—— (2013), 'J. C. Penney Company, Inc. reports 2012 fiscal fourth quarter and full year results', http://www.jcpmediaroom.com/posts/153/J.-C.-PENNEY-COMPANY,-INC.-REPORTS-2012-FISCAL-FOURTH-QUAR-TER-AND-FULL-YEAR-RESULTS. Accessed 29 November 2013.

Kim, Youn-Kyung, Sullivan, Pauline and Forney, Judith Cardona (2007), *Experiential Retailing: Concepts and Strategies That Sell*, New York: Fairchild Publications.

Kotler, Philip (1973), 'Atmospherics as a marketing tool', *Journal of Retailing*, 49:4, pp. 48–64.

Kozinets, Robert V., Sherry, John F., DeBerry-Spence, Benet, Duhachek, Adam, Nuttavuthisit, Krittinee and Storm, Diana (2002), 'Themed flagship brand stores in the new millennium: Theory, practice, prospects', *Journal of Retailing*, 78: 1, pp. 17–29.

Lahart, Justin (2013), 'What's old is new at J.C. Penney', http://online.wsj.com/news/articles/SB10001424127887323820304578411183001562190. Accessed 29 November 2013.

Lee, Thomas (2013), 'Target puts boutique shops on hiatus', http://www.star-tribune.com/business/196634211.html. Accessed 29 November 2013.

Levi-Strauss, Claude (1966), *The Savage Mind*, Chicago: The University of Chicago Press.

Lindquist, Jay D. (1974), 'Meaning of image: A survey of empirical and hypothetical evidence', *Journal of Retailing*, 50: 4, pp. 29–38.

Longstreth, Richard W. (2010), *The American Department Store Transformed, 1920 – 1960*, New Haven, CT: Yale University Press.

Lury, Celia (2004), *Brands: The Logos of the Global Economy*, New York: Routledge.

Lury, Celia and Moor, Liz (2010), 'Brand valuation and topological culture', in Melissa Aronczyk and Devon Powers (eds), *Blowing Up the Brand: Critical Perspectives on Promotional Culture*, New York: Peter Lang, pp. 29–53.

Luvaas, Brent (2010), 'Designer vandalism: Indonesian Indie fashion and the cultural practice of cut 'n' paste', *Visual Anthropology Review*, 26:1, pp. 1–16.

—— (2012), *DIY Style: Fashion, Music and Global Digital Cultures*, New York: Berg.

Mattioli, Dana (2013), 'Penney posts large loss as sales sink further', http://online.wsj.com/news/articles/SB10001424127887323478304578330632060300820. Accessed 29 November 2013.

Moin, David and Clark, Evan (2013), 'Ullman returns as johnson exits', *WWD*, 9 April, p. 1.

Nakassis, Constantine V. (2012), 'Counterfeiting what? Aesthetics of brandedness and brand in Tamil Nadu, India', *Anthropology Quarterly*, 85: 3, pp. 701–22.

—— (2013), 'Brands and their surfeits', *Cultural Anthropology*, 28: 1, pp. 111–26.

Norris, Floyd and Barbaro, Michael (2007), 'This time, housing is taking department stores down with it', http://www.nytimes.com/2007/10/27/business/27charts.html. Accessed 29 November 2013.

Parekh, Rupal and Zmuda, Natalie (2011), 'Love's lost between JC Penney, Saatchi as pair breaks up', http://adage.com/article/agency-news/love-s-lost-jc-penney-saatchi-pair-breaks/231796/. Accessed 29 November 2013.

Pasdermadjian, Hrant (1954), *The Department Store: Its Origins, Evolution and Economics*, London: Newman Books.

Sherry, John F. Jr. (1998), 'The soul of the company store: Nike Town Chicago and the emplaced brandscape', in John F. Sherry Jr. (ed.), *ServiceScapes: The Concept of Place in Contemporary Markets*, Chicago: NTC Business Books, pp. 109–46.

Surowiecki, James (2013), 'The turnaround trap', http://www.newyorker.com/talk/financial/2013/03/25/130325ta_talk_surowiecki. Accessed 29 November 2013.

Thau, Barbara (2012), 'Will in-store mini-shops revive J.C. Penney? Analysts say yes', http://www.dailyfinance.com/2012/09/22/jcpenney-in-store-mini-shops-analysts/. Accessed 29 November 2013.

Thompson, Steven R. (2012), 'Ron Johnson's plan to ditch J.C. Penney's "old lady" store perception', http://www.bizjournals.com/dallas/blog/2012/09/ron-johnsons-plan-to-ditch-jc.html. Accessed 29 November 2013.

Thompson, Derek (2013), 'Who killed JC Penney?', http://www.theatlantic.com/business/archive/2013/02/who-killed-jc-penney/273622/. Accessed 29 November 2013.

Turley, L. W. and Milliman, Ronald E. (2000), 'Atmospheric effects on shopping behavior: A review of experimental evidence', *Journal of Business Research*, 49: 2, pp. 193–211.

Tuttle, Brad (2012), 'JC Penney would be doing great if the stores were less like JC Penney', http://business.time.com/2012/09/21/jcpenney-would-be-doing-great-if-the-stores-were-less-like-jcpenney/. Accessed 29 November 2013.

—— (2013a), 'Can the boutique "Store-Within-a-Store" concept save big box retailers from extinction?', http://business.time.com/2013/04/08/can-the-boutique-store-within-a-store-concept-save-big-box-retailers-from-extinction/. Accessed 29 November 2013.

—— (2013b), 'The 5 big mistakes that Led to Ron Johnson's ouster at JC Penney', http://business.time.com/2013/04/09/the-5-big-mistakes-that-led-to-ron-johnsons-ouster-at-jc-penney/. Accessed 29 November 2013.

—— (2013c), 'Macy's CEO: "Shocked … Stick to My Stomach" after betrayal by former "Friend" Martha Stewart', http://business.time.com/2013/02/26/macys-ceo-shocked-sick-to-my-stomach-after-betrayal-by-former-friend-martha-stewart/. Accessed 29 November 2013.

Wahba, Phil and Gupta, Poornima (2011), 'Penney snags Apple retail executive as next CEO', http://www.reuters.com/article/2011/06/14/jcpenney-idUSN1420751920110614. Accessed 29 November 2013.

Whitten, David O. and Whitten, Bessie E. (2006), *The Birth of Big Business in the United States, 1860–1914: Commercial, Extractive, and Industrial Enterprise*, Westport, CT: Praeger Publishers.

Wieffering, Eric (2011), 'Somebody forgot to tell Macy's that it was extinct', http://www.startribune.com/business/123655999.html. Accessed 29 November 2013.

CONTRIBUTOR DETAILS

Myles Ethan Lascity is a doctoral candidate in Drexel University's Department of Culture and Communication. He earned a master's degree in Visual Culture and Costume Studies from New York University. His current research interests include the cultural formation of brand meaning and consumer interpretation of brands.

Contact: Drexel University, 3141 Chestnut Street, Philadelphia, PA 19104, USA.
E-mail: mel94@drexel.edu

Global Fashion Brands: Style, Luxury & History

© 2014 Intellect Ltd Chapter. English language. doi: 10.1386/GFB.1.135_1

LAUREN DOWNING PETERS
Stockholm University

ANYA KURENNAYA
Parsons The New School for Design

Effortless consumption: The 'Anthropologie' of a brand-focused online shopping community

ABSTRACT

This article examines the dynamics of the brand-focused online community blog Effortless Anthropologie, devoted to the popular retailer Anthropologie, with particular emphasis on how brand values are created, espoused and disputed by its members in a dynamic and interactive online forum. Using relevant literature on the concept of brand community, the net is expanded to capture the activities of a community that exists primarily online. We use examples of posts and commenting activity to demonstrate that it is the existence of the blog that facilitates and maintains such a strong sense of community. This, along with the fact that the blog exists independently from the retailer that it values – that is, it is not a company blog – forces us to reconsider our concept of how brand communities are formed and maintained in the virtual realm. From this analysis, we can learn how brand communities are facilitated by blogs and how they take on a unique dimension online. Consumers use blogs like Effortless Anthropologie to find a community of like-minded users and be a part of a community existing outside of the retail sphere. Retailers and

KEYWORDS

Anthropologie
blogging
branding
brand community
consumption
online retail

marketers might engage with or be aware of the sense of trust, bonding and loyalty that such an online community engenders.

I wouldn't call it a retail store. It's a place where culture and commerce intersect. It's more like the Silk Road – a sense of exploration mixed with the exchange of things and ideas.

(Ron Pompei, Pompei A.D., architect and store designer, Anthropologie)

INTRODUCTION

When Richard Hayne created a retail marketplace in Wayne, Pennsylvania, where his wife and her friends could hang out, shop and sip lattes in 1992, no one could have anticipated the far reaching influence his gesture would have in creating a new kind of shopping experience – one that would transform the practices of basic consumerism into a veritable lifestyle. After hatching the initial idea, Hayne worked closely with architect Ron Pompei for two years. Together they scoured the globe for objects, art and ideas that spoke to the refined, worldly sensibility they sought to cultivate in the first Anthropologie store. In doing so, a two-pronged retail concept emerged that can be attributed to company's meteoric success. As Pompei explains,

[First] we developed Anthropologie as a place for [Hayne's wife and friends] to just be. The way people evaluate themselves and others boils down to three things: what they have, what they do, or who they are. The mainstream culture focuses on what you have. Recently, what you do has become more important. We wanted to respond to the shift toward 'who you are'.

(Labarre 2002)

Hayne and Pompei sought not only to provide a space in which a woman could cultivate her sartorial and aesthetic sensibilities: they also wanted to provide a space in which she could grow. As Hayne and Pompei explained to *Fast Company*, 'We wanted to create an experience that would set up the possibility of change and transformation, where the visitor's imagination was just as important as that of the designer' (Labarre 2002). They explain that they wanted to 'spark interaction on a new level' (Labarre 2002) wherein the experience of shopping at Anthropologie would transcend mere consumerism, turning the store into a space for the communal exchange of ideas, objects and a lifestyle sensibility.

In the two decades since Anthropologie's doors first opened, the company has expanded to 175 retail outlets scattered across the United States, Canada and the United Kingdom. It has also developed a robust online presence through a complementary and often-updated website (Figure 1), making the Anthropologie lifestyle available to more women than ever. Notably, while other stores suffered during the economic recession that began in 2008, Anthropologie has grown; sales increased 22 per cent in the first fiscal quarter of 2010 – a particularly low moment for other women's fashion retailers (Team 2010). Especially important to mention is the relatively high price point of many of these items – $250 sundresses, $400 shoes and $700 end tables – all

Figure 1: The Anthropologie.com homepage, August 2013.

aimed at a target demographic of 'affluent, settled-down career women in their 30s and 40s, with an average family income of $200,000 a year', according to a post from 23 June 2010, on the business and finance website trefis.com. And while the company's growth and profitability is remarkable, what is perhaps more so is the culture that has grown up around it, which far transcends the richly scented candles, vintage-inspired frocks and weighty coffee table books offered up within the stores. Despite spending a whopping average of one hour and fifteen minutes browsing, trying clothes on and chatting (Edelson 2003; Labarre 2002; Palmieri 2004), Anthropologie's legions of consumers have sought out a space in which they could continue to engage with and live the 'Anthro' lifestyle long after walking out of the store's heavy, reclaimed oak doors. With Anthropologie maturing alongside the growth and refinement of the 'Blogosphere' (the constellation of online personal weblogs or 'blogs'), the most logical place for the modern Anthro woman to retreat to would not be Hayne's coffee shop in the first Anthropologie, but the Internet.

In this article, we explore the rise and impact of shopping websites devoted to particular brands, using the blog Effortless Anthropologie as a case study for examining the way such blogs facilitate trends, desires, obsessions and communities in the formation of brand communities on the Internet. Other scholars have examined the experiential nature of online shopping (Jeong et al. 2008; Kwon and Lennon 2009) and the consumptive habits online retail engenders (Kukar-Kinney et al. 2009). With Anthropologie serving as a case study, our article contributes to this growing body of literature by exploring the vibrant character of brand communities that have emerged online in recent years.

Brand communities, as first defined by Daniel J. Boorstin in 1974, are 'invisible [communities] created and preserved by how and what [people consume] that emerged after the industrial revolution' (1974: 89). James H. McAlexander et al. further explain that brand communities in the United States have shifted away from geographically bounded community groups 'into the direction of common but tenuous bonds of brand use and affiliation' (2002: 38). As geographical constraints have come to matter less and less in the formation of such communities, the Internet has emerged as a space in which consumer-fans can congregate. Effortless Anthropologie is the largest 'Anthro-centric' fan blog within a network of over 50 personal blogs dedicated to the retailer. Taken together, the blogs cultivate a space for continued consumerist behaviours outside of conventional retail spaces. Effortless Anthropologie features weekly postings of items that have gone on sale, reviews of products and a community report feature where users can report sightings of rare items in store and online. Such behaviours cultivate what Hope Jensen Schau et al. describe as the collective creation of value within brand communities (2009). However, current research focuses on the experiential aspects of the retailer's website only, overlooking the possibilities for commerce and community inherent in brand-focused external websites. Additionally, previous research into brand communities (e.g. Crewe 2000; McAlexander et al. 2002) has focused predominantly on non-Web-based forms of community building and interaction.

In focusing on Effortless Anthropologie as a site where brand communities are fostered in the online realm by independent, non-corporate actors, this article seeks to provide insight into how the crowdsourcing and commenting inherent in blogs alters the experience of shopping and building fervent brand communities. We begin by addressing the business practices of the brand itself, which lend themselves to adoption into the online realm. We argue that Anthropologie in particular displays the brand characteristics that translate well into the kind of community building that occurs via Effortless Anthropologie. We then analyse the kinds of blog posts that run on the site and separate them into groups: those that facilitate consumption, those that police consumption, those that generate a brand community and those that simultaneously achieve all three of these goals. We situate our findings within the context of existing literature on brand communities and online brand engagement (Schau et al. 2009; Muñiz and Schau 2011). Through this discussion we arrive at an understanding of how the Anthropologie brand community is translated in the online realm and how these practices take on a unique dimension on the blog. Our article advances the discourse on brand communities and adds to it by demonstrating that an online community devoted to creating a dialogue around the brand can flourish even when it is maintained independently of the brand, owing in large part to the particular benefits the blog format affords.

The mechanics surrounding consumer-generated content are of benefit to our analysis. Consumer-Generated Content (CGC), or content relating to a brand that is created by the user rather than the producer of the brand or its products, often takes shape within a collective of brand devotees (Muñiz and

Schau 2011). This kind of content is not necessarily solicited by a company or brand; rather, it is oftentimes laboriously crafted by consumers with no seeming external stimulus. As Albert M. Muñiz and Hope Jensen Schau explain, 'The true reward of CGC is the process and the outcome is not reliant on technical prowess but rather semiotic manipulation, narrative manipulation and complex brand character development' (2011: 211). However, one still questions whether or not CGC can be 'successfully integrated into larger firm objectives, where brand content is harmoniously co-produced' (Muñiz and Schau 2011: 210). In the case of Anthropologie, the answer is a resounding yes.

Before further delving to the dynamics of the online Effortless Anthropologie community, we will first explore the unique brand positioning of Anthropologie itself and how it employs practices that foster a particularly strong brand connection that translates well to the digital realm.

'SHOPPING LIKE A FRENCHWOMAN': CULTIVATING THE 'ANTHRO' COMMUNITY

As quoted by Naomi Klein in her oft-cited text 'No Logo', Walter Landor, president of the Landor branding agency has written that while 'products are made in the factory […] brands are made in the mind' (2009: 201). Similarly, in the introduction to their article 'Concepts and Practices of Digital Virtual Consumption', Janice Denegri-Knott and Mike Molesworth explain, 'commodities and market-based experiences provide opportunities for elaborate consumer daydreams that sustain desire on the basis that they may be actualized via material consumption' (2010: 109). If this is the case, how then is Anthropologie – a constellation of different designers, found objects and one-of-a-kind art pieces – imagined by its dedicated consumer base, and how does it stand out within the diverse market for women's clothing? In short, what is the nature of the Anthropologie 'daydream' and how is it enacted by the Anthropologie brand community?

While other brands and retailers follow the ebb and flow of the fashion system from season to season, changing their merchandise and silhouettes based on current trends, the overall aesthetic of both the Anthropologie store and the merchandise within has changed remarkably little in the past two decades. Selling a reassuringly consistent selection of cardigans, sensibly heeled shoes, A-line skirted dresses and frilly bric-a-brac, the Anthro consumer is loyal to the brand because she knows she will always be able to count on the brand's timeless, feminine look even as hemlines fluctuate and silhouettes evolve. This core consumer, who has been the lifeblood of the Anthropologie brand, is a direct offshoot of that initial 'anthropological' research Hayne and Pompei conducted in 1992 in developing the store's concept. As former company CEO Glen Senk has explained, the Anthropologie woman is

> well-read and well traveled. She is very aware; she gets our references, whether it's to a town in Europe or to a book or a movie. She's urban-minded. She's into cooking, gardening and wine. She has a natural curiosity about the world. She's relatively fit.
>
> (Labarre 2002)

Or, as Laura Compton of the San Francisco Chronicle wrote, this core customer sounds 'like every female friend I have who shops there, all of whom profess a deep love for this place and confess, "Every time I go in there I just want to buy everything"' (2004). Within the Anthropologie community, this woman is known as 'she', and it is 'she' who drives every marketing and merchandising decision within this close-knit retail community. Specifically, this woman is '28 to 45, usually in a committed relationship and has children. She often works in an artistic field and wants to have a unique look', but could not be considered a 'fashion victim [...] She's going to save her clothes and wear them in different ways year to year' (Compton 2004). As many have written (e.g. Compton 2004; Lebarre 2002), if this woman were a movie character, she would closely resemble the quirky, French Amélie from the eponymous 2001 film. In order for a brand community to thrive, as McAlexander et al. explain, it must be 'customer-centric' wherein the 'meaningfulness of the community inhere[s] in customer experience rather than in the brand around which that experience revolves' (2002: 39).

With this kind of intimate knowledge of their core consumer, traditional business acumen would suggest that the Anthropologie marketing team would parlay it into an extensive marketing campaign to draw her into the store. However, Anthropologie prides itself on the fact that the company has never spent a cent on external advertising. As Glen Senk has boasted, 'One of our core philosophies is that we spend the money that other companies spend on marketing to create a store experience that exceeds people's expectations. We don't spend money on messages – we invest in execution' (Lebarre 2002). By execution, Senk is referencing the immersive, homey quality of every individually tailored retail location, cultivated through a mix of new and found objects, large scale art pieces and elaborate window displays. The in-store displays and merchandising are site-specific, as is the architecture of each store, designed with the specific location in mind. Designers at Pompei A.D., the firm that designed New York's Chelsea Market location, took the local character into consideration when designing the store: 'The space references the industrial and maritime nature of the neighbourhood, and at the same time maintains Anthropologie's feminine aesthetic. This personal, location-based store design is aimed at strengthening the customer's identification with the brand' (Mitchell 2010). James Smith, the company's director of store design, added, 'We look at the space we occupy individually and try to react to its inherent character or local architecture style … Aesthetically, we always want to have a connection – however abstract – between the store and the community that it serves' (Mitchell 2010).

As fashion theorist and historian Christopher Breward writes,

> The efforts of style-leaders, advertisers, editors and directors over the past 200 years have all in some way been oriented towards an epiphanic moment of engagement between customer and fashionable product which inevitably happens for the first time within the confines of the retail store.

> (2003: 143)

It is within this space that the meaningfulness of the Anthropologie brand and the legitimacy of the brand community are, in the words of McAlexander et al., 'negotiated through the symbolism of the marketplace' (2002: 38). Yet what is it about this space in particular that has lent itself so well to the formation of a cohesive brand community by the company's loyal consumers? And furthermore, how does Anthropologie engage with this vibrant community base through its own community-building endeavours?

From the moment the woman walks into the Anthropologie store and out of the sterile fluorescence of the shopping mall, her senses are awakened and she is transported to another place. As Polly Labarre describes the Anthropologie experience, it is not unlike shopping at a French flea market: it is not exactly 'efficient', but in the process you 'come away with a story' (2002). Evoking a bustling, global marketplace with its layers, colours and patterns, Anthropologie transforms shopping into a 'multisensory ritual, with its open-ended sense of discovery and the thrill [of what can feel like a] hard-won find' within an otherwise uniform and oftentimes boring shopping landscape (Labarre 2002). However evocative an Anthropologie store is of a quaint vintage flea market though, the core consumer can find solace in the fact that she, as Lebarre writes, will never have to search too hard for that perfect vintage-inspired piece. Rather, Anthropologie caters to a woman who, at one time in her life, trolled flea markets for hours on end, but now, perhaps busy with a family and a career, doesn't have time to do so anymore. The store's wares also cater to a woman who is perhaps too intimidated to seek out authentically vintage items. Within the vintage market, Alexandra Palmer concedes that there exists a steep learning curve that closely mirrors the loose system of hierarchy inherent in the term (2005: 198–99). Alison Clarke and David Miller elaborate in their article 'Fashion and Anxiety' (2002), explaining how within these chaotic spaces, 'individuals are frequently too anxious about the choices to be made to proceed without various forms of support and reassurance' (2002: 209). Thus, the initial Anthropologie experience can prove to be an overwhelming experience to an unacquainted consumer at first glance. However, there is a careful order to what on the surface appears so rustically organic.

Within the friendly space of the Anthropologie store, sales associates and personal shoppers help customers navigate the space, offering assistance where necessary. However, even without the reassuring presence of the Anthro-clad sales associates, the very layout of the store facilitates a broader understanding of the context of the sometimes esoteric goods. As journalist Laura Compton writes, the overall narrative arc of each season is 'interwoven throughout the store' in the form of 'vignettes that put the assortment of merchandise into a homey context' (2004). Anthropologie's creative director Kristin Norris further explains this strategy:

> The front of each store typically shows a gardening or outdoor entertaining 'statement.' Mimicking the movements in one's own home, the customer will decompress as you do in your own home, head to the dining and kitchen areas, then peruse bed, lounge and soaps, so by the time you get to the back of the store, you're as relaxed as you would be by the time you get to bed.
>
> (Compton 2004)

Within Anthropologie's domesticated space, the consumer is enticed to linger. In the process, as Hayne and Pompei had established in 1992, the experience of self-discovery appears to transcend banal consumerism within the shift of 'what you have' to 'who you are' (Lebarre 2002). As one *New York Times* reporter explains, the inside of Anthropologie 'is a kitsch-ridden pastiche of fake leaves, fake moss, bottles arranged like cannon fodder and a cardboard rowboat floating in midair. It all seems so cheery and delightfully illusory, sort of like life itself' (Fair 2010). The woman who is so drawn to the Anthropologie environment and its wares season after season sees herself as an individualist – whimsical, quirky and creative – and the store helps to round out her identity.

Because this woman sees herself as outside of the mainstream, an encounter with Anthropologie can be a revelation, but it can contribute to feelings of otherness or alienation within the consumer marketplace and within her life-style more broadly. Thus there is a tendency for the Anthropologie consumer to retreat back into the world of the store in order to feel as if she belongs. As one consumer explained it, 'I can't help but be wooed by the atmosphere. They seemed to have nailed the exact fantasy so many of my [thirty-something] friends have. They make you feel like … you could actually live a life with 75 gorgeous pairs of pj's' (Compton 2004). In his influential text *The Presentation of Self in Everyday Life* (1959), anthropologist Erving Goffman explains how this sense of community affiliation fostered by the environment of the brand community, expressed by the aforementioned consumers, exists 'chiefly because the tradition of [the] group […] requires this kind of expression [for] vague acceptance or approval' (1959: 6). He goes on to explain that 'everyone is always and every-where […] consciously playing a role […] It is in these roles that we know each other; it is in these roles that we know ourselves' (1959: 19).

In her research on the second hand marketplace in Hong Kong, fashion studies scholar Hazel Clark identified a similar phenomenon in which the vintage shops attracted a niche market of avant-garde consumers (2005). These consumers, disillusioned with mainstream retail, sought to enact performances of individuality through vintage goods. Clark observed that amongst these consumer groups, vintage markets became places to 'be in and be seen in, not merely places to shop, demonstrating the role of consumption as a leisure activity' (2005: 162). Within the Anthropologie store, 'she' not only seeks objects and ephemera to round out her lifestyle but also seeks other Anthropologie-loving women with whom to socialize and to shop. Anthropologist Michel Maffesoli has described this kind of social engagement as the 'undirected being together' in which a given community 'will reinforce the feeling it has of itself' (1996: 79). In her work on the 1960s mod scene in Germany, fashion scholar Heike Jenss has demonstrated that these feelings of community affili-ation within the space of a fashion scene are animated through the use and consumption of clothing (2005: 181). Through this embodiment of a shared affinity for a particular style of dress, social cohesion is generated.

Yet it is not just within the store that this feeling, or the enactment of the Anthropologie fashion scene, occurs. As McAlexander et al. explain, the maturation of the Internet has allowed for this sort of brand community to expand into the online realm. Many marketing scholars have written about this (e.g. Granitz and Ward 1996; Kozinets 1997; Tambyah 1996), yet these studies 'have tended to be situated statically on the dimension of geographic concentration' and not so much on the social dynamics that form and facili-tate them (McAlexander et al. 2002). In the following section, we explore how the Anthropologie brand community has extended into the online realm. We examine how that Anthropologie lifestyle is lived out online, who the principal actors within this community are and how that community shapes consump-tion, both positively and negatively.

FINDINGS: EFFORTLESS ANTHROPOLOGIE AND THE ONLINE LIFESTYLE

The contemporary retail sphere has in the last decade splintered. Understaffed and underperforming stores struggle to draw customers in while savvy, modern consumers escape these spaces by tapping in to online retailers, making an increasingly larger proportion of their clothing purchases on the Internet (Denegri-Knott and Molesworth 2010). Into this venue a number of blogs have emerged to supplement the online shopping experience. Their aim is to aid the consumer in making smart, fashionable choices, as well as to share common appreciation for a brand in a community blog setting. Effortless Anthropologie has emerged to fill this niche, and it has attracted a large number of viewers who use the website to track new, sale and hard-to-find items.

In addition to focusing its efforts on locating goods, however, the blog takes on other functions in line with the experiential mission of the brand itself. This includes posts detailing reader-submitted outfits, community 'fitting room reviews' and styling suggestions. Reviewing these functions, we can loosely group these into three different kinds of activities: those that facilitate consumption, those that police consumption and those that generate a brand community. More important, however, is the fact that even those activities that seem to only revolve around consumption are actually enabling other practices. Conversely, a blog based solely on explicit practices of consumption would not lead to the strong sense of community fostered by a blog like Effortless Anthropologie. Consumption more generally is notable in that it enables other practices, such as building identity or forming communities. All of these different activities take on a unique dimension when performed in virtual spaces as opposed to the lived spaces of the store or the home.

The first set of activities, those that facilitate consumption, is easy to identify: posts of items that have recently gone on sale and sightings of rare and hard-to-find items seemingly exist for the express purpose of communicating the availability of goods to the potential consumer (Figure 2). But the question still stands: is this not one of the primary purposes of advertising, usually undertaken by the company itself? As mentioned previously, Anthropologie as a brand prides itself on not spending a cent on external advertising, instead focusing its marketing dollars on improving the customer's shopping experience through in-store displays that are carefully crafted to elicit emotional response. Largely through its carefully targeted visuals and reassuringly consistent brand identity, Anthropologie has amassed a very loyal following in the two decades it has been in operation. In the online realm, the brand's followers – through subsequent activities occurring on the blog – take on the role of a quasi-advertiser-cum-best-friend by passing on deals and sale tips to their fellow Anthro friends.

In another example of blog activities facilitating consumption, the facetime that particular items garner when they are featured on the website have the opportunity to drive sales, if not incite desire in the minds of the readers. As one commenter named 'shannon' wrote to the head blogger, Roxy, in response to her set of dress reviews that appeared on 5 April 2012,

> I love the Fern & Flower dress on you, and the Paris Halter Dress ... va va voom! Stunning! I think I need the Cordova Maxi Dress. Wow! What a beautiful spring/summer dress. Thank you so much for these wonderful reviews. You're the best!

In this statement, the commenter shares her desire for a particular dress, sparked presumably by the dress review, which brought its particularities to the commenter's attention. Certain items can catapult to the top of this virtual water cooler discussion becoming highly popular within the community. In fact, Roxy even creates a yearly post detailing the top apparel items

Effortless
ANTHROPOLOGIE

Monday, January 28, 2013

Perk Alert: Shop the entire Karen Walker for Anthropologie first.

ᴀNTHRO

FIRST DIBS!

Karen Walker

Never before seen designs, including the stateside debut of her Runaway collection for Made In Kind, and perennial favorite Hi There.

SHOP BEFORE THE REST >

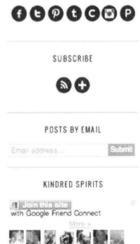

about blogroll blogroll 2 categories
archives

roxy turtle
Slow and steady wins the best closet. I have three playlists on my iPhone: a workout mix, a commuting mix and a shopping mix. Want to know more about me? Head over to the About page.

Email me to say hello or discuss sponsorship and partnership opportunities: snapsparkchik at gmail dot com.

View my complete profile

SUBSCRIBE

POSTS BY EMAIL

Email address...   Submit

KINDRED SPIRITS

Join this site
with Google Friend Connect
More »

If your biggest complaint about Karen Walker's initial Made in Kind for Anthropologie collection was the synthetic fabrics, I've got good news for you. Her Spring 2013 collection, Runaway, is here and it's made from the good stuff. Plus, anthro members get to shop it before anyone else.

Details inside.

Figure 2: 'Perk Alert!' from 28 January 2012 as a type of post that facilitates consumption.

of the year, usually noting their popularity and success within the blog community. Such activities transcend the day-to-day activities of shopping because they instantly place the reader within a large community that can be regarded as what Herbert Gans would call a taste culture (1999). The instantaneity of such interactions and the community approach to brand appreciation shapes the taste culture of its readers in a distinctive way, and in a way that would not be as readily acceptable without the online format that aids its dissemination.

In contrast to the activities that facilitate consumption, there are also those that police consumption. While there are certain items that become popular within the blog community, there are others that get overlooked or are negatively received by the taste culture community of the blog. For example, when Anthropologie made high-level staff changes within its design team in a calculated effort to be more in line with current fashion trends a few years ago, a noticeable shift took place on the blog. A series of wistful, 'those-were-the-days' posts and comments made clear the distaste for the newer items and those that were less in line with the brand's original design aesthetic. Commenter after commenter bemoaned the boxy, 1970s style tops and high-waist flared jeans of spring 2011, noting their inappropriateness for the workplace, their overly youthful nature and their flimsy construction. One in particular – in response to a blog post titled 'What does Anthropologie mean to you?' from 19 May 2011 – included images of Anthropologie garments Roxy adored from seasons past. In the comments section, a reader with the handle 'applesauce23' also included images of garments she considered her 'stand out' pieces (Figure 3). She then proceeded to reflect on how she maintained her shopping habits despite Anthropologie's recent stylistic departures:

> Lately, I feel like I've been settling for pieces that seem to be the best of the worst as I browse through the sale racks. Also, if there is a really nice piece that comes out, I tend to see everyone [...] rave about it, which takes away from the uniqueness I loved about Anthro's clothing in the past. [...] The huge flowy tops, boring basics, and cheaper fabric has made shopping for clothes at Anthropologie a little more difficult these past few months. Even though I had a $250 gift card, I ended up buying two pairs of shoes (Floral Fandango heels and Nelumbo Kitten heels in black) because I didn't really see any stand out pieces. The only purchase I made before that was a mug. The sad thing is that I don't even feel compelled to hold on to my gift card to see future offerings because I've been so unimpressed with the clothing. I really hope that Anthropologie moves away from the trendy styles and goes back to the tailoring, quality, style, and details that it was known for.

Aside from demonstrating her still-avid interest in the brand, this commenter uses the blog as a forum to discuss her decrease in purchases from the retailer. She owes this shift in her consumption habits to the retailer's implicit betrayal of her taste preferences. This reflective posting, as well as the flood-gate of commentary that comes along with it, is part of the taste culture that develops online. Through this enactment of the taste culture, the original Anthropologie aesthetic is further cemented in the minds of the brand community while other, more divergent stylistic impulses are dissociated from the brand's identity.

Lastly, there is the set of practices that contribute to the generation and maintenance of online brand communities. Reader-submitted outfits and fitting room reviews – that while still conforming to the norms of the blog-generated taste culture – create the same reassuring sense of community the brand advocates through its in-store displays. In these posts, readers submit photos of themselves in their 'Anthro best', demonstrating the true diversity of the company's customer base. Within this microcosm of the larger

Figure 3: Comments from the 19 May 2011 post entitled 'What does Anthropologie mean to you?'.

'Anthro' community, women from all over the country (and some abroad) of different ethnicities, varying ages and with non-normative fashion bodies are depicted (Figure 4). Through these posts, readers celebrate both their common taste – signified by their purchase of similar items – and their distinctiveness, evidenced by the unique way they choose to style their looks. From these posts, opportunities to locate and secure items for one another, including placing items on hold at other stores or alerting the community when they return rare items or locate them online, emerge. These activities, more than just facilitating or policing consumption, contribute to the development of a linked community defined by who these women are and how they personally interpret the Anthropologie brand. This sort of community affiliation brings to mind Pompei's aforementioned quote in which he explains how Anthropologie exists as an alternative to mainstream consumerism

Sunday, January 27, 2013

Eye Candy: Effortless Anthro Reader Outfits!

Alyssa
Anthropologie Sashed Sweater Skirt
Anthropologie top

It's Sunday and you know what that means -- Reader Outfits!! Although I'm taking this week off you won't even notice because we've got 20+ lovely ladies decked out in some serious Anthropologie goodness. Please show your love for all of our contributors in the comments! If you'd like to submit a look for Reader Outfits please read through the guidelines and then snap away!

On to the outfits...

Figure 4: Reader-submitted Anthropologie and Anthropologie-inspired outfits as seen on EffortlessaAthropologie. blogspot.com, January 2013.

in shifting the focus away from what you have and 'toward who you are' (Labarre 2002).

Using Schau, Muñiz and Arnold's four categories of value-creating practices within brand communities, we can see how a blog like Effortless Anthropologie continually advances and reinforces the values of the brand through the three types of posts mentioned above. These posts serve to facilitate consumption, police consumption and facilitate brand community. Social networking, or the first category of value-creating practices, is glimpsed in the very format of the blog. Through these social networking channels,

I have noticed a lot of community members sharing in-store deals and spots in the comments of various posts. Inspired by the weekly Seek & Find posts started by the lovely Alexis over at J.Crew Aficionada, I think now is a good time to start a similar weekly post here.

More This Way »

Posted by roxy turtle at 12:05 PM   Comments (81)

Labels: weekend report   M○ ⬚ 🗗 ౣ +1   +2   Recommend this on Google

Figure 5: In-store Community Post, Friday, 25 January 2013.

commenting and following functions allow users to link into a like-minded community of fellow users bonded by their common love of the brand. The second of Schau et al.'s categories, impression management, includes the practices of evangelizing and justifying the brand's values. As the authors write, brand community evangelizers 'act as altruistic emissaries and ambassadors of good will' (2009: 34). This practice is particularly evident in the weekend in-store community posts (Figure 5). These posts, which go live every Friday afternoon, allow members to share their in-store and online 'field research' with the community. As Roxy notes in the body of each post of this kind, members can 'ask for help in finding an item, report back on what you saw in-store at your local Anthro, ask general questions, make a request, or just stop by to say hello'.

Community engagement, the third category of practices that create brand value, includes the activities of staking, milestoning, badging and documenting important moments in the brand's history. Roxy's ruminations about the good and bad of Anthropologie's recent offerings are a clear demonstration of such activities whereby she stakes her interest in the brand and delineates her interest and focus. In one notable post, she recalls her first point of engagement with the brand in 2008. Here, she situates this early moment of engagement as the starting point or milestone for her brand relationship, and she marks the present moment as a deviation from the legacy of the brand. This post therefore not only documents Anthropologie's decline, but also serves a plea for it to return to its glory days.

Brand use is the fourth of Schau et al.'s categories, and it includes activities of grooming, customizing and commoditizing. These practices are best evidenced in the weekly posts devoted to sharing reader outfits: a member who submits her outfit, and many do on a weekly basis, demonstrates her knowledge of how to care for, outfit and rework their Anthropologie garments into unique expressions of their taste.

Each of the twelve practices that create value within brand communities are at play to varying degrees within the Effortless Anthropologie community. These practices are also all undertaken by the consumer rather than by the company – the tasks the brands must perform to create value in the eyes of their target consumers have in this case been taken on fervently by the consumers themselves, an example of Muñiz and Schau's (2011) Consumer-Generated Content. In addition to demonstrating the strength of the Anthropologie brand community, Effortless Anthropologie demonstrates the unique dimension that brand-related activities take on when they occur in the digital realm.

CONCLUSION

As a community-based blog devoted to a particular brand, Effortless Anthropologie reveals the highly successful creation and maintenance of a brand community in the digital realm. In viewing the blog as a site where brand communities are fostered in the online realm by independent, non-corporate actors, we have demonstrated the unique dimension given to the experience of shopping and building fervent brand communities online. Having addressed the affinity between the business practices of the company and the aims of the blog, we have seen how community building plays an active role in shaping meaningful consumer relationships to a brand. However, a few questions remain to be addressed. For one thing, how is interaction on the blog itself policed? What are the hidden aspects of such communities and what are the taboo topics that get swept under the proverbial $600 rug? And if there is such a strong sense of trust that circulates amongst community members, does the anonymity of the Internet breed any kind of malice that has potential to dampen this trust?

All things considered, however, it is through the 'common and tenuous bonds of brand use and affiliation' (McAlexander et al. 2002: 38) that Effortless Anthropologie community members are so strongly linked to one another. Members are linked in ways that transcend mere consumption practices, engaging rather in the collective creation of value and meaning that such practices elicit. Within this context, the Internet serves as the space in which such community members may congregate; a corner of digital space is carved out and metaphorically bedecked in the warm, cosy comforts of home that Anthropologie both represents and offers for purchase.

REFERENCES

Boorstin, Daniel J. (1974), *The Americans: The Democratic Experience*, New York: Vintage.

Breward, Christopher (2003), *Fashion*, Oxford: Oxford University Press.

Clark, Hazel (2005), 'Second hand fashion, culture and identity in Hong Kong', *Old clothes, New Looks: Second Hand Fashion*, Alexandra Palmer and Hazel Clark (eds), Oxford: Berg, pp. 155–73.

Clarke, Alison and Miller, David (2002), 'Fashion and anxiety', *Fashion Theory*, 6: 2, pp. 191–214.

Compton, Laura (2004), 'Seducing us softly: Why women love Anthropologie', *San Francisco Chronicle*, 12 September, http://www.sfgate.com/cgi-bin/article.cgi?f=/c/a/2004/09/12/CMG1L890631.DTL&ao=all. Accessed 14 April 2012.

Crewe, Louise (2000), 'Geographies of retailing and consumption', *Progress in Human Geography*, 24: 2, pp. 275–290.

Denegri-Knott, Janice and Molesworth, Mike (2010), 'Concepts and practices of digital virtual consumption', *Consumption Markets & Culture*, 13: 2, June, pp. 109–32.

Edelson, Sharon (2003), 'Anthropologie's customer-focused culture', *WWD*, 28 July, Gale (A105966480), http://www.wwd.com/fashion-news/fashion-features/anthropologie-8217-s-customer-focused-culture-724230. Accessed 16 June 2013.

Fair, S. S. (2012), 'Samurai shopper: Squatting at Anthropologie', *New York Times*, 7 June, http://tmagazine.blogs.nytimes.com/2010/06/07/samurai-shopper-squatting-at-anthropologie/?scp=3&sq=anthropologie&st=cse. Accessed 11 March 2012.

Gans, Herbert (1999), *Popular Culture and High Culture: An Analysis and Evaluation of Taste*, New York: Basic Books.

Goffman, Erving (1959), *The Presentation of Self in Everyday Life*, New York: Anchor Books.

Granitz, Neil A. and Ward, James C. (1996), 'Virtual community: A sociocognitive analysis', *Advances in Consumer Research*, 23: 1, pp. 161–66.

Gregson, Nicky and Crew, Louise (2003), *Second-Hand Cultures*, London: Berg.

Jenss, Heike (2005), 'Sixties dress only!', in Alexandra Palmer and Hazel Clark (eds), *Old Clothes, New Looks*, Oxford: Berg, pp. 177–95.

Jeong, So Won, Fiore, Ann Marie, Niehm, Linda S. and Lorenz, Frederick O. (2009), 'The role of experiential value in online shopping: The impacts of product presentation on consumer responses towards an apparel web site', *Internet Research*, 19: 1, pp. 105–24.

Klein, Naomi (2009), 'No Logo', in Hazel Clark and David Brody (eds), *Design Studies: A Reader*, London: Berg, pp. 201–05.

Kozinets, Robert (1997), '"I want to believe": A netography of the X-philes subculture of consumption', *Advances in Consumer Research*, 24: 1, p. 475.

Kukar-Kinney, Monika, Ridgway, Nancy M. and Monroe, Kent B. (2009), 'The relationship between consumers' tendencies to buy compulsively and their motivations to shop and buy on the internet', *Journal of Retailing*, 85: 3, pp. 298–307.

Kwon, Wi-Suk and Lennon, Sharron J. (2009), 'Reciprocal effects between multichannel retailers' offline and online brand images', *Journal of Retailing*, 85: 3, pp. 376–90.

Labarre, Polly (2002), 'Sophisticated sell', *Fast Company*, 30 November, http://www.fastcompany.com/magazine/65/sophisticated.html?page=0%2C0. Accessed 14 April 2012.

Maffesoli, Michel (1996), *The Time of the Tribes: The Decline of Individualism in Mass Society*, London: Sage.

McAlexander, James H., Schouten, John W. and Koenig, Harold F. (2002), 'Building brand community', *Journal of Marketing*, 66: 1, January, pp. 38–54.

Mitchell, Lauren (2010), 'Distinctive beauty: Anthropologie makes a statement in New York's Chelsea Market with a creative, elegant store design', *DDI: Display and Design Ideas*, 22: 6, p. 26.

Muñiz Jr., Albert M. and Schau, Hope Jensen (2011), 'How to inspire value-laden collaborative consumer-generated content', *Business Horizons*, 54: 3, pp. 209–17.

Palmer, Alexandra (2005), 'Vintage whores and vintage virgins: Second hand fashion in the twenty-first century', in Alexandra Palmer and Hazel Clark (eds), *Old Clothes, New Looks*, Oxford: Berg, pp. 197–214.

Palmieri, Jean E. (2004), 'A lesson in Anthropologie', *WWD*, 17 November, Gale (A124935872).

Schau, Hope Jensen, Muñiz Jr., Albert M. and Arnold, Eric J. (2009), 'How brand community practices create value', *Journal of Marketing*, 73: 5, pp. 30–51.

Tambyah, Siok Kuan (1996), 'Life on the Net: The reconstruction of self and community', *Advances in Consumer Research*, 23, pp. 172–77.

Team, Trefis (2010), 'Anthropologie more than just a luxury for Urban Outfitters', *Forbes*, 24 June, http://www.forbes.com/sites/greatspeculations/2010/06/24/anthropologie-is-more-than-just-a-luxury-for-urban-outfitters/. Accessed 14 April 2012.

CONTRIBUTOR DETAILS

Lauren Downing Peters in a Ph.D. candidate at the Centre for Fashion Studies at Stockholm University. She graduated from the M.A. Fashion Studies programme at Parsons The New School for Design in May 2012, and received her B.A. from Washington University in St. Louis where she majored in Art History and Anthropology. She is also a founding editor of *Fashion Studies Journal*, an interdisciplinary, peer-reviewed journal for the academic study of fashion design and theory. Her dissertation will build upon her M.A. thesis, in which she explored the relationships between plus-size women, fashion, and their bodies, through an exploration of the political fat body and the ways in which female fat activists employ dress to make their bodies more visible in society.

Contact: Centre for Fashion Studies, Stockholm University, SE-106 91, Stockholm, Sweden.
E-mail: lauren.downing.peters@ims.su.se

Anya Kurennaya is a recent graduate of the M.A. Fashion Studies programme at Parsons The New School for Design, having previously studied linguistics and foreign languages at the University of New Mexico in Albuquerque and at McGill University in Montreal. She is a founding editor of the recently launched *Fashion Studies Journal*, created by students in the MAFS programme to showcase Masters' level work in fashion studies, and teaches undergraduate courses in design, writing, and fashion studies at Parsons The New School for Design. She is currently working to publish selections from her thesis, entitled 'Look what the cat dragged in: Masculinity, sexuality and authenticity in 1980s Glam Metal'.

Contact: Department of Art and Design History and Theory, 7th Floor, 2 West 13th St., New York, NY 10001, USA.
E-mail: kurea091@newschool.edu

Global Fashion Brands: Style, Luxury & History
© 2014 Intellect Ltd Chapter. English language. doi: 10.1386/GFB.1.153_1

CHRISTINA LINDHOLM
Virginia Commonwealth University

Visible status: Couture and designer *abayas*

ABSTRACT

Dress is often consciously used as a vehicle to express personal taste, social status and wealth. Observant Muslim women in the Arabian Gulf are not immune to this phenomenon and are actively treading the narrow path between fashionable dress and conservative religious and cultural dictates. This chapter explores the ways that the abaya, the typical all-covering black outer robe, is being redesigned by both Muslims and non-Muslims. A lucrative new global market has emerged as couturier and designers provide products that are beautiful and modern within the bounds of cultural practices.

KEYWORDS

abaya
veil
hijab
Muslim
Middle Eastern dress
couture
abaya fashion

HISTORY OF DRESS IN THE MIDDLE EAST

Haute couture fashion and traditional Muslim dress seem to be at completely opposite ends of the spectrum of dress choices. Couture is known for astronomical costs and the shopping Mecca for the extremely wealthy with styles purposely designed to attract attention. At the other extreme is the *abaya*, a non-descript traditional garment dating back hundreds of years, specifically made to deflect notice. The prevailing stereotypical image of an observant Muslim woman is one where she is swathed in a black, shapeless garment from head to foot, with all visible markers of age, social status and personal physical attribute erased. These all-encompassing outer robes are typical daily dress for conservative Muslim women from the Arabian Gulf countries including

Bahrain, Qatar, the United Arab Emirates and Saudi Arabia. Although many women from the area consider the abaya and the companion head scarf, the *shayla*, required religious dress, it is in actuality a national or regional dress practice that has carried over since before the nineteenth century.

The basic form of flowing, draped and covering attire dates back prior to Biblical times, when all women, regardless of individual religious beliefs, wore long, loose robes. As time progressed, and people spread out across the globe, the Arabian region became largely isolated from the West and its evolving modernity and technologies. The Arabian Gulf region and its Muslim inhabitants made a very deliberate choice to focus on religion. They accepted very little change and encountered only a few intrepid western explorers until the mid-nineteenth century, adhering instead to traditional ways of living and dressing. Even as Europeans and Americans began to make their way into the Arabian Peninsula in greater numbers during Victorian times, transportation and communication was limited and difficult, so the impact of early visitors on the traditional way of life was minimal. Very few of the western visitors were women, and as there was no interaction permitted between Arab women and western men, Arabian women and how they dressed were not influenced by western dress practice.

RELIGIOUS DICTATES

Religion is often cited as the reason for compelling Muslim women to wear the abaya and shayla. The Qur'an does in fact direct women to dress modestly, as it does men, but nowhere does it require a black over gown, head cover and even facial cover. The most often quoted passage is Sura XXIV:31, which states:

> And tell the believing women to lower their gaze and be modest, and to display of their ornament only that which is apparent, and to draw their veils over their bosoms, and not to reveal their adornment save to their own husbands or fathers or husbands fathers, or their sons or their husbands sons, or their brothers or their brothers' sons or sisters' sons, or their women, or their slave, or their male attendants who lack vigour, or children who [know?] naught of women's nakedness. And let them not stamp their feet so as to reveal what they hide of their adornment. And turn unto Allah together, O believers, in order that ye may succeed.

Thus, Muslim women have been directed since the time of the Prophet Muhammad (560–632 CE) to be modest in public, in both dress and behaviour. However, the verse is somewhat confusing to non-Muslims as it is unclear what constitutes 'adornment'. It has been variously considered to be jewellery, but just as often decorative clothing. Various translations of the Qur'an tell women to 'reduce [some] of their vision and guard their private parts', while others require women to 'keep their gaze low and protect their chastity'. The Yusuf Ali translation says that women 'should not display their beauty'. This reference to beauty is the reason Muslim women cover their hair and, often, their face as well.

Covering women's 'beauty' was and is often still seen as a means of protecting both men and women from behaviour that could bring shame and dishonour to their families. Shirazi quotes Mernissi's famous work from the 1980s, which identifies women's sexuality as the agent of *fitna*, social chaos.

> The Muslim woman is endowed with a fatal attraction which erodes the male's will to resist her and reduces him to a passive acquiescent

role. He has no choice; he can only give in to her attraction, whence her identification with fitna, chaos and the anti-divine and anti-social forces of the universe.

(Shirazi 2001)

By donning a concealing garment, men and women enter a culturally approved, if not required, contract that allows women to slip through public quietly, without causing notice or concern to men while protecting a woman's modesty and privacy.

All Muslim women in the Arabian Gulf States wore the abaya, or a similar type of concealing dress well into the 1930s. The original abaya form was called ar'as, meaning head, abaya. This garment is a large square cloak made from cotton or wool for daily wear, or, more rarely, silk for very special occasions, that is worn atop the head rather than on the shoulders, cascading down each side of the face to the floor. It is made to order from black, opaque cloth and is held closed by hand in front, concealing the wearer's hair, neck, shoulders and basic body shape. It was often worn with a face mask or facial veil. Special occasion abayas were often decorated with gold *zari* embroidery around the neck and down the front openings. As zari is made from beaten gold wrapped around thread, zari embroidery was evidence of wealth and social status.

REJECTION OF COVERING DRESS

After World War I, greater knowledge of Europe and America through travel, newspapers and radio began to impact the culture and way of life in Arabia. Several tribal city states in the peninsula were gathered together under the rule of the House of Saud to form the new country of Saudi Arabia, and the discovery of oil catapulted many parts of the region to instant and immense wealth. Eager to consolidate their control of the government of the fledgling country, the Saud rulers decreed that tribal and regional dress was to be discarded in favour of westernized fashion. This political decision followed the precedents enacted by Egyptian officials in the early 1900s when the veil was banned, by Ataturk who banned all religiously associated garments in Turkey in 1925, and by Reza Shah who required Iranian women to abandon the chador in 1935. Requiring western dress for both men and women in Saudi Arabia served several purposes. First, and perhaps most importantly, it erased tribal affiliations that were evident in specific dress forms. Not all tribal leaders were supportive of the Saud regime, so eliminating visible kinship associations served to limit the potential for political uprising and coup. Second, western dress was evidence of a burgeoning modernity as Arabia became more engaged with international politics. Ahmed states 'The veil-to *Western* eyes [was] the most visible marker of the differentness and inferiority of Islamic societies' (original emphasis). Thus, as the oil monies flowed into the region, the extravagant international haute couture fashions being purchased and worn by many Saudi women were proof of modernity, enormous wealth and the status that usually comes with it.

RE-EMERGENCE OF MUSLIM DRESS

In the 1970s, a wave of politically involved Islam emerged in the Middle East. Called Islamism, members of this movement expressed concern over the continuing and growing secularism that was occurring in the Middle East. The Islamists sought to reject 'corrupt' western practices and to return to lifestyle practices that are guided by the Qur'an and governed by Sharia (Islamic) law. The first evidence of a dress reaction to this movement occurred in Egypt where young, female university students adopted conservative clothing with ankle-length skirts, long sleeves and head covers. These visual cues indicated that they were conservative, observant Muslims and served as a signal that they expected to be treated as such. Attitudes towards the predominance of western-influenced fashionable dress shifted all over the Middle East in the 1980s and Muslim women began to once again adopt concealing dress. In the Arabian Gulf, this took the form of an abaya, but one that was greatly changed from the old fashioned r'as abaya. The new abaya is a closed over robe that is worn like a loose coat over another set of clothing. It is made from a soft, silky fabric, usually polyester or nylon, and had a matching headscarf. It is cut in a slight A-line shape and either pulled over the head or fastened all the way down the front with hidden snap closures. The sleeves are long and straight with a simple braided soutache cord used to turn back and conceal the raw edges. The headscarf is a two-foot-long rectangle about 18 wide and worn wrapped around the head and neck. Many women also wear a *niquab*, a semi-sheer black cloth that completely conceals their face, or exposes only their eyes. The only thing the new abayas have in common with the original r'as abaya is the colour black and the continuing practice of having the garment custom made. Until recently, only the very cheapest abaya of poor-quality cloth was available readymade.

Not all women were eager to adopt or re-adopt covering dress, but social pressure to declare religious affiliation, piety and national pride was sufficient to encourage most women to accept wearing the abaya when out of the privacy of their home compounds. Some young women liked the abaya as proof of maturity since most females don the abaya at the onset of puberty. Others valued it as a social contract where it is understood that Muslim males will not harass women wearing religious dress. Many others chafed under the social expectation and family pressure to cover.

EVOLUTION OF ABAYA STYLE

Several events since the 1970s have contributed to the evolution of the abaya. As both personal and governmental wealth grew in the region, funds became increasingly available for non-essential and luxury expenditures. Leisure travel to Europe and the United States exposed Muslim women to international fashion, and the ever-growing presence of mass media in their home countries kept them up to date on current fashion trends. Coincidental with the re-adoption of the abaya in the 1980–1990s was the increase in the numbers of women in the Arabian Gulf countries pursuing higher education, both within their own countries, and Europe and America, and eventually securing jobs and pursuing careers. The rise in employment triggered an enormous growth in the abaya market across the entire Arabian region. Whereas initially a plain black abaya was suitable to be worn on the relatively rare occasions when women were away from home, working women now were out of the home every day for extended hours, requiring an entire wardrobe of abayas. Their education and professionalism engendered an independence and desire to express personal style that was frustrated by the anonymous black abayas. Since most abayas are one of a kind, made to measure by tailors from Nepal or India, it was a simple step for women to add small, personal details to their abayas.

Embellishment began to appear on the abayas in the late 1990s, first in the form of discreet black decoration, such as subtle black lace applique or black embroidery on the sleeves. This was quickly followed by beaded designs and embroidery that used colour in small areas around the sleeve edges and neckline. The A-line shape of the abaya then evolved into a wide variety of silhouettes and the amount and degree of embellishment mushroomed. Abayas transitioned from purely functional garments, worn to render a woman anonymous and invisible, to active examples of the fashion cycle, requiring seasonal offerings and subject to international fashion trends. Wealthy, fashion-aware Middle Eastern women would no more wear an outdated abaya than a western woman would wear old, out-of-style dress.

Where a woman might have had four or five plain black abayas in the past, and could wear them repeatedly and interchangeably, the newly fashionable abayas were far more memorable, so a wide selection of abayas was needed for the various occasions women attended. Tailor shops abound in the Gulf States and many women took advantage of the ability to express their fashionability and personal sense of style by designing their own gowns. The shops offer a selection of fabrics and 'models' that a customer can examine and try on, and the number of magazines featuring fashion abayas has proliferated. A customer might ask that a style be copied exactly, or she might require a variety of changes. Some customers work closely with the tailor in a partnership to develop attractive abayas, while other forays into abaya design are less than successful. These disappointing garments are often immediately given to charity.

DESIGNER ABAYA SHOPS

A new type of abaya shop emerged in the region early in the twenty-first century. These shops offer an upscale collection of well-designed luxury abayas available as ready to wear, where the only changes performed by the business are adjustments for fit. The shops are luxurious and well appointed with elegant surroundings and often located in modern, western-style shopping malls. Customers select an abaya style and have measurements taken. The garment is then made to her size and delivered to her. This retains the cache of a custom-made abaya, but maintains the integrity of a professionally designed abaya. My Fair Lady, and Mothahajiba, which translates as 'the veiled woman', have been manufacturing abayas under this system for more than a decade. Dary designs, a subsidiary of My Fair Lady, and aimed at a younger clientele, features a stylized *D*, often set in crystals, as an exterior logo. The other companies use an interior label.

Figure 1: Window of designer abaya shop in City Center, Doha, Qatar. Photo: author, November 2008.

The demand for beautiful, elegant and sophisticated abayas did not go unnoticed by the international haute couture. Many Middle Eastern women were already customers, so it was a natural expansion and sound business decision to enter into couture abaya design and production. This was a highly unusual departure from the traditional dictatorial couture practice, where the designer determined what was to be offered, with little regard given to the wants and needs of a customer, so addressing the cultural needs of a specific population was unprecedented. However, the population of customers who could afford and were willing to spend the enormous costs of couture garments has been steadily shrinking and the couturier have had to change their modus operandi.

THE ARABIC FASHION SHOW

In order to promote haute couture abayas, the Saks Fifth Avenue of Saudi Arabia hosted an abaya fashion show at the George Fifth Hotel in Paris in June, 2009. Abayas designed by international fashion superstars John Galliano, Carolina Herrera and Nina Ricci were modelled, runway style, in the manner of all couture fashion runway showings. Nodding to the heritage of the region, an Arabian stallion was also paraded down the catwalk. It is not surprising that none of the models were Middle Eastern or of Middle Eastern descent, as there is still serious cultural resistance to Muslim women drawing attention to themselves in such a public manner. The designer abayas were priced between $5500 and $11,150 and were gifted to Saks Fifth Avenue's most faithful clients. Lesser expensive ready-to-wear versions of the couture abayas were manufactured with price tags of about $2500, and these abayas were available in the Saudi Saks Fifth Avenue stores.

This highly successful event was followed in December 2010 with the Percil Abaya Design Awards in the United Arab Emirates. Persil, a German laundry detergent company, has manufactured an abaya 'shampoo' for washing the delicate, embellished abayas since 2007. Part of its success is that the shampoo retards fading of the black abayas. By sponsoring the contest, Percil associated the brand's abaya shampoo with emerging designers and fashion forward abaya designs in a successful advertising strategy. The Design Awards contest was open to any UAE resident and organized by the team that annually presents The Bride Show Abu Dhabi, a hugely popular fashion event, attracting consumers from all over the Arabian Gulf region. The contest has become a yearly event and launches unknown and often amateur designers into regional fame.

GROWTH OF THE ABAYA MARKET AND ABAYA FASHION

The volume of name brand abayas has been steadily increasing at a brisk pace in recent years. An Internet search under the term 'designer abayas' reveals dozens of options with prices ranging from $25 at the low end to several thousand dollars at the couture end of the market. Many of these are produced under brand names and claim to be 'designer'.

In addition to the blossoming number of abaya designers, manufacturers and shops, there are now numerous websites reporting on the latest abaya fashions. Writers attend the growing number of abaya fashion shows in the Arabian Gulf region and report on the emerging trends and the newest designers. Sites like Trends4ever.Com, youngmagazin.com, hijabstyleandfashion. com, hijabstyletrends.com and hijabtrendz.com post images and discuss the shows. Some of them, like Hijabtrendz, include interviews with designers and suggestions on make-up, fashionable dress to wear under the abaya and accessories. They feature helpful suggestions about different styles of covering practice and how to comply with social requirements in a fashionable way. A few of the sites are also retail outlets for various companies.

Blogs have become another avenue of current information for stylish Muslim dress. Women and men, Muslim and non-Muslim alike worldwide participate in lively discussions about what is appropriate to wear. The advent of designer and couture abayas has generated international discussion and debate, with some applauding individual expression and others decrying the great expense and blatant, attention grabbing, public display. Muslim cleric 'Abd al-'Aziz ibn 'Abd Allah ibnBaaz lectures that adornment is prohibited and should be rejected according to the Qur'an's directive to dress modestly.

All of the concern and discussion over decorative abayas has not deterred the tidal wave of growth in the embellished abaya industry. One of the stand-out new abaya design houses is the DAS Collection from the United Arab Emirates. The name DAS stands for daffa, abba and suwaieya, various types of abayas worn across the Arabian Gulf. Launched in 2008 by sisters Reem and Hind Beljafla in Dubai, the brand has become hugely popular, with interviews and publicity in international magazines including Harper's

Figure 2: DAS Collection model No. 10. Fall 2013. Used by kind permission of DAS Collection.

Bazaar and press from BBS News. The venture started with a spring/summer collection in 2009, and as the company developed a fall/winter collection was added in 2010 and a pre-fall/winter in 2011. Their resort collection debuted in 2012.

The designing sister, Reem, is British educated, holding a degree from the American University in London in Fine Art and Interior Design, with additional classes completed at Central St. Martins College. The sisters have always been interested in fashion and began to customize their own abayas as the trend away from the plain black abayas grew. Receiving acclaim and admiration at events and social activities, they recognized that there was enormous potential for a line of bespoke and couture abayas. Customers especially requested abayas that would compliment their expensive and exclusive name brand shoes and handbags from brands like Christian Dior, Hermès, Chanel and Gucci. DAS developed designs that beautifully coordinated with accessories for a sophisticated, polished appearance.

The DAS brand focuses on femininity, cultural references, interesting cuts and fabrics, and high-quality craftsmanship. They use a black base fabric, usually a crepe or satin and compliment it with lace, velvet, organza, georgette, chiffon or even leather. Delicate embroidery in contrasting colours, or piping in white or other colours highlights unique silhouettes. DAS abayas were among the first Muslim dress to be offered at Harrad's, London's landmark elite retailer, and are now available in five Arabian Gulf countries. Designs are also available on their website www.dascollection.com. The fall 2013 collection featured garments in a price range from about $800 to $1225. In addition to those items online and in the stores, they accommodate custom, special orders.

Since opening, the company has received several awards including H. H. Sheikh Mohammed Bin Rashid Awards for Best Businesswoman for the Year, Best Design Business – 2008, Dubai Fashion Week 2010 – Best Traditional Wear and Harper's Bazaar Best Dressed 2010.

Another highly successful company is Akhawat London, the creation of Muslim convert Aaliyah Hana. After embracing Islam in 2001, she struggled to find a style of dress that she felt was appropriately modest, while still attractive. After relocating to the Middle East, she discovered beautiful and fashionable abayas while living in the United Arab Emirates. Once she returned to London and opened Akhawat, it became one of the first clothing companies in the West to approach abaya design and manufacture with bespoke design, fabric and embellishment choice, and custom sizing.

Akhawat London offers four distinct collections, suitable for different occasions and personal needs. These collections are offered seasonally and shown on runways throughout the world, but especially in the Middle East.

The Signature Collection of fall 2013 ranges in price from about $300 to $725. These abayas and matching shaylas are complex designs highly embellished by intricate embroidery, meant to be worn for special occasion. The Purple Label designs feature unusual silhouettes and matching head wraps. They are highly trendy with contrasting fabrics in bright colours, seemingly aimed at a younger, more avant-garde customer. Prices in this range are between $300 and $475. The Butterfly collection offers several options for the wedding abaya. A few are black, but pink, peach or white is also available. The light-coloured abayas would only be worn in intimate surroundings with family and female friends. These garments cost between about $450 and $685. The fourth collection Noir is a line of discreet and understated black abayas

Figure 3: DAS Collection model No. 3. Fall 2013. Used by kind permission of DAS Collection.

ranging in price from $315 to $445. Although embellished, they are less bold in design and fabrication and seem to appeal to a more conservative, but still fashion-minded woman.

Although completely online, Akhawat London customers are able to select different combinations of the various abayas on the site, choosing a sleeve from one style and a shape from another. There is a moveable scale to determine price and a detailed sizing chart. Once the fabric has been selected and the design details identified, the garment is produced. Akhawat London ships all over the world.

Legions of designers are now producing abayas and other types of conservative dress for the Muslim market. Although the shayla and abaya are typical of the Arabian Gulf countries, Muslims all over the world have adopted the ensemble as emblematic of their adherence to Islam. The market is enormous, as Islam is the second largest religious community after Christianity. A December 2012 report estimates that there are 1.6 billion Muslims and Islam is considered to be one of the fastest-growing religions in the world. The largest concentration of Muslims, 64 per cent, is located in Asia Pacific; however, the Middle East-North Africa still has a population of 341 million and about 93 per cent of them are Muslim. That translates to a very large number of women wearing the all-covering Islamic approved dress. The French Fashion University Esmod in Dubai estimated that the global Muslim fashion industry would be worth $96 billion if half of the world's Muslim population spent $120 a year on dress. In the Arabian Gulf countries, many women spend far more than that on a single abaya, and in fact acquire extensive wardrobes of abayas, many of which are very costly.

CONCLUSIONS

The final debate, in many westerners eyes, remains why do Muslim women wear the abaya at all? It is perfectly possible to dress in modest and discrete clothing that does not reveal body contours and does not require donning a completely separate set of clothing. A highly decorated abaya further complicates the issue as it appears to run counter to the Qur'an's directive to dress modestly and in fact seems to attract attention rather than deflecting it. The branded abaya companies have facilitated the move of the garment from a plain, black utilitarian 'uniform' to a fashionable garment in its own right. Abayas now appear seasonally and follow trends inspired by the same fashion trends as western fashion. They are the subject of fashion writers and fashion bloggers and are shown internationally on runway fashion shows. Yet, why should any community, be it religious, ethnic or political, be expected to adopt western dress? There are complex reasons why western fashion exists as it does, and there are similar reasons for Middle Eastern religiously inspired dress. Both practices use dress to express group membership, age and maturity, as well as socio-economic status.

Name brand abayas appear to be a result of the wealthy Middle East engaging more frequently with the consumer-oriented west, in particular the fashion manufacturing cycle. Educated and well-travelled professional Muslim women are seeking, and, in many cases, finding or creating a balance between their religious and cultural needs and their growing interest in presenting a personal, fashionable and modern appearance. Designers from both the East and the West are eager to tap into this lucrative market. Designer abayas exist in the borderland between the anonymous black ra's abaya and contemporary couture. These abayas allow expression of personal taste, although they are actually less personal than the one of a kind, bespoke garment made by a local tailor. An increasing number of manufacturers have realized the enormous potential profits, so the market is now flooded with distinctive abayas that are quickly available for every occasion, in nearly every price range.

Throughout the recent history of the Middle East, covering dress for women has alternately been required, then discouraged, and even legally banned. It is now socially and culturally encouraged in Bahrain, Qatar and the United Arab Emirates, and in Saudi Arabia and Iran it is required. The fashion abaya and shayla now bridge the gap between traditional ethnic garb and modern international fashionable dress, retaining religious and cultural expression while also expressing fashionability, individuality and wealth. The name brand or haute couture abaya goes further to legitimize the abaya as a fashion item. A recognizable designer name strives to provide the assurance of the highest quality, luxury, taste and sophistication, the same as haute couture or designer brand names work on Euro-American fashion. A designer abaya implies elevated social status, while still self-identifying the wearer as an observant Muslim.

ACKNOWLEDGEMENT

My thanks to DAS Collections for the use of images of their designs.

REFERENCES

'Abaya couture at Harrods' (2010), Newzglobe.com, 15 July.

Ahmed, Leila (1992), *Women, Gender and Islam*, New Haven: Yale University Press.

Al-Qasimi, Noor (2010), 'Immodest modesty: Accommodating dissent and the "Abaya-as-Fashion" in the Arab Gulf states', *JMEWS: Journal of Middle East Women's Studies*, 6: 1, pp. 46–75.

Al-Wahabi, Najla (2003), *Qatari Costume*, London: The Islamic Art Society.

Antonelli, Paola (2000), 'Signature value', in Jane Pavitt (ed.), *Brand.New*, Princeton: Princeton University Press, pp. 52–55.

Berman, Sheri (2003), 'Islamism, revolution, and civil society, perspectives on politics', *American Political Science Association*, 1: 2, pp. 257–72.

Dahle, Stephanie (2011), 'Middle East's fashion week', Forbes.com, 23 February 2011.

Desilver, Drew (2012), 'World's Muslim population more widespread than you might think', Pew Research Center, Washington, DC, http://www.pewresearch.org/fact-tank/2013/06/07/worlds-muslim-population-more-widespread-than-you-might-think/. Accessed 1 October 2013.

Esposito, John (1998), 'Women in Islam and Muslim societies', *Islam, Gender, and Social Change*, in Yvonne Yazbeck Haddad and John L. Esposito (eds), Oxford: Oxford University Press, pp. ix–xxviii.

Martin, Ann Smart (1993), 'Makers, buyers and users: Consumerism as a material culture framework', *Winterthur Portfolio*, 28: 3, pp. 141–57.

Morris, Mary (1997), 'What do women want? Gender and politics in the Middle East', *Middle East Policy*, 5: 3, pp. 155–90.

Odell, Amy (2009), 'John Galliano, Carolina Herrera, Nina Ricci, and more design fashion abayas', NYMag, 15 September, http://nymag.com/thecut/2009/06/john_galliano_carolina_herrera.html. Accessed 30 September 2009.

Pavitt, Jane (ed.) (2000), *Brand.New*, Princeton: Princeton University Press.

Radsch, Courtney (2009), 'Abayas get glam revamp from designers in Paris', Al Arabiya, 28 June.

Shirazi, Faegheh (2001), *The Veil Unveiled; The Hijab in Modern Culture*, Tallahassee, FL: University of Florida Press.

Taylor, Lou (2000), 'The Hilfiger factor and the fexible commercial world of couture', in Nicola White and Ian Griffiths, *The Fashion Business; Theory, Practice, Image*, Oxford: Berg. pp. 121–143.

Wahab, Siraj (2009), 'Amina Al-Jassim: Passion for fashion', Arabnews.com, 3 June.

Walker, Tim (2008), 'Princess Diana designer Bruce Oldfield creates red carpet abaya'. *The Telegraph*, 14 August. http://www.telegraph.co.uk/news/newstopics/mandrake/2560051/Princess-Diana-designer-Bruce-Oldfield-creates-red-carpet-abaya.html. Accessed 1 September 2008.

Yamani, Mai (1997), 'Changing the habits of a lifetime: The adaptation of Hejazi dress to the new social order', in Nancy Lindisfarne-Tapper and Bruce Ingham (eds), *Languages of Dress in the Middle East*, Richmond: Curzon, pp. 55–66.

—— (1976), *The Glorious Koran* (trans. Marmaduke Pickthall), Albany: State University of New York.

http://abayasbyakhawat.com/abayas-online-abaya-shop/. Accessed 1 September 2013.

http://www.arabesque-hc.com/designer.swf. Accessed 5 September 2013.

http://www.alibaba.com/member/qa108039561.html. Accessed 5 September 2013.

http://www.dascollection.com. Accessed 29 August 2013.

http://www.fibre2fashion.com/news/fashion-news/uae/newsdetails. aspx?news_id=93937. Accessed 15 September 2013.

http://www.hijabstyleandfashion.com/. Accessed 30 September 2013.

http://www.hijabtrendz.com/. Accessed 30 September 2013.

http://3abaya.com/our-designers/20/neon-edge.html. Accessed 5 September 2013.

CONTRIBUTOR DETAILS

Christina Lindholm has served since 2008 as an Associate Dean in VCUarts. This follows a five-year position as Dean of the VCU Qatar campus where she managed the transition from a sponsored programme to the first official off-shore branch campus of an American university. Prior to that, she was chair of the Department of Fashion at VCU after a fifteen-year tenure at the University of Cincinnati School of Design.

Dr Lindholm holds a BS and an MS from the University of Missouri-Columbia, and a Ph.D. from the University of Brighton, UK.

She is a member of several professional organizations including the Textile Society of America, the Popular Culture Association and the Phi Kappa Phi Honor Society. Among her publications are articles in the Berg *Encyclopedia of World Fashion* (2010), the 3rd edition of *Dictionary of American History* (Charles Scribner's Sons, 2002) and the 2nd Edition of *The St. James Fashion Encyclopedia* (Visible Ink Press, 2002). She has served as a consultant to many companies, including Proctor and Gamble, DuPont, Play, Timberland, and Olivvi.

Contact: Virginia Commonwealth University School of the Arts (VCUarts), 325 N. Harrison St Richmond, VA 23220, USA.
E-mail: clindholm@vcu.edu

PART III

Brands in the Luxury Market

Global Fashion Brands: Style, Luxury & History

© 2014 Intellect Ltd Chapter. English language. doi: 10.1386/GFB.1.167_1

TASHA L. LEWIS
Cornell University

BRITTANY HAAS
Hermès of Paris

Managing an iconic old luxury brand in a new luxury economy: Hermès handbags in the US market

ABSTRACT

The Hermès brand is synonymous with a wealthy global elite clientele and its products have maintained an enduring heritage of craftsmanship that has distinguished it among competing luxury brands in the global market. Hermès has remained a family business for generations and has successfully avoided recent acquisition attempts by luxury group LVMH. Almost half of the luxury firm's revenue ($1.5bn in 2012) is derived from the sale of its leather goods and saddlery, which includes its handbags. A large contributor to sales is global demand for one of its leather accessories, the Birkin bag, ranging in price from $10,000 to $250,000. Increased demand for the bag in the United States since 2002 resulted in an extensive customer waitlist lasting from months to a few years. Hermès retired the famed waitlist (sometimes called the 'dream list') in the United States in 2010, and while the waitlist has been removed, demand for the Birkin bag has not diminished and making the bag available to luxury consumers requires extensive, careful distribution management. In addition to inventory constraints related to demand for the Birkin bag in the

KEYWORDS

European luxury
Hermès
American consumers
women's accessories
status consumption
aspirational brands

United States, Hermès must also manage a range of other factors in the US market. These factors include competition with 'affordable' luxury brands like Coach, monitoring of unsolicited brand endorsers as well as counterfeit goods and resellers. This article examines some of the allocation practices used to carefully manage the Hermès brand in the US market.

INTRODUCTION

Hermès

Thierry Hermès established the company in 1837 as a wholesale business providing harnesses to carriage builders. By 1879, Thierry's son Émile-Charles had opened the Hermès flagship store in Paris and began production and sale of saddles and other equestrian accessories to an upper-class clientele able to afford the expense of carriages and horses. Eventually, during the Industrial Revolution, Hermès realized that in order to keep up with the invention of the automobile, their breadth of product needed to expand. Hermès then branched into luggage and luxury travel goods, as well as silk scarves for women to wrap on their heads for long car rides. Émile's son, Émile-Maurice, was responsible for the addition of luggage, portable furniture and other travel-related items designed to accommodate the various emerging modes of transportation and travel occasions (ocean liner, safari, airplane), but the company was careful not to forsake its equestrian heritage and still provided the requisite tools for the sport of horse riding, which became even more prestigious once other forms of transportation replaced the carriage (Milbank 2005). The company has remained family owned for several generations with control divided amongst more than 200 family members. Current Executive Chairman and CEO, Patrick Thomas, is the first non-family member to head the luxury firm. The company will return to family leadership in 2014 after Thomas retires and Axel Dumas (a sixth generation descendant of founder Thierry Hermès) assumes the role of CEO.

Design and development of handbags

In the hierarchy of luxury handbags, Hermès is the uncontested leader and its products classified as the 'equivalent of a Rolls Royce or Chanel couture suit' (Thomas 2007: 171). The tradition of bag-making at Hermès evolved with its heritage of equestrian craftsmanship, and one of the earliest styles was the *Haute a Courroies*/High Belts bag. It was designed by Émile-Maurice Hermès around 1900 who drew inspiration for the design from similar bags he saw being used by Argentine gauchos. The design is the genesis of both the iconic Kelly and Birkin bags. The popularity of the Kelly bag is notably tied to 1956, when American movie actress and Princess of Monaco, Grace Kelly, was shown on the cover of *LIFE* magazine carrying a large *Haute a Courroies* to conceal her yet unannounced pregnancy. The bag was in immediate demand and sales soared, earning it the signature nickname associated with the Princess (Milbank 2005). The Birkin bag was the result of purposeful design collaboration with British actress/singer Jane Birkin and then Hermès chairman, Jean-Louis Dumas, who responded to the actresses' desire for a proper travel bag. Also popularized due to the notoriety of its carrier was the Constance bag (1967), a favourite accessory of

Jackie Kennedy Onassis. A single Hermès handbag requires eighteen to 25 hours of labour in Paris workshops with a production output of about five bags per week (Jacobs 2007). Hermès does not outsource production nor does it license its name for other product categories. Its sourcing model is in contrast to other luxury brands that have managed to increase handbag production in order to appeal to global demand for luxury in emerging consumer markets.

Making an icon

Hermès handbags are entirely crafted in France and a single Birkin bag takes approximately two days to complete. The high degree of hand-work combined with the limited availability of precious leather skins does constrain the production output of the bag and thus the quantity allocated to the global market. The quantity of Birkin bags distributed throughout US stores is based on clientele in each location. While most stores receive bags in their inventory, the majority of bags are allocated to stores in New York City, Beverly Hills, Las Vegas and Honolulu. These markets are characterized by a disproportionate number of high net worth individuals as well as tourists (domestic and international) shopping for Hermès handbags.

The Birkin assortment can vary based on the materials used, which include exotic skins such as ostrich, crocodile and alligator. Hermès owns an alligator farm in the Gulf region of the United States to ensure the supply and quality of its exotic skins. Other farms (for crocodile skins) are located in Africa and Australia (Thomas 2007). It takes about three skins to make a bag from alligator or crocodile since Hermès only uses the soft skin from the underside of the animal and skins are matched to obtain similar patterns on a single handbag (Thomas 2007). The number of bags sent to any given store may be based on its high dollar value (particularly for more rare skins like ostrich and crocodile) or based on units. Sizes for the bag are 28, 30, 35, 40 and 45 cm and correspond to the measured length across the bottom of a particular bag. Leather Birkin bag varieties may include five to six per season, each with its own style name (e.g. Togo, Clemence, Swift, Barrenia, Box, etc.). Within a given leather variety, there are approximately ten colors available per season. In addition to this assortment, limited novelty models of the bag are also made available such as the Sailor Birkin, Golf Birkin, Flag Birkin and 2-tone Birkin. To celebrate the twentieth anniversary of the Birkin in 2004, Hermès created the Birkin25 made from *braise*-shaded crocodile, with a white gold clasp and padlock studded with diamonds and priced at $81,000 (Anon. 2004). These novelty bags are presented each season to add variety and exclusivity for collectors of Hermès bags. Their availability depends on the individual store's decision to order the bags for its clients.

OLD LUXURY: SCARCITY AND EXCLUSIVITY

Luxury products are synonymous with exclusivity and scarcity. If luxury products become too accessible they lose their status, which is one of the primary motivations for luxury consumption. Price plays a significant role in who is able to afford luxury products and serves to confirm the degree of rarity and exclusivity of a product (Dubois and Duquense 1993). Luxury products do not conform to the traditional demand curve for products, which predict a decline in product quantity demanded as price increases. Instead, luxury products tend to experience greater demand at higher prices with a diminishing demand as prices decline (Rath et al. 2012). In addition to price or perceived conspicuous value (the Veblen effect), other influences that serve to reinforce the exclusivity of luxury products include perceived unique value (snob effect) and perceived social value (bandwagon effect). With the *Veblen effect,* demand for a product rises because its price is higher and price serves as a conspicuous indicator of prestige and serves to impress others. The *snob effect* describes the perception of price as an indicator of exclusivity and consumers in this category avoid using brands available to the general masses. The *bandwagon effect* is driven by consumer desire to convey membership with a particular group by consuming prestige products (Leibstein 1950; Vigneron and Johnson 1999). Arguably, all of these influences are involved in the demand for Birkin and Kelly bags due to their symbolism of wealth (Veblen), scarcity (snob) and elite class (bandwagon) membership. These influences are more pronounced as luxury products are experiencing global demand and pressures to grow their brands in order to satisfy emerging market consumers eager to display their economic success.

Bernard Catry (2003) notes how some luxury goods companies have consciously created an environment of scarcity, unrelated to any production limitations, which ensures that products are perceived as rare and precious. On the other hand, the scarcity of the Birkin bag is a result of the amount of time (labour) it takes to create each bag (about two days). Undoubtedly, Hermès' handbags embody the brand's equestrian heritage and the craftsmanship associated with each hand-made bag is well known to its customers, not as a marketing tool but rather as a justification for its prestige status and ultra-premium price point (ranging from $10,000 to $250,000). In 2011, in response to bottlenecks in its production, Hermès announced that it would expand production capacity by opening two new factories in France dedicated to its leather goods and saddlery in order to sustain the momentum behind its strong growth (Diderich 2012c).

In spite of its limited production, the Birkin bag has experienced saturation in some international markets, particularly Asia. A July 2012 *Forbes* article (Carreon 2012) discusses how the Birkin bag may have lost some of its exclusive luxury appeal due to its ubiquity in places like Hong Kong and Singapore. However, in mainland China's explosive luxury market, Hermès bags, due to their scarcity, craftsmanship and pricing, are still highly desired as a sign of status and absolute luxury in contrast to brands like Louis Vuitton which has experienced diminished luxury appeal and has shifted to the 'new luxury' position of a prestige brand due to its accessibility and over exposure in the market (Lee 2012). As Birkin consumers increase globally and seek a more luxurious product, Hermès continues to raise the bar on the exclusivity of the Birkin. The most expensive Birkin bags are priced at around $275,000–300,000 and usually feature diamond hardware. The United States is offered a limited amount of these bags per year, and they are only offered to the top spending clients. There is a degree of customer segmentation as well as segmentation among Hermès stores. The demand clearly outweighs the supply, and bags are allocated between all of the different global subsidiaries. Hermès of Paris US retail stores are only allocated a certain number of Birkin bags per year to sell and quantities are less than those allocated to markets in Asia and Europe. In addition, all global customers are only allowed to purchase two Birkin bags annually. The Asia-Pacific region receives the most Hermès bags globally due to the high level of bag penetration in this market.

NEW LUXURY: ACCESSIBILITY AND ASPIRATION

While Hermès handbags are the pre-eminent marker of luxury for its owners, the Birkin and Kelly bags have grown to iconic status among consumers, from the traditional old luxury, wealthy patrons of the brand to new luxury aspirants. Popular media has influenced consumer awareness of Birkin and Kelly bags, which is not that different from its past appearances on the arms of royals and international celebrities, which were images congruent with the old luxury heritage of Hermès. However, the conspicuous consumption of Birkin and Kelly bags by media moguls, hip hop royalty and reality television stars (mainly in the United States) has exposed a new group of consumers primarily in the 'new' luxury segment. Reality television star Kim Kardashian reportedly spent close to $100K in the Paris store that included the purchase of six Birkin bags (Apatoff 2010). Television personality Martha Stewart carried her Birkin bag during her 2004 court appearance and received criticism due to the nature of the accusations she faced (insider trading). However, the bag was seen as a worthy representation of her image as a 'formidable snob' (Warren 2004).

Indeed luxury products have become more visible and accessible to consumers as brands have extended their offerings to aspirational consumers. Michael J. Silverstein and Neil Fiske call this market 'new luxury' and distinguish it from old luxury, which is described as 'aloof, exclusive, expensive, handmade and elitist' (2003: 52). New luxury is characterized as 'engaging, affordable, premium, mass artisanal, and value driven' (2003: 52). New luxury categories include accessible super-premium, old luxury brand extensions and *masstige* products. Accessible super-premium items are priced well above conventional products in the same category but are affordable to the new luxury consumer. Coach handbags were specifically repositioned at the affordable luxury category by its new CEO in 1996 (Thomas 2007). Old luxury brand extensions include product lines created for lower price points by traditional luxury brands, like Mercedes-Benz or Armani. There is also a category of new luxury known as *masstige* (mass+prestige) brands, which are not associated with old luxury by extension, nor do they possess super-premium price tags, but are higher priced than conventional products in the category (Victoria's Secret lingerie). Consumers of new luxury were described as relatively affluent (making more than $50,000 a year), but the spending on new luxury items was distributed across a wide range of income levels in the United States. (Silverstein and Fiske 2003). Median income for households in the United States have hovered around $50,000 since 2003 (United States Census Bureau 2013), making half of US households potential consumers of new luxury products.

Hermès has not embraced any new luxury brand approaches for the US market although it competes with the more accessible luxury brands. However, it has made adjustments to its Asia market strategy and introduced the Shang Xia Chinese brand to provide lower price point items in its largest market (Asia-Pacific). Accessible luxury brands in the United States include American brands like Ralph Lauren, Tommy Hilfiger, Michael Kors, and most importantly, Coach – a major player in the handbag market. It has been estimated that close to 80% of the US luxury apparel market is actually comprised of accessible (new) luxury, 16% of the market is categorized as 'aspirational' luxury (Louis Vuitton, Gucci) and a modest 3% as 'elitist' luxury, which includes Hermès and Chanel (Bernstein Research 2010). These ratios also correspond to the retail presence of the respective luxury categories. Coach has 451 retail locations in the United Staes and by comparison, Louis Vuitton has 122 and Hermès has 36.

Hermès in the United States

Hermès entered the US market in the 1930s and a Vogue advertisement for a store opening reads:

> Now in America – in New York. The famous shop of Hermès where his eminent American clientele most conveniently find those exclusive Hermès originations in fine leather which set the mode of Paris – the handbags, the luggage, the innumerable smart accessories – all under the distinguishing mark of the Hermès name which implies unmistakably a rare craftsmanship directed by creative supremacy.
>
> (Anon. 1930: 98)

Today, there are 27 directly owned Hermès stores in the United States and a handful of select *concessionaire* and licensed locations carrying smaller assortments of Hermès métier products (leather goods, handbags, scarves, ties). Hermès also sells wholesale product categories, which include fragrance, watches and tableware to luxury retailers like Saks Fifth Avenue, Nordstrom and Gumps.

In 2013, amidst strong financial gains in its US stores, Hermès began upgrading its presence in the United States with a larger Beverly Hills flagship store, and new off-mall locations for both its Atlanta (Buckhead) and Miami (Design District) stores (Edelson 2013). Co-CEO, Axel Dumas, commented that the United States, while already an 'established market', 'resembles an emerging country' in terms of growth (Socha 2013: 1). The Americas region is the third largest market for Hermès (after Europe and Asia) and the United States has the most stores and revenue in the region. The current strategy for Hermès in the United States seemed concentrated on engaging its current customer base with a broader selection of its products (i.e. home goods) since Dumas also commented that the company would focus on increasing the size of its existing 27 stores instead of adding new ones (Socha 2013). Hermès also began to move away from the department store distribution model and closed all of its Neiman Marcus sales locations in 2012 (Hermès 2012). The stand-alone store is Hermès' main format in the United States and this is in contrast to the mall and department store locations more frequently used by Coach (Bernstein Research 2010).

Recent studies of luxury consumption by US consumers also suggest a stratification of luxury categories that aligns with the segmentation of accessible, aspirational and elitist luxury (Mintel 2011). Three groups that emerged from the research included *Exclusives*, *Taggers* and *Treaters*. The *Exclusives* segment had a perspective of luxury that most aligned with features of the Hermès brand, which included a definition of luxury as 'brands with a long-standing history of exclusivity and prestige', a greater tendency to associate luxury goods with craftsmanship and premium materials, and avoidance of obvious designer logos or patterns (Mintel 2011). This segment was also older than the other two (over 45 years old), had the highest income ($100K or more), and made up about 20% of the US population (United States Census Bureau 2013). In general, consumers with incomes of $75K were more likely to purchase luxury handbags, which ranked third after their luxury purchases of clothing and beauty products (Mintel 2011). The same research also showed that the purchase of luxury handbags was highest among female consumers between the ages of 18 to 54, with 18 to 34 years olds slightly higher (39%) than women 35 to 54 years old (38%). Additional studies have shown that among US female consumers 18 to 25 years of age, handbags already symbolize status and a means of communicating self-image (Grotts and Johnson 2013).

While Hermès presents Equestrianism as the heart of its brand identity, and unit sales over time may show that silk is the most popular product, popular culture and media presents the Birkin bag as the undisputed icon of the Hermès brand (Boyd 2013). Most notable in US popular media is the television series *Sex and the City* and a specific episode titled, 'Shoulda, Woulda, Coulda' (Frankel 2001) from Season 4. In this episode one of the main characters, Samantha Jones, attempts to secure a $4000 red Togo style Birkin bag by deceitfully using actress Lucy Liu's name to move up the five-year waitlist. After the show aired, the notoriety of the Togo bag skyrocketed and since 2001, the bag has continued to rise in price annually (see Figure 1). Silverstein and Fiske discuss the influence of *Sex and the City* on the consumption of new luxury products and services in the US market noting that the show became a 'key influencer in certain categories of goods, particularly liquor, restaurants, clothing, jewelry, accessories and shoes' (2003: 42) with the greatest impact made on women's fashion. The Birkin's 'appearance' in the show is consistent with its historical association with celebrity, but it also created demand in the show's middle market audience looking to trade-up to the coveted bag.

The influence of *Sex and the City* on sales of the Birkin bag is also representative of the power of brand endorsers, which can include both unintended

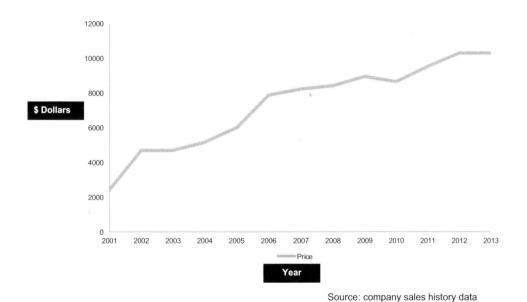

Source: company sales history data

Figure 1: Birkin 35 Togo Leather price, from 2001 to 2013.

and unwanted endorsements. Endorsers can be in the form of *agents*, *semi-agents*, *Amazons*, *free movers* and *hi-jackers* (Radòn 2012). Celebrities can fall into any of the first three categories based on the manner in which the luxury brand supports the celebrity endorsement – ranging from advertisements (agents), free products (semi-agents), and wearers of the brand that are not affiliated via advertising or complimentary products (Amazons) (Radòn 2012). Celebrities may also be among the hi-jackers if they wear the luxury item in a manner that is inconsistent with the brand's image, and free movers are non-celebrity peers who wear the brand and may also introduce inconsistency if they veer from the brand's image. A different example of unintended (but perhaps not unwanted) endorsement is California designer Brian Lichtenberg. The designer has co-opted the Hermès name and logo for his Homiés streetwear line, and the brand enjoys a celebrity following as well as distribution in high-end retail stores. The parody streetwear brand has not yet been subject to trademark-related legal action from Hermès (Lipke 2013).

The association with celebrity or high-end retail does not provide complete immunity from the guardians of the Hermès brand. For example, the potential distribution of 'Jelly Kellys' (replicas of the iconic Kelly bag made in rubber) as wedding favours by Jennifer Lopez, led to a written request to abandon the gifting of the replicas by the law firm representing Hermès. The bags had also appeared in department stores like Henri Bendel and Lord & Taylor, which received cease-and-desist orders from the law firm. Hermès asserted that they were opposed to the exact replication of the bags with the inclusion of unique features that clearly define the Birkin bag's appearance, particularly the belt located at the top of the bag. This signature trademark was omitted from similar rubber replicas that were sold at Bloomingdale's and were subsequently not targeted for legal action by Hermès (Branch 2004).

Allocating the Birkin bag

Despite the rumours of the 'waitlist' (or 'dream list') for a Hermès Birkin bag, it is no longer in existence in the United States. Though each Hermès store is free to manage its business as they see fit, most stores sell Birkin bags on a 'first come, first serve' basis. Many Hermès stores deliberately refrain from displaying Kelly and Birkin bags on the selling floor. Legally, store employees must sell anything that is on the floor. By keeping merchandise off of the floor, Hermès employees can selectively merchandise, or clientele, the bag. Because the demand is so high for the Birkin bag, Hermès store employees rely on customer relationship management and often clientele the bags to their best customers. An optimal Birkin purchaser would be a customer who is already a loyal Hermès client. As a client builds a reputation at a store through the acquisition of opening price point items such as silk, enamel bracelets and ready-to-wear, the client may find it easier to obtain the Birkin.

The Hermès store also serves as a point of customer relationship management around the bag and for the brand, and certain stores do take requests for specific bags. US store directors travel to the Paris market annually for purchasing and will try to place orders according to customer requests they have received. However, because production is so backed logged, the delivery of an ordered bag could take-over a year. It would be impossible to fill every direct request, but at least the store directors have an idea of what bags are in highest demand, and where to place their orders. Dana Thomas (2007) describes the bag ordering process for Hermès clients and states that bags on view in the store are more like display models to present the client with options for a custom-ordered bag:

> You choose the material: cowhide, reptile, ostrich, or even canvas. You choose the color and the kind of hardware: silver, gold, diamond-encrusted. And for the Kelly, you choose if the seams are on the outside or turned in. And then you wait several months while it is made to your specifications.

> (2007: 172)

Re-Distribution, resellers and counterfeits

The difficulty in obtaining a genuine Birkin bag has led to reselling and counterfeiting in certain markets and the United States is no exception. In 2012, an international counterfeit crime ring was uncovered by French police, involving the production of counterfeit Hermès bags with the help of several Hermès employees. The fraud was originally detected by the company's internal monitoring system and resulted in the discovery of hidden workshops filled with precious and rare leather skins. Dollar sales of the counterfeits by one branch of the ring were valued at $22 million (Diderich 2012a). In February of 2013, US Customs and Border Protection agents in Los Angeles seized two counterfeit shipments of Hermès bags imported from China worth $14.1 million (Ellis 2013).

This counterfeiting effect is not unique to Hermès, or luxury items, but occurs with many products demanded by consumers that are available in limited quantities and higher price points. Because of the extremely high rate of reselling and fake bags, Hermès has further restricted how it sells its iconic handbags. Now, each customer is only able to buy one Birkin or Kelly bag every six months (or two bags per year). While some (very, very important) customers are given special 'allowances' for multiple items, this is only after a thorough investigation of buying history has been completed. These practices are implemented not only to be able to offer more bags to more clients, but also, to eliminate the reselling and counterfeit production of the bag.

The Internet has become the most prolific channel for counterfeits and a US court even ordered 34 web sites selling counterfeit Hermès products to pay the company damages of $100 million. As a result of these incidents, Hermès Chief Executive, Patrick Thomas, commented that 80 per cent of goods sold on the internet under the Hermès name are not authentic (Diderich 2012b).

Genuinely authentic bags may also make their way into the resell market after owners sell or donate them. In the aftermath of the recession, consignment shops experienced an increase in inventory as consumers sold off their luxury items. Designer handbag reseller, Fashionpile in Beverly Hills (fashionpile.com), listed bags from Chanel, Louis Vuitton and Hermès as part of its secondhand inventory (Otay 2009). Bag leasing site, Bag, Borrow or Steal (bagborrowsteal.com) specializes in designer brands and occasionally makes direct requests to its subscribers for them to sell the company their Birkin and Kelly bags. The bags are either leased on its primary site (currently all Hermès bags have a waitlist) or sold via its Private Sale site. While Hermès cannot prevent this practice, it does raise concerns around counterfeiting. The issue of selling authentic bags to resellers is that these companies or individuals may distribute authentic bags alongside the counterfeits, and purchasers of authentic bags on the resell market will be able to create such intricate replicas that not even a trained craftsman may be able tell the difference. The more bags they own, the more valid their copies become. Bag, Borrow or Steal provides a statement on its website to assure its subscribers that all of its merchandise has been verified for authenticity, but all sites on the Internet may not be so forthcoming (or legitimate).

CONCLUSION

Hermès entry to the digital space/e-commerce

Uche Okonkwo (2007) points out that e-commerce is a huge opportunity for luxury fashion brands but it can be challenging to recreate the exclusive, sensory nature of the luxury shop in the virtual environment. Hermès recognizes the importance of e-commerce and has adopted an approach that makes a limited range of products available for purchase online (Oknokwo 2007). Even though the company still limits the presence of many leather products on its website, including the elusive Birkin and Kelly bags, it serves as a great catalyst for introducing the mass market to the wide range of Hermès products. Currently, Hermès has extremely high goals for expanding the Internet division in all countries where its products are sold. The company recently entered the social media domain as it moves to attract a younger customer to the brand's opening price point products. Products include the Garden Party tote and Evelyne bag priced at around $2500 to $3500 (hermes.com).

By having a legitimate web presence, Hermès is also able to control its online sales and discourage counterfeiting. The hermes.com website is the only place that consumers can be sure that they are purchasing a genuine Hermès product on the Internet. Even the company's wholesale partners are not permitted to sell Hermès products online. While this strict control does not entirely address the problem of replicas available on the Internet, it is an essential approach to maintaining the image and integrity of the brand.

The availability of the Birkin bag in the US market is based on a carefully balanced determination of consumer demand, status and brand integrity. While waitlists are no longer a part of the Birkin bag purchase process, this does not imply immediate gratification for all consumers, particularly those new to the brand. Consumer loyalty, geographic location and purchase history across the Hermès brand are also contributors to gaining access to the limited inventory of Birkin bags. US consumers unable to obtain a bag through the limited domestic supply may also explore the various resellers (both online and offline) offering authentic previously owned Birkin styles, where prices are still remarkably high and inventories incredibly low. Scarcity in the marketplace has made the Hermès brand vulnerable to counterfeits and new luxury American brands also divert consumer spending to more accessible products. Nevertheless, the appeal of the Birkin lies in its handcrafted manufacture, refined association with heritage and status, as well as its elusive availability, ensuring that demand has not waned even in an uncertain global economy.

REFERENCES

Anon. (1930), 'Advertisement: Hermès of Paris, Inc.', *Vogue*, 5 July, 76: 1, p. 98.
—— (2004), 'Last look: The Birkin 25', *Vogue*, 1 March, 194: 3, p. 604.
Apatoff, Alex (2010), 'Big Spender', *US Weekly*, 4 October, p. 16.

Bernstein Research (2010), 'Black book – European luxury goods: The anatomy of overseas luxury markets', http://search.ebscohost.com/login.aspx?direct=true&db=bth&AN=61232139&site=ehost-live. Accessed 9 October 2013.

Boyd, Annita (2013), 'Oh, honey! It's not so much the style, it's what carrying it means: Hermès bags and the transformative process', *Fashion, Style & Popular Culture*, 1: 1, pp. 81–96.

Branch, Shelly (2004), 'Style & substance: Hermès' jelly ache; rubbery copies of famed bag create a sticky situation; did cracking down fuel fad?', *Wall Street Journal*, 9 April, p. B.1.

Carreon, Blue (2012), 'Has the Hermès Birkin bag lost its appeal?', http://www.forbes.com/sites/bluecarreon/2012/07/17/has-the-hermes-birkin-bag-lost-its-appeal/. Accessed 20 December 2012.

Catry, Bernard (2003), 'The great pretenders: The magic of luxury goods', *Business Strategy Review*, 14: 3, pp. 10–17.

Danziger, Pamela N. (2005), *Let Them Eat Cake: Marketing Luxury to the Masses – As Well As to the Classes*, Chicago: Dearborn Trade Publishing.

Diderich, Joelle (2012a), 'Fake Hermès ring busted in France', *Women's Wear Daily*, 18 June, pp. 1, 12.

—— (2012b), 'Hermès Hails breakup of fake bag ring', *Women's Wear Daily*, 18 June, http://www.wwd.com/business-news/legal/herms-hails-breakup-of-fake-bag-ring-5966863. Accessed 2 December 2012.

—— (2012c), 'Keeping up with demand key for Hermès in "12"', *Women's Wear Daily*, 10 February, p. 2.

Dubois, Bernard and Duquense, Patrick (1993), 'The market for luxury goods: Income versus culture', *European Journal of Marketing*, 27: 1, pp. 35–44.

Edelson, Sharon (2013), 'Hermès making American push', *Women's Wear Daily*, 20 August, http://www.wwd.com/retail-news/designer-luxury/herms-american-spending-spree-7092916. Accessed 20 August 2013.

Ellis, Kristi (2013), '$14.1 M in Hermès fakes seized in L.A.', *Women's Wear Daily*, 7 March, http://www.wwd.com/business-news/government-trade/customs-in-seizure-of-1500-fake-herms-bags-6833954?src=search_links. Accessed 10 October 2013.

Frankel, David (2001), 'Coulda Woulda Shoulda', *Sex and the City*, Season 4, Episode 11, USA: HBO.

Grotts, Allie S. and Johnson, Tricia Widner (2013), 'Millenial consumer's status consumption of handbags', *Journal of Fashion Marketing & Management*, 17: 3, pp. 280–93.

Hermès (2012), '2012 annual report', http://finance.hermes.com/en/Reports-and Presentations/Annual-reports. Accessed 1 August 2013.

Jacobs, Laura (2007), 'From Hermès to eternity', *Vanity Fair*, September, http://www.vanityfair.com/culture/features/2007/09/hermes200709. Accessed 1 December 2012.

Lee, Melanie (2012), 'Louis Vuitton so last season for China's Super Chic', http://www.reuters.com/article/2012/06/07/us-china-luxury-idUS-BRE85602D20120607. Accessed 21 November 2012.

Leibstein, H. (1950), 'Bandwagon, snob, and Veblen effects in the theory of consumers' demand', *The Quarterly Journal of Economics*, 64: 2, pp. 183–207.

Lipke, David (2013), 'Designer parodies test legal boundaries in streetwear', *Women's Wear Daily*, 29 August, http://www.wwd.com/menswear-news/fashion/designer-parodies-test-legal-boundaries-in-streetwear-7103033?src=search_links. Accessed 29 August 2013.

Milbank, Caroline (2005), 'Hermès', The Berg Fashion Library, http://www.bergfashionlibrary.com/view/bazf/bazf00299.xml. Accessed 8 December 2012.

Mintel (2011), 'Consumer attitudes toward luxury goods – US-march 2011', http://academic.mintel.com/display/543136/#. Accessed 26 September 2013.

Okonkwo, Uche (2007), *Luxury Fashion Branding*, New York: Palgrave Macmillan.

Otay, Anne-Marie (2009), 'Secondhand shops see uptick in sales', *Footwear News*, 1 June, http://www.wwd.com/footwear-news/markets/secondhand-shops-see-uptick-in-sales-2151911. Accessed 18 December 2012.

Radòn, Anita (2012), 'Unintended brand endorsers' impact on luxury brand image', *International Journal of Marketing Studies*, 4: 1, pp. 108–15.

Rath, Patricia Mink, Petrizzi, Richard and Gill, Penny (2012), *Marketing Fashion: A Global Perspective*, New York: Fairchild Books.

Silverstein, Michael J. and Fiske, Neil (2003), *Trading Up: The New American Luxury*, New York: Penguin.

Socha, Miles (2013), 'Hermès bullish on America', *Women's Wear Daily*, 3 September, http://www.wwd.com/business-news/forecasts-analysis/hermes-bullish-on-america-7105987?src=search_links. Accessed 3 September 2013.

Thomas, Dana (2007), *Deluxe: How Luxury Lost Its Luster*, New York: Penguin.

United States Census Bureau (2013), 'Historical income tables: Households', http://www.census.gov/hhes/www/income/data/historical/. Accessed 10 October 2013.

Vigneron, Franck and Johnson, Lester W. (1999), 'A review and conceptual framework of prestige-seeking consumer behavior', *Academy of Marketing Science Review*, 1999: 1, pp. 1–15.

Warren, Marcus (2004), 'Martha Stewart goes to court in high style: Totes $7,800 bag for jury selection', *National Post*, 23 January, p. A12.

CONTRIBUTOR DETAILS

Tasha L. Lewis (Ph.D.) is an Assistant Professor in the Department of Fiber Science & Apparel Design at Cornell University. Her current research involves fashion brand management, sustainability in the apparel supply chain, and consumer-facing fashion technologies. Tasha Lewis is the corresponding author.

Brittany Haas graduated from Cornell University with a degree in Fiber Science & Apparel Design. She has worked at top luxury and designer brands including Ralph Lauren, Saks Fifth Avenue and Hermès where her current role is the Hermès of Paris USA Merchandise Manager.

Contact: Cornell University, College of Human Ecology, Department of Fiber Science & Apparel Design, 37 Forest Home Drive, Ithaca, NY 14853, USA.
E-mail: tll28@cornell.edu

Global Fashion Brands: Style, Luxury & History
© 2014 Intellect Ltd Chapter. English language. doi: 10.1386/GFB.1.179_1

OSMUD RAHMAN AND LAUREN PETROFF
Ryerson University

Communicating brand image through fashion designers' homes, flagship stores and ready-to-wear collections

ABSTRACT

The objective of this exploratory study is to examine how the appearance of a designer's home, flagship store and fashion collection might influence consumer perception towards that designer's brand. Convenience sampling and in-depth interviews were used, and six female subjects (aged 23–39) were recruited for this study. Our findings suggest that viewers were able to recall information from their memories and generate meanings through their observations of magazine photographs of designers' homes, flagship stores and fashion styles. When the image perceptions of a designer's personal living space were congruent with the viewer-held brand concept, it reinforced and strengthened the overall brand image. Through various visual cues or 'props', viewers were able to visualize, interpret, query and portray a designer's perceived image. It is evident that viewers can make judgements and predictions of the personality of the home owner/inhabitant based on his/her material possessions. This study suggests that, in addition to the direct communication strategies such as flagship stores and a designer's collection, a designer's personal domestic interior can be used as a communication strategy to further connect with prospective consumers.

KEYWORDS

fashion designers
domestic interior
flagship stores
fashion styles
brand image
consumer perception

INTRODUCTION

Image is one of the significant aspects of brand knowledge. It can be described as the 'consumer perception and interpretation of a cluster of associated attributes, benefits and values' (Batey 2008). K. L. Keller (2003) suggests that brand associations are nodes of information that are perceived and stored in the brain, based on stimuli from any encounter that an individual may have with the brand. From this perspective, what resonates the most with consumers/viewers can be considered a 'touch point' for the communication of beliefs and meanings.

To build a strong image, the integrated marketing communications (IMC) approach emphasizes the importance of creating a consistent brand message across all channels (Rowley 2004). As many researchers have previously suggested (Duncan and Moriarty 1998; Solomon and Englis 1994), the IMC approach can be used to reinforce a brand message and positively influence consumer perception towards a specific brand. In other words, an effective communication strategy must convey a consistent and coherent message to the public regardless of its format – including direct/planned and indirect/unplanned strategies. To understand this complex interplay and congruity among different communication channels or 'touch points', the current study examined messages conveyed by both direct and indirect communication strategies. We chose the visual images of a designer's personal home environment (indirect strategy) and the designer's flagship store and runway collection (direct strategies) as vehicles to assess the salient impact of these communication 'touch points'. Considering a designer's home as an indirect form of communication is grounded in the assumption that one's personal possessions serve as a means of self-expression (Belk 1988; Csikszentmihalyi and Rochberg-Halton 1981).

According to our research, in addition to photos of fashion collections, visual images of designers' homes and flagship stores are increasingly shared with modern consumers through magazines, websites and other media, some examples being *W Magazine, Elle Decoration, Interior Design,* Interiordesign. net, mylusciousLife.com, preciouslyme.com, home-styling.blogspot.com and ft.com, to name a few. In this digital age, people can learn about a designer's lifestyle and persona more easily than ever before. Similarly, designers can present their ideology, lifestyle and image through a range of aesthetic vehicles. One's home and clothing are closely associated with the user/dweller, and are often considered as 'second skins' in which people can gain information of an individual (Jager 1983; Solomon 1986). Thus, it is not uncommon to see many established fashion designers extending their clothing lines to create home collections (e.g., Ralph Lauren Home, Donna Karan Home Collections and Calvin Klein Home) in order to communicate their lifestyles and ideologies.

Although many prior research studies (e.g., Akhter et al. 1994; Fulberg 2003) focused on the retail store environment and the brand image it communicated, no literature currently available relates to the particular topic of the private interior space as a form of communication of designer brand image. Our objective is to examine how a designer's personal home environment, flagship store and fashion collection may all work together to influence consumer perception towards a fashion brand.

Designers' ideologies and tastes can be manifested consciously and unconsciously through different aspects of creation and representation. Although domestic home and retail space serve different functions, we believe that simi-larities can be found in both spatial environments.

A number of research questions were raised to direct and guide this study:

- How do viewers perceive and interpret visual elements in designers' homes (private spaces) in relation to their flagship stores (public spaces) and recent runway seasonal styles (collections)?
- How do these three elements reinforce/enhance viewers' associative network and influence their perceptions towards the brand image?
- How do similarities and differences among visual contents play out in the context of brand association?
- Can these elements be strategically used to complement and reinforce each other?

THE DESIGNER'S PERSONAL HOME ENVIRONMENT

Home is often considered to be 'the "place" of greatest personal significance' (Proshansky et al. 1983: 60). Individuals personalize their personal living spaces with material goods to reflect and communicate their own distinctive personal-ities, tastes and interests (Csikszentmihalyi and Rochberg-Halton 1981; Hauge 2011). However, to feature a designer's home in a magazine does not merely reveal his/her private inner world, but also creates an important touch-point to arouse interest and provide entertainment to the magazine's readers. In other words, when exposed in the public media, a designer's home can raise interest, increase publicity, provoke excitement and arouse emotion. As Richard Salecl points out in his study of the exposure of privacy in today's culture, '[…] we have an increasing desire to see what is supposed to be hidden' (2002: 4).

Consumers often perceive a brand image based on their current or previous knowledge and experience of various associative stimuli. When designers open up their homes through the mass media, this can become part of the associa-tive stimuli, provoking readers to ask, 'Does the name behind the label actu-ally live the image and lifestyle that his or her brand preaches?' In exposing their domestic spaces, designers are figuratively setting the stage for an evalu-ation of their personal lifestyles and private worlds which may – whether they are aware of it or not – influence viewer perceptions and attitudes towards them as well as their brands. Indeed, the display of a designer's home can be deliberately employed as an indirect communicative strategy to manifest personal lifestyle and taste through material objects and their spatial organi-zations. Holbrook et al. (1990) points out that personal possessions often serve as 'props' for the expression of self-image. In other words, the home interior, furniture and decorative elements can be considered to be signifiers, or non-verbal communicators, providing symbolic clues to viewers about the owner's identity, societal status, aesthetic preferences, and personality traits (Cupchik et al. 2003). As E. S. Casey asserts, 'there is no place without self; and no self without place' (2001: 406).

According to E. K. Sadalla et al. (1987), viewers are able to infer a home-owner's self-perceived lifestyle, personality and image to a significant degree when the images of the interior of a home are presented to them. In addi-tion, a study conducted by M. Bonnes et al. (1987) found that the creation of a living-room environment not only conveys the owner's aesthetic values but also reflects his or her interpretation of the social activities that will happen there. Homes, like clothing, can be seen as symbolic vehicles to construct identity, express individual taste and engage social interactions.

Indeed, houses are often chosen, modified and decorated in such a way that they are symbolically appropriate for the inhabitants (Sadalla et al. 1987). It is important to note that although the interior space can be co-created with other individuals such as an interior designer, family members and/or significant others, it is reasonable to believe that a creative person (e.g., a fashion designer) will exert great influence during the co-creation process. As A. J. Clark reported, 'Kelly [informant] sees the room as an expression of her talents as a [dress] designer, […] Kelly views her living room as a testament to her 'know-how' and individual artistic flair' (2001: 34).

Our study investigates whether by considering the exposure of one's home as part of the strategy of brand building, designers could offer consumers entertainment while also helping their consumers to construct and build a relationship with a 'face behind the brand'. However, creating a convincing message is an important yet daunting task in today's hyper-stimulating society.

THE FLAGSHIP STORE

'Flagship stores' can be defined as large or 'mega' establishments located in prime and prestigious locations that offer a full range of merchandise and novel shopping experiences (Kent 2007). There is a growing body of research dealing with the significance of flagship stores in a range of different venues encompassing themed flagship brand stores (Kozinets et al. 2002), high-end fashion flagship stores (Moore and Doherty 2009), flagship hotels (Collins 2009), virtual flagships (Jackson 2009) and flagship supermarkets (Kirby 2009).

In contrast to private and domestic spaces, flagship stores are 'open to the public', linked to shopping activities, and directly associated with brand image. A successful flagship store should manifest an ideal brand image, and offer a memorable and pleasant experience to shoppers.

It is evident that the flagship store is increasingly popular as a marketing strategy to build relationships with consumers (Kozinets et al. 2002), create awareness and interest (Moore et al. 2000), and provide spaces for interactivity, socialization and communication (Kent 2009). Thus, flagship stores do not merely serve as places/spaces for purchases, but also for socializing, leisure and 'shoppertainment' (Edelson 2010). For example, the Aeropostale flagship store in New York's Times Square uses high-tech interactivity (animated LED billboards) to engage shoppers (Edelson 2010).

Although there are many attributes in the retail environment that may influence consumer perception and experience (Brengman and Willems 2009), the present study focuses primarily on a store's interior design and spatial organization rather than its 'ambient factors' (music and temperature), merchandise, service and post-transaction satisfaction. Without a doubt, interior design and decor play a significant role in the experience of customer participation, connectivity and interactivity (Kent 2009). Shoppers often decode and create meaning from the spatial environment through their personal interpretations, perceptions, understanding and imagination (Gieryn 2000).

FASHION COLLECTION

Innovative design does not merely reflect a designer's creativity and vision, but also displays and manifests the designer's personal self, beliefs and values. According to A. Spindler (1997: 11), Marc Jacobs' individualistic signature, for example, 'comes from within, from a life, from a circle of friends and from an awareness of contemporary culture […]'. Y. Kawamura (2005: 35) adds, 'Today's designers place the strongest emphasis in recreating and reproducing their image, and the image that is projected through clothing is reflected on the designer's personal image as an individual. Both the fashion and music industries, in this sense, are image-making industries'. Clearly, the individual designer and brand image play a vital part in selection choices and buying decisions, as they provide inferential and associative meanings to consumers. The runway collection thus becomes an important marketing tool to express designers' ideologies, to build brand image, to communicate with the public, and to elicit a variety of symbolic meanings and psychological responses (Kwang et al. 2008). For example, Marc Jacobs is often associated with 'good creative and aesthetic taste' (Currid 2007: 142), and is considered 'individualistic, hip, detached cool' (Tokatli 2011: 6). His 2010 Marc by Marc Jacobs collection featured a wide array of fun, creative and aesthetic elements encompassing giant bunny head bows, mixed prints (polka dot, plaid, gingham and tribal patterns) and a wide array of colours. As stated on myitthings.com blog, the Marc by Marc Jacobs collection was 'cute, playful, and true to the brand's quirky aesthetic'.

Fashion styles change at a much faster pace than do designers' homes and their flagship stores. Modern consumers are accustomed to the idea that 'clothes come, or go, in and out of fashion' (Bernard 2010: 23). In other words, fashion styles are fleeting and ephemeral, whereas interior design and architecture are relatively more permanent and static (Potvin 2010). Thus, it is interesting and meaningful to find out what role the interior space and fashion style may play in brand communication.

Many research studies of domestic space are rooted in environmental psychology. 'Housing and identity' has been one crucial theme (Cieraad 1999); this concept encompasses such areas as domestic symbols and the self (Csikszentmihalyi and Rochberg-Halton 1981), housing as presentation of self (Duncan and Duncan 1976) and identity symbolism in housing (Sadalla et al. 1987). Over the last twenty years, western domestic space (practice and objects), flagship stores and clothing consumption have all been the subject of consumer studies from diverse disciplines that include fashion, retail management, psychology, sociology and anthropology. Despite the growing body of literature, most prior studies have examined personal home, flagship store and fashion styles individually, rather than investigating how these elements reinforce and interact with each other in order to strengthen the brand image. However, since all three of these areas are concerned with the notion of creativity, they should not be viewed as separate entities. The current study attempts to address a subject that has been neglected in previous research by studying the significance of the relationships among these three areas.

RESEARCH METHOD

Sample selection

Convenience sampling and in-depth interviews were used for this study. In total, six female subjects (aged 23–39) were recruited. Females were chosen because they are in general more fashion conscious than males (Beaudoin et al. 2003), and frequently connect with fashion retailers through various media such as magazines, store displays and the Internet. All informants recruited for this study were interested in fashion, and had some knowledge

and personal experience with our focal designer brands (as shown in
Table 1) – although some of them might have never seen the designers' resi-
dences through magazine or other media before. To ensure that each partici-
pant met these criteria, a series of screening questions was posed before the
interview was conducted.

			Stage 1: Prior to Image Grouping		
Pseudonym	**Age**	**Occupation**	**What fashion and home magazines do you usually read?**	**Focal designer**	**Information source/ familiarity with focal fashion designers**
Sarah	23	Real Estate Analyst	*Vogue, Harpers Bazaar, W Magazine* and *House & Home*	Tory Burch	Owned a couple of items, had read about her, and had seen her products in department stores
				Alexander Wang	Owned a few items, had read about his clothes
Sally	23	Online Account Manager	*Vogue* and *Elle*	Tory Burch	Had been to her store in Florida, read about her in magazines and visited her company website
				Alexander Wang	Less familiar; had read about him in magazine
Jane	24	Store Associate/ Student	*Harpers Bazaar, W Magazine, Vogue* and *Style at Home*	Tory Burch	Had studied in fashion school, seen her designs in the stores, in magazines, on company websites and blogs
				Alexander Wang	Owned his products, studied him in school, had seen his products in stores and magazines, on company website and blogs
Beth	28	Architect	*Wallpaper, Dwell, Lush, I.D., Frame, Vogue* and *Vanity Fair*	Tory Burch	Had read about her in maga- zines during fashion week, in the media, on blogs and websites, and had been to her stores in Las Vegas and Florida
				Alexander Wang	Had read about him in maga- zines, during fashion week, in the media, on blogs and websites, and had seen his products in department stores
Laura	38	Part-time Nurse	*House & Home, House Beautiful, Style at Home, Elle, Vogue* and *Harpers Bazaar*	Tory Burch	More familiar with her accessories and handbags and had read about her in magazines, blogs and websites

				Alexander Wang	Had read about him in magazines, on blogs and websites
Mary	39	Charity Coordinator	*InStyle* and *Allure*	Tory Burch	Had read about her in magazines and TV, been to her stores in Las Vegas, and owned her products
				Alexander Wang	Recognized his name but did not know much about him

Table 1: Summary of informants' profiles and information sources prior to image grouping.

Designer brand selection

The selection criteria of designers' brands was based on a number of factors including the eminence of their brand presence in North America; their substantial exposure in print media; and the presence of a flagship store in New York City. New York City was selected due to its geographic proximity to the researchers and participants as well as its significance as a location for flagship stores (Fernie et al. 1998). The focal designers we chose for this study had appeared frequently in mainstream fashion magazines over the last three years, with at least one article featuring their place of residence and flagship store in New York City. Based on the above selection criteria and the results of a pilot survey, two individuals were identified and selected for this study: Tory Burch and Alexander Wang.

Visual stimuli and photograph elicitation interview

In-depth photography elicitation interviews are deemed to be essential to gaining a comprehensive understanding of how viewers interpret and perceive images. Interviewing with photographs can reduce stress and fatigue, evoke deeper human consciousness than 'words-alone' interviews (Harper 2002), and can generate multiple meanings/'polysemy' (Barthes 1964).

In the current study, three sets of visual stimuli were used as a vehicle to elicit informants' perceptions and opinions (Samuels 2004). In total, 30 digital images were taken from various magazine and fashion websites (see Table 2 for additional information). In order to avoid possible bias and to assist viewers in focusing strictly on the physical objects and spatial environment, three images of the designers' homes were digitally altered to blur the presence of the designer.

Data-collection procedures

Three stages of data collection were undertaken in order to fully understand each informant's reactions towards the visual stimuli. In stage one, interviews began with screening questions about informants' familiarity with the focal designers (Tory Burch and Alexander Wang), and their habitual sources of fashion information (e.g., fashion/lifestyle magazines), as shown in Tables 1 and 2. To establish a general idea about how the informants perceived each focal designer, they were asked to freely elicit their top-of-mind brand association prior to image grouping. Their responses indicated that in general, informants perceived Tory Burch as classic (n=3) and feminine (n=3), and said her designs often consisted of orange colour (n=3) and silk (n=4), whereas Alexander Wang was perceived overwhelmingly as edgy (n=5), and his collection was said to

Focal designer	Visual stimuli	Image source	Selection criteria
Tory Burch	Domestic home (five images)	*Elle* (2009)	Featured at least once online or on the magazine; home in New York City
	Flagship store (four images)	The Tory Blog (2011)	Featured at least once online or on the magazine; flagship store in New York City
	Fashion collection (six images)	Style.com (2011)	Recent collection: Fall, 2011 Ready-to-Wear (RTW) and Spring, 2012 RTW
Alexander Wang	Domestic home (five images)	*W Magazine* (2011)	Featured at least once online or in a magazine; home in New York City
	Flagship store (four images)	America Blog (2011) and *Rose for Lilli* (2011)	Featured at least once online or in a magazine; flagship store in New York City
	Fashion collection (six images)	Style.com (2011)	Recent collection: Fall, 2011 RTW and Spring, 2012 RTW

Table 2: Visual stimuli and image source.

often display black colour (n=5) and leather items (n=4). In stage one, informants were also asked demographic questions such as their age and occupation.

In stage two, informants were presented with the photographic images, which included the designers' homes, their flagship stores, and their recent ready-to-wear collections. Participants were asked to group these images into two categories (Tory Burch and Alexander Wang) with three sub-categories (designer's home, flagship store and collection), according to their perceptions and experiences of each designer brand. Once image grouping was accomplished, the researcher re-arranged the images into the correct clusters and then invited informants to provide comments. In the final stage, an in-depth, semi-structured interview was conducted to collect information concerning viewers' perceptions, reactions, assessments and inferences. For example, interview questions included, 'What kind of elements make you believe that it's Tory Burch or Alexander Wang?', 'What kind of lifestyle do the images reflect?', 'What is your first reaction to his/her home, flagship store and collection?' and 'Do you find consistency or congruency among his/her home, flagship store and collection?'

Data analysis

In order to generate meaningful and significant results, we adopted an interpretive approach and used content analysis for this study. Content analysis is a 'systematic, replicable technique for compressing many words of text into fewer content categories' (Stemler 2001), and it allows us to 'make inferences by objectively and systematically identifying specific characteristics of messages' (Stemler 2001). Qualitative content analysis aims at being structured and systematic but still analytic by looking at the depth and breadth of the data being analysed (McNabb 2002).

Coding is an important tool for qualitative content analysis. This research employed emergent coding conducted by two researchers. Following a preliminary examination of the data, a provisional checklist was devised, based on the interview transcripts and grouping commentary and observations. In Vivo codes (Saldaña 2009) were used to identify and classify significant categories (as shown in Table 3), including atomistic view/specific objects (e.g., furniture, chandeliers, pillows, coats, shoes, etc.) and holistic view/spatial organization (e.g., spacious), perceived associative meanings (e.g., masculine, cool, inviting, comfortable) and viewer's inferential/implicative meanings (e.g., match with the brand logo). Explanations of personal view points will be presented in the following sections (e.g., Social Gatherings/Entertainment: 'It reminds me of someone who would like to have a dinner party').

	Visual Attributes	Associative Meaning	Informant's Perceptions and Responses	
Tory Burch Domestic Home *Line art illustration to show specific objects; not actual visual stimuli*			Traditional/Classic and Modern/Contemporary Co-Exist	Designer/Brand Image
	▪ Orange colour ▪ Chevron pattern ▪ Settee	Traditional Modern	'She always uses the classic orange [...] so overall it has a traditional look, but she mixes with modern accents and more youthful elements such as chevron pattern and little settee. [...] Some rooms are more contemporary and some are more classical.' (Beth)	'Especially orange is associated with her brand. [...] Same thing with her home, like orange zig-zag pattern - the colours and the style really carry through with her personal style.' (Beth) 'That's a Tory Burch colour - the bright orange [refer to her store], and the shape of the chandelier is reminiscent of her logo.' (Mary)
Tory Burch Flagship Store *Line art illustration to show specific objects; not actual visual stimuli*			Traditional and Playful	Coherence
	▪ Orange colour ▪ Purple ikat cushions	▪ Tradition ▪ Playful/ Fun	'Her flagship store is interesting because it's very much like her home - the interweaving of traditional and contemporary, which I think is why Tory Burch did so well.' (Jane) 'Well, it's fun in a way [...] there are playful patterns like the purple ikat on the cushions and chairs; and the bright orange lacquered walls are obviously fun.' (Sarah)	'It's got a lot of detail like her home – it's similar in feel to her home, like lots of contrasting patterns and contrasting colours with the oranges and purples, and gold.' (Laura)

Table 3: Examples of informants' perceptions and responses towards visual stimuli.

FINDINGS AND DISCUSSION

In Stage 1, all informants reported familiarity with the focal designers, although one informant (Mary) said that she only recognized the name of Alexander Wang but not his style. All respondents stated that they purchased and read mainstream fashion magazines such as *Vogue*, *InStyle*, *Elle* and *Harpers Bazaar*.

In addition, most informants read mainstream interior-design magazines, and four informants indicated that they often found fashion information from online sources such as magazine websites and blogs (Table 1).

Image grouping

In each interview, all informants were asked to participate in an image-grouping exercise. The instructions were to arrange all images into two groups based on their judgment of which personal home environment, flagship store and ready-to-wear collection appeared to them as belonging to the individual focal fashion designers.

With respect to the designers' flagship stores, every informant grouped three or more images correctly for Alexander Wang and five grouped three or more correctly for Tory Burch. When discussing the rationale for making image-grouping decisions, informants generally said they had relied on their past perceptions of the designers' image and brand image. They also used visual similarities between images, such as the coherence of colour and style, to guide their decisions on the inclusion or exclusion of a picture from any group.

Once image grouping was completed, the researcher re-arranged the images into the correct clusters and then invited informants to provide comments and an in-depth, semi-structured interview was conducted to collect information about viewers' perceptions, reactions, assessments and inferences. Informants provided a lot of information and insights regarding the interior décor of both domestic home and flagship store, however, they offered relatively less feedback about the collection styles. There are two possible explanations for this outcome. First, it could be difficult to retrieve information from their memory because fashion is ephemeral – the cognitive processing could require more time (Brach 2012). As such, a number of informants stumbled and paused during their responses to designers' collections. For example, Sally expressed, 'I don't really know how to articulate [refer to Tory Burch collection]. Um, it's pretty contemporary and fun, [pause] but there are still some elements that seem more traditional'. Second, some design elements within a garment could be less tangible, and may not be amenable to dissection and easy understanding (Rahman 2011). For example, one informant described Alexander Wang's clothing as cool; however, she was not able to point to the exact design feature to substantiate her view. Clearly, some informants made their judgments based on their holistic views (total/whole impressions) instead of atomistic views (specific design features).

Figures 1–2: Image grouping process.

Symbol of meanings

Tory Burch – traditional with contemporary flair

Many informants found that Tory Burch's apartment was 'super' traditional in its design aesthetic. For example, one of the informants (Sally) said, 'It's like over-the-top traditional, and I just picture like a lady from Connecticut sitting in this living room with the floral upholsteries, and the traditional wood coffee tables, and the crystal chandelier'. Although the overall impression was traditional, some informants stated that there were several elements (e.g., green floors in the kitchen, orange drapery in the living room) that contained a contemporary flair.

Most of the informants also mentioned that Tory Burch's domestic interior felt like a family home belonging to an upper-class person who enjoyed entertaining and hosting dinner parties. They said that the highly functional kitchen with large work surfaces and the inviting dining area with a traditional round dining table conjured up ideas of close social gatherings. Indeed, furniture and interior decorations/accessories play an important role in how an owner's image and identity is projected. As Mary Haweis asserted in her *Art of Decoration* (1881: 17), 'furniture is a kind of dress, dress is a kind of furniture, which both mirror the mind of the owner, and the temper of the age'. In addition, some informants perceived Burch's home as feminine and playful. For example:

> All of [the images of Tory Burch's domestic home] seem very feminine with the colour choice, but the living room definitely seems the most feminine to me. […] The abundance of colour, and fun floral patterns or the zigzag in the closet seems youthful and playful.
>
> (Sarah)

In response to the images of Tory Burch's New York flagship store, all informants described it as luxurious and feminine. They felt that the personality of the store seemed to be fun, yet sophisticated, which was echoed in the description of the design style as a mix of traditional and contemporary. While elements such as furniture style, heavy drapery and indulgent molding represent a traditional aesthetic, the playful mix of bold prints and bright colours created a youthful and contemporary sensibility. These findings clearly demonstrated that physical/material objects can provide viewers with points of reference (Gioia and Chittipeddi 1991), evoke open-ended interpretations (Weick 1995), and generate a multitude of responses including both cognitive and emotional (Oldham et al. 1995). As one informant (Lauren) commented, 'The space is contemporary, not in a way where there are straight lines and hard edges. It is a modern take on traditional design, where new ideas are paired with traditional, formal design'.

Indeed, specific design elements in her flagship store also considered to be playful and fun encompassing the deep purple ikat design patterns, decorative pillows, the leopard carpet, and the brave application of bright orange lacquer on the walls. Another informant (Mary) described the retail space: '[…] the display case and the lighting make me imagine a jewel box. […] It's like in *Pretty Woman* when Richard Gere opens the box and closes it and he makes her laugh'.

In regard to Tory Burch's ready-to-wear fashion runway shows, informants stated that they perceived the wearers to be young and fun, yet desiring to

project a sophisticated image. Both Fall 2011 and Spring 2012 garment silhouettes were described as classic; specifically, participants found that the summer
dresses, tunics and shrunken jackets referenced tried-and-true shapes. Modern
elements, such as glittery surface embellishments, flirty patterns and warm
bright colours, injected a youthful appeal to the outfits. As Sarah stated,

> With the bright colours, [the clothing items] definitely seem like Tory
> Burch to me. The decoration on the bottom of this dress, and the polka-
> dot pattern are fun, flirty and playful [...]. Someone who's urban and
> wants to look classic and sophisticated, but still young and fun, would
> wear these clothes.

With this perspective and analysis, it is reasonable to conclude that the images
projected by Tory Burch's home, flagship store and collection are consistent.
As some informants concluded:

> Tory Burch, I think that her home, her store and her clothes are all
> similar. I think that she likes a lot of different contrasts of textures and
> colours and things that make you look twice, and maybe for a little
> longer to take it all in. I really think she lives the image of her brand.
>
> (Laura)

> She has really strong branding in her stores, and um the way the
> product is displayed is really consistent with her brand, like chandelier
> and even the millwork ... so to me that's really obvious. Same thing
> with her home [...] the colours and the style really carry through with
> her personal style.
>
> (Beth)

Alexander Wang – urban, edgy, indulgent and modern

Alexander Wang's Manhattan apartment was found to be urban, edgy and
indulgent. Our informants said that the décor within his personal living space
conjured a rock-and-roll lifestyle full of heavy socializing and late-night party-
ing. Wang's overall design aesthetic was interpreted as contemporary due to
its experimental mix of hard and soft elements. The blatant display of elec-
tronics (audio speakers) created a space that was also perceived to be masculine; this finding is in accord with the viewpoint of M. Csikszentmihalyi and
E. Rochbery-Halton (1981) that male possessors cherish objects of action (e.g.,
televisions, stereo sets and trophies) more frequently than do females, who
prefer objects of contemplation (e.g., photographs, textiles and plants). The
modern chrome and glass of pieces, such as tables and chair bases, coupled
with the abundant use of animal skins, furs and hides in pieces such as the
zebra rug, fur blanket and shaggy living room chair, created a very distinct
space. Additionally, informants said that the lack of colour, dark look and
high contrast between the overall black and white elements created an uninviting and uncomfortable feeling.

Based on the images shown of Alexander Wang's New York flagship
store, most informants felt that the overall modern and contemporary was
a successful retail environment and that it was more inviting than his home.
The architectural details (high ceilings restored Corinthian columns and a

cage) evoked an edgy and luxuriously designed shopping environment. One informant (Sarah) said that these elements 'add a pop of edginess. It's a little cheeky in such an obviously expensive space to throw up a hammock and a cage'. Overall, informants indicated that the space felt edgy and cool, and it conjured a creative, alternative, fashionable and indulgent lifestyle.

It was perceived that Alexander Wang's customers were confident, youthful, cool, edgy, skinny and rich, with rock-and-roll persona. For example, Alexander Wang's typical follower was described as an 'edgy and cool New Yorker who lives a fast-paced, stylish lifestyle […]. I see wearing [those clothes] daytime into the evening: to work and then to drinks afterwards' (Beth). While informants acknowledged that the fashion was designed for a female wearer, they felt the appearance was decidedly androgynous but yet masculine with unique hard edges. Wang's Fall 2011 fashion collection was seen to be dominated by the use of luxurious black materials such as silk and fur. This contrasted with the Spring 2012 apparel, where the dominant look had a sportswear influence. Although the styles were generally perceived as edgy and cool, many of them were deemed unwearable; which was based on the garments' unflattering and 'different' silhouettes and patterns.

Interestingly, both Alexander Wang's home and collection were perceived edgy and cool, and yet his home was seen as uninviting and his collection as unwearable. Nevertheless, it was agreed that the execution of the design and details was thoughtful and impressive, and his store was perceived to be relatively more inviting and welcoming than his residence. Overall, the image of Alexander Wang's home, flagship store and collection were still considered as consistent according to the vast majority of our informants' responses. For example:

> I'd say the store, the residential space and the Fall line are all similar in terms of colours, level of edginess and youthfulness to an extent… they appeal to a specific demographic. And the Spring line, especially if you mix and match some of those pieces, it could appeal to a much broader range of people, but definitely still edgy, still youthful. […] Residential space, commercial setting and fashion collection of Alexander Wang are so consistent and it strengthens his brand image.
>
> (Beth)

> If you look at his clothes and his actual house they're actually very similar, like, I mean who has a fur chair? And he uses fur for his collection too… a fur coat, fur boots and fur slippers [one of the Fall 2011 images]. I could see him, like… it's very creative, also masculine, which his clothing is so androgynous. But I can see someone in his clothes going to party at his apartment.
>
> (Jane)

Visual elements provoke perceived images

Whether they based their ideas on the designers' homes, their flagship stores or fashion styles from recent runway collections, it was clear that our informants were able to develop and articulate a conceivable persona, lifestyle and/or social tableau for the designers. As stated in the preceding sections, Tory Burch was perceived as classic, fun and playful, while Alexander Wang was perceived as cool, edgy, contemporary and modern. Without a doubt, an individual's possessions can serve as a stage or 'performance' in which one's personality and social characteristics can be displayed and communicated to the public (Goffman 1959). In other words, material objects and spatial organizations can be used as 'props' for the expression of an individual self (Holbrook et al. 1990; Rahman et al. 2012), and through these various visual cues viewers are able to visualize, query, interpret and portray their perceived image of each designer. As such, viewers can make judgements on the personality of an owner/inhabitant based on his/her material possessions (Wilson and Mackenzie 2000).

Perception of Tory Burch – feminine, girly, young and fun

Informants perceived Tory Burch to be a socialite who enjoyed spending time with her family, decorating and entertaining friends. In reviewing informants' responses, it comes clear to us that it is not merely the interior space that creates a perceived or imaginative image of the inhabitant, but also the interior decoration and the social activities that were likely to take place in the private/public space (Pennartz 1999). For example, some statements include: 'She [Tory Burch] likes having guests over and sharing her personality through her space. [....] It really seems like the type of space that she's having people over to fabulous parties [...] with people that use the word fabulous a lot' (Beth). The persona perceived when viewing the Tory Burch store was '[...] a young, fun, flirty girl in her twenties or thirties. The store is sophisticated, but still playful. It's not oppressive, and I don't feel like a young woman would feel out of place in this setting' (Jane). On the basis of Tory Burch's fashion collections, informants imagined the wearer was: '[...] feminine and very girly. She would want to live the classic, traditional lifestyle of settling down with a guy, getting married and having babies' (Jane).

Perception of Alexander Wang – individualistic, cool, urban and edgy

On the basis of viewing images of Alexander Wang's home environment, informants perceived him as cool, urban guy who lived an edgy, rock-and-roll lifestyle. For example, one informant said,

> The fact that these meticulously thrown carpets, the fact that none of the furniture matches – it just goes – it just reminds me of a place where musicians hangout [...] and I guess for successful musicians, I see them as being able to afford, you know, such expensive things, but they do it in a little bit of a nonchalant way.
>
> (Jane)

Images of the Alexander Wang flagship store elicited comments that he was perceived as 'forward-thinking, modern, edgy' and 'slightly alternative'. Based on the images of Alexander Wang's fashion collections, participants imagined the wearer to be a confident, individualistic person who was not concerned with following mainstream trends. Informants said that people who chose to wear these unusual, edgy pieces did not care what others thought of their style.

This research interpretation strongly suggests that viewers were able to cognitively construct an associative lifestyle through knowledge of the designer's home environment, their flagship store and the fashions that they produce. While the home and fashion products were clear examples of the visual cues or 'props' that can serve as an expression of a self-image, it can be argued that the flagship store environment was visually 'read' in the same way. The store atmosphere or 'store design factors' including functional and aesthetic design aspects (layout, style and colour) were the most important elements for viewers/customers in eliciting a brand personality or image (Brengman and Willems 2009: 348).

Totality and consistency of brand image

Based on the visual stimuli for each designer, it is evident that our informants were able to extract certain information (from specific elements and spatial organization) that parallel or 'fit' with their perception of each designer's aesthetic style and brand image. Our results clearly demonstrated that visual stimuli including images of private domestic space and public spaces can trigger brand-related associations and thoughts in viewers' memories (Keller 2005).

The consensus of the study was that the visual and mental congruities were clear among Tory Burch's and Alexander Wang's respective personal homes, flagship stores and runway collections. Other than the visual stimuli, informants also said that both designers' private living spaces fit well with what was perceived to be their brand image, and it was evident that their home interiors strengthened the brand image and identity. For Tory Burch, one informant said that '[the image of her home] strengthens her brand image because everything is so consistent. You're seeing that she's doing what she loves, and her influence affects everything she touches – she's living within a consistent realm' (Jane). Laura echoed that opinion, stating, 'I think that her home and her store and her clothes are all similar. [....] I really think she lives the image of her brand [...] she certainly has a direction'. For Alexander Wang, Sarah said '[...] the home is so indicative of his image and design direction. It reinforces my idea of him because it makes him seem even more authentic – he's living the same image that he's designing for'.

CONCLUSION

We believe that the present study was able to capture and collect subjective interpretations and viewpoints from our informants in order to draw a collective overview of viewers' perceptions and judgments. According to I. Rogoff (2001: 24), every element related to visual culture is 'read on to and through one another, lending ever-accruing layers of meanings and of subjective responses'. It is evident that in viewing the homes of Tory Burch and Alexander Wang, the perceived brand image could be reinforced or strengthened.

According to M. Lindstrom, the more elements a consumer can recognize and relate to, the more effective a brand resonance will be. Thus, consistent communication strategies play a vital role in developing and building a brand image – they foster familiarity, reliability, and ultimately render brand trustworthiness (Lindstrom 2002). Some prior studies (Bornstein 1990; Kohli and Thakor 2002) additionally indicated that repeated stimulus exposure (stimulus habituation) would increase a viewer's familiarity with and appreciation for an object.

Managerial implications of opening personal homes to public display

Based on the fact that the nature of this study was exploratory with a limited investigative scope, the results should not be generalized to a larger population. However, the findings can offer some insights and meaningful recommendations regarding the overt display of a designer's personal home environment in the mainstream media.

It is important to note that viewers often look for visual and cognitive information to match or harmonize with their pre-established/-perceived impression of a brand. This is especially true when designers are the name-sakes of their brands, as their personal 'selves' are inextricably connected with their brand images and product lines. However, when viewers are confronted with frequent incongruity, they are more likely to end up with a cognitive dissonance. Therefore, fashion designers who reveal their domestic living spaces to the public – whether they are doing it as a means of self-expression or indulgence, or because the editorial staff of a magazine is interested in the entertainment value – should consider their overall brand images as part of their ultimate intentions.

Another implication, closely linked to the preceding one, is that the prep-aration and arrangement of private living spaces for photo shoots should be carefully considered. The display of a designer's domestic interior (both contents and contexts) in a magazine is critically important for the formation of the viewer's perception. Even the smallest details can help viewers to paint an elaborate mental picture of the homeowner's lifestyle.

One of the important findings of this research is that once an associa-tion is perceived, it will become part of the information network contributing to a designer's brand image. In other words, props that are brought into the spatial environment may transcend their physical form and gain symbolic and aesthetic meaning. Therefore, those individuals involved with the work on the other side of the camera lens should be aware of how various objects, décor, and spatial organizations can shift perception. In the case of Alexander Wang, many of our informants were affected by several intangible elements such as the lighting and photographic quality. The exposure, camera angles and image cropping ostensibly conjured the image and elusive aura that contributed to a specific interpretation and feeling about the lifestyle and social activities of a designer. Thus, the seemingly simple factor of photography has to be calcu-lated according to a designer's desired image and what their brand managers want to project into the public sphere.

Finally, if designers want to use their home as indirect communica-tive tool, it is imperative for them to make a clear visual link between their home environment and their brand image. This can be done on multiple levels, but ultimately it is important for consumers to connect a designer's home with the lifestyle image that the company wants to offer. Especially when reading a magazine, viewers should be presented with digestible images that clearly communicate intended information. At the most basic level, designers should be shown in their homes – living in their spaces. This simple choice allows a viewer to formulate a quick association between what they know about the designer's brand image and the perception of the designer's home. Even though the viewer may read in the text and find out who is the inhabitant of the featured home, a visual connection (prompted by the designer's presence) will resonate in viewer's memory more effectively.

Besides showing the actual designer in his/her home environment, creating a visual link between the domestic interior, the retail space, and the designer's fashion style can enhance and reinforce the connection. To convey a consistent message, selecting and utilizing cohesive fashion styles and home/store interiors through the layout of the magazine feature can do this. In the present study, we found that once the informants were clear about the images belonging to each designer, they were able to discuss their perceptions with greater ease.

FURTHER RESEARCH

Although the photographic images and settings of a designer's living space may be artificially created or 'staged' for magazine publication, we believe that the observations and judgments made by the viewers have validity, and will provide valuable information on branding and communication strategy. In addition, perceptions of a designer's home, flagship store and fashion collection could be varied across countries, geographical regions and consumer markets. Therefore, further in-depth cross-national study is deemed to be important particularly for fashion designers with multinational brands.

REFERENCES

Akhter, S. H., Andrews, J. C. and Durvasula, S. (1994), 'The influence of retail store environment on brand-related judgments', *Journal of Retailing and Consumer Services*, 1: 2, pp. 67–76.

Barthes, R. (1964), *The Responsibility of Forms: Critical Essays on Music, Art and Representation* (translator: H. Richard), Berkeley: University of California.

Batey, M. (2008), *Brand Meaning*, New York: Routledge.

Beaudoin, P., Lachance, M. J. and Robitaille, J. (2003), 'Fashion innovativeness, fashion diffusion and brand sensitivity among adolescents', *Journal of Fashion and Marketing Management*, 7: 1, pp. 23–30.

Belk, R. W. (1988), 'Possessions and the extended self', *Journal of Consumer Research*, 15: 2, pp. 139–68.

Bernard, M. (2010), 'Fashion statements: Communication and culture', in R. Scapp and B. Weitz (eds), *Fashion Statements: On Style, Appearance, and Reality*, Palgrave, New York, pp. 23–34.

Bonnes, M., Giuliani, M. V., Amoni, F. and Bernard, Y. (1987), 'Cross-cultural rules for the optimization of the living room', *Environment and Behaviour*, 19: 2, pp. 204–27.

Bornstein, R. F. (1990), 'Exposure and affect: Overview and meta-analysis of research, 1968–1987', *Psychology Bulletin*, 106(2), pp. 265–89.

Brach, A. M. (2012), 'Identity and intersubjectivity', in A. M. González and L. Bovone (eds), *Identities through Fashion: A Multidisciplinary Approach*, London, UK: Berg, pp. 48–64.

Brengman, M. and Willems, K. (2009), 'Determinants of fashion store personality: A consumer perspective', *Journal of Product & Brand Management*, 18: 5, pp. 246–355.

Casey, E. S. (2001), 'Body, self and landscape: A geographical inquiry into the place-world', in P. C. Adams, S. Hoelscher and K. E. Tills (eds), *Textures of Place*, Minneapolis: University of Minnesota Press, pp. 403–25.

Cieraad, I. (1999), 'Introduction: Anthropology at home', in I. Cieraad (ed.), *At Home: An Anthropology of Domestic Space*, Syracuse, NY: Syracuse University Press, pp. 1–10.

Clark, A. J. (2001), 'The aesthetics of social aspiration', in D. Miller (ed.), *Home Possessions*, Oxford, UK: Berg, pp. 23–45.

Collins, H. J. (2009), 'Emotion and identity in flagship luxury design', in T. Kent and R. Brown (eds), *Flagship Marketing: Concepts and Places*, New York, NY: Routledge, pp. 32–45.

Csikszentmihalyi, M. and Rochberg-Halton, E. (1981), *The Meaning of Things: Domestic Symbols and the Self*, Cambridge: Cambridge University Press.

Cupchik, G. C., Ritterfield, U. and Levin, J. (2003), 'Incidental learning of features from interior living spaces', *Journal of Environmental Psychology*, 23: 2, pp. 189–97.

Currid, E. (2007), *The Warhol Economy: How Fashion, Art, and Music Drive New York City*, Princeton, NJ: Princeton University Press.

Duncan, J. S. and Duncan, N. G. (1976), 'Housing as presentation of self and the structure of social networks', in G. T. Moore and R. G. Colledge (eds), *Environmental Knowing, Theories, Research, and Methods*, Stroudsburg, PA: Dowden, Hutchingson & Ross, pp. 247–53.

Duncan, T. and Moriarty, S. E. (1998), 'A communication-based marketing model for managing relationship', *Journal of Marketing*, 62: 2, pp. 1–13.

Edelson, S. (2010), 'Aropostale's interactive flagship', *Women's Wear Daily*, 21 October, 200:84.

Fernie, J., Moore, C. M. and Lawrie, A. (1998), 'A tale of two cities: An examination of fashion designer retailing within London and New York', *Journal of Product & Brand Management*, 7: 5, pp. 366–78.

Fulberg, P. (2003). 'Using sonic branding in the retail environment: An easy and effective way to create consumer brand loyalty while enhancing the in-store experience', *Journal of Consumer Behaviour*, 3: 2, pp. 193–98.

Gieryn, T. F. (2000), 'A space for place in sociology', *Annual Review of Sociology*, 26, pp. 463–96.

Gioia, D. A. and Chittipeddi, K. R. (1991), 'Sensemaking and sensegiving in strategic change initiation', *Strategic Management Journal*, 12: 6, pp. 433–48.

Goffman, E. (1959), *The Presentation of Self in Everyday Life*, New York: Doubleday Anchor.

Harper, D. (2002), 'Talking about pictures: A case for photo elicitation', *Visual Studies*, 17: 1, pp. 13–26.

Hauge, A. L. (2011), 'Identity and place: a critical comparison of three identity theories', *Architectural Science Review*, 50:1, pp. 44–51.

Haweis, M. R. (1881), *Art of Decoration*, London: Chatto and Windus.

Holbrook, M. B., Solomon, M. R. and Bell, S. (1990), 'A reexamination of self-monitoring and judgments of furniture design', *Home Economics Research Journal*, 19: 1, pp. 6–16.

Jackson, T. (2009), 'Virtual flagship', in T. Kent and R. Brown (eds), *Flagship Marketing: Concepts and Places*, New York, NY: Routledge, pp. 186–94.

Jager, B. (1983), 'Body, house, city or the intertwinings of embodiment, in habitation', in D. Kruger (ed.), *The Changing Reality of Modern Man*, Pittsburgh, PA: Dusquene University Press, pp. 51–59.

Kawamura, Y. (2005), *Fashion-ology: An Introduction to Fashion Studies*, New York, NY: Berg Publishers.

Keller, K. L. (2003), *Strategic Brand Management: Building, Measuring, and Managing Brand Equity*, 2nd ed., Upper Saddle River, NJ: Prentice Hall.

—— (2005), 'Branding shortcuts', *Marketing Management*, 14: 5, pp. 18–23.

Kent, T. (2007), 'Creative space: Design and the retail environment', *International Journal of Retail & Distribution Management*, 35: 9, pp. 734–45.

—— (2009), 'Concepts of flagship', in T. Kent and R. Brown (eds), *Flagship Marketing: Concepts and Places*, New York, NY: Routledge, pp. 8–19.

Kirby, A. (2009), 'What is a flagship supermarket? An analysis of supermarket flagship in a historical context', in T. Kent and R. Brown (eds), *Flagship Marketing: Concepts and Places*, New York, NY: Routledge, pp. 173–85.

Kohli, C., Suri, R. and Thakor, M. (2002), 'Creating effective logos: Insights from theory and practice', *Business Horizons*, May–June, pp. 58–64.

Kozinets, R. V., Sherry, J. F., DeBerry-Spence, B., Duhachek, A., Nuttavuthisit, K. and Storm, D. (2002), 'Themed flagship brand stores in the new millenium: Theory, practice, and prospects', *Journal of Retailing*, 78: 1, pp. 17–29.

Kwang, J. N., Holland, R., Shackleton, J., Hwang, Y.-Y. and Melewar, T. C. (2008), 'The effect of evaluation criteria on design attributes and brand equity in the product evaluation process', *Brand Management*, 16: 3, pp. 195–212.

Lindstrom, M. (2002), *Clicks, Bricks and Brands*, London: Kogan.

McNabb, D. E. (2002), *Research Methods in Public Administration and Nonprofit Management Quantitative and Qualitative Approaches*, Armonk, NY: M.E. Sharpe.

Moore, C. M. and Doherty, A. M. (2009), 'The flagship store: the luxury fashion retailing perspective', in T. Kent and R. Brown (eds), *Flagship Marketing: Concepts and Places*, New York, NY: Routledge, pp. 63–73.

Moore, C. M., Fernie, J. and Burt, S. (2000), 'Brand without boundaries: The internationalisation of the designer retailer's brand', *European Journal of Marketing*, 34: 8, pp. 919–37.

Oldham, G. R., Cummings, A. and Zhou, J. (1995), 'The spatial configuration of organizations', *Research in Personnel and Human Resources Management*, 13, pp. 1–37.

Pennartz, P. J. (1999), 'Home: The experience of atmosphere', in I. Cieraad (ed.), *At Home: An Anthropology of Domestic Space*, Syracuse, NY: Syracuse University Press, pp. 95–106.

Potvin, J. (2010), 'The velvet masquerade: Fashion, interior design and the furnished body', in Alla Myzeley and John Potvin (eds), *Fashion, Interior Design and the Contours of Modern Identity*, UK: Ashgate Publishing, pp. 1–17.

Proshansky, H., Fabian, A. K. and Kaminoff, R. (1983), 'Place-identity: Physical world socialization of the self', *Journal of Environmental Psychology*, 3: 4, pp. 57–83.

Rahman, O. (2011), 'Understanding consumers' perceptions and behaviours: Implication for denim jeans design', *Journal of Textile and Apparel Technology and Management*, 7: 1, pp. 1–16.

Rahman, O., Liu, W.-S. and Cheung, M.-H. (2012), 'Cosplay: Imaginative self and performing identity', *Fashion Theory: The Journal of Dress, Body & Culture*, 16: 3, pp. 317–42.

Rogoff, I. (2001), 'Studying visual culture', in N. Mirzeff (ed.), *The Visual Culture Reader*, 2nd ed., London: Routledge, pp. 24–34.

Rowley, J. (2004), 'Online branding', *Online Information Review*, 28: 2, pp. 131–38.

Sadalla, E. K., Vershure, B. and Burroughs, J. (1987), 'Identity symbolism in housing', *Environment and Behavior*, 19: 5, pp. 569–87.

Saldaña, J. (2009), *The Coding Manual for Qualitative Researchers*, London: Sage.

Salecl, R. (2002), 'He exposure of privacy in today's culture', *Social Research*, 69: 1, pp. 1–8.

Samuels, J. (2004), 'Breaking the ethnographer's frames', *American Behavioral Scientists*, 47: 12, pp. 1528–50.

Solomon, M. R. (1986), 'Deep-seated materialism: The case of Levi's 501 jeans', in R. J. Lutz (ed.), *Advances in Consumer Research*, vol. 13, Provo, UT: Association for Consumer Research, pp. 520–21.

Solomon, M. R. and Englis, B. G. (1994), 'Observations: The big picture: product complementarity and integrated communications', *Journal of Advertising Research*, 34: 1, pp. 57–63.

Spindler, A. (1997), 'Two take the money and produce', *The New York Times*, 9 April, p. 11.

Stemler, S. (2001), 'An overview of content analysis', *Practical Assessment, Research & Evaluation*, 7: 17, http://pareonline.net/getvn.asp?v=7&n=17. Accessed 19 July 2013.

Tokatli, N. (2011), 'Creative individuals, creative places: Marc Jacobs, New York and Paris', *International Journal of Urban and Regional Research*, 35: 6, pp. 1256–71.

Weick, K. E. (1995), *Sensemaking in Organizations*, Thousand Oaks, CA. Sage Publications.

Wilson, M. A. and Mackenzie, N. E. (2000), 'Social attributions based on domestic interiors', *Journal of Environmental Psychology*, 20: 4, pp. 343–54.

CONTRIBUTOR DETAILS

Osmud Rahman is an Associate Professor and Associate Chair of the School of Fashion at Ryerson University, Toronto. His works have appeared in various journals, including *Journal of Fashion Marketing and Management, Journal of Global Fashion Marketing, Fashion Theory, The Design Journal, International Journal of Design, International Journal of Fashion Design, Technology and Education*. His research interests are consumer behaviour, fashion design, subculture, and branding. He is currently involved in a study of cross-national fashion consumption.

Contact: School of Fashion, Ryerson University, 350 Victoria Street, Toronto, Ontario, Canada M5B 2K3.
E-mail: orahman@ryerson.ca
Tel: 416-979-5000, ext. 6911
Fax: 416-979-5227

Lauren Petroff grew up with a keen eye for fashion and culture. After attending Havergal College and McGill University, Lauren continued her education at Ryerson University, where she earned her Master of Arts degree in Fashion. Today, Lauren has found a position as a design editor for a prominent Canadian shelter publication, allowing her to be inspired by design and architecture on a daily basis.

E-mail: petroff.lauren@gmail.com

Global Fashion Brands: Style, Luxury & History
© 2014 Intellect Ltd Chapter. English language. doi: 10.1386/GFB.1.199_1

RAYECAROL CAVENDER
Ohio University

DORIS H. KINCADE
Virginia Polytechnic Institute and State University

Leveraging designer creativity for impact in luxury brand management: An in-depth case study of designers in the Louis Vuitton Möet Hennessy (LVMH) brand portfolio

ABSTRACT

Luxury goods research is growing in prominence, but the majority of existing research is consumer based and not business focused. This qualitative case provides analysis of an archetypal luxury goods company and an in-depth review of the company's management. Emergent relationships and patterns reveal best practices for successfully leveraging designer impact to achieve sustainability and longevity in a saturated global luxury goods marketplace. Findings indicate that when a creative and innovative designer with a clear understanding of the brand's personality

KEYWORDS

brand management
luxury fashion
case study
designer creativity
brand personality
Louis Vuitton
  Moet-Hennessy

and responsiveness to the unpredictable nature of fashion is paired successfully with visionary management who respect creativity as a process, there are positive implications for the brand. Although limited to biases inherent in one case, relevance of findings can be considered for other luxury goods companies. Field testing in the industry could determine if the findings can be utilized by other luxury companies.

INTRODUCTION

In recent history, the dynamic yet paradoxical nature of the luxury goods industry has garnered attention in the fields of management, marketing and retail research. Robust entry and growth in emerging markets, stalwart sales figures despite global economic recession, and overall growth of demand for luxury goods in the four principle segments (i.e. apparel fashion, perfume and cosmetics, wines and spirits, watches and jewellery; Fionda and Moore 2009) has resulted in an increase in research geared towards determining what drives value for luxury consumers and identifying best practices in management of luxury brands. Although research has grown, some areas of the luxury market are yet unexplored.

One area of study that has received limited attention is the use of designers and designers' names as part of the marketing and creative management of luxury brands. Historically, designers were the originators of luxury brands. Starting with the Father of Couture, Charles Frederick Worth, the *haute couture* houses of Paris (e.g. Chanel, Dior) represented some of the first luxury brands. With the re-emergence of the fashion industry in the post-World War II era, Dior created a dynasty of luxury goods in the 1950s and 1960s that increased the attention of the shopping elite to luxury brands (Charney et al. 1992). Documentation of the power of the famed French and Italian designers abounds in the history of the fashion industry; however, investigating the business process of leveraging the high profile power of the designer into the modern marketing of luxury brands needs further investigation.

The proliferation of luxury brands in the industry, the availability of high fashion items at lower price points through fast fashion retailers, and the propensity of consumers to shop multiple brands to create personal style aesthetics rather than remaining exclusively brand loyal further illustrates the volatility of the fashion sector of the luxury goods industry (Tungate 2008). This postmodern market environment drives the need for luxury companies to continue to demonstrate strong brand identity and unity of marketing vision at all levels of the company, all while leveraging their core competencies such as quality and durability, heritage and creativity in order to be competitive in a saturated marketplace. Current and future luxury companies can learn by studying how successful companies have leveraged this designer power.

The purpose of the qualitative research study was to identify lessons learned by an archetypal company for successfully leveraging designer impact to achieve sustainability and longevity in a saturated global luxury goods marketplace. An in-depth case analysis of a leading luxury conglomerate, Louis Vuitton Möet Hennessy (LVMH), was completed to generate data for the study. LVMH is both a financial success and a marketing leader in the luxury sector of the retail industry and, thus, representative of an archetypal luxury company. In addition to the industry leadership by the company, the business administration of LVMH is also acknowledged as leading edge management. This managerial leadership is due to the business practices of LVMH's Chairman and CEO, Bernard Arnault (Galloni 2009).

With a professional background in financial engineering and property development, Arnault's first involvement with the luxury goods industry began with his acquisition of Dior Couture in 1984 and subsequent ascension to the helm of LVMH following the conglomerate's 1989 formation. Through his countless successes coupled with missteps resulting in lessons learned, Arnault honed a brand strategy for LVMH that avoided 'managerial limit setting', fuelled 'radical innovation', and revered the creative process of his brands' creative directors as akin to that of a 'Leonardo da Vinci or Frank Lloyd Wright', 'an unpredictable, messy, highly emotional activity that the company wholly endorses' (Wetlaufer 2001: 118).

Studying the best practices of a leading company and its visionary management (i.e. Arnault) can provide lessons learned from their successes and failures (Edmonson et al. 1997; Fionda and Moore 2009; Gabriele and Rosa 2009; Givhan 2011). The lessons learned from this study emerged inductively using the following research questions:

1. What are the overarching management strategies used by Arnault in his leveraging of designers' creativity among LVMH brands?
2. What are the lessons learned by Arnault and LVMH through the development of star brands Dior and Louis Vuitton?
3. What are the failures in the Fashion and Leather Goods Group experienced by LVMH and lessons learned from these failures?
4. What are the lessons learned from allowing creative designers to operate brands and their own individual companies (e.g. Marc Jacobs, Christian Lacroix) simultaneously?

REVIEW OF LITERATURE

Before the 1960s

In the years before the 1960s, luxury brands grew from fashion designers themselves, many of whom implemented very advanced business practices at a time when marketing was virtually non-existent (Okonkwo 2007). These designers represented both the creative and commercial sides of their companies and thus, presented a clear and cohesive brand identity to the consumer. The designer as a business manager is considered to originate in 1858, when Charles Frederick Worth established his couture house and created many of the ingredients now used in contemporary fashion marketing (Polan and Tedre 2009). He was the first couturier to give his clients a show (i.e. fashion or runway show) featuring his work and then allow them to choose the garments they liked for purchase. Worth was also an outstanding brand spokesman and was the first designer to put his signature on his creations. His likeness was akin to that of contemporary designers in that he was an elitist, had a flamboyant personality, and was a perfect visual depiction of the brand he represented (Tungate 2008).

'Fashion historians contend that fashion is a reflection of the times in which it is created and worn', and that 'fashion responds to the zeitgeist, or spirit of the times' (Brannon 2006: 13). Like Worth before her, Gabrielle 'Coco' Chanel, another fashion and ultimately luxury brand icon, had an extraordinary ability to identify pertinent elements of the Zeitgeist and incorporate changing societal needs into her designs. This attribute is common to the designers who have been successful over decades and not just short periods of time. An example of Chanel's fashion leadership and marketing acumen is seen in the changes in her designs as a result of World War I (1914–1918). When women's roles in society changed as they worked in the fields and in factories while the men were at war, Chanel responded by creating trousers and other garments using materials and designs that were previously only seen in menswear (Milbank 1985).

In 1947, Christian Dior burst into the Parisian luxury business with the New Look. These decadent and flamboyant designs were reminiscent of pre-war fashions. Although many women protested, lots of women were again ready for feminine, over the top garments. The New Look did its job as a marketing technique; by creating controversy, it put Dior on the map in the fashion world and restored *haute couture* in Paris (Cawthorne et al. 1998). With Dior's dramatic revolutionary change, consumers began to expect seasonal newness and a faster pace for fashion change (Charney et al. 1992).

Beleaguered luxury designers beginning in the 1960s

By the mid-1960s, most fashion designers began to extend their brands along seemingly compatible product lines (e.g. handbags, shoes, scarves) and into ready-to-wear, both of which were often characterized by loosely held distribution and production (Reddy et al. 2009; Tungate 2008). This expansion meant new abilities to reach new markets and expand, but also rendered the former business model of designer-driven strategies irrelevant as financial and market share growth necessitated operating in multiple departments to better manage brands' development. Over time, designers began to further capitalize on the strong brand value of their names by entering into licensing agreements over a wider array of products that eventually left many prestigious luxury brands severely overextended (Brannon 2006; Cawthorne et al. 1998).

In the 1950s, for example, Pierre Cardin began mass producing and distributing cheaper copies of his designs. He quickly made more money selling multiple units of the same design than he did in selling a few single-item *haute couture* designs; however, his name was now a household word instead of an association with elitist luxury. By 1998, Cardin held more than 800 licenses in 94 countries and had lent his name to everything from cigarettes to baseball caps as well as to ready-to-wear apparel (Brannon 2006). Although Cardin had the vision to recognize markets such as China and Russia as emerging powerhouse markets, his ego-driven licensure decisions ultimately led to the dilution of the brand's image. The company saw profit margins drop after he licensed his name to goods that extended too far from the original product category (Reddy et al. 2009). Cardin's licensure strategy illustrates the importance of making management decisions that will preserve the exclusivity and value of the brand.

Additional challenges that continued to trouble apparel designers and the luxury brand industry arose from the 1960s into the 1990s, as the namesake designers of many luxury brands groomed successors to take their place upon retirement while passing actual company ownership to their families. 'The most consistently celebrated and influential designer of the past twenty-five years, Yves Saint Laurent can be credited with both spurring couture's rise from its sixties ashes and with finally rendering ready-to-wear reputable' (Milbank 1985: 308). Saint Laurent, who took over the creative director role at the House of Dior after Christian Dior's death in 1957, not only mastered the Dior aesthetic and the Zeitgeist, or spirit of the times, but also became the first designer to create a unique ready-to-wear line that was not an adaptation of *haute couture*. However, after Saint Laurent's departure from the brand in 1958, the House of Dior also became plagued by over-licensing and unclear designer vision (Christian Dior SA 2012).

The most significant event in the luxury goods sector during the 1980s was in 1989 when Bernard Arnault assumed his role as President of Louis Vuitton Möet-Hennessey (LVMH). Arnault had one goal in mind as he honed the LVMH market process: the creation of star brands. The only way to achieve star brand status, according to Arnault, is to be 'timeless and modern, fast growing and highly profitable all at once' (Wetlaufer 2001).

Continued drama and radical changes for luxury brands in the 1980s and beyond

Throughout this time period, many new creative directors continued to struggle to find a balance between their brands' existing identities and their own unique design aesthetics (e.g. Tom Ford). Furthermore, many of the luxury brands' new creative directors were also designers and gained notoriety of their own. The more importance these designers gained in the marketplace, 'the harder it [became] to pour [their] identity and ego into a brand without [their] name on it' (e.g. Tom Ford for Gucci; Agins 2004: B5).

This challenge was heightened by the early years of the 2000s as many creative directors launched their own labels, some owned by the same parent company and some not, resulting in the creative director's role of managing two unique brand identities simultaneously (Agins 2004).

When the namesake labels of these creative directors were owned by a parent company different from the one under which their primary appointments were housed, additional challenges were posed. Working for two separate, competing parent companies was problematic for many such designers who ultimately left their creative director roles after their contracts expired in order to focus on the development of their own labels (i.e. Alexander McQueen, Michael Kors, Narciso Rodriquez; Agins 2004).

In contrast, many up-and-coming designers successfully leveraged their roles as creative designers at prominent heritage brands to establish their own reputations and successful labels (e.g. Karl Lagerfeld, Matthew Williamson, Marc Jacobs; Brannon 2006; Cawthorne et al. 1998). Although the luxury goods industry achieved positive growth from a business perspective during the 1990s, fashion as an art and a sense of unique design seemed to be lost. In the 1990s, apparel became a commodity as designers created functional, minimalist styles that often appeared bland and old-fashioned (Tungate 2008).

For some luxury brands, hiring up-and-coming creative directors 'reenergize[ed] the house and [made] it relevant to a new generation (e.g. Phoebe Philo at Céline, Narciso Rodriguez at Loewe, Christian Lacroix at Pucci; Socha 2007: 22). This trend had both positive and negative outcomes for designers and for companies. One of the most noted, and earliest, examples of this leveraging of designer creativity for luxury brand management was the acquisition of Dior by Bernard Arnault in 1984 and his subsequent revitalization of the flailing brand through business strategy changes and implementation of trusted input from the appointed creative director. Arnault later assumed the role of Chairman and CEO (1989) of Louis Vuitton Möet-Hennessey (LVMH) and achieved success by employing the same strategy in the development of fashion brands in the portfolio. A study of Arnault's techniques in leveraging designer creativity for impact on luxury brands has potential to inform future companies of best practices.

METHODS

The researchers conducted an in-depth case analysis to delineate the brand management strategies used by Arnault to successfully leverage designer creativity in the luxury brands owned by LVMH. Michael Beverland (2004) indicated that, due to the paradoxical nature of luxury brands, research methods that facilitate deep exploration, rather than surface level observations are preferable. A case study design facilitated an investigation of real world phenomena, pertaining to the sample company, and an examination of 'those phenomena in all their complexity' (Leedy and Ormrod 2005: 133). Recent published research further supports the case study as a valid research tool for examining business practices of leading companies in the luxury sector (Tynan et al. 2010; Kapferer and Tabatoni 2013).

SAMPLE COMPANY

The LVMH conglomerate was selected as a sample company for the case study. Louis Vuitton, a star brand in the LVMH portfolio, was the highest ranked luxury brand by two major brand valuation reports in 2012 (i.e. Interbrand Best Global Brands and Brandz Top 100), which demonstrates the company's financial and marketing leadership in the luxury sector (Interbrand 2012; Milward Brown 2012). Louis Vuitton's role as a benchmark luxury brand suggests that their business strategies are observed and emulated by other luxury goods companies across the sector. Although this research includes only one case study, it does explore multiple brands, beginning with the formation of the LVMH conglomerate in 1987. This allowed the researchers to conduct cross-brands analyses for comparison purposes in which commonalities and differences across brands were sought, as suggested by Matthew B. Miles and A. Michael Huberman (1994).

DATA COLLECTION AND ANALYSIS

Data collection was an examination of the best practices of LVMH, a leading luxury goods conglomerate. This information was supplemented with an in-depth historical review of the luxury goods industry from its inception, and an exploration of theories related to this business environment. Data, as collected and reviewed, was coded revealing emergent themes. Analysis of data collected on designers and related brands in the LVMH portfolio provided insight into how the designers and the brands were managed in relation to one another. This contact with and reflection of data helped the researchers identify successes, failures and lessons learned in the leveraging of designer creativity from the inception of the conglomerate to the first decade of the 2000s.

In order to increase the internal validity of the study, triangulation was employed, as suggested by Gretchen B. Rossman and Sharon F. Rallis (2003). The researchers gathered general apparel business and company data through a comprehensive review of available literature, including both primary and secondary sources. Articles from apparel industry trade publications (e.g. *Women's Wear Daily*), national newspaper publications (e.g. *Wall Street Journal*) and leading business magazines (e.g. *BusinessWeek, Forbes, The Economist*) were surveyed for information relevant to LVMH, star brands and designers, and the luxury goods industry as a whole. Additional data on LVMH was gathered from the company's website and other company documents (e.g. 10-K reports) were obtained from business databases (e.g. Mintel). General business databases (e.g. ABI/INFORM, Business Source Complete) were also employed to identify additional information on the company's corporate structure, business models and marketing initiatives. General and specific Internet searches were used to identify pertinent resources.

FINDINGS

As data analysis progressed, a key variable identified as vital to leveraging designers and their brands within the luxury goods industry was creativity. Creativity was often noted as innovation in marketing strategies or product styles generated by a creative director/designer. The researchers observed that the importance and need for creativity are considerably higher in the fashion segment of the luxury goods industry due to its seasonal nature. This factor requires continual strategic planning and product development for the introduction of new style lines, materials and colours by creative directors and their design teams in order to construe the Zeitgeist of each season successfully.

OVERARCHING MANAGEMENT STRATEGIES FOR LEVERAGING DESIGNER CREATIVITY WITHIN THE LVMH BRAND PORTFOLIO

Adopting a multi-brand acquisition strategy, Arnault, as Chairman and CEO of LVMH, spent the 1990s building the company into a luxury conglomerate and changing the face of the luxury goods industry. Arnault's initial strategy was to acquire undervalued heritage brands, but his desire to impose production synergies in the brand portfolio proved challenging to the acquired companies whose management were concerned about a compromise in brand identity (Gabriele and Rosa 2009). This concern caused Arnault to adopt a more hands-off approach in the area of product development while keeping a tight control on distribution to ensure quality and exclusivity of LVMH's brands. Arnault believed brands that had paired creative and motivated design teams with entrepreneurial management would thrive in this decentralized organizational structure and be valuable assets in the long term (Arnault 2013).

Creativity as a process was central to Arnault's business strategy and creative directors at each brand were given full authority over product designs (Givhan 2011). Arnault believed that in time the small local fashion houses that he was acquiring (mostly Italian and French brands) would improve in profitability and be able to compete on a global scale. The growth process was slow and in some cases competitive profitability and positioning did not develop. LVMH was buying growth through acquisitions but experiencing sluggish sales growth from recurring operations, slipping profit margins, and a high debt-to-equity ratio. During this period, LVMH relied on Louis Vuitton and its star brands from the Champagne and cognac businesses for the bulk of its sales and profits (Passariello 2007).These factors forced the company to refocus their business strategy in the first decade of the 2000s towards digesting and growing their investments (Edmonson et al. 1997).

After the strategy shift from hands on direct management to decentralized designer controlled product development in 2002, LVMH began to implement integration initiatives to aid flailing brands and realize scale economies within the conglomerate. This additional strategy has allowed the conglomerate to increase 'credibility with its brands, because it let its designers continue to design while providing a structure and support system of back office efficiencies that many independent luxury designers lack' (Gabriele and Rosa 2009: 220). Therefore, the acquired brands' creative directors continued to create and drive brand strength within the portfolio.

LESSONS LEARNED FROM STAR BRANDS DIOR COUTURE AND LOUIS VUITTON

Christian Dior Couture (i.e. Dior Couture) was the first luxury brand Arnault acquired in 1984 and the means by which he would later establish the cross-shareholding structure that he would use to gain control of LVMH in 1989. An examination of this company from 1984 to 2011 provides an illustration of Arnault's business formula for success in the management of luxury goods brands while shedding light on his strategy of leveraging designer impact.

Dior Couture was once considered France's most prestigious fashion label, but was significantly diluted by extensive licensing and widespread distribution in the 1970s. The company's most pressing problems stemmed from over-licensing and an increasingly dowdy image compared with that of other hot, young designers (Christian Dior SA 2012). After Arnault took his seat as Chairman of the Board in 1984, he made many employment and management changes at Dior. Arnault believed that his chosen group of executives could successfully carry out his broad mission for the brand,

> [which was bringing] Dior's business model into the modern luxury age, transforming it from a licensing-driven company to one centered on control of production and distribution. That not only meant rebuilding the organization, and launching into the lucrative accessories category, but reenergizing the house and making it relevant to a new generation.
> (Socha 2007: 22)

In 1988, Arnault appointed shrewd businesswoman, Beatrice Bongibault, as managing director of Dior Couture. The hiring of Bongibault is noteworthy as she came to Dior Couture from Chanel, and had been instrumental in the 1982 hiring of German-born designer, Karl Lagerfeld, as Chanel's new design director. This maverick and risky move, of involving innovative designers in the business process, ultimately revitalized the Chanel brand and helped position it to a younger consumer demographic (Goodwin 1990). The Lagerfeld appointment marked the emergence of a new strategy that would save many luxury heritage brands from impending extinction and Bongibault planned to utilize the same strategy to rejuvenate Dior Couture. In 1989, she replaced the house's couturier and design director, Marc Bohan, who had been with the company for 28 years, with the Italian ready-to-wear designer, Gianfranco Ferré (Morris 1989).

With the guidance of Arnault, Bongibault and Ferré aggressively rebuilt Dior Couture's ready-to-wear business that had been a long-term problem area for the company, increased advertising budgets, made a major push into the accessories market, curtailed licensing agreements and re-gained a tight hold on production and distribution (Goodwin 1990). Dior's couture collections, operated by Ferré, also garnered praise and clients that had left after the firing of Bohan, were once again placing orders (Goodwin 1990).

After the departure of Bongibault, Arnault asked Sidney Toledano from Lancel to join Dior Couture as general manager in 1994 (he would later become CEO in 1998). Toledano shared Bongibault and Arnault's philosophy of 'merging subversive talent with dusty historical brands' and giving designer's the reins to be disorganized and spontaneous (Givhan 2011: 53). In 1996, the two managers hired eccentric and creative British designer, John Galliano, to move from Givenchy to Dior. The appointment of Galliano illustrated Arnault's penchant for hiring edgy, critically acclaimed young designers known for captivating, infuriating and exciting the fashion press, a strategy meant to 'bring in the buzz that drives the biz' (Greenfeld and Pascual 2000: 49). When discussing Galliano's avant-garde collections, Arnault stated that 'his ideas are not meant to be worn, but the ideas descend down to prêt-a-porter and to everything in the line. And that's what we sell' (Greenfeld and Pascual 2000: 49–50).

As creative director and fashion designer, Galliano's major accomplishment came in 1999 with his Matrix couture collection and a hip hop inspired ready-to-wear collection. The executives' gamble on Galliano had positive financial and market gains as media hype generated on the runway was facilitating renewed interest in the iconic Dior brand. Beginning in 1999, the company began to have big double-digit increases, with the exception of the drop experienced by most consumer-product companies in 2001. Sales reached $1 billion in 2007 (Socha 2007). Somehow Galliano's fantastical runway shows and edgy designs meshed with the conservative culture of the traditional Dior Couture brand and transformed the couture company into a modern luxury company.

Even more impressive than the revitalization of Dior's brand identity, was Arnault's strategy for the Louis Vuitton brand, whose profits and sales were on the decline in the 1990s. Although the Louis Vuitton brand maintained an indisputable reputation for craftsmanship, the must-have bags of the 1980s were now considered 'the bag[s] your mother bought' (Guyon 2004: 34). Arnault, who in his role as LVMH CEO 'recognized the need to exploit the [Vuitton] company's potential immediately to assure its performance and thereby its longevity' (Pasols 2005: 301) appointed Yves Carcelle CEO of Vuitton in 1990.

Carcelle carried out Arnault's vision of infusing modernity into the heritage brand by introducing new leather lines. However, the pivotal change in the overhaul of Louis Vuitton's brand identity was the move to ready-to-wear and the appointment of a new creative director. Carcelle, with Arnault's support, tapped Marc Jacobs, a 34-year-old designer to become Louis Vuitton's new creative director (Anon. 1996). As an edgy new designer, Jacobs was already generating a high level of consumer and media interest in the apparel industry for his grunge design aesthetic. Since 1997, Jacobs has perfectly channelled the Louis Vuitton brand essence in his collections and is considered by many to be the most influential designer in fashion. Jacobs and his creativity has been a key factor in the success of the Louis Vuitton brand during the first decade of the 2000s.

Analysis of the restructuring and revitalization of the Dior and Louis Vuitton brands' identity confirmed two lessons learned from Arnault's management in leveraging designer creativity. First, creative design talent with a clear understanding of the brand's personality and responsiveness to the unpredictable nature of fashion is the most important driver of brand strength. Second, the creative director must be aided by a visionary manager who can provide expertise in business capabilities and work with the creative director to ensure that the synergized brand identity is accurately projected through the marketing vision.

FAILURES WITHIN THE FASHION AND LEATHER GOODS GROUP EXPERIENCED BY LVMH AND LESSONS LEARNED

Before Arnault made any acquisitions to the LVMH portfolio, he tried unsuccessfully to build a brand internally by underwriting Christian Lacroix's brand in 1987. Pressure to generate a profit in a small time window led Lacroix to subdue his designs in order to reach a larger audience (Donovan 1988). The brand's identity was a casualty of that decision, and it became unrecognizable to consumers in the market. In addition to the Christian Lacroix brand's namesake failing to establish a recognizable brand personality and signature design aesthetic, successful collaboration of the brand's creative design team and management team never occurred.

This failure within the brand portfolio begs the question of why Arnault did not take a more proactive role in selecting a visionary manager for the brand at its inception. A lesson learned from the Lacroix brand failure, was that brands must be allowed to grow and develop at their own pace. Arnault and LVMH learned that they must allow brand's creative directors the freedom to create without limits, trusting that commercial interpretation of the designer's vision will come eventually, and with it, positive financial results (Gabriele and Rosa 2009). Because creative talent is so highly valued within LVMH, the conglomerate now lives by the philosophy that 'if you look over a creative person's shoulder, he will stop doing great work' (Wetlaufer 2001: 118). Since LVMH's company-wide shift, driven by Arnault, from an acquisition strategy to one that fosters internal growth and the development of brands with star potential in 2002, the brands and designers in the Fashion and Leather Goods Group have experienced many successes (e.g. revival of iconic brands Fendi and Céline). This strategy shift involved constant creativity and sustained innovation, focused investments, and disposal of non-strategic assets (Anon. 2003).

LESSONS LEARNED FROM ALLOWING CREATIVE DESIGNERS TO OPERATE BRANDS AND THEIR OWN INDIVIDUAL COMPANIES (E.G. MARC JACOBS, LACROIX) SIMULTANEOUSLY

Supervising creative personalities while simultaneously nurturing a brand's financial and growth capabilities, has proven to be a challenge for Arnault. Occasionally this challenge has had a positive outcome. Marc Jacobs is an example of a designer whose relationship with Arnault and LVMH has overcome obstacles and changes over time, and whose work is still thriving in 2012. Considered the most influential designer within the LVMH brand portfolio, this subversive designer proved to be a potent creative force at Louis Vuitton despite initial culture clashes with the brand's executives and established design teams. The designer's high profile, ingenious designs, and introduction of accessories, ready-to-wear and shoes, helped the company's sales double to $2.4 billion by 2001 and reach $3.5 billion by 2004 (Agins 2004).

In contrast, progress at Marc Jacobs' own label was much slower, and in 2004, as he approached the renegotiation of his contract with LVMH, Jacobs believed that LVMH's minimal investment (e.g., $50 million) in the Marc Jacobs brand was stalling its development. Arnault justified his cautious investment in the Marc Jacobs brand due to the fact that sales of the brand had only recently begun to show real financial promise. The contract negotiations between Marc Jacobs and LVMH in 2004 marked a turning point in the relationship between the designer and the conglomerate. Arnault confirmed his commitment to keeping Jacobs happy as the designer and LVMH directed more support to the development of the Marc Jacobs brand including product development and international expansion. Arnault renounced his handling of previous CEO appointments for the brand and the divestment of Marc Jacobs Perfumes, and vowed to involve Marc Jacobs in future decisions regarding the brand.

The handling and outcome of the Marc Jacobs as a designer and the Marc Jacobs brand example illustrates how LVMH has continued to hone its management of the smaller brands within its portfolio, including brands with namesake designers at the helm. LVMH's contract negotiations with Marc Jacobs in 2004 followed the conglomerate's strategic shift in 2002 to a focus on core brands with star potential. Marc Jacobs' brand has proven to be one of those core brands as LVMH's increased investment in the brand fuelled its growth and subsequent financial success. The brand has demonstrated successful expansion of its distribution network in Europe, Asia and the Americas with strong sales across all geographic regions. A successful second-line, Marc by Marc Jacobs, was launched and has been continually gaining momentum with the excellent performance of its shoe and leather goods collections (Anon. 2013). Marc Jacobs himself has also been a ten time winner at the Council of Fashion Designers of America (CFDA) Awards. His seasonal runway shows, for both his own brand and for Louis Vuitton, generate media interest and excitement among fans for their edgy approach and praise from the international fashion press (Anon. 2013). In fall 2013, Jacobs announced his departure from Louis Vuitton to focus exclusively on his namesake brand. Nicolas Ghesquiére, who previously enjoyed a 15-year tenure as creative director at Balenciaga, will assume the creative director role and is expected to generate buzz-worthy collections like Jacobs has done before him.

The Céline brand also represents successful management by Arnault of the dual and simultaneous roles of designer. After the departure of Michael Kors in 2004, the Céline brand struggled to establish a following and a firm brand identity. Céline's subsequent creative directors failed to convey the French brand's sophistication and emphasis on subtle tailoring and quality materials in their collections. In 2007, British fashion designer, Phoebe Philo, who had previously had success at Stella McCartney and Chloé, was hired as a potential savior for the Céline brand (Dodes and Passariello 2010). In her time at Chloé, Philo had created an 'it' bag, the Paddington, launched many successful ready-to-wear collections, and saw sales double.

In order to allow Philo to develop her vision for Céline, LVMH took several drastic steps to smooth the transition for the new creative director. For example, the entire inventory stock left in stores prior to Philo's first collection was destroyed at a loss of roughly $126 million. In addition, 'Céline also closed all but one store in the U.S., cut ties to less exclusive retailers, stopped producing bags in China and restored the accent to its name, all part of a move to tightly control and elevate the brand' (Dodes and Passariello 2010: B1). These strategic steps are examples of applications of lessons learned by Arnault in order to devise a strategy for Céline's long-term success and profitability.

In October 2009, Philo presented her first collection for the brand. Her minimalist reinterpretation of the Céline aesthetic resulted in influential luxury retailers (i.e. Bergdorf Goodman, Barneys) vying to carry the collection (Dodes and Passariello 2010). The designer's subsequent collections have continued to fuel momentum at Céline and, with a strong new foundation, the label has since begun to increase its distribution across all geographic regions, initiated renovation and expansion projects in numerous store locations, and begun to strengthen other product categories, such as leather goods (Anon. 2013). Philo is also one example of the many designers (e.g. Sarah Burton at Alexander McQueen) with more subdued personalities that have recently taken over and had success at established brands, demonstrating that placing flamboyant types in the creative director role is not essential for a brand to achieve success.

Not every designer hired by Arnault resulted in success; however, lessons were learned from each experience. LVMH's divestment of the Lacroix brand in 2005 and Christian Lacroix's subsequent departure from the creative director role at LVMH-owned, Pucci, illustrate a challenge experienced within the LVMH brand portfolio. 'In the age of luxury-goods conglomerates, star designers' loyalties often are divided between their own brands and the ones they are paid to design for corporate clients' (Agins 2004: B5). Many up and coming designers have worked for big firms while simultaneously gaining notoriety through the development of their own fashion labels, some of which owned by the same parent company, some not.

The negative aspect of this type of designer partnership with major conglomerates, as seen in the case of Christian Lacroix and other designers, has multiple ramifications and lessons to be learned. A designer's own brand can be divested from the conglomerate while the designer is still employed by another brand within the conglomerate. It becomes challenging for a designer (e.g. Lacroix, Kors) to continue working at the second brand or label due to time, and sometimes, ego constraints. Additionally, 'the more famous the designer becomes, the harder it is to pour his identity, and ego into a brand without his name on it' (Agins 2004: B5). Finally, the designer takes on the challenge of maintaining the distinct brand image of each label and separate visions for each season's collections without compromising one brand over the other.

The examples of Marc Jacobs, Phoebe Philo and other creative directors'/ designers' work at LVMH brands confirm Arnault's belief in the importance of finding a creative director, usually an innovative designer, who is a good strategic fit with a brand and a brand's image. By giving the designer creative control to make important decisions regarding product lines and by putting a visionary management team in place that will aid the brand in growth, development and marketing initiatives, a brand has the best possible formula for success (Givhan 2011). For example, trade-offs for the Céline brand such as the closing of stores and the destroying of previous inventories, were necessary short-term steps to achieve desired results for the brand in the long term. In a recent interview, Arnault indicated that he believes Céline to be the LVMH Fashion and Leather Goods Group's next star brand (Givhan 2011).

DISCUSSION AND SUMMARY

Throughout the findings of the case analysis, LVMH CEO, Bernard Arnault, was identified as a visionary manager with a penchant for appointing edgy, critically acclaimed, young designers to creative director positions. These designers were known for captivating, infuriating and exciting the fashion press, a strategy meant to 'bring in the buzz that drives the biz' (Greenfeld and Pascual

2000: 49). Often, the result was that the subversive talents' fantastical runway shows and edgy designs somehow meshed with the conservative cultures of the heritage brands (i.e., Dior, Louis Vuitton, Pucci, Loewe). This integration transformed these heritage brands into modern luxury players and left LVMH brands' management directors to focus on strategic initiatives such as tightening production and distribution, calculating extension of product offerings, and carefully expanding into new locations and emerging markets. Findings showed that the decision to fill the creative director role with strong and eccentric personalities sometimes resulted in disasters for LVMH: culture clashes with management that had to be resolved (e.g., Marc Jacobs); PR disasters when the celebrity designers' personal problems and failure to handle their star power became evident and played out in the media (e.g. John Galliano in 2011); and failure of designers to reach a commercial interpretation of their designs, and thus, reach profitability (e.g. Christian Lacroix). However, the findings also showed that this strategy of appointing designers as directors could be highly successful (e.g. Marc Jacobs).

Analysis of the LVMH case study also revealed that when an individual brand was experiencing declining sales or declining brand image in the minds of consumers (e.g. Christian Lacroix, Dior), communicative differences and clear disconnects between management and the creative team's vision for the company were also present. However, in many instances the vision was realigned with planning and leadership, such as the leadership provided by Arnault. The fact that a company must have a clear brand vision across all departments and business functions is seemingly a no-brainer. However, for luxury fashion brands, as seen in the LVMH case study, a power shift in decision making existed as the creative director made successful decisions regarding the direction of the brand that were then executed across departments through the business capabilities of management.

The important lesson learned by Arnault in leveraging designer creativity is seen in an interview for the Harvard Business Review. In the interview, Arnault stated that 'the last thing you should do is assign advertising to [a brand's] marketing department. If you do that, you lose the proximity between the designers and the message to the marketplace. [LVMH] keeps the advertising right inside the design team' (Wetlaufer 2001: 122). Despite the challenges of forging successful working relationship between brands' management and creative teams, the case study revealed that LVMH is making strides across its portfolio to continually hone these partnerships to better position brands in the minds of consumers. Visionary managers provide expertise in business capabilities and work with the creative director, often a creative and innovative designer, to ensure that the synergized brand identity is accurately projected through the marketing vision. Constant collaboration between brands' creative and business functions combined with cohesion of goals and strategies across all company levels provides luxury apparel brands with a formula for success in navigating this high growth industry (Givhan 2011).

CONCLUSIONS AND RECOMMENDATIONS

In conclusion, two lessons were learned from the study of the management of the most successful LVMH brands (e.g. Louis Vuitton, Marc Jacobs, Céline). First, creative and innovative designers with a clear understanding of the brands' personality and responsiveness to the unpredictable nature of fashion were paired successfully with visionary management that respected creativity as a process. Second, visionary managers are instrumental in providing expertise in business capabilities and working with creative directors to ensure that the synergized brand identity is accurately leveraged and projected through the marketing vision. Current and future companies who wish to emulate the best practices of the LVMH conglomerate should carefully select their management team and creative directors. Visionary leaders with the power to simultaneously control and let go are needed to leverage the creativity of the most innovative creative directors.

REFERENCES

Agins, Teri (2004), 'For Marc Jacobs, a hot partnership needs alterations', *Wall Street Journal*, 9 February, http://online.wsj.com/news/articles/SB107628251050523971. Accessed 20 November 2013.

Anon. (1996), 'LVMH's Bernard Arnault in talks with Marc Jacobs', *Women's Wear Daily*, 172: 1, p. 2.

—— (2003), 'Annual results 2002', LVMH, 6 March, www.lvmh.com. Accessed 23 June 2013.

—— (2013), 'Translation of the French financial documents', LVMH, 31 January, www.lvmh.com. Accessed 23 June 2013.

Arnault, Bernard (2013), 'Chairman's message', LVMH, 31 January, www.lvmh.com. Accessed 23 June 2013.

Beverland, Michael (2004), 'Uncovering theories-in-use: Building luxury wine brands', *European Journal of Marketing*, 38: 3/4, pp. 446–66.

Brannon, Evelyn L. (2006), *Fashion Forecasting*, 2nd ed., New York: Fairchild Publications.

Cawthorne, Nigel, Evans, Emily, Kitchen-Smith, Mark, Mulvey, Kate and Richards, Melissa (1998), *Key Moments in Fashion*, London: Hamlyn.

Charney, Nicolas, Cardin, Marlene McGinnis, and Reeder, Rebecca (1992), *Christian Dior: The Legend*, New York: VideoFashion.

Christian Dior SA (2013), 'Hoover's Company Records- In-Depth Records', *LexisNexis Academic*, 27 November, http://www.lexisnexis.com/hottopics/lnacademic/. Accessed 1 December 2013.

Dodes, Rachel and Passariello, Christina (2010), 'LVMH Wipes Celine Slate clean, opening way for Phoebe effect', *Wall Street Journal*, 9 March, http://online.wsj.com/news/articles/SB10001424052748703954904575110010639056770. Accessed 20 November 2013.

Donovan, Carrie (1988), 'Fashion: The Paris couture; trying times for Lacroix', *New York Times*, 28 August, http://www.nytimes.com/1988/08/28/magazine/fashion-the-paris-couture-trying-times-for-lacroix.html. Accessed 20 November 2013.

Edmonson, Gail, Reier, Sharon and Flynn, Julia (1997), 'LVMH: Life isn't all champagne and caviar', *Business Week*, 10 November, http://www.businessweek.com/stories/1997-11-09/lvmh-life-isnt-all-champagne-and-caviar. Accessed 20 November 2013.

Fionda, Antoinette and Moore, Christopher (2009), 'The anatomy of the luxury fashion brand', *Journal of Brand Management*, 16: 5/6, pp. 347–63.

Gabriele, Carbonara and Rosa, Caiazza (2009), 'Competitive advantage in luxury industry: Is it a question of size', *The Business Review Cambridge*, 14: 1, pp. 216–21.

Galloni, Alessandra (2009), 'Being Bernard Arnault', *Wall Street Journal*, 5 March, http://magazine.wsj.com/features/the-big-interview/being-arnault/3/. Accessed 11 December 2013.

Givhan, Robin (2011), 'Bernard Arnault rethinks the cult of fashion gurus', *Newsweek*, 158: 3, pp. 52–57.

Goodwin, Betty (1990), 'New dior boutique part of long-term strategy: Couture', *Los Angeles Times*, 14 September, http://articles.latimes.com/1990-09-14/news/vw-258_1_rodeo-drive. Accessed 20 November 2013

Greenfeld, Karl Taro and Pascual, Aixa (2000), 'Battle deluxe', *Time*, 155: 18, pp. 48–50.

Guyon, Janet (2004), 'The magic touch', *Fortune*, 150: 5, pp. 34–37.

Interbrand (2012), 'Best Global Brands 2012', www.interbrand.com. Accessed 30 January 2013.

Kapferer, Jean-Noel and Tabatoni, Olivier (2013), 'The LVMH-Bulgari agreement: Changes in the luxury market that lead family companies to sell up', *Journal of Brand Strategy*, 1: 4, pp. 389–402.

Leedy, Paul D. and Ormrod, Jeanne E. (2005), *Practical Research: Planning and Design*, 8th ed., Upper Saddle River, NJ: Pearson Education.

Milbank, Caroline Rennolds (1985), *Couture: The Great Designers*, London Thames and Hudson.

Miles, Matthew and Huberman, Alan Michael (1994), *Qualitative Data Analysis: An Expanded Sourcebook*, 2nd ed., Thousand Oaks, CA: Sage.

Milward Brown (2012), 'Brandz top 100: Most valuable global brands 2012', http://www.milwardbrown.com. Accessed 30 January 2013.

Morris, Bernadine (1989), 'Dior confirms Ferre will replace Bohan', *New York Times*, 11 May, http://www.nytimes.com/1989/05/11/garden/dior-confirms-ferre-will-replace-bohan.html. Accessed 20 November 2013.

Okonkwo, Uche (2007), *Luxury Fashion Branding: Trends, Tactics, Techniques*, London: Palgrave Macmillan.

Pasols, Paul-Gerard (2005), *Louis Vuitton: The Birth of Modern Luxury*, New York: Abrams.

Passariello, Christina (2007), 'LVMH's new fashion: Luxury with restraint', *Wall Street Journal*, 13 February, http://online.wsj.com/news/articles/SB117132546679406525. Accessed 20 November 2013.

Polan, Brenda and Tredre, Roger (2009), *The Great Fashion Designers*, New York: Berg Publishers.

Reddy, Mergen, Terblanche, Nic, Pitt, Leyland and Parent, Michael (2009), 'How far can luxury brands travel: Avoiding the pitfalls of luxury brand extensions', *Business* Horizons, 52: 2, pp. 187–97.

Rossman, Gretchen B. and Rallis, Sharon F. (2003), *Learning in the Field: An Introduction to Qualitative Research*, 2nd ed., London: Sage.

Socha, Miles (2007), 'Steering the ship', *Women's Wear Daily*, 193: 43, p. 22.

Tungate, Mark (2008), *Fashion Brands: Branding Style from Armani to Zara*, London: Kogan Page Limited.

Tynan, Caroline, McKechnie, Sally and Chhuon, Celine (2010), 'Co-creating value for luxury brands', *Journal of Business Research*, 63: 11, pp. 1156–63.

Wetlaufer, Suzy (2001), 'The perfect paradox of star brands: An interview with Bernard Arnault of LVMH', *Harvard Business Review*, 79: 9, pp. 116–23.

Whitworth, Melissa (2011), 'Bernard Arnault rethinks the cult of fashion gurus', *Telegraph*, 18 July, http://fashion.telegraph.co.uk/news-features/TMG8637752/Bernard-Arnault-rethinks-the-cult-of-fashion-gurus.html. Accessed 20 November 2013.

CONTRIBUTOR DETAILS

RayeCarol Cavender, Ph.D., holds the B.S. in Merchandising Management with a minor in Spanish from Virginia Tech and the M.S. in Consumer Affairs with a minor in International Studies from Auburn University. She holds the Ph.D. in Apparel, Housing, and Resource Management from Virginia Tech with a focus on Apparel Business. She also has extensive experience in customer service in the hotel and restaurant industries. Dr. Cavender is an Assistant Professor in the Department of Human and Consumer Sciences at Ohio University and teaches courses in retail merchandising and fashion product development. Her major research interests include brand management of luxury goods, experiential marketing, international marketing and customer relationship management.

Contact: Department of Human and Consumer Sciences, Ohio University, Grover Center E171, 1 Ohio University, Athens, OH 45701-2979, USA.
E-mail: cavendr1@ohio.edu

Doris H. Kincade, Ph.D., is a Professor of Apparel Product Design and Merchandising Management in the Department of Apparel, Housing, and Resource Management at Virginia Tech in Blacksburg, VA. She is a Faculty Fellow with [TC] [2] at the National Apparel Research Center. Her research, using both qualitative and quantitative research methods, involves the examination of best business practices for apparel manufacturers and retailers with emphasis on the strategies of Quick Response, rapid product development and mass customization.

Contact: Department of Apparel, Housing, and Resource Management, Virginia Tech, 109 Wallace Hall, Blacksburg, VA 24061, USA.
E-mail: kincade@vt.edu

Global Fashion Brands: Style, Luxury & History

© 2014 Intellect Ltd Chapter. English language. doi: 10.1386/GFB.1.215_1

ALICE DALLABONA
University of Leeds

Narratives of Italian craftsmanship and the luxury fashion industry: Representations of Italianicity in discourses of production

ABSTRACT

In the last few years many luxury fashion labels like Gucci have emphasized, in their communication, the various types of craftsmanship involved in the creation of their pieces as a means of providing history and additional value to their products. This article investigates this phenomenon with a specific focus on issues of national identity and 'Italianicity'. First, the different strategies concerning representations of craftsmanship in discourses of production that are employed by Italian luxury fashion labels are examined. This phenomenon is investigated through a series of case studies with the aim of identifying situations of dialogue and contradiction between the strategies employed. Moreover, the article examines how both the celebration of Italian handmade craftsmanship in fashion and issues of technological developments are addressed in the discourses of production of luxury fashion goods. Also, the history of

KEYWORDS

luxury fashion
craftsmanship
branding
Italianicity
narratives of
 production
national identity

the Italian fashion system and its distinctive traits will be considered in this respect. However, narratives of Italian craftsmanship are not only present in the communication of the Italian luxury fashion labels examined here. References to craftsmanship 'made in Italy' also feature in the discourses of production employed by non-Italian luxury fashion brands like Marc Jacobs. In this respect, this article considers how Italian craftsmanship is strictly intertwined with connotations of quality, arguing that it can be productively employed by luxury fashion labels both to provide additional value to products and, more broadly, to enhance the reputation of their brands. Moreover, it is argued that luxury fashion labels do not merely capitalize on ideas of Italianicity that are already present but instead contribute, in an ongoing process, to recreate them through narratives that emphasize certain values associated with them. In this sense, the versions of Italianicity proposed by the Italian luxury fashion labels examined here also contribute to reinforce the positive image of their brands.

A QUESTION OF CRAFTSMANSHIP

In recent years luxury fashion labels have extended their brands and associated their names with goods that are not always characterized by a high price tag, extending towards the lower end of the market and making luxury products available to more and more people. Many have argued that this phenomenon implies a democratization of luxury (Mortelmans 2005: 517; Okonkwo 2007; Tungate 2009; Chadha and Husband 2006; Thomas 2007; Taylor and Doug 2008; Kapferer 2012). Masstige strategies can be extremely profitable for luxury fashion brands but they can also be problematic in terms of maintaining the exclusivity and prestige associated with luxury companies (Stegemann 2006: 63; Roux 1995: 1977; Dubois and Paternault 1995: 73; Phau and Prendergast 2000) as they can reduce 'the prestige of the core brand, perhaps because the core brand becomes mentally associated with a lesser quality brand extension' (Kim and Lavack 1996: 28).

In order to avoid brand dilution (Aaker 1990; Milberg et al. 1997; Loken and Roedder John 1993; Lye et al. 2001) and protect the aura of prestige and status associated with their brands, many luxury companies emphasize certain traits that are commonly associated with luxury such as rarity, scarcity and restriction (Berthon et al. 2009: 46; Dubois et al. 2001: 11; Mortelmans 2005: 505; Stegemann 2006: 59; Aiello and Donvito 2006: 2; Appadurai in Spooner 1986: 38). Luxury fashion brands sustain the scarcity of their most prestigious and expensive products through a variety of strategies like limited production and availability (Phau and Prendergast 2000; Dubois and Paternault 1995; Mortelmans 2005: 505; Aiello and Donvito 2006: 2). They employ strategies of limited distribution in order to create a 'well-controlled scarcity' (Chevalier and Mazzalovo 2008: 14) and maintain their prestige and reputation (Okonkwo 2007: 105; Moore and Birtwistle 2005: 268; Mortelmans 2005: 505). However, for other goods associated with luxury fashion brands, like diffusion lines and products of downscale vertical brand extension like fragrances, it is not possible to speak of real scarcity, as they are produced in large numbers. In those cases companies like Armani then try to convey at least an 'impression of scarcity' (Chevalier and Mazzalovo 2008: 49).

Other traits associated with luxury goods that are emphasized by luxury fashion brands in their communication and branding strategies are high quality, which revolves around issues of good design and aesthetic value (Mortelmans 2005: 506; Dubois et al. 2001: 12; Chevalier and Mazzalovo 2008: xi; Aiello and Donvito 2006: 2), high-quality materials (Jackson 2004: 157; Mortelmans 2005: 506) and excellent craftsmanship. In particular, in the last few years many luxury fashion labels have emphasized, in discourses of production, the craftsmanship involved in the creation of their pieces as a means of providing history and additional value to their products. This article investigates this phenomenon with a specific focus on issues of national identity and 'Italianicity' and examines in particular production videos created by Italian and non-Italian luxury fashion labels. The term 'Italianicity' was coined by Roland Barthes (1977) to connote an abstract entity that remains open to new additions that, case by case, are linked to Italy and its lifestyle, not crystallizing into a definitive list of elements that are Italian tout court. 'Italianicity is not Italy, it is the condensed essence of everything that could be Italian, from spaghetti to painting' (Barthes 1977: 48).

NARRATIVES OF ITALIAN CRAFTSMANSHIP IN DISCOURSES OF PRODUCTION

Production videos are becoming increasingly present in the discourses of luxury fashion brands, both in Italy and abroad, and complement established strategies of showcasing craftsmanship in store for a selected public. With regard to the Italian luxury fashion industry only, this strategy has been used by Gucci with its 'Gucci Artisan Corners', that saw Gucci artisans showcasing their skills in a series of selected stores around the world, through purpose-built Gucci workshops. A similar strategy was employed by Fendi for its 'Fatto a Mano' campaign, which saw Fendi artisans collaborate with several artists to create unique pieces in Fendi stores around the world. It has to be noted however that the production videos examined here are rather different, as they are not only directed at the clientele of the luxury fashion brands in question, but more broadly to potential consumers and those who have an interest in such labels. In this sense, the demonstrations of the labels' craftsmanship have gone global, as not only are they featured in official websites but they are, in many cases, also published on Youtube and readily available to anyone with access to the Internet.

Craftsmanship is a distinctive trait that characterizes luxury fashion brands (Berthon et al. 2009: 45; Dubois and Paternault 1995: 75; Fionda and Moore 2009: 349) and, as observed by Michel Chevalier and Gerald Mazzalovo (2008: xii), luxury goods are usually associated with 'specialists working by hand on individual pieces' for a significant amount of time, which makes these products more expensive, but also more unique, than if they were mass-manufactured (Dubois et al. 2001: 11). Italian luxury fashion labels, like their French counterparts, have often emphasized their heritage in terms of craftsmanship in their communication, as in the case of Hermès or Chanel. Many have recently produced a number of videos, in addition to print and TV advertising campaigns, that demonstrate how their products are handmade employing traditional methods, showcasing the workmanship of skilled artisans.

Gucci created a series of videos showing the handmade production of its Jackie and New Bamboo bags. This emphasized how all of the different phases – from dyeing, cutting and stitching the leather to the finishing of the bags – are performed by expert artisans (Prada 2011a, 2011b). Similarly, Ferragamo produced videos that showcase the craftsmanship involved in the production of leather goods. With regard to handbag production, Ferragamo also emphasized how the brand can rely on the 'workmanship made up of slow, careful, encoded gestures that are the fruit of a typically Tuscan artisanal expertise' (Ferragamo 2010a). The same level of craftsmanship and expertise is also showcased in the production of its Tramezza men's shoes (Ferragamo 2010b).

Fendi, on the other hand, published a series of videos illustrating the skills involved in the handmade creation of a greater variety of products, from sofas to watches and fur goods. In one of the videos that focus on its 'Selleria' range, Fendi highlights how the company 'recovered the artisan mastery of the Roman saddlers, composing unique items produced in limited editions and numbered, entirely cut and assembled by hand' (Fendi 2011a). Regarding the creation of its sofas, Fendi's production videos also show how the different phases of production are performed by skilled artisans using traditional methods with regard to stitching for example (Fendi 2011b).

Fendi also emphasized the handmade craftsmanship involved in the creation of its Peekaboo bespoke bags (Fendi 2012a), of the fifteenth anniversary edition of its iconic baguette bags (Fendi 2012b) and of its watches (Fendi 2011c). Similarly, Dolce and Gabbana also focus on the different phases of handmade production of their Sicily bag (Dolce and Gabbana 2012) and jewellery line (Dolce and Gabbana 2011), that also showcases different elements of Italian traditional craftsmanship.

In the videos produced by the above mentioned Italian luxury fashion labels the technology involved in the many phases of goods production is not featured. Instead, they prefer to emphasize the craftsmanship of the artisans that create the products by hand. This resembles the many accounts 'of Made in Italy that romanticizes small, craft-based firms competing against all the odds on the unforgiving field of hardscrabble capitalism' (Ross 2004: 212).

By endorsing ideas of craftsmanship and handmade production of fashion, those luxury fashion brands capitalize on well-established narratives associated with Italy (Steele 2003: 161), but refer to a myth of Italian craftsmanship that hides the reality of how many fashion goods are manufactured using automated production methods.

> 'Craft' is a key term in the promotional rhetoric of virtually every Italian manufacturer, and it is supposed to evoke an unbroken tradition of making things by hand in artisanal workshops as old as the Renaissance.
> (Ross 2004: 210)

Despite the fact that it was fairly recently, in the twentieth century, that Italian fashion gained popularity among consumers and respect in the fashion industry, becoming one of the ideal homelands of fashion (Vaccari 2005: 48), the prestige and reputation of Italian craftsmanship has a long history and was established way before the rise of Italian fashion in the post-war period.

Italian textiles have been appreciated since the Middle Age and are renowned for their quality and colours (White 2000). Embroidery also has a long-established tradition (Steele 2003: 122; Rocca 2006; Giordani-Aragno 1983) and so has tailoring and accessory production, especially concerning shoes and, more generally, leather goods (Jackson 2004: 161). Many Italian luxury fashion labels were actually born as leather goods workshops, such as Gucci, Prada and Fendi, or shoemakers, like Salvatore Ferragamo.

Images of craftsmanship and artisanal traditions are closely intertwined with ideas of Italy and contribute to create and reinforce the corporate mythology of the Italian fashion companies mentioned above, but do not represent a complete account of how the goods produced by those brands are actually made. Nowadays, many Italian luxury brands produce a significant part of their products abroad (Segre Reinach 2005: 49), mostly in Asia and Northern Africa, but nonetheless 'European luxury brands frequently dwell on their "heritage" for marketing purposes, using a tradition of craftsmanship as a way of seducing consumers and justifying elevated prices' (Tungate 2005: 18).

Narratives of Italian craftsmanship are so powerful that they are not only present in the communication of Italian luxury fashion labels, but also feature in discourses of production employed by non-Italian luxury fashion brands like Chanel, Louis Vuitton and Marc Jacobs. Italian craftsmanship is so strictly intertwined with connotations of quality and prestige that it can provide additional value to products and also, more broadly, enhance the reputation of any luxury fashion brands.

Bruno Pavlovsky (Chanel's president of global fashion) revealed that the label produces part of its knitwear, shoes and bags in Italy as Italian craftsmanship in those areas is excellent. Italian artisans are, he explains, better than their French counterparts when it comes to making bags that are not structured or require particular leather work (Pambianco News 2012). The quality of Italian craftsmanship in regard to leather and its worldwide reputation is also recognized by fashion label Marc Jacobs, which designs its bags in Milan and produces them in Florence, as shown in a video posted on the company's website and official Youtube channel (Marc Jacobs 2011). Similarly, Louis Vuitton's shoes are made in Italy, in Fiesso d'Artico, because, as Pietro Beccari (vice-president of marketing and communication for the label) confirms, Italy is the place with the best know-how in shoemaking, whereas the company manufactures its leather in Asnières (France) and watches in Switzerland, in Le Chaux-de-Fonds (Crivelli 2009). It has to be noted that the French fashion system has a long history of being closely intertwined with Italian craftsmanship, as 'Italian artisans were, in fact, often employed by French couture houses to do fine handwork' (Steele 2003: 7) so that this situation showcases a certain historical continuity.

A DIFFERENT TYPE OF KNOW-HOW

In this respect, the strategy employed by Prada for its production movies is different. Whereas other labels focus mainly on the craftsmanship involved in the creation of their product and only marginally, and very briefly, feature manufacturing phases that are not the result of handmade workmanship, Prada shows phases of production that utilize automated processes, such as plotting.[1] This represents a different facet of the Italian luxury fashion industry and a more honest account of how different goods associated with luxury fashion labels are produced. Not all the products created by luxury fashion brands are the result of handmade production or are characterized by the high level of craftsmanship that is showcased in the production videos examined earlier. The videos that emphasize the workmanship of skilled artisans created by Fendi, Ferragamo and Dolce and Gabbana fail to mention a problematic aspect of the contemporary luxury fashion industry in regard to the manufacture and prestige of their products.

Most of the products associated with modern luxury fashion labels are nowadays mass-manufactured, and not only when a brand extension is

1. See http://www.prada.com/en/production-movies.

involved. In this respect, Jean-Noel Kapferer (2004: 70) distinguishes three levels within the production of luxury brands. The level of the griffe, where the products are the result of the unique work of the designer, the level of the workshop and streamline mass production. However 'even if the *products* are mass-manufactured, as in the case of a perfume' people often 'want to believe that the *object* comes directly from the designer's workshop' (Chevalier and Mazzalovo 2008: xii, original emphasis) and consider them as emanations of that very craftsmanship that labels greatly emphasize through their corporate communications.

Nowadays, the democratisation and massification of luxury brands imply that there are different levels of luxury within the luxury industry, which are often a function of different methods of production. Danielle Alleres (1990) distinguishes three types of luxury goods: inaccessible luxury, characterized by very high prices, intermediate luxury, characterized by products that are more accessible than the goods in the previous category, and accessible luxury, characterized by even cheaper prices than the ones associated with the other two typologies of goods. It is the latter that nowadays is the most important financially, as Chevalier and Mazzalovo (2008: xi) argue. Similarly to Danielle Alleres, Michael Silverstein and Neil Fiske (2003, 2005) also recognize that contemporary luxury goods are not always associated with premium prices. Consequently, they identified three typologies of new luxury, all of which 'are not so expensive as to be out of reach' (Silverstein and Fiske 2005: 3), i.e. accessible super-premium products, old luxury brand extensions and masstige goods, which are products that refer to established luxury brands but are sold at much cheaper prices and therefore are accessible to the majority of the population. The more accessible facets of luxury fashion brands are not characterized by the same level of craftsmanship showcased in the production videos by Fendi, Ferragamo and Dolce and Gabbana examined earlier.

In its discourses of production, Prada refers to a different type of know-how that nonetheless is closely intertwined with the Italian fashion system. This includes knowledge that is deeply rooted in the technological progress and the industrial development that the country has experienced since the post-war period. The success of many Italian luxury fashion companies like Prada, but also Missoni, Ferragamo and Gucci, is strictly intertwined with the specific industrial structure of Italy, which revolves around a series of industrial districts. Industrial districts are 'dense concentrations of interdependent small- and medium-sized enterprises (SMEs) in a single sector and in auxiliary industries and services' (Dunford 2006: 27). They are clusters of enterprises that operate in the same sector and they constitute the core of the Italian industrial system. The districts also involve a community of people, companies, institutions and associations that operate in a limited area, so that there are at stake also certain widespread values and knowledges, alongside a series of cultural and social elements (Merlo 2003: 102).

There are more than 150 industrial districts in Italy, mostly located in the North and Centre of the country (Ricciardi 2010: 137), especially in the fashion industry (Brunetti et al. 2002: 52; Dunford 2006: 34; Viesti 2007: 53; Bacci 2004; Merlo 2003) such as Como for silk, Biella for wool and Florence for leather.

> Consider also the Italian leather fashion cluster, which contains well-known shoe companies such as Ferragamo and Gucci as well as a host of specialized suppliers of footwear components, machinery, molds, design services, and tanned leather. [...] It also consists of several chains

of related industries, including those producing different types of leather goods (linked by common inputs and technologies) and different types of footwear (linked by overlapping channels and technologies). […] The extraordinary strength of the Italian leather fashion cluster can be attributed, at least in part, to the multiple linkages and synergies that participating Italian businesses enjoy.

(Porter 1998: 79)

This industrial structure is particularly beneficial for the fashion industry because, as Michel Dunford observes,

in industries such as textiles, clothing, knitwear, and shoes, fashion/ seasonal factors are a stimulus to rapid changes in products: development cycles are short, prototyping is rapid, batches of products are small, the variety of products is great, and costs are spread across a wide range of goods.

(2006: 28)

As emphasized by Valerie Steele (2003: 2), 'the Italian fashion system is characterized by the vertical integrations of production from fiber to finished item'.

In this respect, Prada's production movies refer to a type of know-how that does not revolve around issues of craftsmanship, transcending the established association between Italy and handmade production. Italy has a long history of being considered as being placed outside of modernity (Parkins 2004: 258) both in the discourses of literature and tourism (Vestito 2006: 139). Yet, those narratives coexist alongside the ones celebrating its modern design (Snaiderbaur 2009: 64), showcasing the two facets of the 'made in Italy' phenomenon.

REPRESENTATIONS OF ITALIANICITY

The discourses of production that focus on issues of handmade craftsmanship and the ones that on the other hand feature automated process conjure up ideas of 'Italianicity' through different and contradictory traits, but both versions are nonetheless presented as being authentic to the public. This supports conceptualisations of authenticity as an effect of sense, a narrative construction that transcends any anchoring to reality. It is problematic to conceptualize authenticity in relation to its correspondence to an objective reality. Far from being a self-evident concept, authenticity is a culturally determined entity (McIntosh and Prentice 1999: 593).

Authenticity cannot be determined simply by retailing the objective material attributes of the artefact. It has to do not only with genuineness and the reliability of face value, but with the interpretation of genuineness and our desire for it.

(Spooner 1986: 200)

Authenticity is not an intrinsic quality of objects, but the result of people's projections and expectations (Bruner 1991; Silver 1993) and of narrative strategies. There is an inherent paradox in authenticity, as it is 'seen as the unstageable, the untouched and the real (thing)' (Knudsen and Waade 2010: 22). Yet, nonetheless it can be staged (MacCannell 1973). As observed by Ning Wang

221

(1999: 351) 'things appear authentic not because they are inherently authentic but because they are constructed as such in terms of points of view, beliefs, perspectives, or powers'. In semiotic terms, authenticity is a textual strategy in the same way truth is (Greimas 1984), being conjured up through narratives that support such a modality of discourse.

The myths of authentic 'Italianicity' that the discourses of production employed by the luxury fashion brand examined in this article convey are presented as obvious. However, they are actually the result of a selection of traits associated with coherent communicative strategies that work as a 'lustral bath of innocence' (Barthes 1977: 51) naturalizing connotations of Italianicity. Those myths of authentic 'Italianicity' are in fact constructed entities that hide their nature as social and ideological constructs through an aura of reality (Barthes 1974), translating concepts that are culturally constructed 'into self-evident laws of nature thereby reinforcing social stereotypes and making them appear inevitable' (Bronwen and Ringham 2006: 213).

NARRATIVES OF PRODUCTION AND NATIONAL IDENTITY

Narratives of handmade craftsmanship and high-tech manufacturing are both strongly associated with the Italian fashion industry and imply a contradiction that seems to be problematic for luxury fashion brands that emphasize their heritage in terms of craftsmanship in their communication and focus on issues of handmade production. This is exemplified in the case of a Ferragamo video focusing on the production of its women's shoes, which clarifies that it is true that 'most of the manufacturing stages are done by machine, but the machine is always guided by man's experienced hand' (Ferragamo 2010c). This fosters conceptualizations of the Italian fashion industry as being a 'marriage of traditional craftsmanship, innovative design, and modern industrial technology' (Steele 2003: 117). This phenomenon is often described as the artisanal production of industrial goods (Calabrese 2009: 39). Prada also goes in this direction. Despite showing phases of automated manufacturing, at the same time it aims to reinforce its prestige and heritage through other production videos that focus on the craftsmanship and handmade production involved in their more expensive lines, such as *Haute Couture*. This is epitomized by a video that showcases the handmade finishing of a special edition of the Prada eau de toilette, Amber pour homme that presents the metal casing of the bottle being covered in leather by the hand of a skilled craftsman (Prada 2011c). Despite the fact that this special edition is very different from the average fragrances that are completely produced in automated factories, the video actually suggests that all the Prada products are made by hand by skilled specialists, thus perpetuating the myth of the label and its intrinsic craftsmanship. In fact, the Prada brand was born in 1913 as a workshop specializing in leather products.

The different, and even contradictory, traits associated with Italian fashion are a function of the richness of the Italian identity and the variety of traits of 'Italianicity' it comprises. This reinforces the idea that national identity is not a fixed entity but a conglomeration of different traits, a mutable and fuzzy entity that allows enough diversification for brands to pick and choose the most appropriate characteristic for their ends. For this reason, in this article, Italian national identity is examined in terms of 'Italianicity' instead of 'Italianness'.

As Tim Edensor argues (2002: 17), national identity can be created and reproduced through different mundane elements like landscapes, films or advertising and is grounded 'in the everyday'. In accordance with Michael Billig (1995: 6), he also argues that national identity is reproduced through the apparent innocence of everyday discourses. Edensor argues that national identity can be 'found in a bewilderingly dense profusion of signifiers, objects, practices and spaces' and is 'constituted by innumerable pathways, connections and sources' (Edensor 2002: 33). National identity is not only constructed through discourses of nationalism but also the ones of 'nationnes' (Borneman 1992: 352) that feature in a variety of media, narratives and practices. These are more discreet mechanisms that can actively create nations' identity. In this perspective, national identity is a 'fluid' concept (Cartocci 2009: 184) or a 'liquid' entity (Bauman 2000) that, far from being fixed and established once and for all, remains 'perpetually open to context, to elaboration and to imaginative reconstruction' (Cubitt 1998: 3). In this sense, national identity is constantly evolving and open to be modified by a variety of players, including the brands that are considered here and the discourses of production that they employ.

So, national identity is not static and is 'never complete, always in process' (Hall 1990: 222). Brands also contribute to this process constructing myths of national identity that then circulate worldwide, creating and reshaping, in an on-going process, powerful images whose influence goes beyond the realm of commodities and into culture. In this sense, the products, discourses and narratives associated with luxury fashion labels examined here are pivotal, as they can greatly influence 'popular notions of Italianess, Frenchness and Britishness' (Davey 1999: 121). In this respect, it is not relevant whether those notions of national identity are the result of narratives developed within the boundaries of the countries in question or outside of them, as with the case of discourses of production employed by non-Italian luxury fashion brands that focus on the value of Italian know-how examined earlier. As Edensor argues (2002: 144), 'the production of national identity' can also occur 'outside of the nation'.

From this perspective, national identity is a 'discursive concept, built by different kinds of texts, tourist texts (brochures, leaflets, guides, pictures) and other kinds (movies, newspapers, literature)' (Brucculeri 2007: 1), created by different sources and media, in a comparative perspective based on difference as a salient identity-making tool (Ricoeur 1996). In semiotic terms, nations are texts (Ferraresi 2000: 245), entities created through narratives (Bhabha 1990) where at times reality and mystification merge (Hobsbawm and Ranger 1983). The ideas of national identity that those different elements convey are neither natural nor obvious, but constructions whose strength does not lie in their accuracy.

Discourses of nationhood in branding are intrinsically selective. They do not aim to convey an accurate portrait of nations, but only emphasize certain traits associated with them that are functional in reinforcing the positive image of national brands. This means that they contribute to reshape conceptualisations of national identity by focusing only on the positive characteristics and rejecting less desirable associations, creating 'idyllic' images that in turn contribute to reinforce the positive image of the brands. In this sense, the notions created by brands as a function of this logic can be described as 'benign form of national consciousness because elements that are not benign are not permissible within a nation-branding framework' (Aronczyk 2008: 55).

Far from being parasitic entities that simply capitalize on Italian identity, brands are active players in its constant redefinition. For example Prada,

Ferragamo and Gucci were, alongside other luxury fashion labels, the creators of the association between Italy and fashion. In this sense, the discourses and narratives employed by luxury fashion brands are pivotal sites for shaping and mobilizing notions of Italian national identity.

REFERENCES

Aaker, David (1990), 'Brand extensions: The good, the bad, and the ugly', *Sloan Management Review*, 31: 4, pp. 47–56.

Aiello, Gaetano and Donvito, Raffaele (2006), 'L'evoluzione del concetto di lusso e la gestione strategica della marca. Un'analisi qualitativa delle percezioni sul concetto, sulla marca e su un prodotto di lusso', in Andreani, Jean-Claude and Collesei, Umberto (eds), *Proceedings of the 5ᵗʰ International Conference Marking Trends*, Venice 20–21 January 2006, pp. 1–16.

Alleres, Danielle (1990), *Luxe: Strategies-Marketing*, Paris: Economica.

Aronczyk, Melissa (2008), 'Living the brand: Nationality, globality and the identity strategies of nation branding consultants', *International Journal of Communication*, 2: 1, pp. 41–65.

Bacci, Lorenzo (2004), *Distretti e imprese leader nel sistema moda della Toscana*, Milano: Franco Angeli.

Barthes, Roland (1974), *Miti D'Oggi*, Torino: Einaudi.

—— (1977), *Image-Music-Text*, London: Fontana.

Bauman, Zygmunt (2000), *Liquid Modernity*, Cambridge: Polity Press.

Berthon, Pierre, Pitt, Leyland, Parent, Michael and Berthon, Jean-Paul (2009), 'Aesthetics and ephemerality: Observing and preserving the luxury brand', *California Management Review*, 52: 1, pp. 45–66.

Bhabha, Homi (1990), *Nation and Narration*, New York: Routledge.

Billig, Michael (1995), *Banal Nationalism*, London: Sage.

Borneman, John (1992), *Belonging in the Two Berlins: Kin, State, Nation*, Cambridge: Cambridge University Press.

Bronwen, Martin and Ringham, Felizitas (2006), *Key Terms in Semiotics*, London: Continuum International Publishing Group Ltd.

Brucculeri, Mariaclaudia (2007), 'Nation branding and cultural identity, the case of the tourist logos', *E|C Rivista dell' Associazione Italiana Studi Semiotici On-Line*, pp. 1–15.

Bruner, Edward (1991), 'Transformation of self in tourism', *Annals of Tourism Research*, 18: 2, pp. 238–50.

Brunetti, Giorgio, Micelli, Stefano and Minoja, Mario (2002), *La sfida delle tecnologie di rete: distretti lombardi e veneti a confronto*, Milano: Franco Angeli.

Calabrese, Omar (2009), 'I segni dell'identita italiana', in Fondazione Intercultura (ed.), *Identita' Italiana tra Europa e societa' multiculturale*, Siena: Fondazione Intercultura, pp. 35–46.

Cartocci, Roberto (2009), 'Come si distrugge l'identita italiana', in Fondazione Intercultura (ed.), *Identita' Italiana tra Europa e societa' multiculturale*, Siena: Fondazione Intercultura, pp. 181–97.

Chadha, Radhaand and Husband, Paul (2006), *The Cult of the Luxury Brand: Inside Asia's Love Affair With Luxury*, London: Nicholas Brealey.

Chevalier, Michel and Mazzalovo, Gerald (2008), *Luxury Brand Management: A World of Privilege*, Hoboken and Chichester: John Wiley and Sons.

Crivelli, Giulia (2009), 'La fabbrica globale è sul Brenta', *Moda24 - Il Sole 24 ORE*, 20 June 2009, http://www.luxury24.ilsole24ore.com/ModaStili/2009/06/fabbrica-globale-brenta_1.php. Accessed 1 December 2013.

Cubitt, Geoffrey (1998), *Imagining Nations*, Manchester: Manchester University Press.

Davey, K. (1999), *English Imaginaries: Six Studies in Anglo-British Modernity*, London: Lawrence and Wishart.

Dolce and Gabbana (2011), 'Dolce&Gabbana jewellery: A love story', http://www.youtube.com/watch?v=0axZXFrrn3U. Accessed 1 December 2013.

—— (2012), 'Sicily bag by Dolce&Gabbana', http://www.youtube.com/watch?v=YEme9GwRhAY. Accessed 1 December 2013.

Dubois, Bernard and Paternault, Claire (1995), 'Understanding the world of international luxury brand: The dream formula', *Journal of Advertising Research*, 35: 4, pp. 69–76.

Dubois, Bernard, Laurent, Gilles and Czellar, Sandor (2001), 'Consumer rapport to luxury: Analysing complex and ambivalent attitudes', Consumer Research Working Article No.736, HEC, Jouy-en-Josas, France, pp. 1–56.

Dunford, Michel (2006), 'Industrial districts, magic circles, and the restructuring of the Italian textiles and clothing chain', *Economic Geography*, 82: 1, pp. 27–59.

Edensor, Tim (2002), *National Identity, Popular Culture and Everyday Life*, Oxford and New York: Berg Publishers.

Fendi (2011a), 'Selleria', http://www.youtube.com/watch?v=5bvtNglycy4. Accessed 1 December 2013.

—— (2011b), 'Fendi Casa: A sofa story', http://www.youtube.com/watch?v=x-vqhniLeQU&feature=youtube_gdata_player. Accessed 1 December 2013.

—— (2011c), 'Fendi: Selleria timepieces', http://www.youtube.com/watch?v=CxTfO2r59Yg. Accessed 1 December 2013.

—— (2012a), 'Fendi Peekaboo made to order experience', http://www.youtube.com/watch?v=wDnGWItKW24. Accessed 1 December 2013.

—— (2012b), 'Baguette re-editions: Making of', http://www.youtube.com/watch?v=nADaXbIsdNw. Accessed 1 December 2013.

Ferragamo (2010a), 'The Salvatore Ferragamo bag, a masterpiece of craftsmanship', http://www.youtube.com/watch?v=JlXdElMOYuI&feature=youtube_gdata_player. Accessed 1 December 2013.

—— (2010b), 'Salvatore Ferragamo Tramezza, shoes fit for a gentleman', http://www.youtube.com/watch?v=1oaqN4tQBS0&feature=youtube_gdata_player. Accessed 1 December 2013.

—— (2010c), 'Salvatore Ferragamo women's shoes', http://www.youtube.com/watch?v=hJ5JiGsw5O4&feature=youtube_gdata_player. Accessed 1 December 2013.

Ferraresi, Marco (2000), 'Interpretare la marca Nazione', in Marco Lombardi (ed.), *Il dolce tuono. Marca e pubblicità nel terzo millennio*, Milano: Franco Angeli, pp. 241–76.

Fionda, Antoinette and Moore, Christopher (2009), 'The anatomy of the luxury fashion brand', *Journal of Brand Management*, 16: 5–6, pp. 347–63.

Giordani-Aragno, Bonizza (1983), *40 Years of Italian Fashion, 1940–1980: Original Drawings and Sketches of the Most Famous Italian Fashion Designers*, Roma: Made in Ltd.

Greimas, Algirdas Julien (1984), *Del senso 2. Narrativa, modalita; passioni.*, Milano: Bompiani.

Hall, Stuart (1990), 'Cultural identity and diaspora', in Jonathan Rutherford (ed.), *Identity: Community, Culture, Difference*, London: Lawrence & Wishart, pp. 222–237.

Hobsbawm, Eric John and Ranger, Terence (1983), *The Invention of Tradition*, Cambridge: Cambridge University Press.

Jackson, Tim (2004), 'A contemporary analysis of global luxury brand', in Margaret Bruce et al. (eds), *International Retail Marketing: A Case Study Approach*, Oxford: Butterworth-Heinemann, pp. 155–69.

Kapferer, Jean-Noel (2004), *The New Strategic Brand Management: Creating and Sustaining Brand Equity Long Term*, London: Kogan Page.

—— (2012), *The Luxury Strategy: Break the Rules of Marketing to Build Luxury Brands*, London: Kogan Page.

Kim, Chung and Lavack, Anne (1996), 'Vertical brand extensions: Current research and managerial implications', *Journal of Product & Brand Management*, 5: 6, pp. 24–37.

Knudsen, Britta Timm and Waade, Anne Marit (2010), *Re-investing Authenticity: Tourism, Place and Emotions*, Bristol and Buffalo: Channel View.

Loken, Barbara and Roedder John, Deborah (1993), 'Diluting brand beliefs: When do brand extensions have a negative impact?', *The Journal of Marketing*, 57: 3, pp. 71–84.

Lye, Ashley, Venkateswarlu, Pulakanam and Barrett, Jo (2001), 'Brand extensions: Prestige brand effects', *Australasian Marketing Journal*, 9: 2, pp. 53–65.

MacCannell, Dean (1973), 'Staged authenticity: Arrangements of social space in tourist settings', *American Journal of Sociology*, 79: 3, pp. 589–603.

Marc Jacobs (2011), 'Made in Italy: Marc Jacobs handbags', http://www.marc-jacobs.com/world-of-marc-jacobs/news-and-gossip/made-in-italy—marc-jacobs-handbags/ba3b5144-da75-4752-8550-694eead2d687. Accessed 1 December 2013.

McIntosh, Alison and Prentice, Richard (1999), 'Affirming authenticity: Consuming cultural heritage', *Annals of Tourism Research*, 26: 3, pp. 589–612.

Merlo, Elisabetta (2003), *Moda italiana: storia di un'industria dall'Ottocento a oggi*, Venezia: Marsilio.

Milberg, Sandra et al. (1997), 'Managing negative feedback effects associated with brand extensions: The impact of alternative branding strategies', *Journal of Consumer Psychology*, 6: 2, pp. 119–40.

Moore, Christopher and Birtwistle, Grete (2005), 'The nature of parenting advantage in luxury fashion retailing – the case of Gucci group NV', *International Journal of Retail & Distribution Management*, 33: 4, pp. 256–70.

Mortelmans, Dimitri (2005), 'Sign values in processes of distinction: The concept of luxury', *Semiotica*, 157: 1/4, pp. 497–520.

Okonkwo, Uche (2007), *Luxury Fashion Branding: Trends, Tactics, Techniques*, Basingstoke: Palgrave Macmillan.

Pambianco News (2012), 'Bruno Pavlovsky: Anche Chanel produce in Italia', http://www.pambianconews.com/bruno-pavlovsky-anche-chanel-produce-in-italia/. Accessed 1 December 2013.

Parkins, Wendy (2004), 'At home in Tuscany: Slow living and the cosmopolitan subject', *Home Cultures*, 1: 3, pp. 257–74.

Phau, Ian and Prendergast, Gerard (2000), 'Consuming luxury brands: The relevance of the Rarity Principle', *The Journal of Brand Management*, 8: 2, pp. 122–38.

Porter, Michael (1998), 'Clusters and the new economics of competition', *Harvard Business Review*, 76:6, pp. 77–90.

Prada (2011a), 'The Gucci New Bamboo: The making of', http://www.youtube.com/watch?v=zbrupTKXlKM&feature=relmfu%20,%20http://www.youtube.com/watch?v=85XU7SizykE&feature=youtube_gdata_player. Accessed 1 December 2013.

—— (2011b), 'The Gucci New Jackie: The making of', http://www.youtube. com/watch? v=85XU7SizykE&feature=youtube_gdata_player. Accessed 1 December 2013.

—— (2011c), 'Perfume finishing', http://www.prada.com/en/production-movies/video? videos=perfume_finishing&page=01&index=8. Accessed 1 December 2013.

Ricciardi, Antonio (2010), 'Le PMI localizzate nei distretti industriali: vantaggi competitivi, evoluzione organizzativa, prospettive future', *Quaderni di ricerca sull'artigianato*, 54, pp. 129–77.

Ricoeur, Paul (1996), *Sé come un altro/Onself as Another*, Milano: Jaca.

Rocca, Federico (2006), *Embroidery: Italian Fashion*, Bologna: Damiani.

Ross, Andrew (2004), 'Made in Italy: The trouble with craft capitalism', *Antipode*, 36: 2, pp. 209–16.

Roux, Elyette (1995), 'Consumer evaluation of luxury brand extension', in Bergadaa, Michelle (ed.), *Proceedings of the European Marketing Academy (EMAC)*: Clergy-Pontoise, 16–19 May 1995, pp. 1971–80.

Segre Reinach, Simona (2005), 'China and Italy: Fast Fashion versus Pret a Porter. Towards a new culture of fashion', *Fashion Theory: The Journal of Dress, Body & Culture*, 9: 1, pp. 43–56.

Silver, Ira (1993), 'Marketing authenticity in third world countries', *Annals of Tourism Research*, 20: 2, pp. 302–18.

Silverstein, Michael and Fiske, Neil (2003), *Trading Up: The New American Luxury*, New York: Portfolio.

—— (2005), *Trading Up (Revised Edition): Why Consumers Want New Luxury Goods… and How Companies Create Them*, New York: Portfolio.

Snaiderbaur, Salvatore (2009), '"Made in Italy" in China: From country of origin to country concept branding', *The Icfai Journal of Brand Management*, VI: 3 and 4, pp. 63–74.

Spooner, Brian (1986), 'Weavers and dealers; the authenticity of an oriental carpet', in Arjun Appadurai (ed.), *The Social Life of Things: Commodities in Cultural Perspective*, Cambridge: Cambridge University Press, pp. 195–235.

Steele, Valerie (2003), *Fashion, Italian style*, New Haven: Yale University Press.

Stegemann, Nicole (2006), 'Unique brand extension challenges for luxury brands', *Journal of Business & Economics Research*, 4: 10, pp. 57–68.

Taylor, Jim and Harrison, Doug (2008), *The New Elite: Inside the Minds of the Truly Wealthy*, New York: AMACOM.

Thomas, Dana (2007), *Deluxe: How Luxury Lost its Luster*, London: Allen Lane.

Tungate, Mark (2005), *Fashion Brands: Branding Style from Armani to Zara*, London: Kogan Page.

—— (2009), *Luxury World: The Past, Present and Future of Luxury Brands*, London and Philadelphia: Kogan Page.

Vaccari, Alessandra (2005), *Wig wag: le bandiere della moda/The flags of Fashion*, Venezia: Marsilio.

Vestito, Caterina (2006), *Tourism Discourse and the Representation of Italy: a Critical Analysis of English Guidebooks*, Napoli: Universita' di Napoli.

Viesti, Gianfranco (2007), *Le sfide del cambiamento: i sistemi produttivi nell'Italia e nel Mezzogiorno d'oggi*, Roma: Donzelli Editore.

Wang, Ning (1999), 'Rethinking authenticity in tourism experience', *Annals of Tourism Research*, 26: 2, pp. 349–70.

White, Nicola (2000), *Reconstructing Italian Fashion: America and the Development of the Italian Fashion Industry*, Oxford: Berg.

CONTRIBUTOR DETAILS

Alice Dallabona is a teaching fellow in fashion marketing at the University of Leeds in the School of Design. Her work examines issues related to luxury fashion, fashion communication and marketing, digital media and new technologies but also branding and national identity. Alice has explored such issues, with a particular focus on the Italian luxury fashion industry and Italian national identity, during her Ph.D. at Nottingham Trent University (UK), for which she was awarded the Vice-Chancellor Studentship. She holds a Laurea Magistrale in Semiotic Disciplines (University of Bologna, Italy) and a MA in Critical Theory and Cultural Studies (University of Nottingham, UK).

Contact: University of Leeds, School of Design, LS2 9JT, Leeds, UK.
E-mail: a.dallabona@leeds.ac.uk

PART IV

Brands in Historical Context

Global Fashion Brands: Style, Luxury & History

© 2014 Intellect Ltd Chapter. English language. doi: 10.1386/GFB.1.231_1

SHAUN BORSTROCK
University of Hertfordshire

Do contemporary luxury brands adhere to historical paradigms of luxury?

ABSTRACT

Luxury is a single category that is demonstrably unstable and it is manifested in the changing landscape of the luxury brand market which is considered as part of the fashion cycle. Luxury brands continue to extend their product offerings to satisfy a continually growing consumer market in which branding has become increasingly important. Existing definitions of luxury are unstable due to an ever changing cyclical market and are exacerbated by marketing, branding, advertising and mass production. It is important to remove the façade of marketing and branding in order to provide a perspective that acknowledges the change and importance of fashion business methodologies to ensure business growth. At the same time it is also important to recognize the fundamental significance of luxury brand heritage and the convenient message this sends to the consumer. It is evident that concepts of luxury will continue to be defined as part of a complex structure of understanding and interpretation. In light of this, one must not lose sight of the importance of the knowledge of the craftsmen and women and their ability to communicate the intricacies of their skills in order to provoke and challenge the perpetuating luxury debate. A significant part of the current luxury brands market is predominantly made up of companies that were founded in the seventeenth and eighteenth centuries. In this period, materials and craftsmanship were prioritized. My article traces a shift in the luxury paradigm.

KEYWORDS

luxury fashion
luxury brands
Louis Vuitton
Prada
Ralph Lauren
Louis XIV

> Worldwide luxury goods market revenues were forecast to grow by seven percent in the final three months of 2012 versus the same period in 2011, culminating in full year growth in 2012 to 10 percent, and pushing total luxury goods revenues to an estimated €212 billion.
>
> (Bain and Company 2012)

INTRODUCTION

As the luxury brands market continues to grow, its products are made available to an increasingly wide and diverse consumer group. I intend to set out to explore the changes in definitions of luxury and luxury branded products, and the meanings attached to them. It is important to understand the ways in which international conglomerates promote their products in order to add value to them in what has become an increasingly saturated market. Christopher Berry suggests that 'luxury can without hesitation be tacked on to almost any article of merchandise from pizzas to handbags, from a fountain pen to a dressing gown and done so presumably to make it more desirable and the more likely to be bought' (1999: 10). Berry's argument that luxury can be attached to anything not only challenges, but also questions the value the term has when used in conjunction with goods and or services. One of the challenges faced in an analysis of luxury is addressing the lack of transparency and willingness to disclose the kinds of information that could be seen to question the notion of exclusivity, something that all luxury brands promote in order to increase sales of their products. It is, I believe, the benefits, linked to a growth in industry, and the recognition that luxury products are in fact inextricably linked to economic gain and growth.

It is also apposite to consider the differentiation between mass produced products, those that could be considered luxury brands, and goods that are made by highly skilled craftsmen in limited numbers. What may be needed is a clear market segregation to maintain differentiation between luxury and luxury brands. I suggest that craftsmanship is inextricably linked to luxury. Examples of luxury products could be an *haute couture* dress or bespoke piece of luggage that may be made to order by a highly skilled craftsman or woman using the finest materials. Scarcity, quality and innovation are also characteristics that define a luxury product. To define luxury in this way makes explicit the characteristics of a luxury product as opposed to a luxury branded product that is mass produced. Defining luxury addresses the misrepresentation of luxury brands that do not adopt the characteristics found in a luxury product but are nevertheless marketed and sold as luxury.

I contend that the historical notions of luxury were clearly articulated through notions of craftsmanship, but that although the term is applied to contemporary products they do not carry the same inherent principles of make. A shortcoming of the existing literature is that it takes a partial view and primarily considers marketing and branding in today's luxury brands market at the expense of other considerations such as skill, craftsmanship and materials. Increasingly the number of texts including *Let Them Eat Cake: Marketing Luxury to the Masses – As Well As the Classes* by Pamela N. Danziger (2005) and *The Luxury Strategy: Break the Rules of Marketing to Build Luxury Brands* by Jean-Noël Kapferer and Vincent Bastien (2009), N. Fiske and M. J. Silverstein (2005) and Uche Okonkwo (2007) address luxury in step with branding but fail to create a distinction between luxury and luxury branded products. Within this recent literature there is a distinct absence of analysis of the contemporary designer and luxury markets and their impact on notions of luxury. These texts are predominantly located within the field of marketing and as such focus on strategic sales techniques rather than detailing the material conditions of the luxury market.

THE LUXURY AND LUXURY BRAND LANDSCAPE

The use of the term luxury is widespread. It is therefore useful to set out a broad historical context for luxury and its social significance. The seventeenth and eighteenth centuries demonstrate how luxury was defined by extravagance where royalty and aristocracy established the parameters that have subsequently constituted luxury. The significance of luxury goods and their consumption during the seventeenth and eighteenth centuries is well documented and included in the works of Maxine Berg and Helen Clifford (1999), Christopher Berry (1994), Chandra Mukerji (1997), Carolyn Sargentson (1998), John Sekora (1977) and Werner Sombart (1967).

In order to gain a better understanding of what luxury represents in the current market and how the perceptions of luxury have evolved, historical texts such as Bernard Mandeville's *Fable of the Bees* ([1732] 1988) emerges as a key point of reference. Mandeville was one of the first to defend the notion of luxury as something that would be of economic benefit rather than a social vice. Berry states that

> Mandeville not only regards luxury, characterised by effeminacy and enervation, as one of these vices but also openly admits its close relationship to pride, avarice, fraud, envy and vanity. However – and here is the source of his notoriety – he nevertheless openly points out its connection with public benefits.
>
> (Berry 1999: 128)

Mandeville not only set out to define luxury as being socially and economically beneficial, he also questioned how best to define luxury suggesting that 'if everything is to be Luxury (as in strictness it ought) that is not immediately necessary to make Man subsist as he is a living Creature ...' (Mandeville, B. ([1732] 1988: 107). Within the context of my argument it would be difficult to consider anything not necessary to survive as a luxury but as Berry says, Mandeville draws 'attention to the experientially warranted fact that what is thought superfluous by one rank in society is looked upon as a necessity by another, superior, rank' (1999: 129) This argument has long been a discussion point and clearly articulates social and material aspirations that were evident during the seventeenth and eighteenth centuries, and arguably still exist albeit in modified form today.

During the seventeenth and eighteenth centuries power was asserted through grand displays of wealth. This is evident in France during the reign of Louis XIV in the latter part of the 1600s. During this period, the luxury market led to an increase in trade, expanding markets and created new international trading relationships. Jean Baptiste Colbert, who served as the Minister of Finance in France from 1665 to 1683 was responsible for increasing economic growth in France which he encouraged by supporting industries through subsidies. Although his schemes were not always successful, he oversaw strict manufacturing policies establishing factories producing luxury goods. 'Colbert certainly set out economic policies to make money, but he pursued this goal by improving the quality and variety of French consumer goods' (Mukerji 1997: 116).

The influence of the king and nobility is due specifically to their political significance and was used to establish their power and social standing.

> When Louis XIV ascended the throne, the legitimacy of the French monarchy itself was disputed … hence even the monarch himself, at the beginning of his reign, needed to make social claims about his authority. This he did lavishly with his great palaces and the elaborate parties he staged there. Louis XIV used conspicuous display not just to solidify his reign but to elevate his favourites. The multi-day fêtes he organized were dedicated to new mistresses, and the buildings he built for these mistresses were monuments to their power.
>
> (Murkeji 1997: 442)

The great gardens of Versailles came to symbolize the power of the king 'they testified to the power European politico-economic empire that Louis XIV and Colbert were trying to forge with the offices of expanding state bureaucracy' (Mukerji 1997: 443).

It is evident that the court of Louis XIV was responsible for commissioning luxury goods. These included buildings and items used both internally and externally that would publicly display the king's wealth and power. Examples include furniture, tapestries, statues and fountains. 'The state was the primary entrepreneur of the period, developing crown-controlled international trading systems, and crown-sanctioned manufactures. These politico-economic institutions were the ones that supplied most of the luxury goods at Versailles' (Mukerji 1997: 448).

The increased relevance of the extent and value of land owned in relation to the authority of the king became central to his assertion of power. 'By the reign of Louis XIV, territorial politics entered the French court, not as a threat to the king, but as a way to associate his legitimacy with the management of the state' (Mukerji 1997: 21). In addition to establishing a hierarchy of land, Colbert attempted to restructure the French economy. The hierarchical fashion system was already in place and Colbert ensured that the items that were commissioned for the court were deemed fit for the king. He guaranteed that the court nobles would be dressed in the finest clothing manufactured in France in tribute to the regime. In this way, Colbert's undeniable loyalty to the king caused him to act irresponsibly in economic terms. As a great supporter of industry he used funds from the treasury to help to start businesses and maintain them during their formative years. The result of this was that France became more of a centre for fashion than an industrial power (Mukerji 1997).

This illustrates his desire to underpin the power of the monarchy resulting in its absolute, although temporary, power. Mukerji suggests that 'it is also possible that the end-product of his ministerial policies was not *supposed* to be rational bureaucracy, economic expansion, or efficient tax accumulation, but the glorification of the king and state' (Mukerji 1997: 117, original emphasis). It would appear that Colbert was less interested in financial gain than elevating the royal household and glorifying the French state. He would commission Les Gobelins, the French tapestry and furniture makers, to produce vast numbers of decorative pieces for Versailles, which at the time was instrumental in setting standards of luxury thereby demonstrating the significance of their skills and the role they played. Les Gobelins produced tapestries and furniture of the highest quality greatly elevating French taste and at the same time established France as a centre for luxury and elegance.

In some respects, the tapestries came to symbolize the essence of luxury production in France. The king was the embodiment of all wealth and power and luxury objects were a sign of this. Not only were the Les Gobelins tapestries beautiful pieces, they also 'served to document important events in the reign, such as military victories, the birth of dauphin, or the king's visit to Les Gobelins' (Mukerji 1997: 123). This grand scale commissioning of work by Colbert on behalf of the king, not only for the various palaces but also the Louvre, 'glorified the monarchy as much as any triumphal arch or victory statue in a formal garden or provincial town square' (Mukerji 1997: 123). The commissioning of work by highly skilled craftsman that would be displayed to courtiers or publicly contributed to France becoming known for luxury products all over Europe. This helped France become a centre for luxury and fashion, something that continues today.

The French, 'fashionable aristocrats, who had already been cosmopolitan for generations, were certainly aware of the diversity of cultural traditions in Europe. But their tastes were becoming economically and culturally more influential. Fashions for goods were beginning to be recognized as forces affecting international trade' (Mukerji 1997: 103). According to Mukerji this resulted in Colbert imposing sanctions on the importation of goods so as not to damage the local trade. Luxury was seen to be a 'primary threat to the state, the state was (therefore) obliged to defend itself through sumptuary laws and similar measures' (Sekora 1977: 52) The imposition of taxes and limiting the importation of goods was common throughout Europe and employed in order to control the consuming habits of the populace so the governing bodies could maintain control and power.

However as the consumption of luxury goods was still limited to those of the aristocracy, this would change. Referring to fashion, Sarah Maza (2006: 126) suggests that because:

> [...] the function of clothing evolved over the course of the century: where garments had once primarily marked a person's status, they became increasingly (for women especially) a sign of taste and fashion [therefore it was] becoming increasingly difficult to tell a person's rank from his or her clothing [and] more and more people in the middling and lower ranks of society had access to garments and furnishings once available only to the elites.

Her observation identifies a pattern that also exists today where fashion produced by luxury brands are readily available and do not illustrate ones social standing. In fashion terms, *haute couture* is one of the ways of representing a luxury purchase within the fashion market. This sentiment is echoed by Murkeji who suggests that 'Colbert wanted to make mostly fine goods for aristocrats and financiers, who were the ones who had the money to spend on fashion' (Mukerji 1997: 103). Status was identified through visual markers where despite a certain element of accessibility to fashionable goods, distinction was still created through consumption. Within a contemporary market it becomes more difficult to recognize a luxury good as it becomes assimilated by an increased number of purveyors and consumed at all levels in the market. The luxury branded product lacks the defining factors that make them luxury; these include the knowledge and the skill of the maker and the rarity and quality of the materials.

Luxury, as defined by the eighteenth century luxury debate, was determined specifically by wealth, an accumulation of power and social standing which has translated into a marketing tool for designer and luxury branded products in the twenty-first century. In addition, capricious, extravagant spending and fantastical displays of affluence throughout the eighteenth century by the nobility further defined the concept (Berg and Clifford 1999). The determination of the court to differentiate themselves from the masses was evident and made apparent through their flamboyant lifestyles and magnificent spending. The court, along with the nouveaux-riches, contributed to the expansion of the demand for luxuries. It was during this time that notions of luxury were clearly articulated and socially agreed but although the term luxury is applied to contemporary consumer products, they do not carry the same inherent principles of manufacture. For example the items commissioned by the court were not available to the general public.

In most cases luxury products during the eighteenth century were reserved for those who could afford them; the monarchy and aristocracy. What is evident is that there is no clear definition of what constitutes a luxury product in the contemporary consumer market. This could be seen to be problematic as reclassifying all types of modern goods as luxury diminishes the value of the very clear boundaries of definitions set during the seventeenth and eighteenth centuries.

Much is written about the value of producing and selling luxury goods during the eighteenth century and it is impossible to consider it all. What is evident according to Sargentson is that 'Paris had an international reputation for luxuries' (1998: 99) and that the retail of luxury goods was encouraged. Sargentson goes on to state that the

> organization of the production and distribution of luxury items was complex, characterized by a high degree of specialization in terms of both production and retailing skills, by close relationships of competition and dependence between makers and merchants. The mercers were prohibited from manufacturing, and their expertise lay almost entirely in the sphere of marketing.
>
> (1998: 99)

He also states that their shops 'had become designed spaces for the displays, examination and consumption of goods by a clientele sensitive to fashion' (Sargentson 1998: 99). Despite varying opinions regarding the good and evil of luxury in Europe, views started to change and '… luxury as it had been viewed for centuries underwent a lasting devaluation: from myth to a fiction, from an ethic to a prejudice, and from an essential general element of moral theory to a minor, technical element of economic theory' (Sekora 1977: 53). The economics of luxury would continue to dominate the luxury debate as the markets changed and luxury products became more accessible.

During the eighteenth century in France, the king was responsible for the structures that governed the production and consumption of goods. It was one of the main ways in which the French court differentiated themselves from the lower order. Their flamboyant lifestyles and magnificent spending of the court, along with the nouveaux riches, contributed to the quantitative expansion of the demand for luxuries. 'The nation and state were embodied in the king, and the ruler and the state were represented by the king's things' (Auslander 1996: 80). Although this would of course change,

> the luxury prevailing at the courts spread gradually to all the circles that were in any way connected with the court or saw fulfilment of their ambitions identified with court life. This description, applies to the entire moneyed class which was gripped with the same fondness for luxury as the court circles.
>
> (Sombart 1967: 80)

The determined aspiration of the courtiers transformed consumer culture. Those with enough money and power began to buy into the concept of luxury and the idea of being able to show one's worth through material things became an obsession. The flamboyant lifestyles of the nobility during the seventeenth and eighteenth centuries could be seen to be the starting point for the popular understanding of luxury today but that this contemporary understanding is also based on a distortion of that original notion.

It is important to note that other European countries were also producing luxury goods during the seventeenth and eighteenth centuries. However, luxury in England, was interpreted by certain groups as a licentious vice and this became a dominant theme of some schools of thought during the eighteenth century. There was much debate regarding luxury, *The London Magazine* in September 1754 contained the following;

> … amongst the many reigning vices of the present age none have risen to a greater height than that fashionable one of luxury, and few require a more immediate suppression, as it not only enervates the people, and debauches their morals, but also destroys their substance.
>
> (Aurelius 1754: 64)

Luxury was associated with negative values and there existed a need to illustrate the positive potential of luxury to both society and business. In *The Wealth of Nations* of 1776, Adam Smith '… expressed a sense of the enormity of a passion for individual and selfish possession of a pair of diamond buckles' (Berg and Clifford 1999: 68). N. De Marchi suggests that Smith; '… seems to have regarded wantonness and caprice as the marks of true luxury spending, in this way directing us to means as well as motive and to wealth levels as well as to types of goods as such' (De Marchi and Van Miegroet 1999: 383). This further illustrates how notions of luxury have become defined through the indulgences of the wealthy at that time.

During the eighteenth century, fashion and luxury were only available to those who could afford it and, as Smith argued, had social ramifications. Smith acknowledged the role that the consumer played within a social environment, aspiring to what others have. Smith's writings had considerable impact in the late eighteenth century and still have relevance within contemporary consumer culture. Smith states that within trade there is often the pursuit of interests that results in the promotion of 'society' over and above what was originally intended (Smith 1776: 330). Luxury, aside from causing obvious divisions in class, also caused some to sell their land and worldly possessions in order to acquire luxuries. The divisions in thought and opinion provided a platform for debate. Yet, although luxury was subject to moral criticism in which consumption of such goods was frowned upon as undermining the virtue of consumers, these same consumers were undeterred and continued their pursuit of luxury products.

> Eighteenth century defenders of luxury, on the other hand, chose to deemphasise morality in favour of economics, arguing in the main that luxury could increase and distribute wealth and was therefore a laudable trait in society. Whatever its moral blemishes, they said, luxury served a needful economic function.
>
> (Sekora 1977: 113)

This thought is further discussed in *Consumers and Luxury* (1999) and the conclusions drawn by Berg and Clifford also acknowledge the changes in opinion. They state; 'luxury was all that was not necessary ... as the luxury debate developed over the century; it was disassociated from a moral frame-work, and was increasingly seen in terms of economic advantages' (Berg and Clifford 1999: 3). The luxury debate continues today and continues to be seen as one that drives economic advantages for the producers and providers of products and services.

Sekora suggests that during the eighteenth century 'variations in usage were natural and common throughout the century, for luxury probably was the greatest single social issue and the greatest single commonplace' (1977: 75). It was recognized that luxury products were inextricably linked to economic gain and growth that benefited industry and society as a whole. According to Berry, 'the eighteenth century was the period when the debate as to the meaning and value-laden status of luxury came into prominence' (1994: 126).

Today, it could be said that the consumer understands and interprets what they buy through historical appropriation. When it comes to luxury, the contemporary marketing of goods is reliant upon the values asserted through historically influenced visual narratives that define as well as explain the concept. It is no longer exclusively through individual displays of extravagance that luxury is marketed because the focus has shifted to luxury branded fashion that is produced and consumed globally. The use of aspirational market-ing methods over the past twenty years has resulted in a tremendous shift in the way in which luxury is portrayed. This is in part due to companies such as Louis Vuitton who diversified from their historical product focus to concen-trate on the emerging luxury brand fashion market. In addition, the empha-sis is now on universal consumer lifestyle aspirations. In contrast, luxury as a concept defined by connoisseurs is traditionally and generally understood in the design industry as applying to aspirational goods that are made by highly skilled craftsmen and are exclusive and or rare, usually rendering them expen-sive. However, in contemporary terms and as a result of mass production, it is difficult to justify the use of the word luxury to define contemporary luxury branded fashion products as craftsmen-made, exclusive and or rare.

Luxury is no longer as contained and distinct as it was and has become the preserve of different social groups.

> Demand emerges as a necessary precondition and stimulant to the subsequent growth of mass-production. In particular, the 'trickle-down' effects of the demand for luxury goods, i.e. the gradual percolation and diffusion of upper-class tastes through all strata of society, anticipate and expedite the arrival of mass markets.
>
> (Fine and Leopold 1993: 121)

Despite fluctuations in the markets, luxury and luxury branded products continue to be produced and consumed. The difference is that luxury products are still produced in limited numbers by craftsmen and women whereas luxury branded products are mass produced. There is evidence to suggest that luxury brand conglomerates continue to expand around the world. Financial results released by Bain and Company, the global corporate management company, suggest that the largest luxury brand conglomerates continue to demonstrate year on year financial growth. They suggest that

> worldwide luxury goods market revenues will grow as much as 50 percent faster than global GDP, with an expectation of four to five percent growth in 2013 and five to six percent annual average through 2015, on track to break the €250 billion sales threshold by mid-decade.
>
> (Bain and Company 2013)

Connoisseurs on the other hand have maintained a luxury market that is defined by craftsmanship. Earlier, it was suggested that a product would be considered luxurious in historical terms if it was made by craftsmen, if the products were exclusive, rare (or both) and made from the finest of materials. A contemporary definition of luxury might be something that defines products as hand-crafted, using the finest materials, and in which artefacts maintain their value outside of the global mass consumer market. An outstanding difference between a luxury product and a luxury branded product is that the luxury branded product tends to be fashionable. The notion of fashion is irrelevant to luxury products as they do not come in and go out of fashion. Berry suggests that 'the transient quality of the status "luxury" necessarily means that a particular "luxury good" will move to the snob affect. This means that self-styled purveyors of luxury goods must always be on their guard to maintain the cachet of "exclusiveness"' (1994: 27). He goes on to suggest that clothing provides a good illustration of how this transient quality of luxury may work. He states that

> there are on the one hand, the fashion leaders and practitioners of *haute couture* and, on the other, the mass market ready-to-wear manufacturer. The latter can advertise a 'luxury' silk blouse to be obtained via mail order, while the former rely on stylistic innovation, inherent quality of raw materials and expertise in cutting and stitching, together with the status of a 'name'.
>
> (Berry 1994: 27)

I suggest that it is not only clothing that provides a platform for this distinction to be made but all goods produced by luxury brands today. *Haute couture* as an example of the very top of clothing production is not dissimilar to that of producing a trunk or bespoke bag. What is clear is that the relationship between fashion and luxury is long-standing. Charles Worth is an example of a pioneering couturier during the nineteenth century who collaborated with Louis Vuitton to ensure that the trunks Vuitton produced were fit for purpose and addressed the needs of their clients. Similar relationships still exist today where collaborations between craftsman, milliners and hat box makers, for example, ensure that their products are well packaged and serve their clients in particular ways. The continuing relationships at the top end of the consumer market are distinct and fulfil the demands of those customers whose specific needs cannot be addressed though a simple exchange in a retail environment. When considering the relationships between crafts-men, it serves to clarify, and indeed distinguish the notion of craftsmanship from that of mass production.

Richard Sennett states that 'the craftsman explores dimensions of skill, commitment, and judgement in a particular way. It focuses on the inti-mate connection between hand and head'. He goes on to say that 'every good craftsman conducts a dialogue between concrete practices and thinking; this dialogue evolves into sustaining habits, and these habits establish a rhythm between problem solving and problem finding' (Sennett 2008: 9). What is apparent are the inherent differences between the ways in which a crafts-man engages with his work to that of someone producing goods on a produc-tion line. The craftsman has the knowledge and skill to select materials, work with and produce a product from design concept to end product. The decision making is something that is inherent in the production of the product. This process differs from that of a production line worker who has little or no input into the design and or construction of a product. The production line worker is limited to the task of making the item. This, it could be said is what differ-entiates the maker of a luxury product from that of a luxury branded product.

It has been important to define a period of time when luxury was at its most prevalent to establish the differences that have contributed to the inter-pretations and understandings of the concept today. In order to understand the significance of luxury's history, it is worth taking a brief detour to explain and situate the argument. As has been established the eighteenth century is a significant starting point. During this period 'we see luxury goods distin-guished [as] ornamental building, furniture, collections of books, pictures, frivolous jewels and baubles …' (Berg and Clifford 1999: 5). Today, the luxury brand customer understands and interprets what they buy through historical appropriation. This is evident in the ways luxury brands communicate their messages through advertising, their online presence and in some instances exhibitions in museums across the world. In 2012, two exhibitions opened showcasing the work of two luxury brands; the Louis Vuitton – Marc Jacobs' exhibition at Musée des Arts Décoratifs in Paris and The Metropolitan Museum of Art in New York's Costume Institute exhibition, 'Schiaparelli and Prada: Impossible Conversations'. The marketing of goods is reliant upon the values asserted through historically influenced visual narratives that define as well as explain the concept. In their book, *Consumers and Luxury: Consumer Culture in Europe (1650 – 1850)*, Berg and Clifford portray the seventeenth and eighteenth centuries as ones of extravagance where royalty and aris-tocracy defined the parameters of production and consumption that would come to constitute luxury (Berg and Clifford 1999). The power of the aristoc-racy was asserted through grand displays of wealth, no more evident than at Versailles in France during the reign of Louis XIV who, according to Sekora, was 'opposed to luxury of others' (Sekora 1977: 53). This is in stark contrast to the democratized luxury brands market we see today. Berg and Clifford amongst others acknowledge that through growth, the luxury market led to an increase of trade, expanding markets thereby redefining the process of trade. During the eighteenth century, luxury was defined through materials, craftsmanship and connoisseurship. Lee Shai Weissbach suggests that during the eighteenth century 'artisans … were thus concerned not only with the actual process of production but also with the quality and the value of the products they produced' (1982: 67). In contrast it could be argued, luxury is defined through mass production, mass consumption, marketing and celebrity. Theo Fennell, the jeweller, suggests that 'when we say luxury goods, what that really means is overpriced gegouls some enormous marketing company attached to a worldwide conglomerate weaves its magic and gets ludicrous prices for things that aren't worth a tenth of it' (2010). Fennell's point of view is not uncommon amongst his contemporaries.

The post industrial age has seen a new understanding and shift in definition of the luxury market due in part to the birth of the designer label in the late 1980s. It is however surprising to see the absence of any substantive critical debate about how, during the late 1980's, products defined as designer labels transformed themselves to become luxury branded goods. It could therefore be said that the designer label brought about the commodification of goods and services within what has today become the luxury brands market through the use of modern marketing methods. Over the last twenty years the concept of luxury has developed an additional contradictory definition. The two main strands that define luxury today arguably create a paradoxical understanding in the eyes of the customer of what luxury represents. The visual markers seen in marketing campaigns of the contemporary luxury brands are trading on pseudo eighteenth-century values. This is evident through the creation of 'scenarios' that adopt an aesthetic that will be argued is lavish in its execution. Luxury brands currently confer value on goods and services, otherwise perceived to be of less worth, to encourage consumption. This assertion is evidenced in the work of amongst others, Danziger (2005), Kapferer and Bastien (2009) and Okonkwo (2007).

In today's market, luxury brands have come to embody the shopping experience of the aspirational consumer. Luxury brand commentators do not address the need for differentiation between luxury goods and luxury branded products; they define them as the same thing. An example of this may be a handmade piece of Tanner Krolle luggage that is labour intensive and in which the best quality materials are used. The item is also made by highly skilled craftsmen as opposed to mass produced luggage made by Louis Vuitton on a production line. This lack of differentiation between something handmade and something made on a production line is highly problematic. Distinguishing luxury from a luxury brand is important as they are fundamentally different. M. Chevalier and M. Gutsatz state that:

> underlying the concept of luxury, there is the notion of exclusivity. A luxury product should be rare and slightly difficult to acquire. It should of course be available, but give the feeling that the purchaser is 'in the know', can identify what makes it so different from other products or other brands, and can demonstrate that he or she has better taste and is more sophisticated than the standard customer.
>
> (Chevalier and Gutsatz 2012: 4)

They go on to suggest that 'an obvious characteristic of a luxury object is quality'. Luxury as opposed to luxury brands has roots that come from a very specific remit, one of being grounded in the origins of the maker, craftsmanship and materials. However, the focus of many contemporary authors is the aspiration of the consumer and concentration on the purchasing experience rather than the product. They explore the methods surrounding the implementation of marketing techniques used in order to market goods and experiences in the luxury branded market. They also employ a variety of terms such as old luxury and new luxury in an attempt to create differentiation where it may not exist. They do not develop the distinction between old luxury and new luxury where old luxury emphasize the object and new luxury focuses on the experience, but categorize both within the context of a brand. Danziger for example, suggests that this 'means linking their luxury products and brands with emotional values that epitomise and resonate with the hopes, wishes, and dreams of the consumers when they envision a luxury lifestyle' (2005: 30). It could be argued that this view ignores the designer maker whose sole aim is to produce goods of the highest quality using the finest materials and ignoring mass production and consumption of their products. What is evident is that the ultimate aim of a luxury brand is to increase the consumption of goods. Through the reclassification of premium products redefined as a luxury brand and marketed as luxury, the customer is buying something that is misrepresented in that market. A luxury product is reclassified within the luxury brand remit losing its value through association. Mass production of luxury branded goods is encouraged, defined and communicated as 'luxury' at the expense of the luxury product which is defined by the maker, craftsmanship and materials. What emerges in much of the current literature is confusion between luxury and a luxury brand. Danziger and Kapferer and Bastien, for example, fail to acknowledge that the need for differentiation between product categories is what creates a diverse market and an aspirational customer. A fundamental flaw in their writing is the inconsistent reference to luxury and luxury brands. She considers them to be the same, where in fact, they are different. In addition, and this is where Danziger differs from her contemporaries, she not only defines luxury and luxury brands as the same, but also confuses luxury with luxury brands and brands as a whole. She talks about the 'brand story' (2005: 181) and that it needs to be revised, refined and reinvented as the values of the consumer changes.

Danziger states that

> the brand story needs to be revised, refined, and reinvented as the values of the consumer change, as they inevitably will. Brands must be expansive so that they can become part of many people's life and can change with the times. The lesson here is to look at brands that have longevity and have sustained themselves over time, like Polo Ralph Lauren as well as many other luxury brands that have a history of spanning decades, even centuries, and you find brands that continue to re-invent themselves to stay relevant.
>
> (Danziger 2005: 181)

It is interesting to note that Ralph Lauren unlike Louis Vuitton and Prada do not manufacture any of their own products, rather they outsource all manufacturing. Furthermore, their mode of production is more in line with a high end fashion retailer rather than a purveyor of luxury goods. Fashion designers, such as, Ralph Lauren are concerned with reinvention and change whereas those producing luxury items are more concerned with consistency and stability that is communicated through their product line rather than the marketing that is intended to drive sales.

The notion that luxury brands must sustain themselves over time through reinvention is consistent with contemporary marketing methods (that include those adopted by Louis Vuitton Moët Hennessey group (LVMH)) where increasing customer demand for product through a diverse product offering is at the core of economic growth and potential profitability. This is evident in the monthly advertising campaigns in magazines, such as, *Vogue* where new luxury branded products are advertised as part of the fashion cycle. However, luxury goods manufacturers often do not adhere to these principles; they instil a sense of consistency and continuity associated with the work they do.

Kapferer and Bastien take a different view, one that considers the product. From the outset they state that 'the reason why marketing … doesn't seem to work with luxury goods the same way it does with everyday consumer goods, even top-of-the-range consumer goods, is because the two are funda-mentally quite different' (2009: 5). What is clear from the writing of Kapferer and Bastien is that they do differentiate between what they define as luxury goods and everyday consumer goods. Even though they consider luxury prod-ucts to be different to everyday goods, they do not consider possible differ-ences between luxury branded products and luxury goods.

There is a distinct difference to the approaches of Kapferer and Bastien, and Danziger. However, both continue to refer to luxury and luxury brands as the same thing. The former define luxury products as luxury based on origin and place of manufacture. 'A luxury product, which carries a whole world with it, has to be produced in a place that is consistent with its world' (Kapferer and Bastien 2009: 14). This point of view is consistent with current trends where manufacturing of luxury goods in the place of origin is increasingly important and communicated as part of the heritage of a company.

> Products by Chanel or Hermès, being manufactured in France, truly are luxury products; products bearing a Dior or Burberry label, on the other hand, being manufactured in countries where labour costs are low and not in France (Dior's place of origin) or in the UK (Burberry's place of origin), are no longer entitled to be called luxury products: this kind of relocation for cost-cutting reasons is proof that these do not have (or no longer have) a sufficiently high level of quality or creativity – as regards the products concerned, at any rate – to justify a price level that would allow them to continue to be produced in their country of origin.
>
> (Kapferer and Bastien 2009: 14)

Whilst this point may be of merit, there is evidence that Chanel and Louis Vuitton do not manufacture all their products in France. Chanel have recently bought Barrie Knitwear in Scotland to manufacture their cashmere. I have been to that factory and have seen Chanel products being made there. Louis Vuitton manufactures certain items in America. Louis Vuitton, Prada and Hermès, it is alleged, also manufacture certain products in China. Few of the luxury brands are transparent about where their products are made as the 'Made In' and country of origin label adds value to their products. The issue that remains problematic is that Kapferer and Bastien move away from the luxury product descriptor to that of the luxury brand. The need for a luxury brand to be mass produced, retailed and marketed on a global scale becomes the intention for the brand to have longevity. Kapferer and Bastien argue that

> all of that holds especially true when the luxury brand sets out to conquer the world. Now, as we have seen previously this is something it has to do: a luxury brand that cannot go global finishes up disappearing; it is better to have a small nucleus of clients in every country – because there

is every chance that it will grow – than a large nucleus in just one country, which could disappear overnight. That's the law of globalization.

(Kapferer and Bastien 2009: 15)

This in itself is problematic as Kapferer and Bastien consider the classification of luxury goods and luxury branded products to be the same thing. The quote implies that if a purveyor of luxury goods as opposed to a luxury brand has no intention of tapping into a global market their company will fall short of realizing the ambitions of the luxury brand. Evidence suggests that it is not the intention of purveyors of luxury goods to expand their markets to such an extent that they become global concerns. The implication of trying to satisfy the global market would shift the emphasis from small production runs to mass production and consumption of their products. Mass production and mass consumption are not a realistic proposition for a designer maker where products are made on site in a workshop and not in a factory. The implications of creating a global luxury brand are far reaching and require substantial investment. A conglomerate, such as, the LVMH has the financial means and is able to provide, and communicate the brand values through the explicit use of a logo to create brand awareness. Fennell faced this problem in 2008 when his shareholders wanted to expand the company. In an interview Fennell explains the complexities:

> The reason I had the fall out with the business when I left for the year and a bit involved the owners if you like, who believed the business could be rolled out into what they saw as this pattern without realising that the people who did that had a vast financial support from the holding company and an enormous infrastructure to roll out into these places and suited them so to do. What they were doing was cashing on the years of incredibly expensive advertising worldwide by saying 'Kazakhstan, you have heard of us?' For us to go and do that would have taken enormous effort in reinventing the wheel each place we went. My belief is we either shouldn't do that or certainly not attempt to do that ourselves. If a bigger company came along and said we want to buy your company and we want to expand world-wide then it would not have been my position to say no. Some of the design and branding projects they got into with people who had no idea about our business at all therefore they were assuming a compound of other people's ideas that were incredibly expensive and of absolutely no value to anybody at all. It was incredibly expensive and cost millions of pounds to do and failed.
>
> (Fennell 2010)

Fennell acknowledges the potential problems that may arise should a company choose to stray from the intrinsic values inherent in the philosophy of its craftsman. He also acknowledges the power of global, multinational companies that have the financial means to expand world-wide. LVMH is an example of such a company. LVMH is one of the biggest and most powerful holding companies and owns the largest group of manufacturers and retailers of luxury branded products in the world. They produce goods that incorporate the brand logo in the design of the finished product. Examples of which include Louis Vuitton, Dior, Marc Jacobs, Loewe, Berluti and Kenzo. They have had a significant impact in relation to the global market and vertical integration.

Within the current luxury brands market, there is evidence that consumers acquire products that display the logo of the company that produces them. According to research conducted by Joseph Nunes at the University of Southern California and presented at the In Pursuit of Luxury conference in London in June 2010, Nunes suggests that since 2008 there has been an increase of more than 30 per cent of logo prominence applied to Louis Vuitton bags. This desire on the part of the customer to consume conspicuously suggests that the democratization of luxury brands is a driver not only for financial gain for the company, but also social acceptance amongst consuming groups for the purchaser. As James B. Twitchell suggests, 'the new luxury is the ineluctable result of a market economy and a democratic political system' (2002: 25). This is echoed in Silverstein and Fiske's book *Trading Up* (2005) where they consider definitions of new luxury and old luxury which could also be said to be a result of a market economy. They define new luxury as; '… products and services that possess higher levels of quality, taste, and aspiration than other goods in the category but are not so expensive as to be out of reach' (Fiske and Silverstein 2005: 1). 'Old luxury is about exclusivity' (Fiske and Silverstein 2005: 55) 'where goods are priced to ensure that only the top 1 to 2 percent of consumers can afford them ...' (Fiske and Silverstein 2005: 55). Luxury branded goods as opposed to luxury products are partially reliant on the customer to sell their products for them. This is where the prominence of the logo comes in. The effect of the democratized retail market ultimately relies on the user to 'advertise' a product through the obvious display of the company logo. The product could be anything from a city guide, a t-shirt with a logo on the front, to a bag with logos that cover the surface or even an emblazoned beach towel. Fiske and Silverstein define these products as old luxury brand extensions, 'lower priced versions of products created by companies whose brands have traditionally been affordable only for the rich' (Fiske and Silverstein 2005: 4). These products have effectively become readily available to anyone who wants them. Price is no longer a factor that stands between the customer and their desire to purchase something from a manufacturer of a luxury brand. Louis Vuitton for example offers what could be termed as entry level products. A Louis Vuitton City Guide costs £22.00 and is available to buy from their stores or website. The impact of marketing, mass production and consumption has enabled the luxury brand to become more accessible to more people on a global scale.

The areas that Fiske and Silverstein and Danzinger agree upon is that new luxury is based on emotion. However, Fiske and Silverstein disagree with Danziger by stating that 'new luxury' must connect with the consumer on all levels. They state that:

> Emotional engagement is essential, but not sufficient, to qualify a product as new luxury; it must connect with the consumer on all three levels of a 'ladder of benefits.' First, it must have technical differences in design, technology, or both. Subsumed within this technical level is an assumption of quality – that the product will be free from defects and perform as promised. Second, those technical differences must contribute to superior functional performance. It's not enough to incorporate 'improvements' that don't actually improve anything but are intended only to make the product look different or appear to be changed. Finally, the technical and functional benefits must combine – along with other factors, such as brand values and company ethos – to engage the consumer emotionally.
>
> (Fiske and Silverstein 2005: 6)

The implication here is that product is integral to the success of a luxury brand within the new luxury market. What emerges is the stratification of luxury as a concept where you have luxury, luxury brands and new luxury. In some ways new luxury, luxury brands and old luxury have shared characteristics. In the current retail market they target the same customer, one that aspires to own luxury goods, but with less spending power. What emerges is the overlap of new luxury, luxury brands and old luxury, as defined by Fiske and Silverstein. Their definition of old luxury where reference is made to the price and manufacture, including craftsmanship still needs to be reviewed as old luxury as luxury does not have the same or similar characteristics whereas new luxury and old luxury it could be argued do.

Fiske and Silverstein suggest 'new luxury … achieves high margins at high volumes, and it delivers the ladder of benefits, especially the emotional engagement of its customers' (Fiske and Silverstein 2005: 8). This also applies to new luxury, luxury brands and old luxury as the ultimate aim is to increase consumption of the product. Goods produced under the label of a luxury brand, new luxury or old luxury are arguably not luxury at all; they are merely better quality products that are marketed in a different way opening up a completely new level of sales that has been created through the customer demand for items that are better made and have an increased social and material acceptance. Manufacturers need differentiation as a means of satisfying social constructs within a democratized luxury market. Customers demand differentiation as is evident in the current trend towards purchasing from smaller companies the produce exclusive products. In an attempt to address this Louis Vuitton have opened Haute Maroquinerie salons offering made to order handbags.

It is also evident that purveyors of luxury goods, those makers who define themselves as connoisseurs, craftsmen and women are increasingly attempting to distinguish themselves from luxury brand retailers through their work. Evidence of this has also emerged through various public lectures, seminars, workshops as well as publications and exhibitions that have become increasingly visible over the past two years. In 2011, the Victoria and Albert Museum, as part of the 'Power of Making' exhibition, held a series of talks focusing on luxury and the value of craft. In 2012 The Crafts Council launched Added Value to 'question the value of contemporary craft within the current landscape of branding and luxury' (Added Value 2012). The website suggests that 'a desire for authenticity, quality and craftsmanship is redefining our understanding of luxury. The term craft has been adopted as a validation of quality and value by brands and more widely' (Added Value 2012). This illustrates that the skill of the maker is once again becoming an intrinsic feature used to describe luxury goods.

REFERENCES

Added Value (2012), 'Added Value', www.addedvalue.org.uk. Accessed 20 December 2012.

Aurelius (1754), 'Prevalence and bad effects of Luxury', *The Gentleman's and London Magazine: Or Monthly Chronologer*, Dublin, pp. 457–458.

Auslander, L. (1996), 'The Gendering of Consumer Practices', in V. de Grazia and E. Furlough (eds), *The Sex of Things*, California: University of California Press, pp. 79–112.

Bain and Company (2012), 'Bain projects global luxury goods market will grow overall by 10% in 2012, though major structural shifts in market emerge',

15 October, Bain and Company, http://www.bain.com/about/press/press-releases/bain-projects-global-luxury-goods-market-will-grow-ten-percent-in-2012.aspx. Accessed 20 December 2012.

—— (2013), 'Worldwide luxury goods continues double-digit annual growth; global market now tops €200 billion', 16 May, Bain and Company, http://www.bain.com/about/press/press-releases/worldwide-luxury-goods-continues-double-digit-annual-growth.aspx. Accessed 30 July 2013.

Berg, M. and Clifford, H. (1999), *Consumers and Luxury*, Manchester: Manchester University Press.

Berry, C. J. (1994), *The Idea of Luxury. A Conceptual and Historical Investigation*, Cambridge: Cambridge University Press.

—— (1999), 'Austerity, Necessity and Luxury', in J. Hill and C. Lennon (eds), *Luxury and Austerity*, Dublin: University College Dublin Press, pp. 1–13.

Chevalier, M. and Gutsatz, M. (2012), *Luxury Retail Management*, Singapore: Wiley.

Danziger, P. N. (2005), *Let Them Eat Cake: Marketing Luxury to the Masses – As Well As the Classes*, Chicago: Dearborn Trade Publishing.

De Marchi, N. and Van Miegroet, H. J. (1999), 'Ingenuity, Preference, and the Pricing of Pictures: The Smith-Reynolds Connection', in N. De Marchi and C. D. W. Goodwin (eds), *Economic Engagements with Art*, Durham: Duke University Press, pp. 379–412.

Fennell, T. (2010), 'The Luxury and Luxury Brand Landscape', London, interview, 13 September.

Fine, L. and Leopold, E. (1993), *The World of Consumption*, London: Routledge.

Fiske, N. and Silverstein, M. J. (2005), *Trading Up. Why Consumers want new Luxury Goods*, New York: Portfolio, The Penguin Group.

Kapferer, J. N. and Bastien, V. (2009), *The Luxury Strategy; Break the Rules of Marketing to Build Luxury Brands*, London: Kogan Page.

Mandeville, B. ([1732] 1988), 'While Luxury Employ'd a Million of the Poor, &c', in F. B. Kaye (ed.), *The Fable of the Bees or Private Vices, Publick Benefits*, 2 vols., Indianapolis: Liberty Classics, pp. 107–123.

Maza, S. (2006), 'Luxury, morality, and social change', in G. Kates (ed.), *The French Revolution. Recent Debates and New Controversies*, 2nd ed., New York: Routledge, pp. 113–131.

Mukerji, C. (1997), *Territorial Ambitions and the Gardens of Versailles*, Cambridge: Cambridge University Press.

Okonkwo, U. (2007), *Luxury Fashion Branding; Trends, Tactics, Techniques*, London: Palgrave Macmillan.

—— (2010), *Luxury Online – Styles, Systems, Strategies*, London: Palgrave Macmillan.

Sargentson, C. (1998), 'The Manufacture and Marketing of Luxury Goods; the Marchands Merciers of Late 17th- and 18th-century Paris', in R. Fox and A. Turner (eds), *Luxury Trades and Consumerism in Ancien Regime Paris*, Aldershot: Ashgate Publishing Limited, pp. 99–137.

Sekora, J. (1977), *Luxury. The Concept in Western Thought, from Eden to Smollet*, Baltimore: The John Hopkins University Press.

Sennett, R. (2008), *The Craftsman*, New Haven: Yale University Press.

Smith, A. (1776), *The Wealth of Nations*, vol. 4, London: Methuen and Co.

Sombart, W. (1967), *Luxury and Capitalism*, Michigan: The University of Michigan Press.

Twitchell, J. B. (2002), *America's Love Affair with Luxury*, New York: Simon & Schuster.

Weissbach, L. S. (1982), 'Artisanal Responses to Artistic Decline: The Cabinetmakers of Paris in the Era of Industrialization', *Journal of Social History*, 16, pp. 67–81.

CONTRIBUTOR DETAILS

Shaun Borstrock is in pursuit of luxury, a notion that seems far removed from today's world of excessive consumption. He works as an independent consultant to luxury brands and associations all round the globe. They have included Thomas Pink, Fortnum and Mason, Gucci, Dolce & Gabbana, Unity PR, Turnbull and Asser, Asprey, The World Gold Council, The British Luxury Council and The South African Luxury Association. Shaun has been actively involved in the international design industry as a consultant, educator and strategist. Shaun is a member of the Board of the Cape Town Fashion Council, having been involved in curation and supporting designers as a mentor through his Foundation, Design for Africa. Shaun's international experience extends beyond designing. He has worked with The Countess of Wessex, Sarah Ferguson and includes Rene Zellwegger, the Oscar winning actress as his former muse and model. Shaun has also designed collections for Cabbages and Roses, where he was Managing and Creative Director and has worked for Loewe, the luxury leather manufacturer, The Emanuels who were responsible for Diana, Princess of Wales' wedding dress and Walter Steiger the internationally renown shoe designer. Shaun is writing two books, one that considers and establishes how notions of luxury, designer, consumerism and manufacture have played a role in determining the emergence of the luxury brand market and the other, a series of personal accounts and opinions which explore current perceptions of luxury with the intention of recovering, reviving and disseminating important historical aspects of luxury in order to expose the impact of influence and marketing on the perception of luxury brands today. Some of the worlds leading designers and stylists are collaborating with Shaun and include, Theo Fennell, Stephen Jones, Tanner Krolle, Ally Capellino and Sophie Dean. He regularly tours the world as an authority on delivering design education as well as a Key Note Speaker on subjects that include consumerism, branding and brand strategies.

Contact: School of Creative Arts, University of Hertfordshire, College Lane, Hatfield, Herts, AL10 9AB, UK.
E-mail: s.borstrock@herts.ac.uk
Web address: www.inpursuitofluxury.com; www.designforafrica.org

Global Fashion Brands: Style, Luxury & History

© 2014 Intellect Ltd Chapter. English language. doi: 10.1386/GFB.1.249_1

LINDA MATHESON
University of California, Davis; and the Academy of Art University,
San Francisco

The 'age of enchantment', the 'age of anxiety': Fashion symbols and brand persona

ABSTRACT

This article suggests that a mythical goddess from the 'age of enchantment' may provide an effective brand persona (BP) for postmodern fashions. As the Modern West is believed to have found its civilization – in the Ancient Near East, there too can we find a fashion symbol with which the contemporary consumer may identify. This work builds on recent research that proposes that the persuasiveness of fashion advertising is not always associated with traditional glamour, and that alternate visual narratives – even those that classify as 'discrepant' and 'grotesque' – may be rewarding and self-affirming to some. Using social theory, this study considers the possible contribution of the iconic Goddess Inanna to the notion of a fashion BP. Inhabiting the world of myth, her legend mixes postmodern themes of ambiguity, resignation and fragmentation with more traditional topics like sincerity, strength, and capability, a practice congruent with many fashion consumers in current society. Unlike the impossible-to-attain idealized images that lead to negative comparisons, frustrations and depression and contribute to an 'age of anxiety', Inanna encourages diversity and capriciousness and may offer a kind of re-enchantment to fashion consumers in our increasingly globalized world.

KEYWORDS

fashion
symbol
brand persona
enchantment
anxiety
ambiguity

> The truly symbolic is that in which the particular represents the universal, not as a dream and shadow, but as a living revelation of the inexplicable.
>
> (Verne 2011: vii, quoting Goethe)

This article is based on the premise that since culture is a series of symbolic forms (Verne 2011, summarizing Cassirer), and fashion reflects these forms, an effective fashion brand persona (BP) must represent its culture and consumer symbolically. Because the Ancient Near East provided the first civilization (Kramer 1969; Maisels 1993; Kenoyer 1998; George 2003; Miles 2010), it follows that the first symbols also are to be found in this geographical and historical sphere. Thus I consider the possible contribution of the legendary Goddess Inanna (also called Ishtar) to the notion of a fashion BP. This examination builds on recent research that suggests that the persuasiveness of fashion advertising is not always associated with traditional glamour, and that alternate visual narratives – even those called 'discrepant' and 'grotesque' – may be rewarding and self-affirming to some women (Philips and McQuarrie 2010, 2011). Unlike the impossible-to-attain idealized images that lead to negative comparisons, frustrations and depression (Philips and McQuarrie 2011; Belk 2001), Inanna lies provocatively between the sublime and the ridiculous in the world of myth where arguably more delight than desperation lies.

Despite being written in that thinly recorded period in history that separates Abraham from Noah in the *Book of Genesis*, predating Homer's *Iliad* by about a century and a half, my case study, the Mesopotamian legend: *The Descent of Ishtar to the Underworld* (Pirjo Lapinkivi, 2010) describes qualities and themes sympathetic to contemporary women. This Goddess exhibits traditional qualities like capability, courage, and strength, yet, also embodies postmodern dimensions like ambivalence, ambiguity and fragmentation congruent with many consumers (Hancock 2009a and 2009b; Scott 2007; Wilson 2003; Davis 1992; Kaiser et al. 1991 and Kaiser 2013). Employing social theory (Barthes [1967] 1990, 2006; Oliver 2004; and others) I argue that the themes exhibited by Inanna's visual narrative from her enchanted age may suggest an apt BP for the fashion consumer in our sometimes anxious one.

As a source of inspiration for branding, the Ancient World, particularly the non-western Ancient World, has not garnered much attention: thus with a nod to Goethe, who believed that ancient literature from all over the globe was worthy of study, and that the truly symbolic is 'a living revelation of the inexplicable' (Verne 2011: vii, quoting Goethe), I take up this task with the hope that useful ideas might be mined and mixed with those of today. Although creating a BP was not their goal, the ancient bards deployed dress items to convey sovereign powers, strengthen and solidify culturally ascribed meanings, and simultaneously structure and advance their storylines. These symbolic articles of attire transported their readers into the world of the story being told, while they conveyed culturally constituted meanings and themes; an essential function that rendered them indispensable to their narratives and to their society (Matheson 2012), arguably a status sought by contemporary fashion brands.

STORIES AND THE FASHION BP

The importance of stories and the ability of sartorial images to generate them cannot be overestimated. For Homer, the highest possible form of existence for humankind was to exist as a fictional character within a story; Helen of Troy and Penelope agreed, weaving their stories on their looms. Nietzsche claims that we need stories to relieve our suffering in the non-storied world, and postmodern scholar Martine Prange (2008: 18, quoting Homer and Nietzsche) argues that existence in a story offers durability, and 'what we strive for is to become part of a myth' wherein we find our 'true' fictional existence. Finally, Goethe sums it up well when he writes:

> Every state or condition, every person, every scene of life, needs to be apprehended only purely objectively and made the object of a description or sketch, whether with brush or with words, in order to appear interesting, delightful, and enviable.
>
> (Prange 2008: 29, quoting Goethe)

Storytelling is also important in contemporary fashion marketing where the symbol of the BP must tell a story and/or provoke one in the consumer (Twitchel 2004; Escalas 2004a, and 2004b; Fog et al. 2005; Papadatos 2006; Hancock 2009a; Huang 2010; Phillips and McQuarrie 2010; Lundqvist et al. 2012). And because myth is characterized by its intensity (Krois 2008), it may be that a mythical story is among the most effective storytelling vehicles. In fact, storytelling may never have been so important to fashion marketing as it is in our escalating globalized world. Since swelling numbers of fashion brands translate into increased competition (Rocamora 2002), and intensified attention to brand differentiation (Calefeto 2004), the need for stories to transfer culturally constituted meaning to the brand itself has magnified (McCracken 1986). Because much of this contextual transfer is prompted by the symbol of the brand, the intent of this article is to probe how the ancient tradition of transferring meaning (themes, power and control) through symbols in stories might inform the postmodern fashion BP.

Let me be clear: I do not suggest that aspects of branding that include mass manufacturing, mass marketing and global distribution, existed in antiquity. Rather, I maintain that the ancient bards' assignment of symbolic meanings, along with sovereign/cultural powers, to items of dress is a practice from which contemporary branding might benefit. Indeed, I posit that the mechanics and effectiveness of this ancient practice, including the archetype on which the privileges were bestowed and the method of narrative transfer, merit examination for possible applicability to a postmodern BP. The fact that powers/meanings were ascribed, transferred and maintained through dress-related processes such as arbitration, interaction, negotiation and interpretation, all still in evidence today, suggests commonalities between the Ancient World and ours.[1] It is my hope to gain theoretical insight into consumption practices that involve that 'socially visible, culturally laden, everyday art object known as fashion clothing' (Phillips and McQuarrie 2010: 390) by a careful examination of the symbolic use of dress items in a narrative from the ancient world.

Narratives portray and strengthen agreed-upon meanings, themes and powers within culturally typical settings. Indeed the narrative then as now can be responsible for the engagement that transports thought to other realms (Gerrig 1993; Green and Brock 2000; Phillips and McQuarrie 2010, 2011) an important method of persuasion for a consumer. The idea of play can be invoked by visual stories that convey discrepant images, supplying the counter mode referenced by Roland Barthes in *The Fashion System* ([1967] 1990). As opposed to the sole search for identity with an unattainably glamorous image,

1. E. Matsushima (1993) has written specifically of dress practices in ancient Mesopotamia, as has Houston (1954), McCall (1990) and Holland (2009) has addressed the practice of ascribing power to items of dress in the ancient near east. Also the ancient Sanskrit literary and cultural treatise, the *Mahabharata*; Valmiki's *Ramayana*; *The Epic of Gilgamesh*, Homer's *Odyssey*, and the *Iliad*; Virgil's *Aeneid*; and *The Hebrew Scriptures* are examples of ancient literature that are rich in illustrations of dress items that transferred power and cultural meaning (Matheson 2012). Scholars who have written of dress in the ancient world include Z. Bahrani (1995), A. Batten (2010), H. Bender (1994), C. Brennan (2009), D. Carins (2002), A. Croom (2002), N. Shiv (1969), G. Davies (2007), M. Dewer (2008), J. Edmondson (2008), D. Edwards (1994), J. Elias (2001), R. Faber (2008), E. Fantham (2008), B. Goldman (2008), S. Hales (2005), M. Harlow (2005), J. Scheid and J. Svenbro (1996), and many more too numerous to list.

this counter mode of advertising may engage the consumer who identifies with the ideas (of capriciousness or ambivalence for example) portrayed in the narrative invoked by the BP symbol that conveys much more than glamour. This identification with an idea that does not beg emulation transports thought to fairy-tale-like realms that offers delight rather than despair and in doing so develops a bond with the BP that activates this process (Phillips and McQuarrie 2010). My study builds on this research stream by suggesting that increased opportunity for narrative transport to the land of myth is gained by combining traditional fashion themes such as sophistication, excitement, competence, sincerity and strength (Aaker 1997) with more postmodern countervailing themes like ambivalence, ambiguity, anxiety and fragmentation (those often classified as discrepant or grotesque depending on the criteria involved). This in turn increases consumer identification with the brand persona, whose parameters I will now attempt to define.

BP is 'the articulated form of the brand's character and personality' (Herskovitz and Crystal 2010: 21); it is 'the set of human characteristics associated with a brand' (Aaker 1997: 347; Buresti and Rosenberger III 2006: 5). This definition, which I employ with a slight variation, separates BP into five dimensions: sincerity; excitement; sophistication; competence; and the rather manly one of ruggedness that I replace with a more gender neutral term: strength. I apply these five traditional dimensions to the Goddess Inanna to test her BP potential. I also discuss postmodern themes such as ambivalence, ambiguity and fragmentation that can be induced by thoughts of unsettling subjects such as nuclear disaster, ecological catastrophe, or a problematic relationship, all of which would render a BP more symbolic of its audience. Stephen Herskovitz and Malcolm Crystal claim that the persona comes first, and is essential to the branding process, while other authors (Aaker 1997; Freling and Forbes 2005a, 2005b; Buresti and Rosenberger III 2006) highlight the symbolic facility of the BP construct to gain a competitive advantage among consumers in a variety of contexts, including that of fashion. The next area that calls for clarity is that of periodization, one that is often messy if not problematic.

AGES AND STAGES

Studying dress history means studying the recoverable stock of past dress-related processes and practices and their retrospective assessments within the associated culture. The problem is that most eras of dress history, like eras of any kind of history, are inhospitable to definition. Despite this unwelcoming turf, I wish to be grounded by accountability: hence this effort to be clear. Rather than the neatly contained Marxist/Hegelian assumption that the 'ideal' sets the criteria for the 'material' world, it seems all eras experience continuity, gradual change and revolutionary shifts; they are multi-layered and not concisely coordinated (Corfield 2010: 385). Thus it becomes each writer's charge and challenge to stipulate what is meant by historical eras cited within their work. I begin with the era of 'now'.

My position on *postmodernity* follows that of historical theorist Keith Jenkins (1997), who claimed that it was not an ideology or position to which we could choose to subscribe; 'it was in fact our current state'. Feminist scholar Joan W. Scott (2007) agrees: 'Like it or not we are in a post-modern age' (Corfield 2010: 383 quoting, Jenkins and Scott). The term postmodernity with its associations of globalizing commerce, cultural interactions and increasing technologies of lightning-speed communication apply to our present age; and because many of these trends are identified as root causes of anxiety (as well as ambivalence and fragmentation) the phrase *age of anxiety* is also applied to this era. Yet, this expression was used long before the twenty-first century, and has been the subject of publications from 1899 to 1996. The latter set of essays marks our current set of anxieties and mourns the death of *the age of enchantment,* a phrase I will tackle next (Corfield 2010).

The *age of enchantment* is difficult to pin down. Characterized as magic, charmed, bewitching, fascinating, entrancing, captivating, enthralling , beguiling, spellbinding, and associated with the ancient/medieval world, it can be an antidote for anxiety when, for example, the enchantment of fairy tales like *Hansel and Gretel* (not in written form as we know it until the mid-late 1800s, but present in oral form long before then) help a child get over separation anxiety when he or she comes of age and needs to discover autonomy (Bettelheim 1976). In the *Oxford English Dictionary* the definitions of 'enchant' include 'to hold spellbound; in a bad sense, to delude, befool' as well as to 'delight and enrapture'. With roots in Middle English *enchanten*, from Old French *enchanter*, and from Latin *incantāre*, can mean to utter an incantation or even to sing. Alternatively, disenchantment, its opposite has long been linked to the anxiety found in western *modernity*, the name given to the era prior to the current one, which often, as in this case, actually includes the current one.[2]

Perhaps the most ambiguous of all terms, *modernity* may be broadly characterized as a fusion of political, psychological social, economic, intellectual, and technological systems or trends that have merged in the West, although some originated between the sixteenth and nineteenth centuries. These encompass (but are not limited to) 'the autonomous and rational subject; the liberal and democratic state; the differentiation of cultural spheres; the dominance of secularism, nationalism, capitalism, industrialism, urbanism, consumerism, and scientism' (Saler 2006: 694). Yet, perhaps the most consistently emphasized characteristic of modernity has been its disenchantment (Saler 2006; Porter 2004; Brague 2003; Kloppenberg 1994; Blumenberg 1983).

Max Weber's famous 1917 lecture in which he discusses 'the disenchantment of the world' was a response to the anomie, fragmentation, and alienation felt by 'the loss of the overarching meanings, animistic connections, magical expectations, and spiritual explanations that had characterized the traditional world, as a result of the ongoing "modern" processes of rationalization, secularization, and bureaucratization' (Saler 2006: 693). Morris Berman augments this:

> The view of nature which predominated in the West down to the eve of the Scientific Revolution was that of an enchanted world. Rocks, trees, rivers, and clouds were all seen as wondrous, alive, and human beings felt at home in this environment … Alternatively, the story of the modern epoch, at least on the level of the mind, is one of progressive disenchantment: from the sixteenth century on, mind has been progressively expunged from the phenomenal world.
>
> (1981: 2)

Enchantment was associated with spirituality and purpose, as well as wonder and surprise, while modernity, with its emphasis on unchallengeable natural laws, condemned and threatened to obliterate these qualities. While promoting escalating rationalization and intellectualization the modern project

2. Jean-Francois Lyotard's position clearly states that: 'It [the postmodern] is undoubtedly a part of the modern ...' (cited in Corfield 2010: 385). Among the many works devoted to modernity are (Marshall Berman 1988; Matei Calinescu 1987; Rita Felski 1995; David Frisby 1986; Anthony Giddens 1990; Jürgen Habermas, 1987; and Stuart Hall, David Held, Don Hubert, and Kenneth Thompson 1996).

3. Michael Saler (2000: 123–142) cites the contribution made by Walter Benjamin, Sigfried Kracauer, Humphrey Jennings, and certain French surrealists in finding a place for the idea of enchantment in modern processes and systems, despite more attention being garnered by the 'cultural pessimists'.

4. Anthropologist Ruth Benedict may have been the first to make this claim in 1931 in her article entitled 'Dress', (1931: 235–37); cited in *Fashion Foundations* (Johnson et al. 2003: 11), since then others like Wilson (2003 and 2004), Steele (1988), and Davis (1992), along with other scholars have reached similar conclusions. Alternatively Craik (2009), Lipovetsky (1994) and myself hold different opinions. Lipovetsky believes it to be a mid-nineteenth-century phenomenon, while Craik points out that although the term 'fashion' is specific to European culture (deriving from Latin and French root words), its concept has changed; and thus should not be confined to a definition as European and only existing since the fourteenth century (2009: 21–25). Like Linda Welters and Abby Lillethun, who define fashion as 'changing styles of dress and appearance that are adopted by a group of people at any given time and place', I agree that the idea of fashion in non-European cultures should be given more scholarly examination (2007: xxi).

refused entrance to mysterious incalculable forces, intent on the standard that all things can be mastered by calculation. Thus, western modernity became equated with a rigid rationality and a shallow, expanding secularism (Saler 2006). Enchantment, however, was not to be so easily dismissed.

An emerging school of thought suggests that postmodernity is as enchanted as it is disenchanted: re-enchanted, perhaps, by fruitful tensions that exist between seemingly irreconcilable forces and ideas (Owen 2004; Brague 2003; Dube 2002; Bennett 2001; Cook 2001; Fisher 1999; Daston and Park 1998; Taussig 1997; Berman 1981). Instead of binary or dialectical approaches to the topic, with their 'either/or' logic, a more antinomial approach with its 'both/and' logic is being used. This stream of thought allows *re-enchantment* and suggests a temporal malleability in which time can be considered 'pleated or crumpled' like a fabric that draws 'together past, present, and future into constant and unexpected relations'(Nead 2005: 8). Here time can also become 'entangled' (Chakrabarty 2000: 243) like a fiber with 'a high degree of unevenness [in which] political, economic and social contexts range from premodern to postmodern in almost every corner of the globe' (Corfield 2010: 382, quotes Khan 1998: 83). This viewpoint offers 'alternative vistas to the historical imagination, and … the possibility of pulling new rabbits out of old hats' (Saler 2006: 692).[3]

The Ancient World is unarguably an old hat that having been well used should be well understood; yet when it comes to dates, arguments abound. Some historians credit the beginning of the modern period in Europe with the birth of Christ in year 1 of the Common Era, others argue for the fall of the Roman Empire in 475 CE, and still others hold that the Middle Ages intervened between the Ancient and the Modern (Corfield 2010: 389). I am one of those. For me, the Ancient World encompasses all time before the Common Era, at which point I am happy to relinquish it in favor of the phrase Middle Ages. Yet, I acknowledge that temporal parameters, like the brim of the 'old hat', are wobbly. What is more carefully constructed are some dress-related principles and practices evidenced by the case study I discuss shortly. Before this, however, with the aim of building on what has already been accomplished, here is an abbreviated review of some pertinent work on social theory that grounds the more recent research on the power and meanings of dress related material culture.

ABBREVIATED HISTORY OF RESEARCH ON SYMBOLIC MEANING

Barthes argues that there is little significance to any item of dress that lacks meaning: thus he invokes a fitting mantra for creators of the fashion BP (2006). Since by definition, the BP articulates the brand's character and personality, it must by extension symbolize and articulate meaning. A look at the work of some scholars that precede him suggests that Barthes's premise is well founded; indeed, unwinding the snarls attached to the meaning of things has occupied many scholars over many years. From the fourteenth century onwards, following the emergence of the nation state and the capitalist markets in Europe, when some scholars claim the fashion industry began,[4] textiles and other components of dress became totems and signs of social, economic or moral identity and religious affiliation. These items assumed an importance that has been acknowledged by major thinkers like Karl Marx (1818–1883), Herbert Spencer (1820–1903), Emile Durkheim (1858–1917), Georg Simmel (1858–1918), Walter Benjamin (1892–1940), Andre Breton

(1896–1966) and Roland Barthes (1915–1980). Slowly and methodically social theory was unfolding the meaningfulness of dress related items.

Durkheim introduced the phrase *totemic relevance* (2001), through which the concept of the totem as a material form is imagined to represent an immaterial substance. This principle considered the symbolic form simultaneously as a physical force, a moral imperative and a religious directive, all useful attributes that increase its contextual value. Although Durkheim was not writing about the marketplace, his findings beckon application to a commodified world, as do the findings of others before him. In the mid nineteenth-century Ralph Waldo Emerson (echoing Augustine from the fourth century) declared commodities in the United States as part of the harmonious architecture of the world, proclaiming them 'quasi-sacramental tokens and vehicles of spiritual truth' (McCarraher 2005: 451, quoting Emerson). British philosopher and sociologist, Spencer studied badges (1924), revealing them to be thoughtful trophies; and Simmel extended the premise when he 'views the sartorial commodity as a modern mythology imbued with a mysterious yet radical spirit' (Lehmann 2000: xvii, quoting Simmel).

Later in twentieth-century Europe, Benjamin, who understood how fashion contained within itself 'the dream energy of society' (Wilson 2004: 383, quoting Benjamin), suggests an inorganic nature and a fetish-like quality in fashion (1999) earlier noticed by Marx, who despite his focus on the science of his account, was unable to banish the religious or ideological from it.[5] Marx (1968: 60) writes of the commodity as being 'a very queer thing, abounding in metaphysical subtleties and theological niceties', and French literary intellectual Andre Breton relates it to the Marvellous (1992): 'a form of surrealist Marxism that would dissolve the distinction between the material and the ideal' (Wilson 2004: 381, quoting Breton). Meanwhile Victor Hugo's aesthetic entangles fashion with both the grotesque and the sublime (Phillips and McQuarrie 2010). Thus we see that Barthes, already acknowledged for his distinguished contribution to this premise of symbolic meaningfulness for fashion items, stood on the shoulders of giants (1972, 1990 and 2006).

Continuing with the search for meaning that must attend an effective fashion BP, I turn to postmodern philosopher Kelly Oliver, who uses the term *idealization* to describe a process whereby 'the object, without any alteration in its nature is aggrandized and exalted in the subject's mind' (2004: 157). This process relates to subjectivity and subject position: two postmodern constructs that are relevant to the BP within its cultural context – a context, Kelly goes on to suggest, that can colonize psychic space. Although fashion brand analysis was not the intention for which this theory was indentified, the concept of idealization is helpful when thinking through the BP. It is congruent with the work of brand scholar Matthew Debord (1997), who uses the word *tyranny* to describe the retail catalogues of J. Crew that depict images of idealized or generally unachievable lifestyles, which manipulate undiscerning readers into buying clothes that they may already own. Joseph Hancock (2009b: 104) draws an even more definitive link between idealization and the BP when he uses the phrase *contextual tyranny* to describe how consumers can be seduced by heavy-handed contextual meanings attached to fashion images.

The idea of tyranny, or the populating of psychic space by fashion advertising also fits with the research of Barbara Phillips and Edward McQuarrie, who use a series of content analyses to demonstrate that almost one-third (29–30%) of fashion ads do not follow the traditional trajectory of showing beautiful models, luxurious goods and splendid settings that invite emulation

5. For a discussion on fetishism see Taussig (1980: 13–38,104–09,129–39). Taussig writes that '... [things] are ciphers and signs that echo the meaning of the system that society forms with them' (1980: 138); see also Freud (2007: 553–57); Steele (2007: 576–83), and Lehmann (2000: xviii, 20, 38, 64, 74, 98, 135–36, 165, 189–91, 222, 230, 232-233, 242–44, 246, 265, 282, 301, 324, 367, 370, 392, 398, 402).

(2010: 105). As the general critique of this prevailing type of fashion ads has been relentless, suggesting that it causes negative social comparisons (Bower 2009; Dittmar and Howard 2004; Martin and Gentry 1997; Richins 1991; Shaw 1995; Solomon et al. 1992), or equally negative comment on the roles of women (Busby and Leichty 1993; Faludi 1991; Innes 1999), these more recent findings, based on a controlled survey of 130 women, as well as three in-depth personal interviews, reveal that there is a growing market for Barthes counter mode, or discrepant ads in fashion magazines *Vogue* and *Vanity Fair* (US), and that they may command viewer engagement and interest as well (Phillips and McQuarrie 2011). This alternate mode allows consumers to direct thought to a preferred psychic space.

The focus of their study of fashion images is on three levels: model appearance, model behaviour and ad setting (Phillips and McQuarrie 2011). If any of these levels illustrate non-idealized, non-aspirational elements, the ad is coded discrepant. for example, evidence of bruises, unkemptness, etc., as in both a Prada and a Jil Sander ad in which the models have strangely solemn and unhappy faces, and also a Balenciaga ad that features fly-away hair, and a crazy hat (unusual and probably unwearable for most people). An ad for Jimmy Choo shoes exemplifies a discrepant setting where the model is sprawled in the dirty trunk of a car parked in a desert near a man who resembles a grave-digger; and Yves Saint Laurent models perched on a gritty urban rooftop evokes a similarly discrepant environment. A Versace ad exhibits discrepant model behaviour by featuring the model playing checkers with a panting black hound.

Suggesting discrepancy in all three categories is the fashion feature shot by Annie Leibovitz that highlights clothes from Marc Jacobs's tenure at Louis Vuitton in the January 2012 issue of *Vogue*. Models are precariously placed on tiers of scaffolding in front of a dilapidated and dirty brick wall with exposed pipes and rust (Figure 1).

Figure 1: Suggestions of discrepancy in setting, model behaviour and clothing can be found in this Marc Jacobs fashion photograph. Image courtesy of © Annie Leibovitz/Contact Press Images, originally for Vogue.

Figure 2: Another Marc Jacobs fashion photograph showing discrepancy first seen in Vogue, *2012. Image courtesy of © Annie Leibovitz/Contact Press Images, originally for* Vogue.

This is clearly not a place one would frequent unless it was necessary to further a goal. A steel ladder leans against the scaffolding suggesting that the models, in their fashion finery, must climb their way to the top, even though those who have apparently arrived do not look very safe. None are smiling; there exists an aura of ambivalent resignation. A few of the models cling to the steel bars, perhaps attempting to secure a tenuous position. Most of the clothes would classify as pretty or glamorous, yet some like the transparent nurses' uniforms worn by models whose faces were streaked with black, would not work for most of us as regular street wear. Another photograph in the same spread (Figure 2) features wooden chairs suspended on a wall. One model is seated midway between floor and ceiling with her feet dangling; others are on chairs at floor level. The clothing is light, airy, pretty and gentle, in direct counterpoint to the setting that might inadvertently attack at any time. All of the models look bemused, quizzical or resigned to their fragmented surroundings.

All of these visual narratives (this one and others mentioned above) constitute a distinct departure from the prevailing glamorized images. The consumer is not asked to attain impossible feats, features or thinness, or do anything but perhaps muse over the unusual fashion presentation, and let their minds wander. Indeed, the interest the discrepant images generate hints at the creation of personal narratives invoked by the marketing itself (Phillips and McQuarrie 2011) – an imaginary journey to a mythological place that allows postmodern themes (along with traditional ones) that relate closely to personal agendas, subjectivities and subject positions.

This cognitive journey prompted by the bond between subject (consumer) and object (BP) can provoke ambivalence and ambiguity, two themes that enjoy a useful confusion. While ambiguity has to do with the meaning systems/

6. Two versions of the poem are known: an earlier (eighteenth-century BCE) longer version, assembled from fragments of text primarily found at Nippur, and a latter (eighth to seventh centuries BCE) shorter narrative, found in a library of the palace in Nineveh, the capital of the Assyrian Empire. Inanna's poem may have been performed to celebrate the festival marking the annual journey of the statue of the goddess from her temple in Uruk to Kutha, home of the shrines of the gods of the Underworld. It may also have been recited to celebrate *taklimtu*, an annual ritual that mourns the death of Dumuzi, her consort – a pastoral god also associated with abundance and fertility (Matheson 2012).

processes, ambivalence has to do with emotions. But because meanings and emotions are entwined, emotions often dictate actions or processes, so fusing or confusing the terms. (Matheson 2012). These alternate themes may actually produce fruitful tensions – a kind of re-enchantment – that stimulates transport from advertising narrative to personal narrative, a primary form of persuasion. The richness of the tensions produced by the combination of the initial five dimensions of an effective BP – sincerity; excitement; competence; sophistication; and strength – in tandem with pertinent postmodern themes – ambiguity, ambivalence, resignation and fragmentation – is demonstrated by the sartorial narrative of the Goddess Inanna.

CASE STUDY: *THE DESCENT OF ISHTAR TO THE UNDERWORLD*[6]

Although other female deities were worshiped and adored throughout Sumerian history, 'the goddess who outweighed, overshadowed and outlasted them all was a deity known to the Sumerians by the name of Inanna'(Kramer 1979: 71). Called Ishtar by the Semites who lived in Sumer, the 'First Daughter of the Moon and the Morning and Evening Star' (the planet Venus) and Goddess of Fertility and Sexuality upstaged all other deities, male or female, in myth, epic and hymn. In short, Inanna was a superstar. Yet, accompanying this regal reputation, we have the slightly suspect story of her rise to fame. To achieve the ultimate power and position, she capriciously challenged the great 'God of Wisdom', her father Enki, in a drinking contest during which she convinces him to give her his gifts, including wisdom and knowledge. In keeping with conventional Mesopotamian practice, these gifts are housed in, or take the symbolic form of articles of dress. This legendary goddess, who by all accounts is both resourceful and aggressive, absconds with these powers in her 'won' items of adornment and refuses to give them back, even when Enki, presumably in a more sober state, requests their return.

These symbolic forms become of significant consequence during Inanna's journey to conquer the Underworld, a feat which would render her Queen of not just Heaven and Earth, but also of the 'Great Below'. Here the knowledge of death and rebirth is believed to reside; the very knowledge that will make Inanna an 'Honoured Counselor' and guide (Wolkstein and Kramer 1983: xvii, 156). She dresses carefully before starting out on this quest where none have dared to go, acknowledging the power inherent in each of her articles of attire, which taken together will ensure her success. Alas, her cousin Eriskigal, the Queen of Death and Inanna's nemesis, hears of this venture and commands her gatekeeper, Neti, accordingly: at each of the seven gates between the two realms, Inanna must surrender an item of dress until stripped of all her clothing and accessories – which also signify all of her worldly powers and goods. The idea of giving up the material to seek a higher good is not unique to these ancient Near Eastern people; but what is distinctive is the idea that pieces of material culture – particularly elements of dress – inscribe, hold, and convey meaning and power so definitively that their removal equates to the relinquishment of the meaning and power itself. This distinction would be powerful indeed for a fashion BP.

The association of fashion symbols and 'fashioning' with the activities of 'making' and 'doing' (both derived from the same Latin root for fashion) begins with the Goddess Inanna's first literary appearance in the *Epic of Gilgamesh* (considered the oldest poem to date). Here a sartorial tradition attaches itself in the form of the protagonist's father who is attributed to be Nudimmud, the Man-Fashioner, and continues in the tale of her descent to the Underworld, our case study, with the cultural custom of situating sovereign powers and ideologies in articles of dress.[7] This practice invites comparison to Durkheim's totemic principle that explains the universe as animated by forces represented in material forms with an ideological aspect that dictates deific respect, ranking the physical form as sacred. It also recalls Emerson, Spenser and Simmel, who compare the sartorial commodity to a modern mythology that houses a radical and mysterious spirit (Lehmann 2000); and fits into that strain of Marxism, either original or in its Surrealist adaptation, that blurs the boundaries between the material and the incorporeal, as well as the secular and the sacred (Wilson 2004). Had Benjamin read this legend, he might have compared fashion's making and doing to its capacity to accumulate the 'energy of its society', including its fetish-like aspect (Wilson 2004: 383, quoting Benjamin); Barthes ([1967] 1990) follows with his claim that clothing is idiosyncratic and parochial, while simultaneously clarifying and revealing of its world; and perhaps most applicable to our ancient goddess's items of dress is Oliver's theory of idealization – how an object is aggrandized in a subject's mind without any change in its physical appearance. With these acknowledged distinctions of dress attached, I return to the consideration of Inanna's BP dimensions, yet must first supply you with a material picture of her image.

INANNA'S PHYSICAL IMAGE

For a number of reasons, securing a physical image of Inanna is challenging. The first difficulty is that there are no extant textile garments of this period, though some fragments do exist; second, it is not an era that dress and art historians have favoured; and third, the existing evidence, that of seals, statuary and other images must be analysed and interpreted, a task that is encumbered by trying to match linguistic terms and their various translations to the different pieces of dress. The fact that this epic is thought to originate around 2700 BCE, and continue as performance, or in writing, through 800 BCE, thus encompassing an evolution of clothing styles with the passing centuries, presents a further challenge. Yet, there is some exciting research available, and I turn to this to find the 'probable' materiality of Inanna's image (Matheson 2012).

Because Inanna's image like all other written images, is culturally derived and contingent upon interpretation, both textual and archeological evidence enhance our understanding. A Mesopotamian clay plaque from the Old Babylonian period (c. 2000–1600 BCE) at the Louvre in Paris demonstrates this. It measures 11.9×6.6 cm. and depicts our Goddess in full regalia; on her head sits a crown adorned with the multiple horns of divinity, the flounced garment covers her body, and around her neck lay rows of beads. In an outstretched hand she holds a scepter flanked by lion heads, her emblem and sacred animal (Wolkstein and Kramer 1983; Ornan 2005).[8] This image is consistent with tomb paintings, sculptures and other representations of goddesses that are usually shown wearing elaborate headdresses with long dresses that bare the right shoulder (Houston 1954; Black and Garland 1975; Ornan 2005). Starting with this general description, I will be as specific as possible as I move on with her journey, while working around the noted restrictions.

7. A second such distinction comes when clothing is used as a prerequisite to becoming civilized (George 2003: 285).

8. Ornan tells us that another emblem for Inanna, traced back to the second half of the fourth millennium, is the looped door-post alluding to her temple (2005: 169), and the star with its number of points varying from six to eight, is also identified with her under her Akkadian name, Ishtar (2005: 151). Ornan also discusses the horned crown worn by deities, as do Houston (1954: 128), and Black and Garland (1975).

There are two versions of Inanna's descent to the Underworld, a Sumerian one and a later Akkadian one, each with their own version of her dress items. In the hope of enriched meaning, I offer them both:

<u>Akkadian Version</u>

Gate I: the great tiara
Gate II: the earrings
Gate III: the egg-shaped beads
Gate IV: the dress pins
Gate V: the girdle of birth-stones
Gate VI: the bangles of her wrists and ankles
Gate VII: the garment of dignity

<u>Sumerian Version</u>

shugurra, crown of the steppe
the small lapis beads
the double strand of beads
her breastplate
her gold ring
the lapis measuring rod/line
her royal robe
(Lapinkivi 2010: 60)

The initial excitement of Inanna's brave adventure to the Underworld is halted at Gate 1 by the command to relinquish her great tiara/crown with its associations of royal power. The word for crown, *agu*/aga is equated with Sumerian men, but when taken together with the word for kohl and that for

Figure 3: Crown of Queen Shubad. Object number: B17710. Provenience: Iraq, Ur. Near Eastern, Materials: Gold, Lapis, Carnelian. Description: with eighteen gold leaves CBS housed at the University of Pennsylvania Museum of Archeology and Anthropology.

the *palla*/gown they combine to constitute the attire of the high-priestess. Leo Oppenheim finds evidence in cuneiform writings from the Third Dynasty of Ur (2094–*c*. 2047 BCE) of Inanna having a golden miter; and archeological digs have produced magnificent crowns from graves at the same place believed to have belonged to Queen Shubad (Figures 3 and 4), possibly similar to the one Inanna was asked to relinquish. Housed at the University of Pennsylvania Museum, these striking examples of highly developed skill in design and execution are so large as to require wigs, as thick as those worn in Ancient Egypt, in order to fit the normal size head. The design displays masterful work in precious metals and jewels along with 'an exquisite appreciation for the beauties of leaf and flower' (Houston 1954: 113–14).[9]

The fact that in much of recorded history monarchs are formally given the realm by the crowning ceremony, suggests that the removal of this 'Cap of Power' constitutes a crucial step in relinquishing sovereignty, and must have caused some *ambivalence* in Inanna's thought and possible *ambiguity* in her actions as she resigned herself to the commands. These mandates from Ereskigal weaken, or *fragment* her ability to forward her quest and test her *sincerity*, the first dimension of Aaker's effective BP (1997), and a test I suggest she passes by her undaunted persistence.

9. Houston describes this crown in detail, discussing its ornament of thin beaten gold raised high above the diadem.

Long-pointed rays like those of a star rise some inches above the head, and at the tip of each ray, hangs a rosette-shaped flower with a jewel in its heart. Then round the head itself the design consists of rows of hanging leaves executed with great truth to nature. The first row is willow leaves, narrow and elegant; the next row is of beech leaves, beautifully veined and with a crystal jewel like a dew drop, at the tip of each leaf. Below these leaves there hangs a row of golden rings which overlap one another in their profusion.
(1954: 113–14)

Black and Garland describe the leaves on this same crown as mulberry leaves, with intertwining tubular lapis beads. They refer to the ensemble as 'the most breathtaking gold-work ever discovered from the ancient world'.
(1975: 22)

Figure 4: The Crown of Queen Shubad. Object number: B17710, Provenience: Iraq, Ur. Near Eastern, Materials: Gold, Lapis, Carnelian, Description: with one gold leaf, CBS Register: Queen Shubad's headdress. Third crown. Twenty gold leaves. Two strings of lapis and carnelian. Gold comb CBS 16693. Housed at the University of Pennsylvania Museum of Archeology and Anthropology.

At Gate II our goddess is ordered to hand over her earrings (Figures 3–5), or in the Sumerian version, her small lapis beads (Figure 5). The so-called 'treasure-list' of Nippur describes eight golden earrings with the term *hyasu*, which pertains to their decoration, and translates as a seasoning, the medicinal plant that we call thyme (Oppenheim 1949): another reminder of the skill of these ancient Mesopotamian artisans in rendering plants in intricate gold. Yet, besides this physical beauty, these earrings infer something beyond their golden circles. Because of the ear's mostly internal location and labyrinth shape, it takes in sounds and changes the imperceptible to the perceptible, thus establishing meaning (Wolkstein and Kramer 1983: xvii, 156). As the Sumerian word for 'ear' is the same as the word for 'wisdom', both of which relate to 'mind' (McCall 1990: 70), Inanna is allegorically asked to remove the rings from her mind, her worldly intelligence and intellectual prejudices that need to be eliminated if she is to reach higher levels of

Figure 5: Object number: B17711. Provenience: Iraq, Ur. Near Eastern. Materials: shell, gold, lapis, carnelian. Description: CBS Register: U.10936-10934 (ribbon) Queen Shubad's headdress. Fourth crown. Fourteen gold flowers, inlaid petals, blue lapis and paste. Thirteen groups of willow leaves of gold with tips of carnelian, three strings, gold, laps and ribbon. Housed at the University of Pennsylvania Museum of Archeology and Anthropology.

understanding. This demand that could easily provoke *ambivalence* and *ambiguity* and might be equated to the postmodern demand to accept an increasingly globalized, multi-ethnic world with competing ideologies and traditions.

In the Akkadian version, the command at the third Gate is to relinquish the twin egg-shaped beads from her neck. This suggests a fertile womb being given up, passed over, rendered useless; an image that may be extended to all people, animals and plants for which Inanna was the 'Goddess of Fertility', or to our postmodern woman who faces a relationship crisis. The Sumerian version uses a double strand of beads that again suggest pairing and by extension fecundity adding more themes of *physical intimacy* and *rights of reproduction*, and at Gate IV *gender relations* is introduced. Here both versions of the legend employ the phrase 'come, man, come' to describe the removal of dress-pins (the word *d/tudittu* has been identified as a 'dress-pin' or 'toggle-pin', (Lapinkivi 2010: 64) from her breast (Akkadian), or a breastplate (Sumerian). This recalls Herodotus's (1942) later claim that Athenian women of the early sixth century used these pins to stab to death a messenger who brought bad news about a battle involving their soldier/husbands. Thus both disguised weaponry and troubled gender relations could be inferred; while the 'come, man come' invitation suggests the pleasures and dangers of sex. Again, these are themes that are familiar to today's fashion consumer.

Gate V features the undoing and removal of the girdle of birth-stones at our Goddess's waist (Akkadian) or her gold ring (Sumerian). William Sladek (1974: 84) suggests that we relate these to 'stones that cause birth' or '*conception*' now translated to mean cowrie-type shells that resemble a woman's sexual organ, which have an apotropaic use in rituals:recall the current themes of contraception, childbirth and abortion, completely appropriate for Inanna (Ishtar) the Goddess of Sexual Love, and equally appropriate for many postmodern women. The idea of encircling or all-encompassing, as Inanna's talents seem to be (and what today's woman is supposed to be), is evident in the girdle and the gold ring. This encircling motif continues with her wrist and ankle bangles (Akkadian) and the lapis measuring rod and line whose images are shown in ring form (Sumerian) and are removed at Gate VI. This leaves only the dress between our goddess and total nudity-dress alone separates Inanna from the underworld, and our modern woman from hers. It seems probable that the so-called postmodern themes of fragmentation and fear of failure are present.

The final order from Neti at Gate VII is for 'the garment of dignity of her body' (Akkadian) her 'royal robe' (Sumerian). Here again I take up the probable materiality of this highly symbolic dress. That it may have featured the flounced skirt is likely, as cuneiform writings from the Third Dynasty of Ur tell us that it was worn up to the Kassite period, (1595–1160 BCE). The same texts suggest that it may have had gold ornaments – stars (see stars of Figures 3–5), rosettes, square cuts or lions sewn on it, and point to these ornaments weighing one-third to half shekel each, and attached so that they could be removed for polishing and repair. The later Neo-Babylonian texts from Nebuchadnezzar II, (604–562 BCE) 32nd year, corroborate this evidence referring to sixty-one golden stars weighing almost nineteen shekels from a *kusitu* garment belonging to the 'Lady of Uruk'(another title for Inanna) at the goldsmith's for repair. And yet another text agrees listing: '703 golden stars (and) 688 *hy-se-e* from the *kusitu* garment of the Lady of Uruk' (Oppenheim 1949: 176). This 'garment of the sky' referred to in both descriptions has also been connected with the sparkling star-strewn dress of the late Assyrian kings (Oppenheim 1949). As the head of the pantheon, Inanna had a monopoly on

10. The reference to Kate Moss is http://omg.yahoo.com/blogs/a-line/inside-kate-moss-model-wedding/886, accessed 14 August 2011. For images see http://www.popsugar.com/Kate-Moss-Wedding-Dress-Pictures-Husband-Jamie-Hince-18104178, accessed 1 January 2013. *The Daily Mail* reference is from www.dailymail.co.uk/.../Kate-Middleton-Duchess-Cambridge-glitters-floor- and was referenced December 12, 2013.

11. From Inanna's priestly lover Dumuzi, the King of Sumer, described as clad in 'his shinning *me*-garments', (Wolkstein and Kramer 1983: 71, 161–62; Oppenheim 1949: 181, 189); to the *Rāmāyana's* references to 'cloth-of-gold' as meaning woven with silver and gold; to the starry corselet of Achilles armour in the *Iliad* (1974); and Virgil's instances in the *Aeneid* of gifts of inestimable value (1992). This love of gold travels from antiquity to postmodernity with ease and carries with it many of the same inferences.

12. John, T Molloy is believed to have written the first book on power dressing, *The New Dress for Success* (1988).

the heaviest and most elaborate embellishments, and spangled in this manner her garments must have been shimmering and impressive, quite as exciting and sophisticated perhaps, as our still-golden gowns of today.

Excitement and sophistication, traditional dimensions of the effective BP attend the beginning of Inanna's narrative and are evident in the opulence of her dress (Lapinkivi 2010; Wolkstein and Kramer 1995; Katz 1983). They are intensified by the systematic disrobing that juxtaposes them with postmodern themes of fragmentation and anxiety. The anticipation, agitation, thrill and tension as well as complexity, cleverness, superiority and style, evident in this narrative sustain both dimensions, and the continued choice of gold textiles – spangled, encrusted, embossed, adorned, woven and worn for celebratory occasions today adds additional support to the importance of these qualities now. That these dazzling pieces of sartorial splendor are still prized is evidenced by model Kate Moss's choice of wedding gown for her marriage to rock guitarist Jamie Hince in 2011. For this momentous occasion Kate donned a John Galliano gown spangled with tiny golden paillettes, reminiscent of Inanna's glittering web of golden stars. Further evidence was seen in March 2012 at the Academy Awards when Oprah Winfrey arrived resplendent in a gold encrusted gown, as did a leading Hollywood actress Meryl Streep, in a gold silk by Lanvin. Furthermore on Sept 12th, 2013, London's Daily Mail described the Duchess of Cambridge as glittering 'in pale gold sequins'.[10] Yet perhaps the link that ties gold spangles and encrustment across the ages is to be found in the ready to wear collections of Dolce and Gabbana fall 2012, and 2013 inspired by religious iconography with its roots in ancient world Byzantine and Venetian mosaics. This penchant for golden glitter that has spanned the millennia is sophisticated and exciting, both visually and viscerally, and provides a recurring site where spiritual aspirations interact and negotiate with contemporary tastes.[11] I posit that Inanna fulfills the first two dimensions of Aaker's effective BP (1997), excitement and sophistication and move to the next aspect that I will attempt to quantify – that of competence.

Because *competence* relates to ability, proficiency and aptitude, I revisit Barthes's conclusion that clothing specifies, clarifies and reveals its culture (2006); and with this in mind, consider how Inanna employed her dress to ensure her place in the hierarchy. As established, elements of dress symbolize powers, meanings and control. Inanna's adornments constitute not just her image, but her attributes and power as well. Far beyond mere representation and identification, they determine and even dictate the position she holds in society, (her subject position in postmodern terms), and what authority she exerts there. By putting on the items endowed with the powers that she needs to succeed, she is equipping herself in a manner deemed competent within her society. This ancient Mesopotamian practice suggests 'power-dressing': another trend of the postmodern that relates to competence and is an intimate associate of branding.[12]

Scholars who have written about *power-dressing* agree that material objects, especially articles of dress, wield some degree of control over their surroundings because they carry messages and serve as symbols (Entwistle 2007, 2000c; Wilson 2003, Roach-Higgins and Eicher 1995; Davis 1992; Goffman 1959; McCracken 1988; Stone 1995 and others too numerous to list). Yet to exert the kind of power that when removed causes weakness to the point of death, and when replaced strength for restoral to life (as happens in our legend) is a critical amount of power, and a potentially potent association for a fashion BP. That this phenomenon existed prior to the era that coined the phrase is made clear by John Carl Flugel (1950), who observed that the heavy silk robes worn by the ancient Chinese rulers acted as both physical and psychological extensions of the body/self. A study of seventeenth-century rulers of the Ming and Qing Dynasties conducted by this writer concurs (Matheson 2008, 2011). Yet the competence associated with this practice of power-dressing, so solidly established with Inanna in one of the oldest legends known to humankind, appears far more extensive in Ancient Mesopotamia than in its future applications.

As in the modern practice of power-dressing, the competence exercised in the Ancient Near East depended on meanings: both attributed and acknowledged. Barthes remarks that 'the knowledge on which the sign depends is heavily cultural'; each member of society must identify, determine, or be aware of the belief system and its expected social practices ([1957] 1972: 35). Postmodern scholars Carolyn Turner and Rebecca Holman (1980) concur stating that 'things' in the environment take on meaning in relation to their implications for individuals' plans. There must be consensus about the meaning of these 'things', and the execution of plans is contingent upon this meaning. Indeed this agreement of meaning may be a byproduct of the synchronicity between images and the society that generates them (Benjamin 2002). Had Eriskigal been unaware of the attributes ascribed to Inanna's adornments, her plan to strip away her power by confiscating her clothes would have failed. Like any skilled defense attorney, Ereskigal seized upon a loophole to protect her territory. Clearly Inanna had miscalculated her cousin's shrewdness; yet, this error in judgment is one we can empathize with, especially on a sartorial level. Any occasion for which we are under or over prepared (dressed), or without a position (badge) that holds the power to reject our hoped for entrance to a desired venue provides a relevant parallel. Then as now, clothes mark the troubled border between inside and outside and as such affect events far beyond their physical state (Wilson 2003). As we dress appropriately, carrying and using items such as our iPod, iPad, and iPhone (Apple has created an allure around its BP with human desires and feelings in mind, including a feeling of competence that supports its premium prices), we are deemed equipped to succeed. So too would Inanna be expected to claim victory in her quest: using the resources available she had equipped herself appropriately. Like the recurring failures on the part of technology to deliver what is promised, the interception of Eriskigal should not colour the competence revealed by Inanna's preparation for and continuance of her journey.

Reviewing the list of traditional dimensions for a fashion BP, I finally posit that Inanna exhibits both *sincerity* and *strength* in perusing her goal despite her increasingly fragmented condition caused by the command to relinquish clothing/power at each of the seven gates. Only one sincere about one's goal would continue in the face of systematic diminishment: Only someone of strength would persist despite apparent danger and defeat. Here, I believe we might agree that the five traditional dimensions of the effective BP – excitement, sophistication, competence, sincerity and strength – have been demonstrated. We have also seen postmodern themes: ambivalence, ambiguity, resignation, and fragmentation. I suggest that this juxtaposition of traditional and postmodern narrative motifs equips Inanna to be a symbol for a fashion BP. For further analysis of these alternate themes and their usefulness in fashion marketing, I return to the work of Phillips and McQuarrie (2010, 2011).

13. In the first case Joseph is sold to the Egyptians where he has an auspicious beginning; in the second he is falsely charged and thrown in prison; and in the third, after correctly interpreting the Pharaoh's dream, he is released and promoted: either for good or bad, a significant life change occurs. For more on ritual of a consumer good see Frieze (1997).

DISCREPANT AND GROTESQUE

Using the criteria from their studies, I classify Inanna's image on arrival in the Netherworld as discrepant (Phillips and McQuarrie 2011) and grotesque (Phillips and McQuarrie 2010). Despite its exciting beginning with an ambitious, competent and carefully clad goddess on a quest to conquer an uncharted realm, fragmentation creeps in at each of the seven gates with the undignified ritual of undressing. In response to Neti's commands Inanna's image changes from one of a richly adorned deity to that of a rotting corpse. Like the metamorphosis of a caterpillar that sheds its outer layers, there is a surrealist quality to this scene in which we can imagine a dialectical exchange between Inanna and her material embellishments. Her crown, jewels and royal robe function as '… visual emblem[s] … telescoped into a punctual image', a description by the French Symbolist poet, Stephane Mallarmé when writing of an object's ability to suggest or allude (Wayland-Smith 2002: 901, quoting Mallarme). Benjamin's reflection that fashion is 'the eternal deputy of Surrealism' (2002: 63), compares it to a parody of the motley cadaver, an opinion inferred by Giacomo Leopardi's 'Dialogue between Fashion and Death' and his memorable phrase 'Fashion: Madam Death! Madam Death!' (Benjamin 2002: 62, quoting Leopardi). Benjamin continues his defense of the grotesque in fashion by musing that: 'every fashion couples the living body to the inorganic world … and defends the rights of the corpse' (2002: 79). Inanna is transformed from exciting, sophisticated, sincere, strong and competent to discrepant and grotesque, as the narrative provides a fitting example of Barthes's counter mode of fashion advertising referenced in *The Fashion System* ([1967] 1990).

Barthes' counter mode of fashion advertising ([1967] 1990), already tested by Phillips and McQuarrie (2010), evokes ideas such as playfulness (fantasy, mythology, ambivalence, ambiguity, etc …) and engages the consumer in this manner, as opposed to engagement by the search for identity with an unattainable glamorous image. The identification with an idea that does not beg emulation allows transport to the land of myth where delight rather than despair await (Phillips and McQuarrie 2010). In the case study, the disrobing process that occasions this transport develops and strengthens a bond with the Goddess. If this were a fashion ad, the bond would be with Inanna, the BP.

The disrobing ritual with which many can identify, has been repeated throughout history and appears to often be instigated by those in positions of power. One of the most illustrious occasions involved the 14-year-old Marie Antoinette, who, before arriving in Paris to marry King Louis XVI, is unceremoniously commanded to remove all of her attire in an effort to rid her of 'Austrianness' (Weber 2006). Disrobing often precipitates a life change; for example, in the Hebrew Bible, Joseph is stripped of his coat of many colours before being thrown in the pit; stripped again by Potiphar's wife when he refuses to bed her; and stripped yet again when crowned Egypt's chief overseer. Each act of undressing is the result of an order by someone holding power over him, and after each disrobing his life changes (Matheson 2012).[13] In many religious traditions, the fallen soul is purified by being undressed, and the Torah itself is revealed to us by a process of undressing, the significance of which lies in a return to a supernal position before descending to the material world (Lipinkivi 2010). Prisoners today are required to remove their clothes before being incarcerated, and finally, fashion models, too, must remove all personal belongings before donning the clothes that they will parade down the runway. So despite the discrepancy and grotesqueness of being slung naked on a hook and left to die – the allegory of defeat and death – the ritual that precedes this sorry state embodies an active dress practice, a force that could add significant intrigue and intensity to a fashion BP.

Feminist scholar Jane Burns refers to this active force of disrobing as the 'sartorial body' (1993: 12). Like any force it ebbs and flows within the narrative as within life. Although Inanna's character motivation may not be selfless when she agrees to remove her crown, or indeed any of her other adornments, the narrative or BP function, besides showing us her character, is to precipitate her defeat by undressing her – thereby elevating the clothing to centre stage. When the narrative or BP function changes to precipitate her rebirth and restoral to life and queenship, the force of her 'sartorial body' is again acknowledged and its coverings systematically reappear. In this manner, the power of dress is equated to matters of life, queenship, and death: powerful connotations that could also be transported from a fashion BP to the consumer.

NARRATIVE TRANSPORTATION

The themes conveyed by Inanna's legend provoke a process called narrative transportation in the fashion consumer. Research into this idea began in the psychological experimental tradition spearheaded by Richard Gerrig (1993), Melanie Green and Timothy Brock (2000), with further studies by Phillips and McQuarrie (2010) who add literary and aesthetic theories to support their consumer research. The legend of Inanna supplies the opportunity for increased narrative transport by its combination of traditional fashion themes with postmodern ones. Present in Inanna's visual narrative, they offer points of entry that involve suggestion, identification, interaction and negotiation, yet, all activity is in the land of fantasy. We are not asked to emulate: indeed, we could not. Nor is there the demand to achieve a proposed state, or deal with unfamiliar themes. Rather it is the very familiarity of these themes that lets time 'pleat' or fold in upon itself (Nead 2005: 8) and 'entangle[s]' the ancient with the postmodern in a kind of re-enchantment (Chakrabarty 2000: 243). Transported by myth, we are invited to create our own fashion stories, an act that strengthens our bond with the BP that extends the invitation (Phillips and McQuarrie 2010). As Inanna's images transport or immerse us in her story – two processes that can prompt persuasion in consumers (Phillips and McQuarrie 2010) – they are interpreted subjectively so that they voice, implement and control peculiarities and ambiguities specific to individual subject positions. With Inanna's combination of themes, this potential fashion BP offers 'custom-made' consumer identification that varies in intensity depending to significant extent on the effectiveness of the narrative transport.

THE REALM OF MYTH

Like Phillips and McQuarrie, I suggest that the element of discrepancy or grotesqueness fosters in some consumers a more intense experience (2010, 2011), augmented by being transported into the realm of myth where emotional intensity is the outstanding feature of thought (Krois 2008: 5). Following Josko Brakus et al. (2009), who demonstrate that the more intense the experience the closer the relationship between brand and consumer, I posit that a fashion BP would benefit from the intensity aroused by this mix of contemporary and traditional themes tussling for top position in their mythic setting.

THE BLURRY LINE BETWEEN SUBJECT AND OBJECT

The BP challenge to have objects with their ascribed power define subjects, could gain strength from the Inanna story where objects are closely entwined with life and death. Although she is pictured as a corpse, the rest of the narrative implies that the powers resident in Inanna's items of dress defend her rights, and assured of their restorative authority await her release from death's grasp. As these adornments are still embedded in her mind even when absent from her body, they act paradoxically as both sign and signifier of conqueror and conquered. Although hanging naked, alone and probably grappling with fears of failure, fragmentation and death, Inanna imagines reclaiming her power. Because her confiscated articles of dress convey intentions and norms of cognition, they form part of her agency and she uses them to resist her oppression. With the systematic reclamation of her dress item at each of the seven gates, her sense of agency and power is restored, her escape facilitated, and the oppressive situation overcome. Linking the restoral of agency and empowerment and the subsequent combating of oppression with a fashion BP and its objects would be powerful connection to boast.

CONCLUSION

This study shows that the ancient Mesopotamian world, with its Goddess Inanna and its use of articles of dress as symbols of power, meaning and control, may offer suggestions to the postmodern construct of a fashion BP. Because 'symbolism extends the phenomenon of feeling beyond the moment' (Krois 2008: 13) the most useful BP must adopt the most representative symbol, which I suggest depicts the rich tensions produced by intermeshing traditional qualities with countervailing postmodern themes. Indeed it is thematic tension that produces the individual narratives that images can conjure, and in so doing supply 'the volcanic ground' for the consumer's story (Krois 2008: 3, quoting Cassirer); if inspired, this story can create re-enchantment, and host delight instead of despair.

As a fashion BP, Inanna acknowledges the brilliance and blitheness of the human spirit, as well as its continual struggles. In keeping with the healthier trend of fashion advertising that has been the bases for recent research (Phillips and McQuarrie 2010, 2011) she is symbolized by images that prompt personal narratives and capriciousness rather than the generally unachievable aspirations of wealth, glamour and and thinness, and the ensuing frustration from negative social comparisons (Bower 2001; Dittmar and Howard 2004; Martin and Gentry 1997; Richins 1991; Shaw 1995; Solomon et al. 1992), or equally negative gender aspersions (Busby and Leichty 1993; Faludi 1991; Innes 1999). That the intensity of these consumer created stories is increased by the mythic aspect of the Age of Enchantment (Krois 2008) has been demonstrated, and that this intensity fosters a closer relationship between brand and consumer has also been established (Brakus et al. 2009; Phillips and McQuarrie 2010, 2011).

Beginning with the Ancient World, fashion's symbolic meaningfulness has been documented by scholars, modern and postmodern, and their combined work attests the significance of this function of dress. This study acknowledges this framework, and applies the social theory to the Mesopotamian narrative. The result is the suggestion of a provocative, discrepant, capricious, heroic and potentially enchanting fashion BP in which ambivalence, ambiguity and anxiety court sincerity and strength, while fragmentation and disenchantment bait excitement, sophistication and competence. I posit that if effectively marketed a fashion BP symbolized by the Goddess Inanna can forward hopes and aspirations, negotiate boundaries and barriers, subvert and divert oppression, celebrate victory and extend empathy in defeat. She encompasses a postmodern persona that awaits adaptation in fashion marketing. She is a potential source of re-enchantment.

This study suggests the birth of an extended BP construct; one that more closely represents the global postmodern consumer. Fashion advertising, with its attendant social themes and meanings extends a challenge to conventional thinking about how BPs are constructed. A key limitation in much of the current research is its restriction to the contemporary, affluent Western European/North American woman. Since both culture and ethnicity are important influences in response to brands, and clothing the body is a gendered activity (Entwistle 2000a, 2000b and 2000c), this situation needs to be rectified. I suggest that consideration of the narrative image of the Near Eastern Goddess from the Age of Enchantment in the postmodern BP construct would be taking a small step in this direction.

REFERENCES

Aaker, John (1997), 'Dimensions of brand personality', *Journal of Marketing Research*, 34: 3, pp. 347–56.

Bahrani, Zainab (1995), 'Jewelry and personal arts in ancient western Asia', in Jack Sasson (ed.), *Civilizations of the Ancient Near East, 1635–1645*, vol. III, New York: Charles Scribner's Sons, pp. 685–86.

Barthes, Roland ([1957] 1972), *Mythologies* (trans. Annette Lavers), New York: The Noonday Press.

—— ([1967] 1990), *The Fashion System* (trans. Matthew Ward and Richard Howard), Berkeley: University of California Press.

—— (2006), *Language of Fashion* (trans. Andrew Stafford), Andrew Stafford and Michael Carter (eds), Oxford: Berg.

Batten, Alicia (2010), 'Clothing and adornment', *Biblical Theology Bulletin: A Journal of Bible and Theology*, 40: 3, pp. 148–59.

Belk, Russel (2001), 'Specialty Magazines and Flights of Fancy: Feeding the Desire to Desire', in Andrea Groeppel-Klein and Franz-Rudolf Esch (eds), *European Advances in Consumer Research*, Provo, UT: Association for Consumer Research, pp. 197–202.

Bender, Henry (1994), 'De habitu vestis: Clothing in the *Aeneid*', in Judith Lynne Sebesta and Larissa Bonfante (eds), *The World of Roman Costume*, Madison, WI: University of Wisconsin Press, pp. 146–52.

Benedict, Ruth (1931), 'Dress', in Edwin Seligman and Alvin Johnson (eds), *Encyclopedia of the Social Sciences*, vol. 5, New York: Macmillan, pp. 235–37.

Benjamin, Walter (2002), *Arcades Project,* Rolf Tiedemann (ed.), (trans. Howard Eiland and Kevin McLaughlin), Cambridge, MA: Harvard University Press.

Bennett, Jane (2001), *The Enchantment of Modern Life: Attachments, Crossings, and Ethics,* Princeton: Princeton University Press.

Berman, Marshall (1988), *All That Is Solid Melts into Air: The Experience of Modernity*, New York: Penguin.

Berman, Morris (1981), *Reenchantment of the World*, Ithaca and London: Cornell University Press.

Bettelheim, Bruno (1976), *Uses of Enchantment: The Meaning and Importance of Fairy Tales*, New York: Random House.

Black, Anderson and Garland, Madge (1975), *History of Fashion*, New York: William Morrow.

Blumenberg, Hans (1983), *The Legitimacy of the Modern Age*, (trans. Robert Wallace), Cambridge, Mass: Harvard University Press.

Bottéro, Jean (1980), 'La mythologie de la mort en Mésopotamie Ancienne'/ 'The mythology of death in ancient Mesopotamia', in Bendt Alster (ed.), *Death in Mesopotamia*, Copenhagen: Akademisk Forlag, pp. 33–34.

Bower, Amanda, and Grau, Landreth (2009), 'Highly attractive models in advertising and the women who loathe them: The implications of negative affect for spokesperson effectiveness', *Journal of Advertising*, 30: 3, pp. 51–63.

Brague, Re'mi (2003), *The Wisdom of the World: The Human Experience of the Universe in Western Thought*, (trans. Teresa Lavender Fagan), Chicago: University of Chicago Press.

Brakus, Josko, Schmitt, Brendt and Zarantonello, Lea (2009), 'Brand experience: What is it? How do we measure it? And does it affect loyalty?', *Journal of Marketing*, 73: 3, pp. 52–68.

Brauner, Ronald (1974), 'To grasp the hem and 1 Samuel 15:27', *Journal of the Ancient Near Eastern Society*, 35: 6, pp. 35–38.

Brennan, Corey (2009), '*De Pallio* and Roman dress in North Africa', in Jonathan Edmonson (ed.), *Roman Dress and the Fabrics of Roman Culture*, Toronto: University of Toronto Press, pp. 258–70.

Budge, Wallis (1900), *Assyrian Sculptures in the British Museum: Reign of Ashusnasir-pal, B.C. 885–860*, London: British Museum.

Buresti, Fabio and Rosenberger III, Phillip (2006), 'Brand personality differentiation in the Australian action-sports clothing market', *Marketing Bulletin*, 17: 1, pp. 1–16.

Burns, Jane (1993), *Courtly Love Undressed: Reading through Clothes in Medieval French Culture*, Philadelphia: University of Pennsylvania Press.

Busby, Linda and Leichty, Greg (1993), 'Feminism and advertising in traditional and nontraditional women's magazines 1950s–1980s', *Journalism Quarterly*, 70: 2, pp. 247–64.

Calasibetta, Charlotte and Tortora, Phyllis (2007), *The Fairchild Dictionary of Fashion*, 3rd ed., New York: Fairchild.

Calefeto, Patricia (2004), *The Clothed Body*, Oxford: Berg.

Calinescu, Matei (1987), *Five Faces of Modernity*, Durham, N.C.: Duke University Press.

Carins, Donald (2002), 'The meaning of the veil in ancient Greek culture', in Lloyd Llewellyn Jones (ed.), *Women's Dress in the Ancient Greek World*, London: Classical Press of Wales, pp. 73–93.

Chakrabarty, Dipesh (2000), *Provincializing Europe: Postcolonial Thought and Historical Difference*, Princeton: Princeton University Press.

Cook, James (2001), *Arts of Deception: Playing with Fraud in the Age of Barnum*, Cambridge, MA: Cambridge University Press.

Corfield, Penelope (2010), 'Post-medievalism/modernity/postmodernity?', *Rethinking History*, 14: 3, pp. 379–404.

Craik, Jennifer (2009), *Fashion: The Key Concepts*, Oxford: Berg.

Croom, Alex (2002), *Roman Clothing and Fashion*, London: Tempus.

Cuisenier, Jean (1991), *Préface to Mille ans de Costume Français*, Thionville: Klopp.

Dar, Shiv (1969), *Costumes of India and Pakistan: A Historical and Cultural Study*, Bombay: Tarporevala.

Daston, Lorraine and Park, Katherine (1998), *Wonders and the Order of Nature*, New York: Zone Books.

Davies, Glenys (2007), *Greek and Roman Dress from A-Z*, London: Routledge.

Davis, Fred (1982), 'On the "symbolic", in symbolic interaction', *Symbolic Interaction*, 5: 1, pp. 111–26.

—— (1992), *Fashion, Culture and Identity*, Chicago: University of Chicago Press.

Debord, Matthew (1997), 'Texture and taboo: The tyranny of texture and ease in the J. Crew catalogue', *Fashion Theory*, 1: 3, pp. 261–78.

Dewer, Michael (2009), 'Spinning the trabea: consular robes and propaganda in the Panegyrics of Claudian,' in Jonathan Edmondson and Alison Keith (eds), *Roman Dress and the Fabrics of Roman Culture*, Toronto: University of Toronto Press, pp. 217–236.

Dittmar, Helga and Howard, Sarah (2004), 'Professional hazards? The impact of models' body size on advertising effectiveness and women's body-focused anxiety in professions that do and do not emphasize the cultural ideal of thinness', *British Journal of Social Psychology*, 43: 4, pp. 477–97.

Douglas, Mary and Isherwood, Baron (1979), *The World of Goods: Toward an Anthropology of Consumption*, New York: Basic.

Dube, Saraubh (ed.) (2002), 'Enduring enchantments: Tradition/community, colony/modernity' (special issue), *South Atlantic Quarterly*, October, 101: 4, pp. 729–55.

Durkheim, Emile (2001), *The Elementary Forms of Religious Life* (trans. Carol Cosman), New York: Oxford University Press.

Edmondson, Jonathan (2008), 'Public dress and social control in late Republican and early Imperial Rome', in Jonathan Edmonson (ed.), *Roman Dress and the Fabrics of Roman Culture*, Toronto: University of Toronto Press, pp. 10–11.

Edwards, Douglas (1994), 'The social, religious, and political aspects of costume in Josephus', in Judith Sebesta and Larissa Bonfante (eds), *The World of Roman Costume*, London: University of Wisconsin Press, pp. 153–59.

Elias, Jamal (2001), 'The Sufi robe (*khirqa*) as a vehicle of spiritual authority', in Stuart Gordon (ed.), *Robes and Honor: The Medieval World of Investiture*, New York: Palgrave, pp. 275–328.

Entwistle, Joanne (2000a), 'Fashion and the fleshy body: Dress as embodied practice', *Fashion Theory: The Journal of Dress, Body & Culture*, 4: 3, pp. 323–47.

—— (2000b), *Fashioned Body: Fashion, Dress and Modern Social Theory*, Cambridge: Polity Press.

—— (2000c), 'Fashioning the career woman: Power dressing as a strategy of consumption', in Maggie Andrews and Mary Talbot (eds), *All the World and Her Husband: Women and Consumption in the Twentieth-Century Consumer Culture*, London: Cassell, pp. 224–38.

—— (2007), '"Power dressing" and the construction of the career women', in Malcolm Bernard (ed.), *Fashion Theory*, London: Routledge, pp. 208–19.

Escalas, Jennifer (2004a), 'Narrative processing building conscious connections to brands', *Journal of Consumer Psychology*, 14: 1 and 2, pp. 168–80.

—— (2004b), 'Imagine yourself in a product: Mental stimulation, narrative transportation and persuasion', *Journal of Advertising*, 33: 2, pp. 37–49.

Faber, Reimer (2008), 'The woven garment as literary metaphor: The peplos in Ciris 9-14', in Jonathan Edmonson (ed.), *Roman Dress and the Fabrics of Roman Culture*, Toronto: University of Toronto Press, pp. 205–16.

Faludi, Susan (1991), *Backlash: The Undeclared War against American Women*, New York: Anchor Books.

Fantham, Elaine (2008), 'Covering the head at Rome: Ritual and gender', in Jonathan Edmonson (ed.), *Roman Dress and the Fabrics of Roman Culture*, Toronto: University of Toronto Press, pp. 158–71.

Felski, Rita (1995), *The Gender of Modernity*, Cambridge, MA: Harvard University Press.

Fishbein, Martin and Ajzen, Icek (1975), *Belief, Attitudes, Intention and Behavior: An Introduction to Theory and Research*, Reading, MA: Addison-Wesley.

Fisher, Philip (1999), *Wonder, the Rainbow, and the Aesthetics of Rare Experiences* Cambridge, MA: Harvard University Press.

Flugel, John Carl (1950), *Psychology of Clothes*, New York: Hafner Press.

Fog, Klaus, Dudtz, Christian and Yakaboylu, Baris (2005), *Storytelling: Branding in Practice*, Copenhagen: Springer-Verlag.

Foucault, Michel (1988), *Technologies of the Self: A Seminar with Michel Foucault*, Luther Martin, Huck Gutman and Patrick Hutton (eds), Amherst, MA: University of MA Press.

Freling, Traci and Forbes, Lukas (2005a), 'An empirical analysis of the brand personality effect', *Journal of Product and Brand Management*, 14: 7, pp. 404–13.

—— (2005b), 'An examination of brand personality through methodological triangulation', *Journal of Brand Management*, 13: 2, pp. 148–62.

Freud, Sigmund (2007), 'Fetishism', in Malcolm Bernard (ed.), *Fashion Theory: A Reader*, London: Routledge, pp. 553–57.

Frieze, Susanne (1997), 'A consumer good in the ritual process: The case of the wedding dress', *Journal of Ritual Studies*, 11: 2, pp. 51–62.

Frisby, David (1986), *Fragments of Modernity: Theories of Modernity in the Work of Simmel, Kracauer, and Benjamin*, Cambridge, MA: Harvard University Press.

George, Andrew (ed.) (2003), *Babylonian Gilgamesh Epic: Introduction, Critical Edition and Cuneiform Texts*, vols I and II, Oxford: Oxford University Press.

Gerth, Hans and Mills, C. Wright (eds) (1915), *From Max Weber, Essays in Sociology*, New York: Oxford University Press.

Gerrig, Richard (1993), *Experiencing Narrative Worlds*, New Haven, CT: Yale University Press.

Giddens, Anthony (1990), *The Consequences of Modernity*, Stanford, CA: Stanford University Press.

Givins, David (1977), 'Shoulder shrugging: A densely communicative expressive behavior', *Semiotica*, 19: 1/2, pp. 13–28.

Goffman, Ervine (1959), *Presentation of Self in Everyday Life*, Garden City, NY: Doubleday.

—— (1967), *Interaction Ritual*, New York: Doubleday.

Goldman, Bernard (2008), 'Greco-Roman dress in Syro-Mesopotamia', in Judith Lynne Sebesta and Larissa Bonfante (eds), *The World of Roman Costume*, Madison, WI: University of Wisconsin Press, pp. 163–81.

Green, Melanie and Brock, Timothy (2000), 'The role of transportation in the persuasiveness of public narratives', *Journal of Personality and Social Psychology*, 79: 5, pp. 701–21.

Habermas, Jürgen (1987), *The Philosophical Discourse of Modernity: Twelve Lectures*, (Frederick Lawrence trans.), Cambridge, MA: Harvard University Press.

Hall, Stuart, Held, David, Hubert, Don and Thompson, Kenneth (eds) (1996), *Modernity: An Introduction to Modern Societies*, Oxford: Blackwell.

Hancock, Joseph (2009a), *Brand Story: Ralph, Vera, Johnny, Billy, and other Adventures in Fashion Branding*, New York: Fairchild.

—— (2009b), 'Brand storytelling: context and meaning for cargo pants', in Peter McNeil, Vicki Karaminas and Catherine Cole (eds), *Fashion in Fiction: Text and Clothing in Literature, Film and Television*, Oxford, NY: Berg, pp. 85–104.

Hales, Shelley (2005), 'Men are Mars, women are Venus: Divine costumes in imperial Rome', in Liza Cleland, Mary Harlow and Lloyd Lewellyn-Jones (eds), *The Clothed Body in the Ancient World*, Oxford: Oxbow, pp. 131–42.

Harlow, Mary (2005), 'Dress in the *Historia Augusta*: The role of dress in historical narrative', in Liza Cleland, Mary Harlow and Lloyd Lewellyn-Jones (eds), *The Clothed Body in the Ancient World*, Oxford: Oxbow, pp. 142–53.

Herodotus (1942), *Persian Wars* (trans. George Rawlinson), New York: Random House.

Herskovitz, Stephen and Malcolm, Crystal (2010), 'The essential brand persona: storytelling and branding', *The Journal of Business Strategy*, 31: 3, pp. 21–28.

Holland, Glenn (2009), *Gods in the Desert: Religions of the Ancient Near East*, Lanhan: Rowman and Littlefield.

Homer, Robert Fitzgerald (1974), *Iliad*, (trans. Homer, Robert Fitzgerald), New York: Doubleday.

Houston, Mary (1954), *Ancient Egyptian, Mesopotamian and Persian Costume and Decoration*, 2nd ed., London: Adam and Charles Black.

Huang, Wen-yeh (2010), 'Brand story and perceived brand image: evidence from Taiwan', *Journal of Family Economic Issues*, 31: 3, pp. 307–17.

Innes, Sherrie (1999), *Tough Girls: Women Warriors and Wonder Women in Popular Culture*, Philadelphia, PA: University of Pennsylvania Press.

Jacobsen, Thorkild (1976), *Treasures of Darkness: A History of Mesopotamian Religion*, New Haven: Yale University Press.

Johnson, Kim, Torntore, Susan and Eicher, Joanne (eds) (2003), *Fashion Foundations*, Oxford: Berg.

Kaiser, Susan (2013), 'Navigating cultural anxiety: Strategic ambiguity in Lizbeth Salander's style-fashion-dress', in Joseph H. Hancock II, Toni Johnson-Woods and Vicki Karaminas (eds), *Fashion in Popular Culture*, pp. 23–47.

Kaiser, Susan, Nagasawa, Richard and Hutton, Sondra (1990), 'The semiotics of clothing: Linking structural analysis with social process', in Thomas Sebeok and Jean Umiker-Sebeok (eds), *The Semiotic Web*, Berlin: Mouton de Gruyter, pp. 603–23.

—— (1991), 'Fashion, postmodernity and personal appearance: a symbolic interactionist formulation', *Symbolic Interaction*, 14: 2, pp. 165–85.

Katz, Dina (1995), 'Inanna's descent and undressing the dead as a divine law', *Zeitschrift für Assyriologie und Vorderasiatische Archäologie*, 85: 2, pp. 221–33.

Kenoyer, Jonathan (1998), *Ancient Cities of the Indus Valley Civilization*, Oxford: Oxford University Press.

Kloppenberg, James (1994), 'Democracy and Disenchantment: From Weber to Dewey to Habermas and Rorty', in Dorothy Ross (ed.), *Modernist Impulses in the Human Sciences, 1870–1930*, Baltimore: Johns Hopkins University Press, pp. 69–90.

Kramer, Stanley (1960), 'Death and the nether world according to the Sumerian literary texts', *Iraq*, 22: 1, pp. 59–68.

—— (1969), *Cradle of Civilization*, Boston: Little Brown.

—— (1979), *From the Poetry of Sumer*, Berkeley: University of Berkeley Press.

Krois, John (2008), 'The pathos formulae of mythic thought', in Paul Bishop and Roger Stephenson (eds), *The Persistence of Myth as Symbolic Form: Cultural Studies and the Symbolic*, vol. 3, Wakefield, UK: Maney, pp. 1–17.

Lapinkivi, Pirjo (ed.) (2010), *The Neo-Assyrian Myth of Ishtar's Descent and Resurrection*, Helsinki: The Neo-Assyrian Text Corpus Project.

Latour, Bruno (2005), *Reassembling the Social: An Introduction to Actor-Network-Theory*, Oxford: University Press.

Law, John and Hassard, John (1994), *Actor Network Theory and After*, Oxford: Wiley-Blackwell.

Lehmann, Ulrich (2000), *Tigersprung: Fashion in Modernity*, Cambridge, MA: MIT Press.

Lindner, Katharina (2004), 'Images and women in general interest and fashion magazine advertisements from 1955–2002', *Sex Roles*, 51: 7/8, pp. 409–21.

Lipovetsky, Gilles (1994), *Empire of Fashion, Dressing Modern Democracy* (trans. Catherine Porter), Princeton: Princeton University Press.

Lundqvist, Anna, Liljander, Johanna, Gummerus Veronica and Riel, Allard, van (2012), 'The impact of storytelling on the consumer brand experience: the case of a firm-originated story', *Journal of Brand Management*, 30: 2, 2 March, http://www.palgrave-journals.com/bm/journal/vaop/ncurrent/full/bm201215a.html. Accessed 26 September 2012.

Maisels, Charles (1993), *The Near East: Archaeology in the 'Cradle of Civilization'*, London: Routledge.

Martin, Mary and Gentry, James (1997), 'Stuck in the model trap: The effects of beautiful models in ads on female pre-adolescents and adolescents', *Journal of Advertising*, 26: 2, pp. 19–33.

Marx, Karl (1968), *Capitalm Vol 1* (trans. Frederick Engels), New York: International Publishers.

—— (1970), *The Social and Political Thought of Karl Marx*, Cambridge: Cambridge University Press.

Matheson, Linda (2008), 'Imperial material: Textile fashions and identities in transitional China', master thesis, Davis, CA: University of CA Davis, pp. 1573–1722.

—— (2011), 'Imperial material: Modern western fashion theory and a seventeenth-century eastern empire', *Dress, the Journal of the Costume Society of America*, 37: 1, pp. 57–82.

—— (2012), *Divinely Attired*, Ann Arbor, MI: UMI Dissertation Publishing.

Matsushima, Eiko (1993), 'Diving statues in ancient Mesopotamia: their fashioning and clothing and their interaction', in Eiko Matsushima (ed.), *Official Cult and Popular Religion in the Ancient Near East*, Heidelberg: Universitatsverlag C. Winter, pp. 209–19.

McCall, Henreitta (1990), *Mesopotamian Myths: The Legendary Past*, London: The British Museum.

McCarraher, Eugene (2005), 'The enchanted city of man: the state and the market in Augustinian perspective', in John Doody, Kevin Hughes and Kim Paffenroth (eds), *Augustine and Politics*, London: Lexington, pp. 261–96.

McCracken, Grant (1986), 'Culture and consumption: A theoretical account of the structure and movement of the cultural meaning of consumer goods', *Journal of Consumer Research*, 13: 1, pp. 71–84.

—— (1988), *Culture and Consumption: New Approaches to the Symbolic Character of Consumer Goods and Activities*, Bloomington: Indiana University Press.

—— (1993), *Decoding Women's Magazines: from Mademoiselle to Ms*, London: Macmillan.

Mead, George (1934), *Mind, Self, and Society*, C. W. Morris (ed.), Chicago: University of Chicago Press.

Miettinen, Reijo (2001), 'Artifact mediation in Dewey and in cultural-historical activity theory', *Mind, Culture, and Activity*, 8: 4, pp. 297–308.

Miles, Richard (2010), *Ancient Worlds: The Search for Origins of Western Civilization*, London: Allan Lane.

Molloy, John (1988), *The New Dress for Success*, New York: Grand Central Publishing.

Nead, Lynda (2005), *Victorian Babylon: People, Streets and Images in Nineteenth-Century London*, New Haven, CT: Yale University Press.

Oliver, Kelly (2004), *The Colonization of Psychic Space: A Psychoanalytic Social Theory of Oppression*, Minneapolis, MN: University Press.

Oppenheim, Leo (1949), 'The golden garments of the gods', *Journal of Near Eastern Studies*, 8: 3, pp. 172–93.

Ornan, Tallay (2005), *Triumph of the Symbol: Pictorial Representation of Deities in Mesopotamia and the Biblical Image Ban*, Fribourg, Switzerland: Academic Press.

Owen, Alex (2004), *Place of Enchantment: British Occultism and the Culture of the Modern*, Chicago: University of Chicago Press.

Pantelia, Maria (1993), 'Spinning and weaving: ideas of domestic order in Homer', *American Journal of Philology*, 114: 4, pp. 493–501.

Papadatos, Cariline (2006), 'The art of storytelling: how loyalty markers can build emotional connectors in their brands', *Journal of Consumer Marketing*, 23: 7, pp. 382–84.

Peirce, Charles (1935), 'Scientific metaphysics', in C. Hartshorne and P. Weiss (eds), *Collected Papers of Charles Sanders Peirce*, vol. 6, Cambridge, MA: Harvard University Press, pp. 272–77.

Phillips, Barbara and McQuarrie, Edward (2010), 'Narrative and persuasion in fashion advertising', *Journal of Consumer Research*, 37: 3, pp. 368–92.

—— (2011), 'Contesting the social impart of marketing: a re-characterization of women's fashion advertizing', *Marketing Theory*, 11: 2, pp. 99–126.

Poloian, Lynda (2003), *Retailing Principles: A Global Outlook*, New York: Fairchild.

Porter, Roy (2004), *Flesh in the Age of Reason: The Modern Foundations of Body and Soul,* New York: W.W. Norton.

Prange, Martine (2008), 'Why do we need myth? Homer, Nietzsche, and Helen's weaving loom', in P. Bishop and R. Stephenson (eds), *The Persistence of Myth as Symbolic Form: Cultural Studies and the Symbolic,* vol. 3, Leeds, UK: Maney, pp. 18–33.

Richins, Marsha (1991), 'Social Comparison and the Idealized Images of Advertising', *Journal of Consumer Research* 18: 1, pp. 71–83.

Roach-Higgins, Mary-Ellen and Eicher, Joanne (1995), 'Dress and identity', in Mary-Ellen Roach-Higgins, Joanne Eicher and Kim Johnson (eds), *Dress and Identity*, New York: Fairchild, pp. 1–7.

Rocamora, Agnes (2002), 'Fields of fashion: Critical insights into Bourdieu's sociology of culture', *Journal of Consumer Culture*, 2: 3, pp. 341–62.

Saler, Michael (2006), 'Modernity and enchantment: A historiographic review', *The American Historical Review*, 111: 3, pp. 692–716.

—— (2000), 'Whigs and surrealists: The "subtle links" of Humphrey Jennings' pandaemonium', in George Behlmer and Fred Leventhal (eds), *Singular Continuities: Tradition, Nostalgia, and Identity in Modern British Culture*, Stanford: Stanford University Press, pp. 123–142.

Scheid, John and Svenbro, Jesper (1996), *The Craft of Zeus: Myths of Weaving and Fabric* (trans. Carol Volk), Cambridge, MA: Cambridge University Press.

Scott, Joan (2007), 'History-writing as critique', in Keith Jenkins, Sue Morgan and Alan Munslow (eds), *Manifestos for History*, London: Routledge, pp. 19–38.

Shaw, Julie (1995), 'Effects of fashion magazines on body dissatisfaction and eating: Psychopathology in adolescent and adult females', *European Eating Disorder Review*, 3: 1, pp. 15–23.

Simmel, Georg (1990), 'Fashion', *International Quarterly*, 10: 11, pp. 130–55.

Sladek, William (1974), *Inanna's Descent to the Netherworld*, Ann Arbor, MI: University Microfilms.

Solomon, Michael, Ashmore, Richard and Longo, Laura (1992), 'The beauty match-up hypothesis: Congruence between types of beauty and product images in advertising', *Journal of Advertising*, 4: 21, pp. 23–34.

Spencer, Herbert (1924), 'Badges and costumes', in John Gillin (ed.), *The Principles of Sociology*, New York: Appleton, pp. 102–59.

Steele, Valerie (1988), *Paris Fashion: A Cultural History*, New York: Oxford University Press.

—— (2007), 'Fashion and fetishism', in Malcolm Bernard (ed.), *Fashion Theory: A Reader*, London: Routledge, pp. 576–83.

Stone, Gregory (1995), 'Appearance and the self', in Mary-Ellen Roach-Higgins, Joanne Eicher and Kim Johnson (eds), *Dress and Identity*, New York: Fairchild, pp. 19–39.

Taussig, Michael (1997), *The Magic of the State*, New York: Routledge.

—— (1980), *The Devil and Commodity Fetishism in South America*, Chapel Hill, NC: University of North Carolina Press.

Turner, Carolyn and Holman, Rebecca (1980), 'The concept of situational self image', *Advances in Consumer Research*, 7 : 1, pp. 610–14.

Twitchell, James (2004), 'An English teacher looks at branding', *Journal of Consumer Research*, 31: 2, pp. 484–89.

Van Meter, Jonathan (2012), 'Fashion and features: A man for all seasons', *Vogue* magazine, 15 December 2011, http://www.vogue.com/magazine/article/marc-jacobs-a-man-for-all-seasons/#1. Accessed 19 January 2012.

Verne, Donald (2011), *Origins of the Philosophy of Symbolic Forms: Kant, Hegel and Cassirer*, Evanston, IL: Northwestern University Press.

Virgil (1992), *Aeneid* (trans. Robert Fitzgerald), New York: Random House.

Wayland-Smith, Ellen (2002), 'Passing fashion: Mallarmé and the future of poetry in the age of mechanical reproduction', *Modern Language Notes*, 117: 4, pp. 887–907.

Weber, Caroline (2006), *What Marie Antoinette Wore to the Revolution: Queen of Fashion*, New York: Picador.

Weber, Max (1958), *The Protestant Ethic and the Spirit of Capitalism* (trans. Theodore Parsons), New York: Scribners.

Welters, Linda and Lillethun, Abby (eds) (2007), *The Fashion Reader*, Oxford, NY: Berg.

Wilson, Elizabeth (2003), *Adorned in Dreams: Fashion and Modernity*, New Brunswick, NJ: Rutgers University Press.

—— (2004), 'Magic fashion', *Fashion Theory, Fashion Dress and Consumption* (special issue), 8: 4, pp. 375–386.

Wolkstein, Dianne and Kramer, Stanley (eds) (1983), *Inanna: Queen of Heaven and Earth: Her Stories and Hymns from Sumer*, New York: Harper.

CONTRIBUTOR DETAILS

Linda Matheson holds an Individual Ph.D. in Humanities with Critical Studies in Material Culture from the University of California, Davis (2012), from which she also holds an M.S. in Textiles (2008). Her dissertation entitled 'Divinely attired' examines the contribution of dress to the narrative process of the ancient epics and sacred texts. After having enjoyed a career as a costume designer that spanned more than two decades and two continents, including Hollywood, London and Vienna, she returned to school to engage in academic research. She currently lectures at UC Davis and the Academy of Art University, San Francisco. Linda has participated in numerous conferences, including those of the National Popular Culture Association, ITAC and The Berkeley Ancient Italian Roundtable. She has published in a number of venues such as *Dress* magazine, and while working on a book project, has a publication in process in *Global Textile Encounters: China, India, Europe* (Copenhagen: The Danish National Research Foundation's Centre for Textile Research, 2014).

E-mails: matheso@gmail.com; lfmatheson@ucdavis.edu

Global Fashion Brands: Style, Luxury & History

© 2014 Intellect Ltd Chapter. English language. doi: 10.1386/GFB.1.279_1

ELLEN ANDERS

Independent researcher

Louis XIV, 'Le marketing, c'est moi'

ABSTRACT

Modern personal branding and innovative fashion merchandising has its origins in a seventeenth-century Monarch, Louis XIV, King of France. Louis XIV was the first to create a global mark of distinction, a brand, for his Royal-firm through cleverly devised visual strategies that can be compared to contemporary advertising and marketing strategies. Similar practices are used, presently, to bring billions of dollars into the textile and luxury markets each year. In this article I will explain the underlying need for and the process behind his branding style. In the 'Age of Discovery' he strove to define what is the best for existing intangible and tangible items, including fashion, theories of government, economics and methods of production. He helped usher in techniques to categorize and classify new commodities that were arriving from the new world almost daily, which included everything from cinnamon to fabrics. He improved production, such as the manufacturing of textiles, by evaluating and setting standards of excellence that among other things opened up a network of communications. This form of networking and collaboration is alive today in business as executives or companies come together to assess and analyse current market trends and needs of customers to make their brand distinguishable and successful.

KEYWORDS

branding
Louis XIV
marketing
visual symbols
luxury brands
Louis Vuitton

INTRODUCTION

What do Louis XIV, Elvis Presley and Steve Jobs have in common? Each pioneered modern branding and marketing practices. When it comes to creating awareness for luxury products, the fashion industry creates skilfully designed advertising and marketing practices today that earn billions of dollars each year and contribute to the garment industry and global economy. The origins of these business practices date back to the seventeenth-century French Bourbon Dynasty and the royal court of Louis XIV, the King of France and his need to keep his kingdom safe from invaders.

Some of the key facets of the business practices used by Louis XIV are:

- Creating a well-designed portrait of the court through coded fashion symbols.
- Achieving global recognition for his kingdom through his glamorous style of governing.
- Developing a national identity that distinguished the nation as an enviable state.
- Devising a pyramid ideal with divisions and subdivisions of his government, that gave him authority to brand and promote his interests.
- Establishing Royal Academies for research in many subject areas that led to inventions such as the Jacquard loom; precursor to the computer.
- Inviting collaboration and debate within academies to raise the awareness of the court by asking questions.

Figure 1: Painting, Louis XIV, Father and Protector of the Nation *by Henri Testelin, 1666, Chateau of Versailles, France © RMN-Grand Palais/Art Resource. NY p. 1.*

- Establishing standards of excellence that stemmed from discussion and debate within the royal academies that led to a successful line of French luxury products that serve as an archetype for luxury brands today.
- Capitalizing on his charismatic leadership, Louis XIV inspired a fresh perception and enthusiasm in the business industry as a whole that unleashed opportunities for entrepreneurship that had not existed before.

HISTORICAL BACKGROUND

In 2015, France will celebrate and commemorate the 300th anniversary of Louis XIV's death and his legacy. To describe his legacy and how and why Louis XIV was able to complete the above, it is necessary to discuss some background information on his life. He was born in 1638, died 1715. His father, King Louis XIII of France, descended from the Bourbon dynasty. His mother, Anne of Austria, was from Spain – at this time, Spain belonged to the House of Austria, hence the name, 'Anne of Austria'. After the death of Louis XIII in 1643, five-year-old Louis XIV succeeded his father to the throne. His mother Anne and Cardinal Jules Mazarin served as regents until his coronation, when he was sixteen years old. He ruled on the throne for 67 years. He fought a number of battles, but there were also relative periods of calm in which he was able to accomplish a great deal.

From experience, he always worried about a rebellious takeover. Rebellious nobles of The *Fronde* attempted to kidnap and kill him when he was ten years old. His mother rescued him, but the event left an indelible mark on him to be aware of a revolt. Geoffrey Treasure states:

> The *Fronde* arose from pressures felt by particular groups to be intolerable: *parlementaires* and other members of sovereign courts, holders of financial office, and *rentiers*. With old feuds and rivalries, great nobles became involved. Motives were as various as the personalities involved. In general, the *frondeurs* were not so much reacting against the growth of royal government as seeking to share in it and benefit from it. The *Fronde* became essentially a struggle for the state.
>
> (1998)

Previous ancestors Henri III and his successor Henri IV were both assassinated. His foremost need was to save both himself and the Kingdom. The question was, 'How?'. The answer was to create and promote himself as an immortal god through fashion emblems that emphasized his divinity and power. James H. Sheehan states:

> To add to the support of his position, the King of France emphasized his special relationship with God. At his coronation each king was anointed with sacred oils and with the title of His Most Christian Majesty, became God's representative in France, rule by divine right.
>
> (1983)

FASHION SYMBOLS

By using fashion symbols as a method of self-promotion, Louis XIV was able to identify himself with the government ideal but broader than that, the nation itself. The emblems, logos and colours, chosen to identify himself with government ideals revealed many inconsistencies in his brand, one being a celestial star that embodied Louis XIV as the ancient Greco-Roman god Apollo, and sole decision-maker of the nation that could be read as a conflict with Catholic Church doctrine. However, much of the problem had been worked out in earlier medieval times as stated below.

Ernst H. Kantorowicz (1997) states that from medieval times there was an accumulation of metaphorical thought that was used to define a King's divine nature and immortality. The King or Crown had two aspects to its nature; one was the natural, or religious body and the second was the political or administrative body. In order for the King not to compete with the Pope, who was also considered divine and immortal, an agreement was reached between them that the King would attend to the administrative part of the kingdom and the Pope would attend to the religious teachings. To make sure the King was held accountable to the teachings of the Church, the King was always under scrutiny to make sure he followed the Christian doctrine and to fail to do so he would be forever damned to hell.

The issue of immortality was upheld by stating that the instant the King died, his legacy would be passed on to his son and, therefore, 'The King Never Dies'. It might also be noted that in the sixteenth century the Catholic Church endorsed the Society of Jesus –The Jesuits – that allowed religion and scientific investigation to be a part of their teachings. The Church, fearful of losing its followers to other sects, allowed religion and science to be conjoined by stating that the thrust of Jesuit teaching is 'to find God in all things' (Jongalekar 2013).

Louis XIV chose a universal symbol of the sun and the colour red to represent the crown and divine right of absolute rule. He called himself, 'Le Roi Soleil', The Sun King, also known as Apollo, in Greco-Roman mythology. Apollo was the god of light and the warrior son of Zeus. As an exclusive symbol for the sun, Louis XIV incorporated the colour red in court dress to signal the King's unrestrained power of absolutism. Why the colour red and the symbol of Apollo? Red was a part of the Roman zodiac calendar and it showed that (as Romans believed) the sun, a celestial star, was closest to Earth in July, the hottest time of the year, hence the strong, forceful colour red. Apollo, the mythical sun god, with his assertive warrior characteristics were needed for Louis to advertise his military strength.

Sheehan describes how establishing an identity helps a nation's stability: 'States want above all, to be identified with heroism, self sacrifice and duty that has made victories possible and their defeats endurable' (2009: 77). He then quotes, Michael Walzer: 'A nation must be personified before it can be seen, symbolized before it can be loved, imagined before it can be conceived'. This is the ideal Louis XIV wanted to convey to his subjects by using allegorical images to personify the ideals of his Kingdom.

The colour red also stood for 'Flames of Inspiration', or divine wisdom, associated with the Monarch's celestial power. Flames represented the wisdom and knowledge given directly to the King by God. It is suspected today that the flames of inspiration metaphor was a way of dealing with intuition, 'A-ha' insight and psychological workings of the mind. Perhaps it represented a part of the unconscious mind in the seventeenth century. The red flames became a visual logo to designate that only he had a direct channel to a godly force and insight. It could also be interpreted as a way to use the eternal flames metaphor to remind the nation of the brilliance of the Bourbon dynasty that would pass on to future kings.

In most official portraits of the King or his family members a red inner lining of their robes are displayed, which is a reference to the 'Flames of

Inspiration'. The colour red became an exclusive copyright of the King and less than a hundred people were allowed to wear it. For the most part, red was reserved for his family alone.

T. C. W. Blanning (2002) explains that Louis XIV, in a letter to his first born son, stated why he chose the sun for a symbol of his reign: 'By its unique quality, by the luster which surrounds it, by the light which it shines on those other stars [planets], which surround it like a court, and how it benefits all life'. Fashion emblems aided in spreading the message of absolutism. Still, he needed help to advance his vision. He drew up a plan for a visionary team to head the empire.

THE 'VISIONARY TEAM'

The 'Visionary Team' members assembled to create the profile of divine ruler were as follows. Cardinal de Richelieu, 1624–1642, was on board for four years and was the first to promote the term 'Supreme Ruler', or 'the King rules alone', with Louis' father, Louis XIII. Louis was a small child when the Cardinal was alive, but it was Richelieu who laid down the legacy of an absolute monarch that was retained by the next Cardinal, Jules Mazarin. Cardinal Richelieu was both a religious leader and political leader of France who was responsible for forming the modern state of France. He was able to earn the loyalty of his subjects through his management of appearance and propaganda. He understood how a distinguished image could produce the success of a King. Anthony Levi observes that: 'Kings and Queens were commonly portrayed and promoted as mythological figures with superhuman powers' (2000). Richelieu saw the office of the King as Herculean god.

Cardinal Jules Mazarin, 1642–1666, was with Louis XIV for nineteen years and continued the theme of 'Supreme Ruler'. Mazarin respected the King's authority. As statesman, he heavily taxed the nobles, which led to civil disturbances by The *Frondeurs* and his exile in 1649. He returned when the King called for his assistance in 1653 and he remained there until his death.

Jean-Baptist Colbert, 1665–1683, was with Louis XIV for eighteen years and oversaw the finances and all manufactured French products. He was the 'King-Pin' of the team and essential to the success of it. He saw to it that the King's projects were financed and enacted, such as the Gobelin textile factory and the academies. Colbert's parents were textile merchants in Reims. He became famous for his economic strategies called 'Colbertism', meaning he wanted to grow and keep money in France, otherwise known as mercantilism. Author, Joel Félix tells of his rise to power and fame in his story of *The Economy, Mercantilism and Colbertism*, in France.

> After helping Louis XIV assume personal power in 1661, Colbert first managed in the name of maintaining financial confidence and of enforcing strict obedience to the King. Colbert's authority was also reinforced by taking on key positions such as the supervision of royal manufactures in 1664, the controllership-general of finances and the superintendence-general of commerce in 1665.
>
> (Félix 2011)

William Doyle's (2001) writings on Colbert, enable us to learn that Colbert in overseeing the academies, took over where Richelieu left off in knowing how to exploit the academies as instruments of cultural propaganda and used them to unify the crown and the nations of France.

Charles LeBrun, 1661–1690, was with Louis XIV for 29 years and was the artist hired by Colbert to be responsible for the visuals; paintings, sculpture, monuments and interiors. LeBrun was in charge of the Arts Academy and did most of the designing, although he hired the artist, LeNotre, to do the gardens and other artists as needed. LeBrun used ornamentation to exalt the image of Louis XIV in the Salon de Venus. Chateau de Versailles, France. Jean Francois Berrielle presents a summary of the art of the time and explains, 'The ornamentation retains its robust and vigorous appearance. Naturalistic Subjects: cock, fleur de lys, head of Apollo. Robust forms are masterful interpretations of the desires of the king' (1982). All of these images were made available in as many private and public spaces as possible. LeBrun's allegories and paintings were to personify the King's character as noble, universal and to place in the minds of his subjects the glory of the Ancient Regime.

The Cardinals were from Rome and knew of the importance of visual images in promoting Christian beliefs. Each team member supported the 'Apollo Myth', the eternal celestial star, the Apollo/Hercules warrior, which all translated into an enormous power. It was Colbert, the finance minister, whose first job was to notify the nation that Louis XIV, age 23, was now the King and 'Supreme Ruler'. Colbert, in 1666, installed an obelisk in Paris defining an actual location and a political marker that stated the King's position (see Figure 2). 'The King Rules alone'. The obelisk, which was a

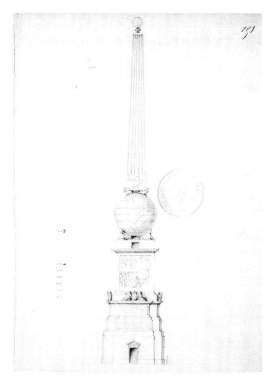

Figure 2: Drawing of Obelisk *by Charles Perrault, BNF, Dist. RMN-Grand Palais/Art Resource. NY p. 4.*

representation of an Egyptian sun ray, a sign of eternal light and a portrayal of the Pharaoh's unconditional power and long lasting dynasty. Colbert was using it as a symbol of Louis XIV's supreme authority.

GOING PUBLIC AND A NEED FOR A MARKER

The installation of the obelisk in Paris was both a distinguishable marker and a ceremonial event to announce that Louis XIV was the new ruler and now in charge of the nation's economy. He was offering the public a chance to buy into his vision of a perpetual, prosperous growing French economy. It was akin to going public and entering the market. Louis XIV offered a royal buy-in to the rebellious nobles. It is as if he were saying: 'The nation's best interest, is my best self-interest. Business revenues are a part of the crown. If I prosper, you will prosper as well. You (the nobles) will receive a title, pension and land for life'.

Today's shareholders are given dividends if the stock rises and the revenues are distributed. Present day companies also need a brand strategy to set themselves apart in a competitive economy. There is still a need for a 'Here I Am', marker, used both as a ceremonial event and a long lasting symbol of a legendary brand. Louis Vuitton, in 2004, announced the reopening of the Paris store by placing large oversized trunks on the storefront. A real advertising marker that could not miss, with a cool selection of suitcases that puts one 'in a class above', when travelling.

The company's position is to promote a luxury brand associated with excellent craftsmanship and references essential features of quality established by Louis XIV's Royal Academies. The marker is a form of seduction that pulls one into Louis XIV's validation of 'What is the best', and represents the pinnacle of refined taste. Today the symbol of the trunks on a store front reveals the company's presence as well as conveying a long lasting brand identity that has traversed nearly two centuries (1854–2013). The LV monogram even mimics Louis XIV's logos of LXIV, LXV or LXVI.

Figure 3: Photo, Louis Vuitton flagship, *Paris, renovation and reopening of store, October 2005. Three months later, L'Espace Culturel, top floor, opened for contemporary art exhibitions. © photographer Marc Plantec, 2005, p. 4.*

PYRAMID CONCEPT

To insure his status as Supreme Ruler, Louis XIV created a hierarchy of authority, known today as a 'Pyramid Concept', or a structural tower of power. The greatest power is concentrated at the top of the pyramid with the least number of people (the King) in control of the authority. A 'pyramid brand' structure is more of a transparent model of layers that allows the company or organization to prioritize and understand its goals to develop the brand. However, the pyramid brand concept is part of a larger business pyramid of authority and depending on the organization that consists of an owner of a company, or board of directors or CEOs (chief executive officers). They all may or may not have the final say in the development of the brand.

A similar pyramid of authority occurred when the owner and founder of Men's Wearhouse, George Zimmer, was eliminated as chief manager of his own establishment. Mr Zimmer was the very public face of Men's Wearhouse, he appeared in numerous commercials and TV spots.

Walter Loeb, contributor to *Forbes* magazine, reported that,

> In a spectacular turn of events, George Zimmer was dismissed as Executive Chairman and subsequently resigned from the Board. In the retail industry, George Zimmer, owner of Men's Wearhouse, was forced out by his board of directors because they said that, 'Mr. Zimmer does not support management and that in their view, his goal is to be sole decision maker which the board could not support'.
>
> (2013)

Louis XIV, the leader of a top down structure of authority, built into his brand framework guarantees that the monarch would be the sole ruler. However, if a rebellion were to occur, the Kingdom would have to worry about a replacement. So the question is, 'Why does it pose a threat for a leader to leave his country or company?' Because, if so much of their personality and talent are embedded in the brand, it poses a threat and a period of uncertainty that can be viewed as a weakness until a successful replacement can be found.

In regards to George Zimmer, Mr Loeb continued to state,

> In my opinion, dismissing the founder and spokesperson – a very high profile and difficult decision no doubt – is in the best interest of the company. I am sure a new spokesperson who will effectively market the company will be found and that Men's Wearhouse will move forward successfully from this unfortunate moment in its history.
>
> (2013)

Louis XIV had some luck on his side. His personality and authority was clearly entrenched in his brand, but he took years to build such a solid front and he had some room to experiment. Louis XIV had 67 years to demonstrate his aims and achievement. However, in the Silicon Valley tech world, a CEO often has only eighteen months to establish his or her success. This can prove very risky for a company's reputation. It can also be noted that after Steve Jobs was forced out of his own Apple company, he started another successful one called Pixar. He later returned to Apple, and much of its success was based on his previous visionary reputation that persuaded customers to support the brand.

Louis XIV's appeal came from a broad range of concepts that were incorporated into his government in which he was in charge: administration, army, trade, Chateau de Versailles, academies and more. Louis XIV, as King, was at the top of the pyramid and was responsible for all departments and subdivisions. Louis XIV's divisions and subdivisions run parallel with today's companies such as one sees in the pyramid structure of Apple Computers. Steve Jobs held the CEO status at Apple located at 1 Infinite Loop in Cupertino, Califoria and established its culture informed by a variety of 'i-products': iPhone, iPad, iTunes, iMac computers. Steve Jobs was responsible for all final decisions.

Elvis Presley, acting as a Celebrity CEO, was chief manager of his divisions: music, albums, videos, Hollywood movies, Graceland.

The personality and fame of these CEOs defined the brand and was totally dependent on visual logos to announce their identity. Louis XIV needed this signification for dominance and he needed it right away to suppress a mutiny.

A VISUAL NARRATIVE OF LUSTRE AND SHINE

A visual narrative was necessary for control. By using the Apollo sun theme, Louis was able to promote the state's wealth by advantageously tying the sun's radiance to the radiant silk worn by the court. Everywhere is one word. On his mother's bedchamber door at Fontainebleau the sun theme emerges with a cornucopia of flowers to reflect the King's virtue and good raining down on the earth. Lustre and shine, reflections of the sun, all metaphorically referenced the Sun King. This sparkle and gloss visibly advertised the state's wealth and separated the classes. Silk dress and textiles reflected a shiny surface and were considered the messengers of good. They were seen everywhere at Versailles. Silk costumes enhanced the royal brand by endorsing the nation's prosperity. Sunshine defined the message; lustre and shine became a major motif.

Men were the first fashion plates to wear silk.

Figure 4: Painting, Claude Henri Watalet, *artist, Jean-Baptiste Greuze, 1696, Chateau du Versailles, France © RMN-Grand Palais / Art Resource, NY, p. 6.*

Figure 5: Painting of Femme de Rohan *by Nicolas de Largillière, 1696. Image copyright © The Metropolitan Museum of Art. Image source: Art Resource, NY.*

The routine of wearing silk was not only essential to protocol, but if one went against it, one would lose their court status and become unimportant. The boastful silk dress of men was to claim that fashion was not a frivolity, but a policy to ensure the protection of the Kingdom. Phillip Mansel in *Dressed to Rule* states, 'Splendour was the basis of court dress. Monarchs considered lace, velvet, silk and embroidery to be necessary and agreeable at court as nobles names and large, lavishly decorated palaces' (1995). He further states, 'Not to wear expensive clothes would be demeaning for the courtier, insulting for the monarch'.

A woman's job was to show up at court and show off a silk garment. Their legal voice may have been muffled, but their ability to create a visual marketing coup went beyond the court. Their elegant style of silk dressing called '*frou-frou*' at the time, was the buzz word at court, and it went viral globally. In 1738, Le Petit Robert, a French dictionary publication, assigned the term '*frou-frou*', to the sound a silk dress made as a woman walked into a room. It was said that she passed by with great '*frou-frou*', meaning in an elegant style.

HERITAGE BRAND STANDS FOR THE TEST OF TIME

The ambassador's role was to wear and flaunt as much refined silk ensembles as possible so that they could literally transport the grandeur of Versailles to far away lands by wearing representations of the court on their backs. It was successful in that it made other countries want to emulate Louis XIV's royal firm, rather than attacking it and gave the brand an exalted reputation. It aided in keeping the nation in a relative period of peace for many years, a time in which many things were accomplished. Voltaire stated: 'That not only were great things done during his reign, but he did them himself'.

Keeping peace among nations through trade and commerce began with 'Les Compagnies des Indes Orientales', the French East India Company, 1664, promoted by Louis XIV himself and directed by Colbert. The company succeeded and grew until it was interrupted by the French Revolution in 1789. France developed a taste for artistic forms derived from Chinese art and narratives called '*Chinoiserie*'. The French textile industry was strongly influenced by Asian style. The '*Tapis de Savonnerie*'/'the tapestry factory', especially exemplified this tradition and was further developed at the Gobelin factory, which is still in existence today. The tradition spread to Great Britain and revived the British carpet industry.

The effects of Louis XIV's marketing practices were carried forward by the transfer of ideas that circulated around the globe and created a kind of fashion diplomacy.

BRANDING INSIGHT

Louis XIV was a branding genius in having his designers create official court dress that was succinct and sharp in describing government principles and policies and the nation's identity. Pierre Arizoli Clementel and Pascale Borguet Ballesteros reveal that, 'Only three pieces of clothing were needed to display the guidelines of the nation; royal cloak with red lining, vest and culottes. The vest and culottes were covered by the cloak and adorned with the Royal Collar' (2000).

The pervasive blue colour represented the army and the powerful force of the military. The blue colour was adopted from the heraldry of the 'Ordre du Saint-Esprit', a military order originating from Henri II, but made important by the court of Henri IV, first Bourbon monarch. Scattered over the silk velvet blue robe were embroidered golden *fleurs de lys*. The *fleur de lys* was a symbol of the nation of France and the Christian trinity. It announced to the world that France was clearly a Catholic, Christian nation. An ermine fur collar was attached to the top of the robe and was adorned with the royal necklace, often referred to as 'The Royal Dog-tags', because of the charm-like medallions that identified the King's victorious battles.

The artist, Charles LeBrun, was to produce portraits of the King and display them throughout Versailles as well as sending them as gifts to other countries to promote the propaganda of the court. Cloth, embellished with symbols of court policies, became a form of fashion literacy and a great storyteller of history. It is necessary today for enterprises to give a clear, concise visual statement of their brand to their clientele in order for them to be persuaded to buy their collections. It is called, 'Staying On Message', and can be challenging.

THE CHALLENGE OF STAYING ON MESSAGE

It is ironic that the academies, by seeking ways to improve arts and goods in order to bring more revenues into the court, unexpectedly undermined the King's rule. One of the most significant parts of his legacy was that of posing questions such as: 'What is the best? How do you know it? How do you disseminate the French culture?'. These questions were asked to raise the standards of excellence for the manufacturing of French products and led to the luxury trade.

Questions and debate spread through contacts the nobles had with colleges, tradesmen, local businessmen and guilds. These contacts were done through their correspondence in letters, newspapers, gazettes, salons, cafes and social affairs such as the theatre. Daniel Roche makes known the scope of how far reaching this communication was that took place and the impact it had on the circulation of information and ideas.

> Humble folk knew how to write and did write letters for utilitarian purposes. What was to prevent them from achieving a degree of introspectiveness, an ability to analyze feelings? Evidence of this can be seen in Parisian estate inventories: papers, letter and writing implements became increasingly common as the century progressed. Ordinary people exchanged letters, infrequently to be sure, but that made them and the people who wrote them that much more important.
>
> (Roche 1998)

Although, the court resided at Versailles, Paris was still the cultural centre. Discussions led to more production and production to more consumption. Colbert held a tight fist over the academies and guilds that produced the luxury products to make sure the increase in production of silk textiles standards were not interfered with. Colbert sent spies out to watch over and report back to him if quality and excellence were not upheld. Aspects of capitalism were creeping in to the market, side by side with mercantilism; something Colbert had to deal with in trade negotiations. The continuing questioning and dialogue among designers is what creates a distinguishable brand. It is the underpinning and foundation that keeps industry alive and productive. The King had not foreseen how a world of mathematics and scientific investigation would bring into question the theories of absolutism. With advances in discoveries and inventions, a new scientific age arose and the mythological emblematic images began to be altered by mathematical symbols. A shift was taking place, the age of Enlightenment was approaching. New forms of thinking and knowledge were on the horizon and would transform former metaphorical explanations of natural phenomenon into scientific justifications.

With the study of nature, portrait painting became landscape painting. Cartoon-like drawings of plants that appeared on textiles were transformed into anatomical drawings of flora and fauna. Descartes' discoveries in mathematics were based on proof, reason and logic. How was the King to produce data and evidence that he was God on earth when the evidence was based on an ancient myth? It was a tale with no physical proof and made the court look out of sync and illogical.

How did the marketing of textiles fit into this scientific picture? It started with the need for transportation and communication. Roche (1998) revealed that the demand for textiles and the imports needed to create them, such as wool, cotton, silk and linen, required roads to be built. To complete this task, maps and mathematical survey instruments were needed. To calculate the demand for goods, more accurate accounts of the population would have to be completed and for the first time, people would need to travel out of their familiar boundaries to more distant regions to gather information, and attend markets and fairs. Publishing snowballed and people had a keen interest in travellers who wrote about their adventures as well as new trends in the trades. The markets brought all the classes together – farmers, entrepreneurs (some of the nobles were slipping down out of the upper class into the new bourgeoisie) bankers, shopkeepers and tradesmen. The lower classes desired to move upwards by buying a title so that they could marry into the aristocracy. Conversations that had never taken place between the classes, because of court protocol, were now slipping into the culture due to the link between commerce and trade.

Caroline Larroche (2004) denotes how the shift in science was taking place in art by natural forms in paintings and sculpture being replaced with more elongated and distorted shapes. Geometric shapes were introduced into many of these designs as in the case of a drawing of a Crown of Christ in 1568 (artist unknown). The crown was made up of concentric circles interlaced with triangles with a protruding conical shaped nail rising up through the crown. A long rectangular cross rests beside it. Many of these shapes take on a geometric reference to mathematical forms rather than organic natural ones. Crossovers of mythological and scientific themes (1783) created by the Montgolfier Brothers made their way into society as evidenced by a ceramic sculpture designed to celebrate the event of the Montgolfier Brothers' invention of the first airship in space, the hot air balloon. The globe attached to the gondola compartment was decorated with little mythological Greek and Roman cherubs placed on top of and around the balloon. It was a mix of myth, art, religion and science. Objects of art were now covered with anatomical figures of specimens such as insects or small animals and showing people's interest in the new science of biology. At the same time that there was collaboration and hybrids of myth and science coming together, there were clashes as well.

With the new discoveries, conversations and debates regarding these changes, the hidden form of individual expression and thought were being set free. Fabrics, textiles, ribbons and trims and the demand for them appear to have been a major driving force in these changes.

COLLABORATION AND DEBATE, MYTHOLOGY TO MATHS

Through collaboration and debate, questions surfaced that put the integrity of the court in doubt by lack of proof, reason and logic. Newly found fossils began to question the age of the earth and came into direct conflict with religious teachings. Was this a question the court was ready to debate?

Not without throwing the brand out of alignment with the coordination and consistency of absolutism. As Roche points out, posing questions was necessary: 'It pointed up the absurdity of and relativity of all customs and beliefs and affirmed the power of the mind to free itself from traditional values by saying no to the status quo' (1998). It should be acknowledged that the King preferred questions, and so did the court, because an answer might be viewed as going against the King and one would risk being sent in exile and have to forfeit pension, land and title. Worse yet, one would become socially insignificant.

Presently, *Le Chambre syndicale de la couture de France* (a trade union) collaborates and networks with other countries, such as Italy, Switzerland and Holland, to enquire and discuss future trends in colours, designs and fabrics. By increasing their awareness of various diverse economic levels, occupational status or cultural values of people, they try to ensure that they are satisfying the needs of the market and its customers.

Fashion companies today try to connect with trends such as going green or respecting labour laws. Now and then, findings emerge that place the organization in a predicament and the brand has to deal with the crisis by realigning the brand or possibly losing their status and consumers. Scandals arise when companies do not follow child labour laws or when workers' lives are put in jeopardy due to building codes not being met, which cause physical injuries or deaths. Increasingly, companies are becoming aware of the public's concern with air or water pollution that can harm the environment and endanger the planet.

Fashion houses, in creating their brand, have to deal with ongoing change and the need to keep up with market trends. Some have been very successful in building 'immortality brands', while at the same time navigating through the transformation yet keeping their core features untouched. An example I have already mentioned is Louis Vuitton, who kept the motto, 'Family, Home and Quality', alive after Louis Vuitton died and was no longer the patriarch of the company. The family legacy passed on to his son, Georges, who was able to keep the message together by slowly introducing subtle changes in the trunk products. Georges had a fascination with Japanese art. He added the Japanese royal colour blue and a geometric kimono flower to the already established stripes and checks on the canvas covering of the trunks. The main purpose was to distinguish the cases from others in the market. The idea back-fired, in some sense, when the stripe, check, flower motif became extremely popular and other companies began to copy it.

Georges used the blue colour and the kimono flower motif in ceramic art to decorate the family home. Family, home and quality became synonymous with the luxury brand. As part of the fashion house of Louis Vuitton, former artistic designer Marc Jacobs incorporated the emblems, originally printed on the suit-cases, introducing more colours along with the checks, stripes and flowers in clothing designs. The designs morphed slowly into new forms, yet still retain the original brand features. By moving in a careful movement into the next century, the brand took on immortality through the legacy of Louis Vuitton. Louis XIV's legacy appeared immortal, but was altered when succeeding generations were unable include changes that would have supported the new rising middle class.

CONCLUSION

The legacy of Louis XIV has influenced not only our lives and western culture, but has had an impact in shaping the direction of the fields of fashion and marketing. Louis XIV formed a visual media of his day to communicate. He invented emblematic silk fashion symbols to give identity to and to promote and advertise his brand. The daily rituals of catwalks that could be seen down the Hall of Mirrors at Versailles, are still going forward today in fashion houses, fashion week displays, TV and movies, newspapers, and magazines.

Louis XIV created a heritage brand of fashion literacy, by making fashion into a visual language and media, with coded messages that educated his subjects to his policies and made his brand popular as a means of distribution. Through his clever placement of silk lustre as a dominant look necessary in court, its broad appeal took his court from relative obscurity to global recognition through the distinction of his brand. He created a global market for French fashion and the luxury trade that generated products with logos and markers for the industry, and revenues for his Kingdom.

Louis XIV sponsored academies to do research and to set standards for fashion, art, architecture, science, theatre, literature and manufactured goods, all of which became known as innovative brands of France, par excellence. He produced a commanding, centralized government that made people want to emulate his style rather than attack the nation. It created a relatively long period of peace in which he was able to accomplish many things. It was by his leadership in overseeing the treaties that ended the 100 years religious wars and economic ventures in the new world that gave the world untold of products such as coffee and fabrics. By the commercial spin-offs from scientific discoveries such as the Jacquard loom that was a precursor to the computer, the technology developed in the seventeenth century has evolved today into a technological revolution.

He devised brilliant marketing strategies, using celebrity endorsement and the allure of glamour and seduction as a form of persuasion to have people believe in and be loyal to the brand. Many celebrities and performers today owe their success to Louis XIV's attention to marketing strategies that he invented to advertise his court.

He devised a system of collaboration and networking within the academies. Through this collaboration much research information was shared that produced positive results for the nation. For example, by strapping a weight and measurement device on the back of his statisticians that went out into the field, they were able to measure the size of the population, how much wine or wool would be produced and sold, and even forecast the weather. They could foretell trends and in doing so gave a feeling of trust to the citizens in the future of the nation.

Had Louis XIV been more aware of how the diverse growing markets brought together the classes, such as the aristocratic land owners with the sheep farmers and silk producers, the artisans who wove the wool and silk and ultimately the merchants who sold it, the Bourbon dynasty might have had a different ending in 1789. Had he been able to conjoin the new independent thinking of the Enlightenment, and the ideas of absolutism, as the Catholic Church was doing by establishing the Jesuit order that included science and religion as a part of their teachings, the Bourbon dynasty might have lived past the crisis in 1789. Louis XIV was busy establishing himself as a God in his elitist community, by using the lustre of silk and other exclusive and awe-inspiring regalia to point out his divinity and economic status.

Year 2015 will be the 300th anniversary of the death of Louis XIV and the 300th year of marketing practices that gave survival, hope and a future to the nation of France. Today, there are many global enterprises that can trace their marketing practices back to Louis XIV and his royal-like firm. The historian Francois Bluche reports that Louis XIV probably never said, 'L'état, c'est moi'/'the state, it is me' but on his death bed, with hundreds of candles lighting up the night sky of Versailles, and an orchestra of violins playing outside his room on the terrace, he did say, 'I am dying, but the state remains'. A century later the dynasty died but the branding practices remained. Louis XIV was able to amass and maintain a recognizable legacy of refinement and faithful followers. He inspired future generations to successfully adapt his marketing ideals to modern day fashion brands.

ACKNOWLEDGEMENTS

Stéphane Houy-Towner, Fashion Historian, Branding expert.
Véronique Belloir, Galeria Mode du Textile, Paris, France, Conservatrice, Collections de 1800 á 1939.
Sophie Grossiord, Galleria, Musée de la Ville de Paris, Conservateur

Général au Musée.
Alexandra Bosc, Galleria, Musée de la Ville de Paris, Conservateur
BNF Paris.

REFERENCES

Arizoli Clementel, Pierre and Borguet Ballesteros, Pascale (2000), *Fastes de Cour et Ceremonies Royales, Le Costume Dy Ciyr En Europe 1650–1800*, Paris: Editions du la Réunion de la Musée Réunion National.

Berrielle, Jean Francois (1982), *Le Style Louis XIV, La Grammaire des Styles*, Paris: Flammarion.

Blanning, T. C. W. (2002), *The Culture of Power and the Power of Culture Louis XIV and Versailles*, Oxford: Oxford University Press.

Bluche, Francois (1984), *Louis XIV*, Oxford and New York: Basil Blackwell Ltd.

Dossier de L'Art (2003), 'La Galerie d'apollo', no. 120, Juin, Plan of the Gallery of Apollo, Chateau du Versailles, pp. 5–6.

Doyle, William (ed.) (2001), *The Short Oxford History of France, Old Regime France, 1648–1788*, Oxford: Oxford University Press.

Félix, Joel (2011), 'France 1500–1648, "The Economy, Mercantilism and Colbertism"' (original article '*Finances*'), in William Doyle (ed.), *The Oxford Handbook of the Ancien Regime*, Oxford: Oxford University Press, pp. 75–92.

Jongalekar, Ashutosh (2013), 'Jesuits, Science and a Pope with Chemistry Degree: A Productive Passing', *Scientific American*, 13 March.

Kantorowicz, Ernst H. (1997), *The King's Two Bodies*, Princeton, NJ: Princeton University Press.

Larroche, Caroline (2004), *Le Manierisme, Une Avant-Garde au XVI Siecle*, Paris: Gallimard.

Le Petit, Robert (1983), *Dictionnaire de la Langue Française* (ed. Paul Robert), Paris: Le Robert.

Levi, Anthony (2000), *Cardinal Richelieu and the Making of France, Churchman and Statesman: Aims and Ambitions*, New York: Carroll & Graf Publishers.

Loeb, Walter (2013), 'Why Men's Wearhouse Was Right To Oust George Zimmer', *Forbes*, 2 July, http://www.forbes.com/sites/walterloeb/2013/07/02/mens-wearhouse-a-storm-in-a-teacup/. Accessed 1 December 2013.

Mansel, Philip and Perrot, Philippe (1995), 'Le Luxe, Une Richess, Vestimentaires Entre Faste et Confort, XVIII-XIX Siecles', in *Dressed to Rule, Royal Court Costume from Louis XIV to Elizabeth II*, New Haven, CT: Yale University Press.

Roche, Daniel (1998), 'Mastery of space, "Manifestations of the Individual"', in *France In The Enlightenment*, Cambridge, MA: Harvard University Press.

Sheehan, James H. (2009), *Where Have All The Soldiers Gone? The Transformation of a Modern Europe*, New York: Houghton Mifflin Company.

—— (1983), *France Before The Revolution*, New York: Routledge.

Treasure, Geoffrey (1998), *Mazarin and the Fronde*, New York: Routledge.

CONTRIBUTOR DETAILS

Ellen Anders is a researcher, lecturer, fashion history teacher and retired High School teacher. She has a B.A. in Art and French Language and Civilization from San Jose State University, CA and is a former fashion designer for major department stores in San Francisco. She has studied and researched at BNF,

Louvre, Les Arts Decoratifs, Margurite Durand Library, Parsons School of Design – summer programme and Institute Catholique, Paris.

E-mails: eanders5@earthlink.net; fashionwall@me.com